SELECTED ORAL HISTORIES OF THE MAY 18 GWANGJU UPRISING

VOL 1. TESTIMONIES FROM VARIOUS LOCATIONS

First published February 2023
CO-EDITORS: **KIM Yeon-Min, Robert Grotjohn**
Publisher: **Sungtaek Jung**

ISBN: 978-89-6849-953-1 (93300)
Price: 27,000 Won

Published by Chonnam National University Press,
77 Yongbong-ro, Bukgu, Gwangju,
Republic of Korea, 61186
Registration: 21 May 1981 No. 53
Tel: 82-62-530-0571~3, Fax: 82-62-530-0579

Printed and bound in the Republic of Korea

SELECTED ORAL HISTORIES OF THE MAY 18 GWANGJU UPRISING

VOL 1. TESTIMONIES FROM VARIOUS LOCATIONS

The BK21 FOUR. Education & Research Program for Fostering Cultural Memory Curators
The Department of English Language & Literature, Chonnam National University
The May 18 Institute, Chonnam National University

Chonnam National University PRESS

TABLE OF CONTENTS

ACKNOWLEDGMENTS

For this translation project, we have many colleagues we wish to thank. First of all, we are deeply grateful to thirty-six translators, including the faculty, lecturers, and graduate students of the Department of English Language and Literature at Chonnam National University. We are also grateful to the May 18 Institute at CNU, especially to Dr. CHOI Jeong-Gi who accepted the translation proposal and obtained copyright permission, and to Dr. KIM Hyeong-Joo who carefully selected the twenty-six testimonies from the abundant pages of the original Korean versions and answered all our questions regarding unclear expressions in the original. We would like to express our gratitude to Tim Shorrock, the distinguished journalist who declassified the so-called Cherokee Files, documents on US policy in South Korea in 1979 and 1980. He generously agreed to write a Foreword to this volume and collaborate on our further projects on the May Uprising. We would also like to add a heartfelt word of gratitude to Dr. HAN Seung-Hee at Hankuk University of Foreign Studies. She gave a series of lectures on translation in the summer of 2021, through which we could establish guidelines of the translation project. We are also grateful to CNU Press. It was pleasure to work with the general editor SONG Mi-Sook, who provided useful guidance as we worked on many drafts. And finally, special thanks to the Brain Korea (BK) FOUR Project funded by the National Research Foundation of Korea. Without its generous support, the plan for this translation project could not have been imagined or realized.

INTRODUCTION

In "Waiting for the First Bus, Again," a popular song composed and sung by Korean singers JEONG Tae-Chun & PARK Eun-Ok, the speaker waits for someone at the bus stop. They were supposed to meet there, but the other person never appears, though the speaker waits until the last bus comes running in the rain. No clues are provided as to what happened to the speaker's friend. The speaker has been wandering around the bus stop in dreams since that spring, still remembering all the warmth and scent of the lost friend.

We are just like the speaker nervously waiting for our friend at the bus stop. To keep our promise to wait for and meet the ones who have been coming to us, we have launched this translation project under the working title, "At the Bus Stop." Waiting for those who have been lost, forgotten, and marginalized from contemporary Korean history and politics, we long for a reunion with them through the translation of *Selected Oral Histories of the May 18 Gwangju Uprising*, originally published in 1990. However, we are well aware of a danger in exaggerating our importance, as if we could mediate between the dead and the living, because we acutely and painfully recognize the limits of language and the cultural differences between Korean and English. Instead of a sense of fulfilment, we are troubled by a sense of failure, especially when subtle nuances in the words of the testimonies have to be generalized and contextualized in the course of translation. The more we feel frustrated with the translation, the stronger our longing for the past becomes. Some may make the criticism that we are so nostalgic about the May Uprising that we imprison ourselves in the melancholic past and even pathologically glorify the traumatic event. As many recent scholars have claimed, however, we need no longer see nostalgia as a pathetic sentiment to be considered a disease. It is neither politically conservative nor merely escapist. Instead, nostalgia opens up lost potentialities of the past, brushing against the grain of both regressive essentialism and teleological state ideology. In that sense, with our translation project, we may be called nostalgists as long as the term refers to those who desire to open up the unrealized past toward multiple futures.

There have been many wonderful translations regarding May 18, such as *The May 18 Democratic Uprising* (2020) published by the May 18 Memorial Institution and *Gwangju Diary: Beyond Death, Beyond the Darkness of the Age* (2017), written by LEE Jae-Eui and translated by SEOL Kap-Su and Nick Mamatas. These fantastic translations successfully arrange several events chronologically to acquire historical significance. The previous translators' chronological representation of the several events of the May Uprising was necessary to provide a perspective from which historical and political responsibilities can be claimed, and through which the people can envisage a step toward reconciliation. Those translations also provide vivid photos and detailed maps to help readers better understand the historical context. Needless to say, readers gain an "overview" of the May Uprising with the help of the previous translations. *Selected Oral Histories of the May 18 Gwangju Uprising* pursues an "underview" of the Uprising in rearranging personal narratives of witnesses who construct their heterogeneous stories in different locations during the Uprising. The witnesses, in fact, find themselves puzzled, baffled, and frustrated because they do not have any overview on the event. Fragmented, inconsistent, and even contradictory, their underviews can be more truthful than so-called historical facts, as Dori Laub's analysis of a Holocaust survivor's testimony proves how the survivor's distorted memory can be truthful because a survivor tends to exaggerate his or her memory after going through a traumatic event. *Selected Oral Histories of the May 18 Gwangju Uprising* willingly risks containing many errors in the witnesses' testimonies. It rather aims to reveal personal narratives of the May Uprising that have been sweepingly generalized and marginalized in favor of a linear model of historical development primarily based on cause-and-effect.

Vol. 1 Testimonies from Various Locations is thematically arranged by locations from which twenty-six witnesses' underviews are revealed. Watching, smelling, hiding, walking, running, crying, and shouting, the witnesses struggle to comprehend and interpret what is going on around themselves while moving from one place to another. Setting aside a chronological order, Volume 1 as a whole is reconstructed as if it were a narrative of an individual witness who encountered a traumatic event. Beginning *in medias res*, "Chapter II. Trauma" covers testimonies about tragic narratives of torture and suffering that take place in Sangmudae and Gwangju Prison. In tracing back to what happened to the witnesses, "Chapter III. Murderous Oppression" revisits the sites of the massacre in Geumnam-ro and in front of the Jeonnam Province Hall. Mercilessly persecuted by martial law forces, Gwangju citizens develop political consciousness to defend Gwangju and democracy around Chonnam National University, in front of Gwangju Munhwa Broadcasting Corporation, around the Fountain Plaza, and in the Province Hall, as illustrated in "Chapter IV. Critical Consciousness." With the heightened consciousness of the citizens in mind, in "Chapter V. Fierce Battles," the readers are guided to the sites of armed struggles, such as the Gwangju Station, Gwangju Park, the Province Hall, and Gwangju Young Women's Christian Association, in which the citizens risk their lives for democracy. Finally, "Chapter VI. With the Dead" shows countless corpses in Sangmugwan of the Province Hall and the Red Cross Hospital, where the dead are guarded by the living who are willing to tell the world the stories of the dead.

We tried to adhere to the translation and spelling guidelines for Korean names provided by the Korean Ministry of Culture, Sports, and Tourism. Basically, we follow the Korean word order for the Korean names in this volume: A family name comes first in capital letters followed by a given name. For instance, LEE Young-Hee for 리영희, and SONG Ki-Sook for 송기숙. However, we keep using some names as they are conventionally spelled, such as CHUN Doo-Hwan for 전두환 and PARK Chung-Hee for 박정희, primarily because they are key figures who should not be confused with any others in the May Uprising. We would also like to note that each testimony has its own number that was originally included in the Korean version, such as "3020. The Hell of Sangmudae." We leave the numbers as they are just in case readers want to use them for cross-checking for further research. As indicated in the title, this volume is arranged by major locations during the May Uprising. Regrettably, however, we do not include maps of Gwangju, not only because our primary focus is a translation, but also because there are many wonderful publications with detailed maps that show a comprehensive overview on the citizens' movements. In that sense, *Gwangju Diary* would be a good reference.

"At the Bus Stop," our translation project of *Selected Oral Histories of the May 18 Gwangju Uprising* will continue in two more volumes: *Vol. 2 The Perspectives of Various Subjects* and *Vol. 3 The Aims of Heterogeneous Communities* in the next four years. As we wait for the appearance of those volumes, we hope this first one will be a valuable resource for researchers, teachers, and students who may not be prepared to read the original Korean versions. Besides those academic audiences, however, this book presents for the general reader gripping personal stories of the Gwangju People's Uprising. These stories can help any reader consider the human potential of ordinary people faced with the oppression of an authoritarian state. They also offer a darker glimpse into the potential for inhuman behavior of those who have surrendered to the false narratives of such a state. The current rise of authoritarian tendencies and sympathies in today's world makes this translation an even more valuable contribution to a hope for a more egalitarian and democratic world.

Because English makes these histories available to an international audience, democratic struggles throughout the world can find transnational solidarity with these histories and perhaps some hope in the fact that the events narrated in these histories led to a more democratic nation, however contentious its democracy may sometimes be. These histories are of a particular time and place, and are particular to a particular people, but from the stories, a non-Korean reader may begin to get some sense of the Korean people's heart and the *han* of their historical suffering. These particular histories also transcend their historical moment, however, connecting the Gwangju people to a more broadly shared human desire for freedom from state oppression. These histories make available in their English translation, the great, though sometimes flawed, fundamental human dignity that the Gwangju people claimed in their rising up. Revisiting that dignity might echo with nostalgia, but it also resounds with the possibility of a better future.

Co-editors KIM Yeon-Min & Robert Grotjohn

February 2023

FOREWORD (1)

On the morning of May 18, 1980, I woke up in Eugene, Oregon, to the distant sound of a giant explosion. Mt. Saint Helens, a majestic volcano in the North Cascade mountain range, had blown its top in a violent eruption that spewed fire, ash, and lava for miles around. But as I watched the news unfold on television that night, I saw the first glimpse of another eruption thousands of miles away in South Korea, in the city of Gwangju. Earlier that same day, hundreds of people had been brutally assaulted by soldiers dispatched to the city by a renegade general, CHUN Doo-Hwan, who had just seized control of the country in a military coup.

As a graduate student in Korean studies at the University of Oregon, I wasn't surprised at this news. Id been closely following the human drama unfolding in South Korea since the October 26, 1979, assassination of PARK Chung-Hee, and understood that CHUN had slowly been consolidating his power in the Korean military and the government. I also knew, from living in Seoul during the 1960 revolution against Syngman Rhee, that the South Korean people would not stand for another dictatorship. But I, like many Koreans, was unprepared for the ferocity of CHUN and his military allies.

According to the first, grim reports from churches and human rights groups, there had been a massacre of protesters by CHUN's black-bereted paratroopers. Students, young people, and ordinary citizens had been shot in cold blood, and others had their bodies torn apart with bayonets; one horrific report said that soldiers had even sliced the breasts from two women. Scores, possibly hundreds and even thousands, might be dead. Desperate messages began streaming out of Korea, pleading for help from the United States, whose president, Jimmy Carter, had promised to make human rights the cornerstone of U.S. foreign policy.

But as I wrote later in an essay about the uprising, the citizens of South Korea quickly learned that President Carter had no desire to offend a friendly military dictator at the height of the Cold War. On the morning of May 27, with approval from the U.S. commander of the joint U.S.-South Korean military command, the 20th Division of the Korean Army invaded Gwangju and crushed the ragtag army of young students and workers who had taken up arms against CHUN's martial law forces. As the press flashed images of dead and shackled rebels being dragged through the streets, President Carter's military and security advisers coldly explained they had instructed U.S. commanders to release the Korean troops from the joint command to restore "stability" in South Korea. Their words conveyed the message, well understood in Korea since the 1940s, that American officials viewed the Korean peninsula as a problem child of U.S. foreign policy, its people and their democratic notions an annoyance at times of global tension.

Shocked by Carter's response to the uprising, I began investigating the circumstances of the Gwangju Massacre. In February 1981, I visited Gwangju and met my first eyewitnesses, an American missionary couple who had been working in the Christian Hospital. A few years later, I read the now-famous book *Gwangju Diary,* and learned of the incredible bravery of the students, workers and citizens who came together in anger, sorrow, and hope to do battle with CHUN's paratroopers. Eventually, through the use of the Freedom of Information Act, I revealed that that the U.S. government had given a green light to the Korean government to use Korean army troops against the huge pro-democracy demonstrations that had rocked South Korean cities in the spring of 1980 - and then, when the Gwangju uprising appeared out of control, backed CHUN's use of army troops to retake the city. My stories shocked and angered many Koreans. Years later, in 2015, Gwangju granted me an honorary citizenship, drawing me even closer to the city.

The oral history you now hold in your hands is the true story of the Gwangju people who resisted CHUN's martial law army and stood up for Korean democracy. As I read through their stories, I'm struck by how closely their memories match those first reports I heard immediately afterwards. Here again are the horrific tale of bayonets tearing through women's flesh; the bodies crushed by clubs and boots, making it impossible to distinguish men from women; the shock at the cruelty of Koreans towards other Koreans; the *Taegukgi* draped across the bodies and faces of the dead; and the despair at the realization that America, publicly committed to democracy, would do nothing to help. It's a history that demands to be told and understood. The voices of Gwangju remind us that defending democracy is a constant struggle and that people under repression will eventually rise up and explode, just like Mt. St. Helens and the Korean people did in 1980.

Tim Shorrock

Humanitarian Journalist
Washington, DC
January 23, 2023

FOREWORD (2)

"We'd like to translate to English *Selected Oral Histories of the May 18 Gwangju Uprising*." One day, Professor KIM Yeon-Min of the Department of English Language and Literature, with whom I was not acquainted, came to the May 18 Institute and asked me for help with these words. It was a very unexpected suggestion that I had never thought of before, and at the same time, it was a refreshing shock to me.

Selected Oral Histories of the May 18 Gwangju Uprising is one of the most important references for those who undertake research on the state violence and people's resistance during the May 18 Uprising. However, it has a reputation as a source difficult to access due to the vast amount of testimonies of up to 500 witnesses and the detail of the testimonies that cover the entire process of May 18. It was surprising and fresh because Professor KIM suggested that he would cover even part of the formidable material in his Brain Korea project.

The first result came out after two years. The translation of twenty-six testimonies has been published under the title of *Vol. 1 Testimonies from Various Locations*. To this end, the BK 21 project of the Department of English Language and Literature has been working steadily for the last two years with twenty-one professors and lecturers and fifteen graduate students. It can be said in a way that the translation project, impossible at an individual level or with such a small workforce, could not be done without the national support of the BK 21. Nevertheless, the enthusiasm and hard work of the professors, lecturers, and graduate students directly in charge of the project deserve considerable respect because the English translation of *Selected Oral Histories* provides the foundation for the May 18 People's Uprising to become an asset of all people and to be sublimated into universal value.

The three key concepts surrounding May 18 in recent years are *investigation* of the truth, *preservation* of the original form, and *forgiveness and reconciliation*. These key concepts may seem obvious at first glance, but they are very controversial concepts in some respects. This is because questions such as what the truth is, whether an original form exists, and, furthermore, who is entitled to forgive whom require ideological and historical consideration. I believe the English translation of *Selected Oral Histories* will lead us to rich debates on those issues.

I participated in the project to publish *Selected Oral Histories* from 1988 to 1990. The colleagues who joined the project tended to consider *Selected Oral Histories* a sort of translation because that publication was a result of rendering from the spoken style of the witnesses' Jeolla dialects, which were unfamiliar to some of the researchers, into a written style close to the standard Korean language. With the aid of the conversion, *Selected Oral Histories* has been able to be shared nationwide beyond the Gwangju region. Now, the first step in translating *Selected Oral Histories*, although only part of it, is being completed. The translation project lays a foundation for international communication beyond a single country. For that reason, I look forward to the further publications of *Vol. 2 The Perspectives of Various Subjects* and *Vol. 3 The Aims of Heterogeneous Communities* in the next four years. I wish the BK 21 of the Department of English Language and Literature steady enthusiasm for the ongoing translation project.

CHOI Jeong-Gi, Ph.D.

Director of the May 18 Institute, Chonnam National University
August 30, 2022

Ⅰ. PREFACE

1. "Records of Blood beyond Death"
   by **LEE Young-Hee**

2. "In Historical Succession to the Spirit of the Uprising"
   by **SONG Ki-Sook**

I PREFACE

1. Records of Blood beyond Death

LEE Young-Hee
Chairman of the Board for the Modern Korean History Institute May 1990

In commemoration of the tenth anniversary of the Gwangju Democratization Movement, which began in Gwangju and the Jeollanam-do area in May 1980, the year of the thirty-fifth anniversary of the division of the nation, the Modern Korean History Institute collected vivid testimonies about the scenes of struggle and has at last published a collection of historical records. I am confident that it is the largest and most meaningful project since the establishment of this institute.

Compared to the hard work, enthusiasm, and great expectations of many people who dedicated their time and energy for many years to the purpose of this project, I think the result is still limited and leaves a lot to be done in the future. However, in the political situation of today when the main culprits who perpetrated the massacre in May 1980 are still in power even though ten years have passed, the difficulties that the participants in this project, researchers as well as eye-witnesses, had to go through while giving and recording testimonies cannot be overlooked. There is nothing more to be desired from our institute if those who are trying to read this collection understand the difficulties that permeate each word, each sentence, and each page of this record.

Every word of testimony in this collection is made not of letters but of fresh blood. It was not easy to get a line of an eye-witness account or a word of direct experience from the mouths of those who are reluctant to testify out of fear, even though ten years have passed since that time. Testimony from the victims of the military dictatorship, who are to remain disabled for life, is not merely an account of their own desperate experiences, but in itself becomes the blood testimony of countless bitter, traumatized souls, the exact number of whom may never be revealed. Therefore, those who are to read the entire collection of this historical record will hear the cries of the heroic fighters of the day, whose souls are wandering between heaven and earth with their eyes still open.

"The history of blood cannot be obscured by the history of ink."

The spirit and sacrifice of Gwangju in May 1980, the year which marks the thirty-fifth anniversary after the division of Korea and its people, can be recognized as the event of the "Gwangju National Democratic People's Armed Resistance" through an academic and historical assessment. It is a rightful and natural assessment. Today's regime, representing the parties who carried out the anti-human indiscriminate slaughter in Gwangju, has finally and officially recognized the event as a "democratic struggle" rather than as a "riot by violent mobs," which was the blatant mischaracterization they had tried to invent at first.

The current significance of the May 18 Democratization Movement in Gwangju is immeasurable. It has caused enormous changes over the past decade in military, political, social, ideological, and economic areas as well as in the sense of life and culture. It also has had a great effect on problems of national division and relations with foreign countries. Furthermore, it has created a strong influence on the national identity of Korean people in terms of international politics and diplomacy. It is true that its ideologically explosive power is constantly amplifying. In that sense, May 1980 in Gwangju lasts forever. This is so because it has become a symbol of the spirit of Korean people inherited through such historical events as the Donghak Peasant Revolution, the March 1 Independence Movement, the armed struggle for liberation from Japanese colonial oppression that took place overseas, and the April 19 Anti-Authoritarian Struggle led by students. The May 18 Gwangju Democratization Movement has become a comprehensive representation of the struggle for human liberation from injustice and oppression. The true image of the people who had to take up arms for life, freedom, and democracy is vividly revived in this collection. I hope it will be a general reference for the voices of humanitarian values.

Finally, I sincerely appreciate the effort of Professor SONG Ki-Sook, director of the Korea Modern History Institute, who has been working on the whole business from planning to completing this project. And I also give credit to the hard work of the researchers who were directly in charge of all the activities on the front line.

I PREFACE

2. In Historical Succession to the Spirit of the Uprising

SONG Ki-Sook, Ph.D.
Director of the Modern Korean History Institute May 1990

In celebration of the tenth anniversary of the May Uprising in Gwangju, the publication of *Selected Oral Histories of the May 18 Gwangju Uprising* is very rewarding for those who have participated in this project. It seems that our Institute is the first to attempt to compile all data, including the oral testimonies of the participants, for a single historical event.

For the decade since the Uprising, political reality has constantly betrayed the great spirit of the Gwangju People's Uprising. Consequently, we have reached the tenth anniversary without even enacting a compensation law. Furthermore, the process of political discussion on the compensation law made the mistake of greatly distorting even the spirit of the Uprising. However, no matter how much politics betrays the spirit of the People's Uprising, the spirit of it is neither faded nor damaged. The more politics betrays, the more the spirit of the Uprising will shine brightly as an indicator of our historical development. The May People's Uprising in Gwangju proves that the people are the substance of the nation and the subjects of history. The people stand tall in our history as a model and symbol of the resistance that faithfully fulfills the legitimate demands of the nation in protecting our nation from the forces of wicked imperialism and fighting against comprador dictatorships relying on a foreign power.

Along with the project of collecting the oral testimonies during the Gwangju People's Uprising, our Institute is planning a larger-scale conference than that of the last year. While continuing to collect important data on modern history centered on the Gwangju Uprising, we plan to hold an annual conference to continually examine the idea and spirit of the Uprising as the original starting point for the development of modern Korean history.

The reason our Institute planned to collect data on the May People's Uprising in Gwangju as the first project, and put special emphasis on transcribing the testimonies of the participants, is to vividly record each individual's noble spirit of resistance and uncorrupted passion at the time of the Uprising and pass them on to future generations. Their testimonies, therefore, may serve not only as historical material but also as a living lesson in itself. Every one of them is as beautiful and precious as a flower, as they willingly threw their lives at daggers and rifles. As a mere historical document, transcribing 500 people's testimonies of a single event may seem to be too much. Still, all investigators tirelessly visited them, listened to their stories, and recorded them because all the stories were as beautiful and precious as flowers.

Such direct oral statements by the participants are bound to have fundamental weaknesses in terms of historical records because it is a natural human psychological symptom to exaggerate or reduce in some cases as one is talking about what one has done. We reviewed the method from various angles in our own way before recording, but we have to admit that there was a lack of sufficient methodological review from a more scientific point of view of oral history. In this respect, this collection is meaningful as an attempt; therefore, the problems that emerge here with this attempt will bring a further task to the academic world. In the course of the development of modern Korean history, data on people's resistance are bound to depend on government circles and will be distorted from the perpetrators' point of view. Since the limitations of such data can be supplemented to some extent through oral transmission and oral dictation, I think that there should be a more in-depth investigation into the method of collecting such oral data and a scientific review of the data. In considering that the truth of such a dreadful event like the nearby Jeju April 3 Incident is revealed by oral statements of the survivors, the academic world should pay attention to oral data.

Our second project is in the planning stage, but considering the various conditions of our Institute, topics like the Gwangju Student Independence Movement may be an accessible subject of investigation. And given the current academic interest, data on small and large events of national and democratization movements since August 15, 1945, the Independence Day of Korea, will be the subject of investigation. We plan to collect and organize the remaining data on the Gwangju Uprising and continue the investigation into other cases. We hope for a lot of interest and encouragement from academia and the general public.

It is the result of the active cooperation of many people that this first project has accomplished even this much. Many professors participated on the research committee, and many young people joined as researchers, sparing no dedication. And most of all, many philanthropists offered decisive help with financial support. I intend to reveal them properly some day and express my deep gratitude for their generosity.

In particular, I can't help but be very grateful for the goodwill of NA Byeong-Sik, the CEO of Pulbit Publishing House, who was in charge of publishing this collection. He also once revealed the full details of the Uprising to the world by publishing *Beyond Death, Beyond the Darkness of the Age,* which was the first comprehensive record of the May People's Uprising in Gwangju. While serving as a board member of the Institute, he is participating in publishing this collection, though he has nothing to gain from it personally, as an extension of the enthusiasm that he already showed in the previous publication.

Ⅱ. TRAUMA

II TRAUMA

1. Sangmudae

3020. The Hell of Sangmudae
Name: PARK Tae-Sung (male)
Date of Birth: August 14, 1959 (aged 20)
Occupation: College student (currently unemployed)
Date of Record: October 1988

Research & Arrangement by YANG Nan-Hee

Overview

PARK Tae-Sung, a student at Chosun University, joined May 18 while struggling against the University Foundation.[1] On May 18th, he was caught while throwing stones at paratroopers sent to suppress the protest. That afternoon, he was taken to the Chosun University stadium and to Sangmudae after going through all kinds of beatings and inhumane treatment. He was released on July 3rd but suspended from Chosun University. He returned to school in 1984 and graduated.

The News of the Extension of Emergency Martial Law

In 1980, I was a sophomore in the Department of Public Administration at Chosun University and was the president of the student association of the department.

[1] Similar to the Board of Trustees of an American university, such a foundation is unique to private universities in South Korea, which are usually proprietary.

As the struggle against the University Foundation had continued since March 1980, professors began to mediate between students and the Foundation. During the course of the mediation, professors responded to the Foundation's unilateral exercise of physical force against them and eventually joined the fight against the Foundation as their opinions were completely inclined toward the students'. The fight lasted from the beginning of the semester until the end of April. At the end of April, external situations changed rapidly, and the military dictatorship conspiracy centered on CHUN Doo-Hwan became known to universities across the country. People began to sense the seriousness of the problem. Student executives agreed to postpone the fight against the Foundation for the time being and cooperate with other universities. At the same time, the Chosun University Committee for the Democratization Struggle (hereinafter referred to as Mintu[2)]) was organized with about twenty members. Mintu appeared as the form of student councils of each college. At that time, the student councils of Chosun University started a fight with the Foundation as a way to regenerate its student movement capabilities that had become stagnant and to strengthen public solidarity. Until May 8, little had been said about the current situation outside the campus.

After the organization of Mintu, we felt the need to change the issue of our struggle to prepare for the urgent issues without consuming our capabilities on campus problems.

Although we had not gained anything from the fight for two months, we agreed to postpone it for the time being and deal with the situation by keeping pace with Chonnam National University. There was a request that the student executive council, which had been active until then, should step back and let Mintu lead street protests, starting with the school gate fight. The two parties, Mintu and the student executive council agreed to disband

---

2) An abbreviation formed from the initial syllables of the Korean words for "democratization" (*minjuhwa*) and "struggle" (*tujaeng*).

the sit-in protest, which had been prolonged for more than fifty days, and held a termination ceremony with 8,000 students gathered at the university stadium. It was a developmental disbandment by temporarily shelving the school issues and moving toward a struggle to prevent the re-establishment of military dictatorship, which was a more urgent issue. As soon as it was disbanded, the initiative of the student movement was transferred to Mintu.

After that, I stayed in Gwangju until May 12th and then fled to Suncheon. It was to avoid terrorizing individual students by the Foundation through acts such as kidnapping and assault. As the terrorizing of individuals began, we ended personal actions for two days and got together. On May 12th, seventeen students went to Hwasun Station and went to Suncheon by train. We stayed at Seonam Temple for one night, and to that point, people hired from the Foundation pursued us. As the Foundation mobilized professors and even gangsters in three vehicles, we went to Jeonju. On May 14th, 15th, and 16th, we heard the news of street demonstrations in Gwangju on television and discussed our plans after May 17th. At the Nana Inn in front of Jeonbuk National University High School, we analyzed the situation while discussing what to do, without knowing anything about the nationwide extension of emergency measures to be pronounced in the early morning of May 18th. Even though we couldn't analyze the situation properly, most of us were optimistic. We certainly expected that it would end in a victory for the democratic forces because we believed even if the military force reappeared, the level of public consciousness was different from that of May 16th. We thought there would be a conflict in the process, but we concluded that the situation would turn out to be favorable to us as the conflict itself would end in the defeat of the military dictatorship. At that time, in fact, it was very cumbersome for the seventeen of us to move all together, and the expenses could no longer be covered.

In the end, we decided to go back to Gwangju individually and had a termination ceremony on May 17th. During the meeting at 12:00 a.m. on May 18th, we learned about the news of the extension of martial law on TV. The previous decision to terminate our meeting was rescinded because of the nationwide extension of emergency martial law, including Jeju Island, and the closure of schools across the country. After we turned off the TV, we heard the sound of tanks in the distance. It was around 1:00 a.m. The inn was located along the local route from Namwon to Jeonju. At the sound of the roar, we peeked out the window but couldn't see anything yet. We guessed that soldiers stationed in Namwon were coming to Jeonju. About an hour later, a huge group of tanks and armored vehicles passed by. All the roads we could see were occupied with tanks and armored vehicles. It was around 2:00 a.m. on May 18th. After witnessing the scene, we kept calling ten professors who had been in contact with us then, but they said that nothing had changed in Gwangju at that time.

On the morning of May 18th, we decided to go to Gwangju. Some students who were wanted because of school issues decided to go to places where they could hide for about two weeks. There was no particular reason for the two-week period of flight, but we judged that it would be difficult for the soldiers to hold out for more than two weeks no matter how heavily they were armed. Each of the seventeen shared our contact information, decided to keep in touch and ask after each other, and then parted.

On the morning of May 18th, I headed to Gwangju. I arrived at Gwangju Express Bus Terminal around 12:30 p.m. Up to that point, the area near the terminal was calm as usual. I took the bus No. 5 to go home in Bangrim-dong, but the road was blocked in front of Gwangju Jeil High School. Looking at Geumnam-ro from the bus, the number of students was about 500, and the number of riot police suppressing them was much more. At that time, Geumnam-ro was covered with fog-like tear gas. The bus driver said he could not move anymore. When everyone got out of the bus and looked toward the Province Hall, there were barricades near the entrance, and Geumnam-ro 2nd and 3rd Streets were filled with tear gas as the sound of tear gas bombs reverberated, making it difficult to distinguish things properly, even what was right ahead. In the midst of that, I could dimly saw one or two students running around and combat police who wore iron helmets dragging students toward the Hanil Bank. The combat police surrounded the areas in front of the YMCA and the Hanil Bank, and toward the Intercity Bus Terminal in three layers. About 2,000 to 3,000 citizens were watching the demonstration surrounding the combat police. In other words, about 500 students were surrounded by the combat police on Geumnam-ro 2nd and 3rd Streets, and the police were surrounded by the citizens.

The Fight on the First Day

It was unclear whether it was the students in Geumnam-ro that began to incite citizens who were just watching from the outside. Encouraging the citizens, saying "You can't just look at it like this, can you?" they joined the citizens, singing songs and forming a scrum. Although there was no direct participation, two to three thousand citizens gradually began to stir, yelling out and throwing stones. The combat police fired tear gas at the citizens nervously as they felt agitation from their rear. From this point on, as citizens voluntarily threw stones, chanted slogans, and pushed in line with the students' lead, the blocking line of the combat police was slightly disrupted. I remember that the students inside joined the citizens. After a while, citizens and students were dispersed around Geumnam-ro 5th Street as the combat police rushed toward them. When more and more students continued to be beaten and dragged away, citizens who were seeing it from the outside supported the demonstration by screaming. Following the riot police and throwing stones at them when the riot police were pushed back, the citizens participated in the demonstration in the form of disturbance operations from the rear.

I had barely gone home since I participated in demonstrations on campus issues in March. So I was still wearing a thick winter parka. It was warm, and I thought I couldn't go around wearing such an outfit, so I headed home to change my clothes. Taxis were no longer running, and buses were running off their routes. I turned to Chungjang-ro, thinking that I had no choice but to walk. From Chungjang-ro 5th street to 4th street, I could hardly find people but there was tear gas. At that time, there were a lot of stones and rubble that could be used as weapons for the protesters around the construction site of the Chunggeum Underpass. When I went to the Chungjang-ro Police Box, a fight with the police was going on fiercely. Unlike the fight at the Hanil Bank, there were citizens and students joining in and fighting by throwing stones. Fierce fighting developed on both sides around the road dug for the underpass construction, and the police continued to broadcast pacification messages. The police told us to go home quickly rather than to linger there. Until then, the demonstration was somewhat romantic, not realizing the hostile situation that would develop later on, in that the combat police said, "Is throwing stones democratization? Go home quickly!" which was followed by the citizens' responses with jokes.

After fighting for about an hour in front of the Chungjang-ro Police Box, we were pushed back by the combat police and went to the entrance of Chosun University through the back alley of the Province Hall. There were paratroopers, but there were no tanks, and they did not yet start suppressing the protestors. At about 2:00 p.m., when the combat police were temporarily pushed back, perhaps because of a lack of tear gas to shoot, the crowd of protesters destroyed the Chungjang-ro Police Box. I went back to Chungjang-ro 2nd Street through the alley in front of the former Patriots Affairs Office and Baekje Hotel. The street was already blocked off by the combat police. When I went back to the front of the American Cultural Center, I noticed a lot of college students from Chosun University I knew. I went to the front of the Daedo Hotel with them. There were also many Chosun University students there. From then on, slogans were rarely shouted except when they were pushed back after throwing stones. They retreated outside the range that the tear gas canisters could reach and shouted slogans again. I could feel the situation getting intense as time went on. There, I found tear gas bombs that had not exploded with their tops open and the powder spilled. So I collected them to put into buckets of water supplied by the nearby houses and shops and dissolved them.

The ongoing fight almost seemed like hand-to-hand combat. There, too, being pushed back by the combat police, I went to the back wall of the Province Hall and saw that the road was filled with citizens. There were probably about a thousand people. After taking a break there for about ten minutes, I joined a scrum that formed again and headed toward the Daedo Hotel, where a lot of tear gas was fired, which pushed people back toward Yangyeong Academy. As many people ran to get out of the way, combat police resting near the Labor Office hurriedly put on gas masks and fired tear gas, and another battle broke out there. I stepped back for a moment and made a phone call to my home in Bangrim-dong. I was living in my aunt's house at the time, so my aunt answered the call and told me not to come back home. The previous night, four or five plain-clothes police officers came and searched the whole house, asking where the Chosun University student council executives were and urging her to tell them right away while making a mess. She told me not to come home for a while. But I didn't have money at the time, so I planned to meet my cousin in front of the Labor Office and get some money. Roughly calculating the time to meet my cousin, I rejoined the demonstrators again. Being pushed together with the demonstrators, I went to Sansu-dong and saw many citizens there. Students were arrested at the Dongmyeong-dong Police Box. But as the protesters pushed toward Sansu-dong, they surrounded the police box. About eight police officers in the Dongmyeong-dong Police Box who had held the students were literally caught by the protestors. Seeing the situation, I went to Yangyeong Academy to meet my cousin. I met the cousin and received 30,000 won, put on a spring jacket my cousin brought, and sent the winter parka home.

Coming back to the street in front of the MBC station, a helicopter hovered and started pacification broadcasting. It was a few minutes before 3:00 p.m. Tear gas, fragments of tear gas bombs, and stones were scattered around the place where demonstrators had passed by. Until I was caught around 4:00 p.m. by paratroopers who were first deployed to suppress the demonstration, I went back and forth in front of Dongmyeong-ro, the Labor Office, and the MBC station. When I couldn't endure the tear gas during a stone-throwing demonstration, I washed my face and got some fresh air before joining the protesters again. After protesting for a while, I wiped my tears behind Gwangju Girls' High School and came out to Dongmyeong-ro. And the demonstrators were nowhere to be seen. According to the citizens looking at the protest there, demonstrators were chased toward Sansu-dong. As I was heading toward Sansu-dong to follow the main demonstrators, I saw people crowded near the Jang-dong Intersection. I went there and I found that they were citizens who were just watching. A helicopter was continuously making a pacification broadcast along Dongmyeong-ro on the way to Sansu-dong. It said citizens should return home quickly. When I looked ahead, I couldn't see the demonstrators, so I went to the Jang-dong Intersection again. The scattered demonstrators were gathering again in front of the MBC station on a small scale. As a middle-aged woman said, it seemed true that the majority of earlier demonstrators had gone somewhere else.

The Atrocities of the Paratroopers with Bayonets

At around 3:30 p.m., several military trucks came in a row from the Intercity Bus Terminal. I felt like I was watching a movie when the trucks made a sudden stop in front of the MBC station and soldiers jumped off like springs from both sides of the trucks at the same time. I was wearing glasses stained with tear gas, dust, and sweat, so I was washing my glasses among some women because I couldn't see well. When I saw the soldiers jumping out of the trucks, someone shouted they were reserve forces. It was difficult to suppress the protests only with the riot police, so it was said that they took reserve forces near Gwangju and trained them to use clubs in the 31st Division, and they finally appeared that day. Until then, I was carefully observing their actions, remaining defenseless. There were forty to fifty demonstrators in front of the MBC station. As paratroopers spread moving in circle, screaming, "Ya!" all the people there ended up lying on the ground. They ran around carrying M16s with bayonets fixed. Seeing the movement, I sensed that they were something different from the combat police I had seen. Still, I was about 50 meters away from the MBC station, and I was standing and watching among the women, thinking that I would not be caught if I stood with citizens standing on the sidewalk as the paratroopers passed by. But it seemed that they had already lost their minds. Running among the people and striking them with buttstocks, they came right in front of us. I saw the fallen people grabbed by the hem of their pants from both sides and dragged and loaded into a truck. I started to run away with all my might, thinking that I would be killed on the spot if I was caught by them.

At that time, fleeing from the University Foundation due to the school protest issue, I walked about 70 kilometers from Suncheon to Gurye, which caused blisters on my feet. And I was very tired because I could hardly sleep at all when I watched the martial law forces entering Jeonju on the night of May 17th. Moreover, as soon as I arrived in Gwangju, I went with the protesters, so the fatigue was indescribable. Along with some other people, I ran away to the front of Gwangju Girls' High School, and when I turned around, seven or eight paratroopers were chasing after us. When I got to the main gate of Gwangju Girls' High School, I saw that other paratroopers with clubs were looking at me from the Education Committee Building. As I tried to turn back and run away again, the paratroopers were already close at hand. I couldn't run away any longer, so I ran into an oil shop right in front of me. There, four or five ladies were squeezing oil and opened the side door leading to the main house when they saw us running in a hurry and told us to pass through quickly. All the people who ran with me entered the main house through the door. Instead of going inside, I was hiding behind the oil press. I was hiding for only three or four minutes, but it felt like an age. At that time, the ladies in the oil shop went out to the door to see what was going on outside. I also joined them to look out. The paratroopers found me and mercilessly hit me in the head with their clubs. After that, I was dragged out, being hit in the head and shoulders by two paratroopers several times. I lost consciousness for a very short time. The ladies who saw the scene screamed and yelled, "Don't you have a younger brother?" When I came to my senses and tried to run away, the two of them hit me and grasped me harder. Then, when they shouted at their colleagues, other paratroopers rushed to me and kicked me in the chest with their military boots. When I was almost unconscious, kicked and beaten by clubs, they dragged me toward a truck in front of the MBC station. If there was any sign of resistance, they beat people instantly. Being dragged, I glanced at the Labor Office and saw people, caught and unconscious, being dragged by the hem. I didn't think I could resist anymore, so I told him not to hit me because I would follow him faster from then on. When I boarded the truck in front of the MBC station, another paratrooper who was watching from above hit me more times than I could count.

I was lying on the floor of the truck with my head down. Unconscious people kept being thrown into the truck like luggage. After a while, the truck we rode moved back and forth between

Jang-dong Intersection and Dongmyeong-ro toward Sansu-dong, picking up citizens and students. Every time the truck stopped, the paratroopers stomped on us and beat us, and cruelly hit the people in the truck. When we were so crowded in the truck that we could not move, people could talk to the person next to them for a few moments. The truck stopped somewhere in Dongmyeong-ro, and they started beating us one by one from the inside again. The people next to me whispered that they would question each person one by one and beat students when their student IDs came out. So I ducked down and swallowed my student ID. There were two pieces of paper with the phone numbers written down when we parted with other student council executives in Jeonju, one of which I swallowed. At the moment I was about to chew and swallow the other one, I was caught. I was forced to stand up and started getting hit again. At that time, my chin was cut and I bled a lot. Their faces got red, and they smelled of alcohol, so they must have been drunk.

After being beaten individually one by one, we were taken to the Chosun University stadium three to four hours after being caught. When we got off in the middle of the stadium, about 300 people who had already been arrested were there. As soon as I got off the truck, the paratroopers began to beat me ruthlessly. It was probably about 6:30 p.m. when I arrived at Chosun University stadium. In order to prevent people from running away, the paratroopers were gathered in circle surrounding the people in the middle of the stadium, forcing them to put their hands on their heads. The paratroopers kept beating the people who were outside, so people kept coming inside the group not to get hit. As I looked, the circle became smaller and people piled up. It looked as if maggots were moving.

I saw the paratrooper who had taken a note with the phone numbers from me going to his commander. I was so scared that I secretly took off my jacket and threw it away so that he wouldn't recognize me. After a while, the paratrooper who brought the note called names on the note and ordered the people of the names to come out. No one went out until three or four names were called. But someone went out answering probably because he had the same name. Then the paratrooper beat him up until he was unconscious and couldn't move.

There was no more beating after 9:00 p.m. The paratroopers told us to raise our hands if anyone wanted to go to the toilet. But no one answered because of what they had seen. The paratroopers told us to come out three or four times, saying it was okay. Then, one person went out and they took him across the stadium without beating him. Seeing them bring others one by one without beating them, I thought I could run away because a single paratrooper led each person, although I didn't have to go to the toilet.

But I couldn't escape because I felt like they were going to shoot me. For the first time since I was caught, I was allowed to rest for about an hour without being beaten. At this time, other people's faces no longer looked human. Beaten and swollen, covered in blood, they could hardly be recognized.

At about 10:00 p.m., a military police truck arrived. They tied us together in a row like weaving dried croaker fish and about fifty people were tied up with long ropes. With our hands tied behind our backs, we were beaten while they forced us to climb into the military truck. We all rode in such a way that the person in the back supported the person in the front with one's shoulders or head. There were so many people in the truck, and I felt like I was suffocated. The truck was locked up on all sides, so when the back door was closed, the light completely disappeared, and I couldn't see anything.

The Hell of Sangmudae

Soon, we got off at the Gwangju Police Station around 10:00 p.m. In the Gwangju Police Station, they only checked our names, addresses, and identities. Before we split up and were loaded into the vehicles, the combat police boarded; the police officers told us in worried looks that we should keep ourselves safe. We stayed at the Gwangju Police Station for more than two hours and were sent to Sangmudae. As soon as we arrived at the Sangmudae drill ground, they ordered us to take off our clothes except underwear and made us do the tadpoles crawl. A soldier was assigned to each of us, continuing to beat us in the back with baseball bats. And the soldiers pushed us into the guardhouse just at dawn. There were six cells in total in the guardhouse from Rooms 1 to 7, and there was no Room 4. I remember that the size of each cell was about eight *pyeong*.[3] About 80 people were locked in a cell. Since each room spread out in a fan-shaped radial form, soldiers could see each room at a glance if they sat in front of them and monitored them.

The individual interrogations began on May 19th. From waking up at 6:00 in the morning until going to bed at 10:00 at night, life was a series of punishments. And when the investigation stopped for a while, we were required to sit and stay still. If someone moved even a little, they were to be called out of their cell and forced to walk to the furthest cell and back to their cell while being hit. Meanwhile, I was called in for questioning.

On the night of May 20th, there was a strike to refuse the punishments in Room 6. They did it while singing the national anthem. Everyone got up holding on to the iron bars and asked why they were treated like prisoners even when they had not yet been judged in court. But the strike was immediately suppressed. On that day, during the search for the leaders, Professor PARK Dong-Cheol at Chosun University and a student at Sungkyunkwan University were taken to a punishment room of 0.5 *pyeong* and returned 24 hours later. But the Sungkyunkwan University student did not return after that. Rumors said he was

---

[3] One *pyeong* is about 35.6 square feet or 3.3 square meters.

dead, but no one knew the truth. After that, no complaints were made.

We who came from the Gwangju Police Station had meals from the Gwangju Police Station until May 21st. But from May 22nd we were told that they could not bring the meals because of strict traffic controls, so they gave us food from Sangmudae. In the lunch box, there were only two pieces of pickled radish and soybean paste. On May 21st, the release process began. In the morning, a major came in and called out about 80 people who belonged to class D out of classes A to D, as classified during the individual investigations. In the afternoon, the people of class D were called back again and given the clothes and shoes they had taken off when they first entered Sangmudae. At that time, it seems that they released only those classified as class D as protests spread demanding the release of arrested citizens and students. After arriving at Sangmudae, we stayed only in underwear until we were released. There was a rumor inside that if you were dragged out, you would die. So when the 80 or so left, we saw them getting on the bus. And the person who watched them through the bathroom window told us that they seemed to be released since they were leaving by bus. After that, the atmosphere inside became a little better.

On May 22nd, the second release was held. I think it was about 180 people. After the second release, I felt more spacious and comfortable in the room that had been so cramped that we had slept half leaning against each other.

On the morning of May 23rd, the major came in and called the roll of those to be released. I remember the exact number of the released was eighteen. LEE Seung-Ryong, vice president of the CNU student council, WI Kyeong-Jong, the student president of the College of Natural Sciences, and I were also called out to check the numbers and names. We thought we were going to be released because it was just like the previous roll call for release. After lunch, the major came back and called us out and asked,

“There are eighteen people, right?” So, I remember the number was exactly eighteen. They told us to bring the bags of our belongings that had been confiscated. When I brought my bag, they opened the door of Room 7 and pushed the eighteen of us in. At that time, there were already about ten people who had committed common crimes in Room 7. After opening the other five doors of the cells, the soldiers loaded all the other people into a truck to release them. The rest of us gave up hope for our release. Two days later, many people began to be arrested and detained on a large scale.

On the night of the 27th, the room began to be as crowded as when we first came in. A high school student who was released on the 23rd came back again on the 27th. According to the boy, he was sent back by bus and handed over to the citizen militia in Hwajeong-dong, and the citizen militia greeted them with applause, so he just cried. After being handed over to the citizen militia, some of the released who wanted to go home went home; some who wanted to stay joined the protest. The boy had been beaten and punished by the soldiers every day at Sangmudae, so he was scared to see the military uniforms. However, when he was released and welcome by the citizens just like himself, he was so moved by the fact that there were people on his side. So he couldn’t go home and was caught again on May 27th. We heard from the boy about the process by which the arrested were handed over to the citizen militia. There was an accident in which JEONG Dong-Nyeon hurt himself in the guardhouse of Sangmudae, which is unclear whether it was May 27th or not. At first, I wasn’t with JEONG Dong-Nyeon, but on May 23rd, when the eighteen people were left in Room 7, I was with him. Each was given a spoon hung around their neck. He sharpened it and hurt his belly with it. After that accident, we were unable to go to the toilet freely. We had to report to a guard to go to the toilet in pairs. And they took away all the spoons that each of us was given. On May 27th, a large number of protesters were arrested and detained. Those injured by gunshots and shrapnel were all transported to the Integrated Hospital the next day. At that time, the people who were caught had their deeds written on their backs with red marker pen, such as gun possession, KIM Dae-Jung followers, pistol possession, and members of the mobile strike force. When I saw the people arrested at that time, I could sense the situation outside. Those of us who had been captured earlier took off our shirts and tore them into pieces so the words were unrecognizable. We threw and pushed them into the squat toilet. Because the toilet in the guardhouse of Sangmudae was a flushing type, it didn't go in well. So we put our hands inside the toilet and pushed it away. There were too many pieces to fit in the toilet, so we put them in our mouths and chewed them, so nobody could recognize the letters. At that time, it was said among us that if one had letters written with the marker pens on the back, he would be executed. Our actions were discovered, and we were beaten and punished again.

From May 23rd, there were hardly any side dishes. On the plate that the soldiers used, we were distributed about three spoons of barley, soup with soybean paste and salt, and three or four anchovies. Because many of us couldn't endure punishment and beatings, falling down in a faint, they gave us a lot of salt to prevent fainting. I couldn't stand eating like that for several days. There was not enough rice, so I started to feel hungry from the moment I put the spoon down. I remembered that the side dishes improved slightly from May 27th.

It was probably around the end of May. While we were sitting in the guardhouse, a guard called out Professor OH Byeong-Moon of CNU as he moved a little. Then CNU students appealed to the guard, "He is old and our professor, so we will be punished instead." However, the guard (JEONG Geun-Seok) pushed the students away and ordered the professor to put his hands out of the cell. He hit his palms ten times with a club, but the professor did not scream even a word in front of his students. When he returned to his seat, he held his hands between his knees. His face was distorted, but he said nothing. We had a lot of hostility toward Private First Class JEONG Geun-Seok. And whenever the guy was on duty, we stared at him, his insignia of rank, and his name tag as we reported that we wanted to go to the toilet. It was the greatest hostility we could express ever toward him.

From June 3rd, the atmosphere has eased slightly. That night they told us to write a letter home. We were expected to be released by the end of June. On July 3rd, several people including myself were released. At first, we were classified as class A. But on May 27th, when a large number of the citizen militia were captured, we seemed to be reclassified and released. We left the guardhouse on July 3rd and signed a memorandum to Martial Law Commander SO Jun-Yeol that we would never disclose our experiences at Sangmudae. We were handed over to the school after a two-hour lecture.

After release, I rested at home for fifteen days and took care of myself. I was badly hurt from all kinds of beatings and punishments. For a few days, my whole body was so swollen that people couldn't recognize my face. As soon as I could move around, I went to school and found that I had been suspended. I continued to go to school, but my professor asked me to take a leave of absence because of an order from the Ministry of Education. I delayed it but eventually took a leave of absence. I was allowed to return to school in 1984 and graduated in 1986.

I can't help but feel sorry for those who fought to the end, passed away, and suffered from injuries because I couldn't even fight properly at the time of May 18. When I met my friend PARK Chae-Young, who was arrested on May 18th while protesting elsewhere, we still pledge to requite them by living hard and passionately to compensate for the lack of our participation in the May 18 People's Uprising.

II TRAUMA

2. Gwangju Prison

7143. A Place Where a Man's Life Is as Trifling as a Fly's

Name: KIM Ok-Hwan (male)
Date of Birth: November 3, 1963 (aged 16)
Occupation: High school student (currently unemployed)
Date of Record: December 1988

Research & Arrangement by PARK Jong-Shin

I was born in Sinji-myeon, Wando-gun, Jeollanam-do on November 3rd, 1963, as the youngest son among three sons and two daughters. My father worked at the local district (*myeon*) office at the time, then at a local branch of the National Federation of Fisheries Cooperatives. And my family also worked in the agriculture and fishery industry, so we were well off in the countryside. Therefore, I lived without much difficulty until I entered high school.

When I entered high school in 1978, I lived with my sister, who got married and lived in Unam-dong, Gwangju, to go to school. I lived with the allowance that my father and my eldest brother working for a bank in Wando sent me regularly. Living at my sister's place, I never felt any financial difficulties. Until the day I was arrested on May 19th, 1980, I was able to attend school and live in my sister's house without any difficulties.

Attending CNU High School in 1980, I was able to witness several demonstrations of college students in May 1980. It was such a time when college students ran away to the high school stadium and went back when there was a bang sound. And then we had to close the windows because of tear gas.

May 19th was the midterm day. As I entered the classroom early in the morning, my classmates were telling stories about the trouble they experienced with the paratroopers as they entered the school through the main gate. It was the time when school liberalization was implemented. So some seniors didn't wear school hats and some wore dress shoes. Then, some of the classmates were caught by the paratroopers, slapped on the cheek for not wearing hats, and beaten for having long hair as they entered the main gate. However, since I lived in Unam-dong and walked around through the side gate of the CNU College of Agriculture, I became curious about what the paratroopers looked like when I heard such stories.

I came back home after taking exams in the morning and was studying for the subjects for the next day. Around 6:00 p.m., my classmate KIM Chan-Yong, who lived in Gwangcheon-dong, stopped by my place. He said, "Let's go to the Mudeungsan Stadium. It will be fun." Out of curiosity about the paratroopers, we left the house wearing sneakers and sweat suits. I heard that the paratroopers were beating people, so I put on and wore a sweat suit and a belt so that I could run away quickly. When we arrived there, there were a lot of people gathered, and in the meantime, I happened to part with my friend. There, I heard that "a pregnant woman was stabbed to death by the bayonets of the paratroopers on her way to hospital." I was not myself at those words. The demonstrators were already in a rage, and they sang a hoola song[4] as they protested, "CHUN Doo-Hwan, Resign, Resign."

As time went by, people boarded a truck that came from the highway exit around 8:00 p.m., and I also got on the truck. It was

[4] Hoola Songs refer to the songs sung at demonstration scenes, accompanied by melodies of Irish or American folk songs. The lyrics were adapted from protest slogans.

loaded with plowshares used for plowing. The truck drove toward Gwangju Station. However, I got off the truck because of a traffic jam near the Gwangju Branch of Lotte Confectionery on the way to the CNU Intersection. When I got off, I found the reason for the traffic jam: the paratroopers were controlling traffic at the CNU Intersection. At that time, there was a sit-in demonstration in the road near Lotte Confectionery, where two people led the protest in front of the crowd.

Joining the protest for a while, I came across KIM Seung-Cheol (whose name I didn't know at that time but later found out). He was a truck driver and asked me to go for a negotiation saying, "The paratroopers are blocking the CNU Intersection. So let's demand that they move away." Eleven high school students, including me, followed him. From Lotte Confectionery, we walked along the Taebong-dong Stream to the main street leading to CNU. He cried, "We've come to negotiate because the vehicles cannot move."

"Then come here. Let's talk."

The paratroopers responded to us. As we approached, however, the paratroopers pointed their guns at us and surrounded us. Eventually we could not say anything but were beaten up. And we were loaded on to a truck with no chairs like dogs. Ten people, including KIM Seung-Cheol and me, were caught. One jumped into the stream before being caught, and another slipped away on the way.

On the truck, two paratroopers were guarding us with M16s. When we moved even slightly, they hit us mercilessly with buttstocks. I was on my knees, my head down on the floor. And I felt like something was happening. It turned out that a 12-ton truck rushed to the paratroopers and crashed into a paratrooper who was about to be discharged, and he died on the spot. After that, the paratroopers became more brutal. As I kept my head down like that, I clearly heard gunfire (three or four shots), though

I don't know if any others remember that.

Around 11:00 that evening, the truck moved to somewhere and dropped us off after a while. Because it was dark, I did not know where we were going. I was dragged down a gravel road and found ten other people held there. They were swollen almost all over as they had been beaten. Some of them were forced to support themselves by only their heads and feet, while others were forced to kneel, place their foreheads on the ground, and lift up their feet. We were also kneeling with our feet lifted up.

How long had I been kneeling like that? Some of the paratroopers came up to me and told me to stand up. And I got up, feeling my legs shaking. It was probably because the blood didn't circulate. But he hit me for standing awkwardly. And soon I went for an interrogation. Some paratroopers sat in chairs and asked me questions such as "What's your name?" "How did you get caught?" and "How many stones did you throw?" When I told the truth about how I came by truck to the Mudeung Stadium and how I was caught after going for negotiation, they cursed and hit me for not telling truth. So, I said I had thrown about twenty stones, and he then said, "Get down" and hit my butt mercilessly with a birch cudgel. It felt like my skin was falling off. Then he kicked me everywhere again with his military boots. After receiving such an interrogation, I had to sit on my knees in line again. There were three rows and I was in the front row. Suddenly, one of the paratroopers stabbed KIM Seung-Cheol, who was sitting next to me, in the head with a bayonet. Suddenly, the paratrooper said, "This bayonet is the one that cut off several female breasts during the Vietnam War" and "I will kill all of you." I heard a scream. I thought, "It's my turn next." But fortunately, he didn't stab me. I got goosebumps all over my body. After a while, they called in KIM Seung-Cheol to cut out the hair from the stabbed area and sewed it without anesthesia. I stayed up all night in such fear and fell asleep in the middle of the morning while I was standing on my head.

It was the morning of May 20th. At dawn, I could see the surrounding area roughly, and it seemed to be a building of CNU (it turned out later that it was Auditorium 100 of the CNU College of Medicine). I was familiar with the surroundings because I had attended CNU High School for three years. From that day on, paratroopers began to become very vicious. Sometimes they came in bleeding, and civilians kept coming in, many of whom were bleeding. Perhaps something serious happened out there. The paratroopers, like madmen, said, "Enough of us had died. You guys must die too," throwing chairs at us, striking us with buttstocks, kicking our chests with military boots, and stomping on our legs while we were sitting on our knees. I was beaten up like that countless times.

At around 4:00 p.m. on May 21st, we were tied up with a rope in pairs and loaded into a truck. It was a sealed vehicle, a 4.1-ton vehicle like an armory repair car, and we could not even move our feet since everyone in the classroom was packed into the truck. It was fortunate that we survived there since we could have all died unless we helped each other to untie the ropes as soon as we were loaded in the truck. The truck moved slowly. It was the end of May, so the weather was already very hot. We could not breathe properly due to hypoxia and we panted. After a while, the paratroopers poured down tear gas powder through a small space in front of the truck. People were screaming and about to die from coughing. And there was a scramble to put our heads to the small opening on the ceiling of the vehicle to breathe. In the meantime, I fell to the floor, and I was able to stand erect because my friend who attended Kumho High School supported me and helped me get up. If I had collapsed that way, I would probably have been trampled to death. As I woke up, I realized there was a seat inside the vehicle. And I suddenly remember my teacher had said in the military drill class, "If you do not have enough oxygen, don't move much." So, I sat still in the seat right behind the driver's seat and did not move.

The vehicle stopped after moving for about three or four hours. When the door opened, people tried to get off first to breathe. I was sitting in the inner seat, so I got off later, and then I stepped on three dead bodies as I got off the truck. They must have suffocated and been trampled on in the tightly shut vehicle.

Hundreds of people gathered in one place and were standing supported with just their heads and feet, and then kneeled while keeping their heads on the ground. An old man was so thirsty that he took off his rubber shoes he was wearing and asked my friend who attended Kumho High School to pee in it. And then he drunk it making the sound, "Gulp, gulp." People seemed to be able to do anything if they were pushed to extreme conditions. I heard a man in his 40s threw money in the air and was killed. Also, a man talked to a member of the paratroopers there, saying, "You know me, don't you?" He said the soldier was his cousin, but the paratrooper said no and beat him up hard. Perhaps the paratrooper had a low rank. That's why he denied the fact and beat the man even though he was his cousin.

After a while, they told us to lift our heads. When I looked up, I saw a military vehicle with a machine gun installed standing in front of us. The paratroopers were pointing their loaded M16s at us. I heard, "I will kill you" from one side to the other. At that time, the highest-ranking paratrooper officer, I guess, said, "Enough of our troops died. If we shoot here, the person who is to die will die and the person who is to live will live." There were screams and shouts from all over the place. Then, my friend (HWANG Gil-Ryang) who attended Kumho High School asked me to tell his girlfriend that he died because of this. I also asked him to tell my family that I died like this. It was a situation where we didn't know who was going to die. Therefore, it was not strange to make such a promise. Our promises would have been meaningless if both of us would die. And I dozed off again. My friend woke me up, and I saw that no one was dead. That means we had crossed by the threshold of death once again.

When the sun was almost set and it became dark, they gave out biscuits and told us to share them with two people. I didn't know when I would die, but I was so hungry that I ate some biscuits. Then I had time to look around. I thought to myself, "It was only a prison that I was dragged to for that many hours." Since I used to go to dig a well around the area near the prison in the summer of my sophomore year in high school, I was sure that the tall walls and watchtowers belonged to the prison. I thought they might drag us into the depths of the mountains and shoot us, but it was fortunate in a way that we were brought to prison. I moved with my head down and found that it was a warehouse (outside barracks). It looked like a large warehouse like the one belonging to a local branch of the National Federation of Agricultural Cooperatives, and there were straw bags on the ground. Inside, a metallic barrel was split into two to use one as a urine container and the other as a feces container. We ended up staying there.

On the day I was transferred to the prison, they did not let us sleep and ordered us to sit in a row. Then they forced us to repeat certain sentences to brainwash us, such as "You guys are definitely rioters. And you did this and that wrong. You will do this and that from now on." In the meantime, many people were beaten, and a person who gave the wrong answer was called out and beaten up with a long club until he collapsed; and when he stood up, they forced him to get down supported by only his head and feet. Even at that time, they repeated verbal abuse, such as "I scrape your intestines and serve them with drinks," while kicking the people with military boots. And a paratrooper, for no reason, rubbed a cigarette he was smoking in the face of a person sitting in the front row to put it out. That was cruelty beyond description. We couldn't even go to the bathroom when we wanted, and we had to raise hands until the one who went before came back to take turns. A few days had passed after I was arrested, and I went for an interrogation. When going for questioning, five people were usually called in, while others were waiting outside, and two people entered and were questioned. I was also taken to somewhere for questioning and waiting. At that time, a paratrooper who was guarding us came to me while I was kneeling and asked. He stamped on my knees and said,

"You bastard, who are you?"

"I'm in my third year at CNU High School."

"Then you are going to enter CNU next year."

He beat me and kicked me with his military boots, saying that I would definitely take part in a protest when I entered CNU. It was ridiculous.

After waiting for a while, I went in with KIM Seung-Cheol to be interrogated, and two investigators (from the Defense Security Command?) in plain clothes were there. They talked to each other and said they came from Seoul. One of them asked us if we were Christians or if we went to church. KIM Seung-Cheol replied that he attended church. I answered that I did not attend church (KIM Seung-Cheol is currently a deacon of a church). Still, they treated me fairly well, maybe because I looked young and was a high school student, and they gave me a lower grade (class C or class D?).

After the investigation, we were taken back to another place, where high-leveled groups (class A and class B) were forced to beat each other in the chest. It was done with resentment and sadness, but they had no choice but to follow the order. They hit each other because paratroopers handed over clubs and scared us, saying, "If you hit him lightly, then I will hit you hard." People pounded their fellow men hard. It was truly a sight that I couldn't see with my eyes open. It was discrediting humans and turning them into animals. And the people with light judgments (class C, class D) were watching the scene. Fortunately for me, I was asked to memorize the "National Education Charter" quickly. When I entered the warehouse after waiting for a while, those with the lightest judgments were on the side closest to the door and those with the heavier judgments went inside.

From then on, as we became more familiar with the paratroopers, there were fewer beatings, and they didn't treat us that badly.

Then one day, about four people (?) with gunshot wounds came in. They were served porridge, while those who were being held there were served rice. I was in charge of feeding porridge to the patients who were shot, but I didn't know why. At that time, I wondered, "I thought people would die if they were shot, but they can live like this." I still remember what a paratroop officer said while I was feeding porridge to them:

"My guys are good at shooting guns."

After that, I don't know whether the wounded were taken to the Integrated Hospital for treatment, or they died and were buried somewhere. One day, a woman came in, who was said to be caught during a date and was locked up in the next room. Indescribably abusive language came from that room. It was such as "I will cut out your vagina" or "I will cut off your breast with a bayonet."

Life in prison with the paratroopers was once again brutalized as they were replaced by ordinary soldiers (troops from the 20th Division). It was because the soldiers consistently said, "Do you think only paratroopers are scary? We are no less than them," and then they called people in, made them stand in front of the wall, ordered them to "parade rest," and then kicked them and beat them with clubs. And they were more vicious at bedtime. The paratroopers allowed us even a little movement during bedtime, but these soldiers did not allow even a little. If anyone moved a little bit, the order "to the position" fell. And the person who moved had to jump up and run to the wall beside the door and took a "parade rest." Then, the soldiers kicked him with their military boots, beat him with clubs, and made him half-dead. Most people stayed up all night with their eyes closed because there were a few people who were taken to Integrated Hospital. I was beaten like that once. A man lying next to me was pressing down on my arm, so I moved my arm quietly, and the order "to the position" fell. So, I ran, repeating "to the position" and stood at parade rest, leaning against the wall. I was hit on my stomach and chest with a club, and again in the chest, stomach, and leg with military boots for a long time before I suddenly fell down, losing consciousness. After a while, when I came to my senses, I went back to my seat with an order of "back to the seat" after being pounded on the stomach and chest. And it was morning. The most heartbreaking thing that happened in the prison happened that day. I'm still shuddering, thinking about it even now. The people took turns beating the other people with a big club. At that time, I was holding one arm of a person who was beaten, and all I could think about was that my heart would be hurt less if it were me that was being beaten.

A few days later, the soldiers (from the 20th Division) who had been with us went somewhere, and other soldiers (from the 31st Division) came. They didn't treat us that badly, but they punished and beat us to maintain discipline.

I was transferred to Sangmudae after a while. At that time, there was a branch office of the Martial Law Command in Sangmudae. During the transportation, we couldn't look out of the window and sat down looking at the floor. The sun was setting when we arrived at Sangmudae. Immediately after we arrived at Sangmudae, we went straight into the church. There were a lot of people there, too. They also seemed to be released soon. When we were a little loose-minded, soldiers from the Gyeongsang Province punished us. It seemed to be more difficult than the previous violence of the paratroopers since we were in a relatively relaxed state.

While I was staying at Sangmudae for a few days, I sent letters home. I had to copy the phrases the martial law forces gave me, which roughly stated that I was held in the branch office of the Martial Law Command and was in good health. However, the letter was returned to me because I wrote the wrong home address in Unam-dong. However, on the day I was released, my father, my homeroom teacher, and the principal of my school somehow came to see me. I heard later that they also had to submit a written promise to control my behavior. So, I was released on June 4th. When I look back on my life there, human life was not as good as a fly's. I heard that my friend HWANG Gil-Ryang, who attended Kumho High School and stayed with me in prison, was released around July.

Since then, I have deliberately avoided soldiers in such camouflage military uniforms because I could not control my agitation, and my anger revived by just looking at the uniform of the paratroopers. For almost a month, I kept having nightmares of the paratroopers coming after me with guns. Immediately after my release, I did not feel any particular signs of illness, but I took oriental medicine and herbal medicine from the countryside. But after a while, I found it hard to concentrate and my whole body hurt when I sat at my desk to study, so I couldn't study for a long time. When I studied with my head drooping for a long time, my right back and shoulder blade area became numb and stiff. And when the weather was cloudy or about to rain, my legs hurt. Meanwhile, I failed to study properly for the second semester of my third year of high school, but I got admitted to the CNU College of Agriculture in 1981. However, I took a leave of absence to try the college admission examination again because I didn't want to go to the College of Agriculture. I had the pain during the period I prepared for the exam, but I thought I would get better soon as I had never been seriously sick or gone to hospital until then. However, I returned to school in 1982 because I didn't get a good result in the exam.

After I returned to school, I had pain in the back of my right shoulder while studying for the midterm and final exams in the first semester of the first year. I studied with my back bent over for fifteen minutes and then straightened my shoulders repeatedly.

However, I couldn't tell my parents that I was sick because they were in the countryside. And the school break began. I didn't go to hospital in that condition, and a new semester started.

A few days after the new semester started, I felt severe pain around the right side of my neck. The pain lasted for about ten minutes, and the sensation from the right side of the neck to my entire right arm and shoulders became numb. I bought a pain relief patch and put it on, but it was no good. I was thinking of going to hospital when I got my allowance from my parents. But on September 8th, 1982, a shock to my right arm caused the pain again. The same pain soon spread throughout the body and caused me to become paralyzed. Eventually, I went straight to the emergency room of the CNU Hospital. I stopped breathing, so I had a heart massage, which did not work well. And I had to have a bronchotomy the next day. So, I was hospitalized at the CNU Hospital for about three months. However, I did not receive a definitive diagnosis at the hospital.

I was transferred to Wonkwang University Oriental Medicine Hospital in Wolsan-dong. The doctor said that I was sick because I had been beaten a lot during the Gwangju incident, and the beatings caused a blood clot, which prevented blood circulation. After being hospitalized for one month in the oriental medicine hospital, I recovered significantly. Still, the right half of my body is still numb even though I have been taking medicine. Especially on my right arm and shoulder, I don't feel anything hot or cold, and I don't even feel any pain when pinched. Until now, I can't sleep because of the pain in my body if it's cloudy.

Ⅲ. MURDEROUS OPPRESSION

1. Geumnam-ro

2. In Front of the Jeonnam Province Hall

III MURDEROUS OPPRESSION

1. Geumnam-ro

3038. The Truth Must be Revealed

Witness: LEE Hee-Seung (male)
Date of Birth: October 7, 1954 (aged 26)
Occupation: Retail business (currently working at a liquor agency)
Date of Record: November 1988

Research & Arrangement by LEE Hyun-Joo

Overview

On May 19, LEE Hee-Seung was beaten all over his body by martial law forces near the Catholic Center, resulting in a fracture to his right middle finger.

An Ordinary Soy Sauce Seller

I was born and lived in Sanmak-ri, Masan-myeon, Haenam-gun until I graduated from elementary school. My family was an ordinary family that had been farming for generations. Our wealth was only four *majigis*[5] of rice paddies and four *majigis* of fields, but I had never thought we had a difficult life.

My father died at the young age of thirty-one in an accident while undergoing military "re-training" (which lasted for about a month a year) during the times of the Liberal Party, similar to

---

[5] *Majigi* refers to a traditional Korean unit of area of farmland. One *majigi* can be converted to 661.16 m^2.

the current reserve force training. At that time, I was five years old and had only one younger sister. I remember nothing about my father because I was so young.

I graduated from elementary school in Haenam and came to Gwangju to enter middle school. In Gwangju, I lived alone and went to school. I was young at that time, but I felt burdened by the thought that I was the actual breadwinner of my family, and those things began to come to me as real matters. It was a time when what to do to make money was more important to me than studying. The thought that I should support my grandmother, mother, and sister made my mind more dark and shaded compared to my friends.

After graduating from middle school and giving up going to high school, I immediately got a job at a soy sauce factory arranged by my uncle, who was a grocery wholesaler. The monthly salary was 20,000 won, and the factory provided accommodation and meals, so I saved money regularly because I didn't have to spend much on living expenses. I saved the money while living in the factory for four years, then I bought a bicycle and started a business of buying things from wholesale stores and handing them over to retailers. There were many people who I had gotten to know while working at the soy sauce factory, so I managed the business one way or another.

After two years of business, I received a draft notice in 1978, so I had a physical examination. But because I was the only son in my family, I served as a community military officer. I lived in Seoul for about a year after being discharged from the military. I worked as a laborer at an apartment construction site in Dunchon-dong, and I also worked as a basement pumping worker at Dongah Construction. Life in an unfamiliar place made me easily tired.

When I came down to Gwangju in the spring of 1980, I had my grandmother, mother, and sister come up to Gwangju. I did so because I felt sorry and guilty for my family who had lived apart from me for more than ten years.

In Gwangju, I resumed what I did before joining the military. Now, I was like a middleman who took things from factories and handed them over to stores.

I was spending the spring of 1980 with expectations and new determination for a new environment. In May of that year, the political situation was unusually bad. For me, livelihood was the most important thing, so I didn't know what was going on in the world, and I didn't have much interest in it. Although I was indifferent to the political situation, I was sometimes stimulated by the demonstrations of college students that continued every day in May.

Beaten Up with a Club

I don't know if it was May 15 or 16 when I delivered soy sauce to a store near a park by bicycle. But I saw many students in a scrum pass by. Among them, I saw some with shaved hair and others in *Hanbok*[6]. The students protested in an orderly and peaceful manner. I didn't think the students were that bad. But I had no intention or desire to join their protest.

I was at home on the morning of the 18th. My house was on the way up to Sajik Park, so I was relatively quick to hear the news from the city. Rumors circulated in our neighborhood that "The paratroopers take all students away" and "They beat the students randomly and stab them with bayonets." I had a suspicion, "That's nonsense. How can soldiers stab innocent civilians with bayonets in broad daylight?" I thought I couldn't believe it until I saw it with my own eyes. I thought it would be okay to go out because I didn't do anything wrong and above all I wasn't a student, so I did not listen when my grandmother

---

[6] Korean traditional clothes.

and mother tried to stop me from going out. It was when I reached the bridge in Bulo-dong. The paratroopers were really there. The paratroopers tied students caught somewhere to a rope and dragged them away. They didn't even let a taxi pass by. They hit the taxis several times with clubs. Seeing that, I was afraid and at the same time I thought that I couldn't predict what would happen if I was caught. As I was on my way home by bike, the paratroopers came after me. I was horribly scared at that time. I went blindly into a briquette shop to hide. I knew the shop owner well because I provided soy sauce to the shop. About five paratroopers followed me to the briquette shop. Two of them came in and abruptly tried to beat me. I said out of urgency that I was not a student but a soy sauce seller. When the briquette shop owner said "I can assure you this is the seller who provides soy sauce to my shop," they responded, "What the hell are you?" and were about to hit the owner, too.

When he begged them to believe him, one of them said, "Are you kidding me?" and hit him several times with a club and just left the shop as another soldier who came together with him called to him from outside. They probably looked at my bike and thought I wasn't a student. The paratroopers I saw had bloodshot eyes. I could neither afford to look around nor concentrate. I was stunned sitting for a while, and the shop owner told me to go home quickly. When I got home, I didn't let a word about the incident out of my mouth for fear that my grandmother and mother would be worried.

On the 19th, while I was having lunch, a friend of mine came to visit. The friend, who got married early and had a child, lived near my house. He advised me:

"They hit and kill people as they see them, so don't go outside."

I told my friend about what I had suffered.

It was a little painful for me to stay at home after my friend left, and I was impatient to know what was happening. I left my house without telling my family. Along the side of Gwangju Stream, I went out to the downtown area through the 3rd Street and 4th Street of Chungjang-ro. Many people gathered in front of the Catholic Center in Geumnam-ro. I went into the crowd, after putting my bicycle in a building where Daehan Fire & Marine Insurance was located. There seemed to be only a few members of the airborne forces in the Catholic Center. With a sudden roar of "Waa," angry citizens chased the paratroopers in the Catholic Center. I was nervous looking at them from below, and a young man on the rooftop held high an M16 rifle that he took away from a member of the airborne forces. After seeing it, I came out to the intersection of Gwangju Bank's main branch and looked at the Province Hall, and there were many soldiers and vehicles that sprayed pepper fog in front of the Tourist Hotel. They hadn't fixed bayonets, and, as I recall, they were in military uniforms.

As citizens began to throw stones at the paratroopers, the forces began to push ahead. At that time, I was between Commercial Bank and Jeil Bank, and when they pushed ahead, citizens began to run away. On one side, some of the crowd prepared to fight the soldiers instead of running away, but citizens who knew the cruel atrocities of the paratroopers were busy running away. I was also caught in the middle of the people running away and ran about ten meters, but the person running in front of me fell and I stumbled, too. Several people fell down in a row. From then on, I was out of my mind. Before I knew it, the troops chased and began to trample the fallen people with military boots. There were the sounds of hitting with cudgels and groaning. I thought only that I had to live, so I covered my head with both hands and threw my head in the crowd. Being in this situation brought me a memory of catching frogs in the countryside when I was young. At that time when I caught frogs and hit them with a whip, they stretched out, and now I thought we were just like those frogs back then.

I don't know how long it had been, but I am sure we were

beaten for about ten minutes. The surrounding area became quiet and I could hear groans everywhere. When I opened my eyes, the road around me was full of people. Right near me, the paratroopers stood with fixed charging bayonets every five meters. A truck came from somewhere and stopped near us. Then the paratroopers grabbed the fallen people in pairs from both sides, and threw them into the truck as if they were throwing straw bags. I crawled toward Commercial Bank thinking that I would be doomed if I got caught here. Just as I was walking around Commercial Bank, I found a woman dead with her eyes popped out of their sockets. In the midst of that, I thought I had to get my bike back. The bike was the most important thing for me because I made a living for my family by using it, so I went into Daehan Fire & Marine Insurance building to get it. I rode my bike out of the downtown area along the river and returned home.

Even though I was badly beaten, I didn't even know where it hurt until I got home. As soon as I arrived home, I lost strength all over my body, and the pain began from then. My fingers were swollen and my whole body was throbbing. My swollen fingers did not even bend. I went to KIM Sung-Soo Clinic next to Yangrim Bridge and got treatment for my right finger first. I was diagnosed with the injury that would take five weeks to heal completely. Then I got treated at the clinic for five weeks. The clinic learned that I had been beaten by the paratroopers and did not require payment for the treatment. Even though there was no external wound on my body, I had a headache and backache, so I took herbal medicine for three months, got acupuncture, and took various medicines, but they did not work at all. Whenever it was cloudy, the pain got worse, and if I did a little hard work, my whole body became numb and sore, and these aftereffects still remain to this day. Of course, I can't use my finger normally and naturally. Even though I suffered a lot like this, I went to the Red Cross Hospital on the 21st because I heard that there were many people who died in the hospital. The hospital was literally a scene of chaos with people looking for their family members who had left their homes. They came to the hospital wondering if they could find their family members, and when they found their family members who had turned into corpses, they either lost consciousness or wailed.

From the next day, nothing special happened. When I heard that the Citizens' Army had occupied the Province Hall, I was relieved even though I didn't know anything.

My younger sister Hye-Sook was running a small store at the entrance to the current KBS broadcasting company. My house was right in front of the Women's Center, and when I went there on the 27th, there were many soldiers in the center, too. During the day, I came up to my younger sister's store to see if everything was okay, and the soldiers who were standing guard called me at the entrance of Women's Center. Then, they asked me where I hurt my hand. I felt like I should not say that I was beaten by the martial law troops, so I said I got hurt while riding a bicycle, and they bullied me into saying the truth.

While I was scuffling with them, a jeep drove up. When the lieutenant colonel in the jeep asked what was going on, I said that I was a person living in the house over there, and that I fell riding a bicycle and hurt my finger, assuring him he could check my hand for himself. And then he let me go.

During May 18, I passed through several difficulties in this way. When May passed and June came, a commander of the local reserve forces visited me and told me to report what I experienced. He said I would be provided with rice or something if I reported it, but I didn't. At that time, I thought that I might have encountered retaliation if I had reported it.

As time passed by, everything began to settle down. Everyone returned to their original positions as if nothing had happened. I also started the soy sauce business again from June. By 1981, an acquaintance of mine urged me to get married, saying that he would arrange a matchmaking for me. I was not that old but got married.

There is a difference of two years between my actual age and my age on my family register. I had an older brother, but he died less than a year after he was born. When we were young, there were many babies who died as soon as they were born, so most people were registered late in their family registers. My parents also worried that I might die soon after I was born, so they registered me on the family register only two years after my birth, so there is a difference between my actual age and the official age.

I have a son and a daughter. My son, Tae-Yang, is seven years old, and my daughter, Mi-Ji, six years old. I wanted to have many children because I didn't have a brother. But I couldn't afford it, so I decided to have only two.

My grandmother passed away three years ago, and now there are five people in my family, including my mother, my wife, my two children and me. My sister is married and lives a happy life.

I quit my soy sauce business in 1982 and after that I worked as a street vendor in Chungjang-ro where I usually sold clothes and socks. But there were severe crackdowns on street vendors, and officials extorted us this way and that. They didn't explicitly ask for money, but it was hard for me not to give them money in order to make the business a little easier. It was customary to give money in this business, though it was heartbreaking for me because I couldn't even do business on any day I lost their favor because I didn't pay them to save some money.

I worked as a street vendor until 1985. It costs much more money than you think to be a street vendor. You need some cash, so if you earn money and use it that day, there are many difficulties in getting more goods. For various reasons, I quit the business in 1985.

The place where I got a job after that was the OB Beer agency where I work now. Here, I deliver beer and earn about 300,000 won as a monthly salary. It was only recently that I received this amount of salary. Since the June Uprising[7)] last year, the salary has also risen a lot. It was really great in June last year. I also went to the downtown after work to "protest against the government's attempts to protect the Constitution," shouting with a loud voice until 2:00 or 3:00 a.m. I was almost hit and seriously injured by a tear gas canister last year. At that time, we hit rebar or steel pipes with stones as a way to gather people, so that people could gather after hearing the sound. In the evening, there were many people in the alley on the side of Jungang Daegyo Bridge, and the riot police were next to Taepyeong Theater. I hit an iron pipe supporting a traffic light with a stone under the traffic light to get the people gathered in the alley out onto the street, and it was loud because it was evening. The riot police seemed to have heard the sound, so they shot tear gas at me. I was standing behind the traffic light post, and fortunately the tear gas hit the steel pipe and fell down to the ground, so I didn't get hurt.

I think that the June Uprising led to an amendment of the constitution for a direct presidential election system, and a partial democratization although not a complete one.

In June this year, I reported myself as a person injured during the May 18 Uprising to the YMCA May 18 Injured Association. When I went to the Association, I was given a questionnaire and participated in a survey. In the survey, there were questions such as how much compensation I wanted, but I didn't just report for the compensation. I reported it because I thought the truth must be revealed with the passing of time. At the time of the Uprising, I couldn't think about uncovering the truth or restoring people's honor because I was worried about the disadvantages I would face, but now I don't worry.

---

7) The June Uprising refers to a series of democratization movements against the CHUN Doo-Hwan regime that took place across the country in June 1987.

The truth must be revealed for those who lost their lives or were injured for no reason at that time. This is not for my personal benefit. But I think it's still a long way off before the truth comes out.

Even now, the TV does not show students getting hurt at the protest sites, but it only shows riot police getting hurt.

1. Geumnam-ro

3024. Fighting by Throwing Stones, But There was Nowhere to Escape

Witness: KIM Si-Do (male)
Date of Birth: January 10, 1956 (aged 24)
Occupation: Electrician (currently a van driver)
Date of Record: February 1989

Research & Arrangement by AHN Eun-Jeong

Overview

On May 17, 1980, I witnessed paratroopers beating citizens on Geumnam-ro and, in anger, joined the protest from the 18th. On May 20, I was beaten with a club by paratroopers on the road behind the head office of Kwangju Bank and got injured.

Join the Protest as an Electrician

I was born as the second of three sons and one daughter in Juwol-dong, Gwangju.

In 1980, I was a 25-year-old, energetic young man and worked as an electrician at Gukje Electric store. In addition to this job, I was busy with various other jobs.

In May, I often went to the area of the Province Hall for various business purposes. At that time, whenever I encountered any protesters, I usually stood there looking on them. But I just turned away from them, telling myself, "Because I'm a worker."

It seemed that many rallies were held at the Province Hall.

In mid-May, I saw students and professors from Chonnam National University and Chosun University marching on Geumnam-ro. In the very front row, they were holding large banners and led the long procession in line, desperately shouting for democratization.

On May 17, the place that I was responsible for was an unpainted building. At that time, the construction of the building was in the finishing stages. On that day, I had to go to the construction site as the person in charge. In the morning, I went to work and then my four colleagues and I headed for the unpainted building behind the head office of Gwangju Bank by riding two motorcycles. We saw many men in military uniforms on Geumnam-ro. At first, I thought they were community military officers, but they were combat police.

On one side of the road, we heard the cries of an old women, saying "Give me my son back," and there was a lot of commotion around there.

Watching this scene, I assumed, "Students are demonstrating today as usual," and turned back impassively, thinking that I had to do my own job.

On May 18, my four colleagues and I went out to Geumnam-ro by motorcycle as usual.

On the way to Geumnam-ro, I stopped by one of my acquaintances who was running an electric store near Gwangju Jaeil High School. I was talking with him for a while and looked out at Geumnam-ro because it was very noisy out there.

Paratroopers stood on guard in front of Hanil Bank and near the Catholic Center. Another fifty paratroopers were confronting a few students.

I deliberately wore black work clothes with my colleagues and went to the place where the paratroopers and the students were confronting each other.

The reason why I wore a work uniform was to indicate that I was not a student; in other words, that I was not a demonstrator. Near Hanil Bank, a lieutenant among the paratroopers was leading the troops with a megaphone, and the soldiers in army combat uniforms were holding clubs, with their guns hanging horizontally on their backs.

At this time, more than fifty students poured out of the alley of Daehan Theater and that of Hanmi Confectionery with a sudden sound of "boo." It didn't seem to be long, but the demonstration continued in the midst of a push-and-shove battle as the students and citizens, who were looking at the scene, were throwing stones at the soldiers together.

Until this time, I was standing and watching all this near the tailor's shop in front of Hanmi Confectionery without throwing stones. After a while, the students who were protesting were quite pushed back by the paratroopers' tear gas. At that moment, the troopers rushed after the students, and the citizens and students were scattered. The students ran away with all their might but they could not escape the trained soldiers. A student ran away into the tailor's shop in front of Hanmi Confectionery. I was watching the scene through the tailor's glass door. Inside the tailor's shop, two or three people were working by ironing clothes.

However, two paratroopers chased the students into the tailor's shop to catch them. The paratroopers grabbed one of the students by the collar and suddenly took an iron from the worker ironing in the shop and struck the student mercilessly. They beat the student ruthlessly with the hot iron, indiscriminately on his head and face. People watched this, gaping with anger. Young people were standing speechless, and the older people felt bad for the student, saying "Damn you! Damn you!"

The two paratroopers grabbed the student by the collar, pulled him out like a dog, and threw him into the road in front of the tailor's shop.

Including that student, other citizens and students were captured and stuck in the middle of the road. One of the paratroopers was shouting with a megaphone: "Citizens, hurry back home."

I swallowed my resentment and returned to the house of my acquaintance who was running an electric shop.

"Let's stop doing our work or anything else and go out and fight."

Thus, I walked out to Geumnam-ro with my colleagues. As a fellow citizen and as a human being, I couldn't sit by and watch the unbearably inhuman deeds.

The Two Black Objects were Innocent Citizens of Gwangju

On Geumnam-ro, citizens and students were completely pushed back by the paratroopers.

Around 6:00 p.m. I was pushed by the paratroopers and went to the Intercity Public Bus Terminal. The terminal intersection was packed with citizens and students. The protesters shouted, "CHUN Doo-Hwan, resign," "Lift martial law," and they sometimes sang songs. There were no paratroopers in the direction of Gwangnam-ro, and about one company stood guard only on the side of the fire station.

I was in the lead and was willing to take any risk. When tear gas flew toward us, I quickly avoided it and picked it up and threw the canister back at the paratroopers.

At that time, the tear gas did not explode when it fell on to the ground but poured out white tear gas as it moved. Then, people used the tear gas as a weapon and threw it at the paratroopers without knowing that their palms were burning.

As I kept throwing the tear gas, both my hands were burned and the skin peeled off. Nevertheless, I trapped the moving tear gas with my feet and threw it quickly with my hand. When I grabbed it wrong, I felt the pain of touching a hot pot.

As time passed, the crowd protesters did not shrink. The battle between throwing stones and firing tear gas intensified. Cargo trucks that looked to be about twelve tons arrived from Gwangnam-ro to the public terminal. The license plate read "Gyeongnam." The citizens and students stopped the trucks. The trucks were full of stones, and there seemed to be about three trucks in total.

As far as I remember now, I think we burned up all three cargo trucks. I came home late at night after fighting against the paratroopers near the public terminal.

At around 10:00 a.m. on May 19, I went to work and came out to Geumnam-ro with my four colleagues as we did on the previous day. I could not find the colleagues who came out together with me since we were scattered while protesting. I first walked to the front of Hanil Bank. Protesters were gathered, and I fought in the front row throwing stones while inhaling a lot of tear gas.

The paratroopers were stationed near the Catholic Center in front of Housing Bank, and protesters were at the intersection of Jungang-ro and Geumnam-ro. The protestors mainly fought in the middle of the construction site in the underground shopping mall, and I rested for a while in front of Hanil Bank and got up again. For a while, the protesters pushed back the paratroopers, but eventually they were pushed back by the paratroopers and ran away.

At around 5:00 p.m., fiercely chased by the paratroopers, I couldn't attack anymore and escaped to the underground garage of Hwani Department Store. Many people besides me were chased here, and the paratroopers fired tear gas violently.

The garage was filled with tear gas, and we couldn't see anything. I kept coughing and felt nauseous, and I thought, "I'm dead now," and I thought of the old days momentarily.

I crawled to find a bright place and barely found a door. I caught my breath at the door and began to vomit. After breathing hard, I sat down feeling alive, and it seemed to be quiet outside.

When I walked back to the Geumnam-ro Intersection, the paratroopers were back to their original place. When I felt tired from throwing stones, I would sit down for a while and get up again to attack. I saw that in front of the Catholic Center the protesters were facing the paratroopers by rolling large metal drums used in construction sites.

It was past 10:00 p.m. The paratroopers mobilized a huge number of troops to chase the protesters in taking advantage of the late hour at night. I entered the alley next to Trust Bank and ran away over the wall. Each of the people ran away desperately because they believed that they were likely to die if they had been caught by the paratroopers.

A little later, I came back to the road because it seemed to be quiet outside. The paratroopers were in front of the Catholic Center. People looked around and made a commotion. A black object was seen near Jungang Church. I went to the place where the object was with a few people and turned on a lighter. There were two people lying there. One person's head seemed to have been stomped on with military boots as the marks of the boots were clearly revealed on the head and the marks remained white on his clothes. The person was almost senseless and lying down.

People who saw this scene got angry, saying that the motherfucking bastards stomped on them with the military boots. Everyone was talking.

The other person was making what sounded like a dying moan.

He seemed to shout, "Please save me," and when I looked at him closely, there was a lot of blood on his groin. We took him to a private hospital.

There was no response from the hospital. Then, one of us, in anger, broke the glass door at the entrance and supported the two injured people into the hospital.

Only then did the hospital director and his family came out.

"What happened?"

"We have patients. Please treat them quickly." We got out of the hospital after saying this.

I was so angry that I would have wanted to open fire if I had a gun. It was late at night, and I came home and lay in my room but couldn't sleep. With so much resentment, I was seized with the urge to make an improvised firearm and shoot it.

There's No Way to Escape

On May 20, without going to work, I went to the house of my older close friend who lived near Gwangju Jeil High School. Even my colleagues and the company owner were going out to Geumnam-ro to protest.

I went to his house, and his wife told me a story.

"The paratroopers stopped a bus passing by and pulled students out and took off the girls' clothes and cut off their breasts."

I was so shocked and thought it was a lie, saying "Oh, don't say that." But his wife insisted "I saw it myself."

I left his house and went out to Geumnam-ro. The situation was similar to what happened the day before. The protesters and the paratroopers were confronting each other fiercely. I looked at this scene and then went to the Intercity Public Bus Terminal. There all the protesters said and agreed that the story that the wife of my older friend told me, which seemed to me like a lie, was true. There were some other people who said they were there and had witnessed that scene as well. Citizens and students were crowded in the vicinity of the Public Bus Terminal. After staying there for a while, I went to Daein Market.

When I went to the vicinity of Gyerim Theater, the paratroopers were just rushing up there. At that time, the old ladies who were doing business in Daein Market were busy leaving their things behind and running away. Black smoke and flames rose in the sky. I thought there was a fire coming from near a telephone company, but later found out that the MBC broadcasting station was burnt down.

I moved back from Gyerim-dong to Geumnam-ro. The paratroopers and the protesters continued to engage in the fierce battle, pushing back and forth. Students were once terribly pushed back by the paratroopers. I ran to the alley behind Gwangju Bank. After running for a while, the paratroopers blocked the Catholic Center alley and the Gwangju Bank alley at the same time and forced the protestors to a dead end. There was no way to escape, and I was standing in the middle of the area blocked by the paratroopers.

There was no way to avoid them, so I stood in a noncommittal attitude as if I wasn't participating in the demonstration.

The paratroopers slowly approached me and slammed my knee with their clubs relentlessly. I toppled down on the spot. The troops continued to beat me with clubs. I almost fainted and was beaten down. My face was torn by the asphalt, the skin peeled and blood spurted. I was kicked in the stomach by their military boots, so I couldn't breathe.

They hit me with clubs for a long time and fortunately disappeared somewhere without taking me away as if they were done with me.

After a while, I was rescued by an acquaintance. He pulled me out and took me to one side. It was only in front of Hyundai Wedding Hall that I could breathe and walk with help around the alley of Choheung Bank near Gwangju Park.

In front of Gwangju Park, I returned home in someone's car.

But I couldn't remember how on earth I came back home and how I got out of Geumnam-ro. I was just in a daze.

I had some simple physical therapy at home in Juwol-dong. There was no hospital for me to go to. After a few days, the pain in my legs worsened, resulting in severe swelling. I had no choice but to go to a hospital near Korea Electric Power Corporation (KEPCO) and receive simple treatment before returning home.

After that, my mother would go to the hospital and get medicine for me.

I am Happy, Though

It was around May 22 when I was resting with treatment at home. Near Juwol-dong, there was gunfire at night that sounded like roasting beans. The sound of guns from Songam-dong and Mudeung Mountain terrified citizens.

When people went outside their houses, they could see bullets cutting through the leaves and flying away, and those who saw this quickly went back into their houses in fear.

Standing on the floor of my house and looking outside, I saw that citizens were busy coming and going, riding in several cars. In addition, I sometimes saw young people living in Juwol-dong coming home with rifles and then leaving again.

Some young people living in Juwol-dong were caught by detectives from the Seobu Police Station about a month after the May 18 Uprising was settled, and they were taken to Sangmudae. I heard they were released after about two months.

The wound on my legs was almost healed and I could walk around. But I stumbled forward when stepping down to lower ground. I couldn't dare to do any hard work at all.

I rested at home for about two months and eventually quit my job. When I went to hospital, there was no special treatment. Doctors consistently said that I needed physical therapy.

At home, I treated my knees with a massage and steam every day. But it was difficult for me to walk on cold and windy days because my knees stiffened.

But I couldn't afford to live idle forever even though I was sick.

I got a driver's license in 1981, so I worked as a private driver for my relative.

I couldn't even do this job, so I quit. After getting married in 1982, I used to work by using my skills for electric work. However, I did this job only as a daily employee in charge of paperwork of KEPCO.

I have been living with the help of my brothers without earning a living even after my marriage. It's a little less difficult because I live with my parents, but I'm ashamed to see them.

In 1987, I joined the May 18 Injured Association and have been involved in its activities.

At the end of the additional reporting period, the government sent me a notice telling me to go to a Health Association and have a physical examination.

I went to the Health Association for a checkup, and they told me to go to a general hospital for a comprehensive checkup. So I went to several hospitals, but they told me that there was nothing they could do for my health.

To this day, the aftereffects of my injury are still getting worse. It is painful enough for me to lie down even if I catch a cold. I can't do anything on a day when my knees hurt severely to the bone. If just one part of my body is uncomfortable and sick, my knees ache, and the pain spreads all over my body.

I make a living by driving a van. I pick up the people who go picnicking on weekends, and I earn a living with the daily pay like that.

But I still think I'm happy. When I visit the May 18 Injured Association, many injured people gather to talk about the situation at that time.

There are so many people who were injured worse than I am and have a harder life than I do. There are people who can't walk, who can't move because they can't even afford to pay daily transportation fees, who don't have arms, and who temporarily become mentally ill due to schizophrenia on cloudy days.

I reflect on May 18, 1980 often and talk about it repeatedly: I can never forget and forgive those days when the things that human beings should have never done happened.

Actually, I don't care much about politics. But these days, when I read newspapers and watch television, I can feel that all of these things are controlled by just a few people.

The same is true as to May 18, 1980. I think a handful of people, around five, massacred Gwangju citizens, mocking the whole nation. I can neither forgive nor forget them. I think finding the truth of May 18 must be the first priority.

1. Geumnam-ro

3052. Participating in a Vehicle Protest

Witnesses: WOO Eok-Goo (male)
Date of birth: June 24, 1948 (aged 32)
Occupation: Driver (currently a driver)
Date of Record: January 1989

Research & Arrangement by LEE Hyun-Joo

Overview

WOO Eok-Goo, who was a taxi driver at the time, participated in a vehicle protest on May 20 and got beaten and injured. Currently, he is working as the deputy secretary of the Democratic Driver Association.

Engaged in a Transportation Business before May 18

I was born and still live in Gyerim-dong, Gwangju. I was born in 1948 as the eldest son of three sons and one daughter. When I was young, my parents sold rice, but my father passed away when I was in the third grade of elementary school.

When I attended Gyerim Elementary School, I was quite mature compared to other children. My mother started to sell vegetables to support us in any way she could. As soon as my mother started to work, I had to help her. It was really hard for me to buy vegetables in Mokpo, sell them to each market, and deliver them. My daily routine started at 4:00 a.m. and ended with collecting bills in the evening, jumping from task to task.

After graduating from Salesio Middle School, I continued to trade vegetables with my mother until I turned twenty.

When I was twenty, I thought I could survive in the future only if I learned at least one skill. So I joined Daeyang Industrial Co., Ltd. at the intersection of the current Intercity Public Bus Terminal and learned automobile maintenance skills. The company was run by my older cousin.

At that time, my uncle was driving a commercial taxi. I thought I should learn how to drive, so I did my best to learn.

I got my driver's license in 1968 and drove my uncle's taxi before enlisting in the military in April 1969.

In March 1972, after being discharged from the military, I started driving as a job. Back then, I had a driving job not for a company but for a private car owner. At that time, the transportation industry was not organized, so it was easy to move from one place to another by driving for a day and then going somewhere else to work.

After that, in 1976 I took over a small service center specializing in battery repairs and operated it for about three years although it was difficult. At that time, battery repair service centers also repaired carburetors. But in the summer of 1978, I had to go down to Busan for family issues. After driving a city bus in Busan for seven to eight months, I moved to Seoul, but eventually, I came down to Gwangju again in January 1980. I had nothing, so I borrowed money here and there and bought a Hansi taxi in Gwangju.

Injured at a Vehicle Protest

It was really impressive for me to see the torchlight procession of college students while I was driving downtown on May 16th. Watching the demonstrators marching in good order with serious and solemn looks on their faces and the police in uniform escorting them from the front and back, I thought that it was a good example of democratic citizens and democratic police officers.

I can't remember what time it was on May 18th, but I saw, while driving, a military truck pulled over on the road in front of Soochang Elementary School. Already in front of the school there were many people lying in the road. I couldn't tell whether they were students or ordinary people. The paratroopers were throwing them into a military truck as if they were loading luggage. I trembled at the sight.

Every passenger in my taxi commented on and shuddered at the atrocities of the paratroopers. Each passenger said something about them.

"If it continues, there will be no one left in Gwangju." "Why the hell are they doing that?" "The soldiers are murdering bastards."

Some of them told me that it would be better for me to go home early on a day like this and to be careful. When I drove around the city and reached the vicinity of the Intercity Bus Terminal, I saw citizens and paratroopers were confronting each other. Citizens who were chased by the soldiers ran into the terminal or got out and ran onto a bus.

Until then, I thought ordinary people would not be attacked by the soldiers. But when I saw the citizens being dragged out of the bus, I was terrified.

On the next day (19th) when I went out for taxi service, there were not so many customers compared to other days. There were not many cars on the road, either, and it was desolate rather than quiet. In the morning I took on a few passengers and went home in Gyerim-dong for lunch. After lunch I was playing *hwatu*[8] with some friends, and at around 5:00 or 6:00 p.m. I suddenly heard gunfire. At that time, I couldn't go outside because I was scared but heard later that an armored vehicle had fired at citizens in front of Gyerim Police Box.

---

[8] *Hwatu*, literally "'Flower Battle," is a card game with a deck of forty-eight cards used to play various trick-taking games.

On the 20th, when the atmosphere in the city got more serious, I still operated my taxi service. At around 6:00 or 7:00 p.m., I accidentally drove to the front of Gwangju Station. In the plaza of Gwangju Station some taxi drivers parked their taxis and stopped the other taxi drivers passing by, telling them that our fellow taxi drivers were beaten by the paratroopers while trying to rescue students. Some taxi drivers said,

"What did the citizens do wrong? We must not tolerate this."

"They killed bus attendants."

"They killed bus drivers with a bayonet."

"We have to show the sons of bitches something."

"Soldiers from Gyeongsang Province come here to kill all the people in Jeolla Province." Most of the taxi drivers there had the same idea.

So, we agreed to gather at Mudeung Stadium according to the shared idea that we needed to do something.

However, the taxis could not go to Mudeung Stadium because the paratroopers blocked them. We changed direction and joined demonstrators as we passed by the Intercity Bus Terminal. When we entered Geumnam-ro, there were already a lot of citizens, and a citizen was in my taxi. I drove the car a little ways at a time and went to the front of the Catholic Center.

I didn't know much about the situation in the city before then, and I just thought that the paratroopers treated students too cruelly and mercilessly. At that time, it was already dark, making it difficult to see the surroundings clearly. My taxi was a new car, so I was sitting with the customer and locked the doors tightly, without even realizing that tear gas would leak into the car. And I suddenly heard something thumping the windshield. I was surprised and looked up, and some troops were trying to break the window with their clubs. The windshield of the car is originally quite thick and does not break easily. Still, when a couple of paratroopers rushed onto it and hit it repeatedly with clubs, it couldn't help but shatter.

After being cut by the glass fragments and beaten by clubs, I quickly opened the car door and ran away because I couldn't endure it. I ran around cars here and there only with the intention of running away from the soldiers who chased me. And I finally ran toward the Tourist Hotel, where I found the paratroopers were stationed, which I had not expected. Eventually, I was caught by the paratroopers there and beaten almost to death.

They hit only my knees and ankle bones over and over, and I got beaten practically to death and collapsed. They beat me so terribly that even the martial law troops who were watching me from the side stopped them from hitting me. The paratroopers pulled me from the ground and laid me down on the sidewalk in front of the YMCA coffee shop. There were many people around me who were beaten but not enough to die and dragged just like me.

The people next to me pointed at me and said, "I think this person is going to die."

Left in the Car

After a long time, they put about ten people in a vehicle that looked like a police van, and the driver seemed to be a police officer. Perhaps they only carried those who were thought to be seriously injured. I was taken to the van without knowing what time it was or where it was heading. I guessed they were going toward Gwangju Police Station.

That day I had to stay in the police van. I was very thirsty because I bled a lot. But they didn't give me water, saying I would die if I drank water. I thought that I must drink plenty of water even if I should die now. So I asked for water, saying I didn't care if I died. Then someone handed me a wet towel in my mouth. Even in this situation, I felt terribly sleepy, but I struggled not to fall asleep. I thought I would die if I fell unconscious.

In the middle of the night, a nurse got in the van and cursorily treated the injured and got out.

On the morning of the 21st, the van began to move. I thought they might take us to the hospital, so I looked outside to check that out. But we were inside the Jeonnam Province Hall.

All the patients inside the van were told to get out, but then the police told us to wait in the vehicle because we couldn't go to the hospital now.

After a while, they told us to get out again and took us to a place that looked like an auditorium. About fifty to sixty citizens were taken there by the police, and they looked so terrible that I couldn't even look at them.

The paratroopers, who occasionally came in with citizens they caught, never just left but always struck those who had already been beaten once or more. Fortunately, I looked like a severely ill patient because several parts of my body were bandaged. So they didn't beat me. There were also people who looked over fifty years old.

After a while, the police told only patients to come out, so I went out and they got me into a car.

I was waiting, thinking that this time I would really be taken to the hospital, but I was told to get out again. Then I was taken back to the warehouse. What the heck! They should take me to the hospital or should not tell me to get out... It was hard for me to move, but I managed to drag my body out to stay alive somehow, but it was continually like that. After I had meal that the police prepared with their own money, they told us to get in the car and leave again.

I was determined not to leave, but the police asked me, "Didn't you serve in the military?"

"I did."

"If you know how good the military hospital is, hurry up and let's go."

I got into the car, half-reluctantly being assisted by other people. But the car didn't move again. The police came up and said that we couldn't go to the hospital now, but a helicopter was scheduled to come from the Headquarters of the National Police an hour later. So we should wait until then.

I waited for hours. Long after the afternoon, the police put our car on standby in front of the main gate of the Province Hall. At that time, when I looked at the square in front of the Province Hall, citizens and martial law forces were confronting each other. After a while, a helicopter came. But the first helicopter just passed by as it probably was loaded with something else, and the second helicopter came and we were loaded onto that one. After many twists and turns, we managed to be transferred to the Korean Armed Forces Integrated Hospital.

Three or four days later at the hospital, I asked a military sergeant to call my home. However, my family could not visit me. I heard that my family thought I was dead, so my younger brother went looking for me the next day when I didn't come home. It was said that my younger brother found my car abandoned on Geumnam-ro and my watch was dropped in the car. I think I dropped my watch there in the course of my struggle while being beaten by the paratroopers.

While in the hospital, we were investigated. I firmly denied participating in the protests and said I got injured while picking up a customer.

The Aftermath and Life Afterwards

I was discharged from the hospital on June 3rd, but they didn't just send me home. They gathered us in the training ground of Sangmudae. And only after the chief of a *dong*[9] stood surety for me, they sent me home. After that, I tried all kinds of medicines that were good for health but ineffective. I used to like drinking and drank a lot, but I didn't even touch alcohol at all for about a year. My health barely improved. Sometimes, I can't even remember my home phone number because my memory had completely dwindled.

Even now, my whole body shakes and my head is killing me when I'm angry. Still, I had to make a living, so I bought a Gubaek cargo truck with the help of my family, but the company went bankrupt and I suffered great economic losses. Now I make a living by renting 12-seater vans. These days, there are many different opinions on the compensation issues, but speaking frankly, there would be few people in Gwangju who did not participate in May 18. Almost all citizens participated, and countless people were injured and killed. There are probably a lot of people who were beaten up like me.

In my opinion, first of all, the truth about the May 18 Uprising should be thoroughly investigated and the honor of Gwangju citizens who were falsely accused of being rioters and rebels should be completely restored, and then the compensation issues should be dealt with.

I am currently serving as the deputy secretary of the Democratic Drivers' Association for the May 18 Uprising. I'm not as good at speaking as others, but I think this role was given to me because I attend the meetings diligently.

Although the Democratic Drivers' Association for the May 18 Uprising has not been fully established because it is still in its infancy, we have a determination to work hard in our own way.

---

[9] *Dong* is a local administrative unit in Korea.

1. Geumnam-ro

3056. I Cannot Believe My Bus Crushed Four Police Officers

Witness: BAE Yong-Joo (male)
Date of Birth: March 3, 1946 (aged 34)
Occupation: Gwangju Express Bus driver (currently same occupation)
Date of Record: May 1989

Research & Arrangement by KIM Jeong-Ki

Overview

On the night of May 20th, Gwangju Express provided about ten buses to the protesters at their request. BAE Yong-Joo, who returned from a regular bus service between Gwangju and Namwon, joined the protest with his bus. At around 9:00 p.m., BAE Yong-Joo was passing through the line held by the soldiers and police from the five-way intersection of the Labor Administration to Sangmugwan, carrying a few protesters and another Gwangju Express driver KIM Gap-Jin. Just then BAE Yong-Joo became frightened and confused due to the reckless firing of pepper fog and tear gas from the military and police, and let go of the steering wheel. But the bus run straight toward the line, as it was already moving. Because of this accident, four police officers including KANG Jeong-Woong (aged 39), PARK Gi-Woong (aged 40), LEE Se-Hong (aged 31), and JEONG Chung-Gil (aged 40), who belonged to Hampyeong Police Station and were mobilized to suppress protests in Gwangju, were run over by the bus, and five people were seriously injured on the spot. BAE Yong-Joo was sentenced to death for this accident but was later pardoned and released from Daejeon Prison in December 1982.

Worked as a Bus Driver at Gwangju Express Corporation

I was born in Hwasun, Jeollanam-do as the eldest of two boys and three girls. After graduating from Chunyang Middle School in Hwasun, I helped my parents with farming due to difficult family circumstances.

After being discharged from the army in 1970, I obtained my driver's license. Mostly I used to work as a truck driver, and the pay was very low. I also worked at Gwangshin Passenger Bus Company but sometimes did not receive my monthly salary on the payday, and the pay was only 150,000 won because it was a small company.

In 1979, I got a job at Gwangju Express. I had to do a lot of work and was very busy due to the lack of drivers at this company. Instead, the company offered good conditions for the drivers because it was a big company. I received about 300,000 won per month, so I saved money and lived in hope day by day, envisioning my future.

However, this simple dream was shattered by May 18. Since 1980, the incident has kept haunting me, and`I haven't been able to do anything very well.

Participated in Protests with a Bus

In May 1980, I was working as a driver at Gwangju Express. At that time, I mainly operated between Gwangju and Namwon. With such a busy job, I didn't even have time to pay attention to what was going on in the world. Regarding the situation of Gwangju around that time, I only occasionally saw brief demonstrations taking place in various places and soldiers taking away citizens in the terminal whenever I loaded passengers from the Intercity Bus Terminal and left Gwangju.

At 7:00 p.m. on May 20th, I carried seven or eight passengers from Namwon and headed to Gwangju. At that time, the situation of Gwangju was completely unknown in Namwon. I briefly told the people in Namwon the situation of Gwangju that I had witnessed and heard about from fellow drivers.

When you come to Gwangju from Namwon, you will pass through Gokseong. Usually around this time, bus drivers from our company come out to Gokseong to stay and eat, but, strangely, there were no buses visible that day. At first glance, I thought, "Something happened in Gwangju."

What made me even more anxious was that even though we were near Gwangju, there were few cars on the highway.

Just as I expected, when I was entering Munhwa-dong, people around me said that cars could not enter the city. I had no option but to drop off the passengers in Munhwa-dong, and I reached Gwangju through Ochi-dong by going back to the highway with only the bus attendant in order to go to the Intercity Bus Terminal anyhow.

After passing through the intersection in front of Chonnam National University and coming near Gwangju Station, I saw a platoon of soldiers camped out there, so I went back to Yu-dong Intersection.

Broken stones were scattered all over the street. I felt like I was passing through a gravel field.

When I came to the Yu-dong Three-way Intersection, protesters told me to turn off the light of the bus and drive. I went through Geumnam-ro with the light off and entered the Intercity Bus Terminal.

I saw three or four buses of my company leaving the terminal. Inside the terminal, my company executives were hanging around. And when they saw my bus, the executive director said, "I was worried because there was no bus, but it's good that we have a bus. Follow the bus going out in front of you."

Without knowing the reason, I dropped off the attendant and

left the terminal, thinking, "Maybe I am going to carry people," because it was the company executive's order.

However, there were so many people on the road that buses couldn't get out of the terminal. I was barely able to move toward the city as people almost pressed against my bus. I came out of the terminal without knowing the reason for the crowd, and when I heard the protesters say, "Now Gwangju Express is with us," I found out that my bus was being mobilized for the demonstration.

Cannot Believe My Bus Crushed Four Police Officers

Even though it was almost 9:00 p.m., the street was full of people. I drove to the MBC broadcasting station through the alley by the Gwangju Police Station, following the bus in front of me, which had also been mobilized by my company. My colleague KIM Gap-Jin and several protesters got in my bus.

In front of the Labor Office, I turned the bus toward the Province Hall. Soldiers and police were camped in front of the Province Hall and Sangmudae. It seemed that my company buses had already passed through the line held by the soldiers and police in front of Namdo Arts Center, and several buses of my company were stuck on the road.

People kept pushing my bus, so I slowly entered the blocking line. As I got closer to the soldiers, I couldn't stand the tear gas. Pepper fog and tear gas continued to fly toward us. I was no longer able to drive because of the gas in front of Sangmugwan, so I let go of the steering wheel and crouched under the driver's seat. My face was covered with tears and my nose was running because of the tear gas, and I blacked out. My bus slipped to the corner of the road, being left in gear. Screams from all over the place were driving me crazy.

When the bus stopped, I jumped off it, thinking that I should escape somewhere quickly. Soon I entered a nearby underground restaurant with a few citizens who were on the bus. I ate food given by a lady of the restaurant, and when it seemed to have become quiet outside, I crossed over the wall behind the restaurant and came out to the street. I slept at an inn near Gyerim Police Box with a truck driver I used to work with and some people I had met on the street.

On the 21st, I was curious about what happened the night before, so I went to the front of Sangmugwan and met a bus driver named OH Seok-Gu, one of my colleagues, in front of Munhwa Broadcasting. He was surprised to see me.

"*Ohmea*![10] You're in trouble. Last evening, your bus killed four police officers."

"What? What do you mean by that? Tell me in detail."

I heard a detailed story from him. I couldn't believe it. I was so shocked. Something unexpected happened, but I didn't know about the deaths and had a good night's sleep. Now, it was as if I were having a nightmare.

I immediately went to my company because I thought I had to take some measures. At the company, people who didn't live in Gwangju gathered to stand guard for the company. I asked the people what to do, feeling as if I were a great sinner. The executive director of the company said to comfort me, "Don't worry too much. If we hire a lawyer to defend you, you will serve for about six months in prison and be released."

But it was easier said than done. How could I handle such a thing all by myself? That kind of huge thing happened because I was just ordered to drive my bus out by the company.

---

10) *Ohmea*, an exclamation and a dialect used in the area of Gwangju city or in Jeonnam Province, expresses a sense of wonder, translatable as "Oh, my." It can be interpreted in many ways, depending on the situation. It refers to a sense of embarrassment, sadness, or despair. It can also express an overwhelming feeling of joy.

Sentenced to Death

I only stayed at work after that day feeling frustrated without any kind of plan. Where should I run away and how would I live after that? I wished that someone had come and got me quickly. However, I heard that KIM Gap-Jin, who was in my bus that day, was arrested by soldiers on the spot. Another colleague was said to be shot in the leg.

On May 29th, two detectives from Gwangju Police Station came to the company. I was dragged away by them, giving up all hope.

In the police station, there were many people who were arrested in connection with May 18, including a lady who was arrested for cooking for protesters.

I wrote a report at the police station and was immediately transferred to Sangmudae. I was transferred from Sangmudae to Defense Security Command, back to Gwangju Police Station, and back to Sangmudae again after being required to do nothing for a whole month but write reports of my activities during the Uprising. Before I came to Sangmudae, KIM Gap-Jin, who was caught during the demonstration, was alone held to account and suffered tremendous torture and beating. So when I saw him there, he was like a dead body. I told the truth as it was to investigators. It was only then that he was able to be acquitted of murder. However, after his release, he died in 1986 after suffering from severe torture and beating in prison.

At the guardhouse of Sangmudae, it was bedtime at 9:00 p.m. However, the investigators called out inmates after 9:00 and began what they called "work." They tortured the prisoners by beating them up and preventing them from sleeping.

I was tried at Sangmudae. LEE Doo-Ho, the managing director of Gwangju Express, and the president of the Gwangju Express Union came as my reference, but how helpful could they be? Eventually, I was sentenced to death.

I was moved to Gwangju Prison and stayed in a 0.75 *pyeong* solitary cell in handcuffs made of leather.[11] I was in Cell No. 1. PARK Noh-Jeong, who was sentenced to death as a person involved in May 18, was in Cell No. 2, and SEO Man-Seok was in Cell No. 3.

I was also sentenced to death in a high court trial. My whole world seemed to be collapsing, and I thought, "I am going to die like this." How could I explain this feeling in words?

If I were to die anyway, I wished I could die after seeing a good world where no one was dying unfairly like me.

After the high court trial, I was transferred to Daejeon Prison together with HEO Gyu-Jeong—the Chairman of Domestic Affairs Department in the Province Hall at the time of May 18—and AHN Cheol.

Later, PARK Noh-Jung and I had our sentences commuted to life imprisonment at a Cabinet meeting, and on April 3, 1981, my sentence was again reduced to twenty years in prison, and then I was released from Daejeon Prison as the last person involved in May 18 on Christmas in 1982.

After my release, I tried to work again at Gwangju Express, but they refused to accept me. The president of Gwangju Express just gave me 500,000 won in compensation. I heard that my wife visited the company when I was in prison, and the company said, "We ordered him to take the bus out, not to kill people," avoiding their responsibility for me.

I was worried about my deteriorating body and thought no one would hire me, so I farmed five or six *majigis* with my wife. And then I got a job at Hwasun Mining Station as a manual worker. It was to carry logs needed for the coal harvesting industry from

---

[11] This method was referred to as *Hyuk-su-jeong* in Korean, which was designed to fasten a leather belt around the prisoner's waist and then put both of their wrists in handcuffs that were attached to the belt.

the mountain by using *jige*[12]. However, I was even kicked out of this kind of manual work after three days. They suddenly fired me without telling me the reason. Perhaps they heard that I was involved in May 18.

I got my driver's license again in 1984, as I felt like there was no other way to make a living. I got the license again because my previous license was automatically suspended when I was in prison.

I tried to get a job at Gwangju Express again with the new driver's license, but the high-level staff of the company told me to wait a little longer.

I had no option but to drive my friend's car for months, but I got sick and stayed at home after that.

I have been working at Gwangju Express since I took the test as a Gwangju Express driver in April 1988. However, I am at home now after being suspended because I recently had a fender bender. I don't understand why I don't want to do anything every May when everything goes worse, and my body and mind get sick.

Even if I try to forget May 18, the nightmare of the day has not disappeared for the last nine years. Above all, I may be able to escape from the nightmare only when May 18 is correctly defined.

---

[12] *Jige* is an A-frame back carrier used in Korea to carry wood from mountains, crops, heavy things, etc.

III MURDEROUS OPPRESSION

2. In Front of the Jeonnam Province Hall

3087. A Flower Seed Planted in a Broken Body

Witness: KIM Yong-Dae (male)
Date of Birth: April 15, 1952 (aged 28)
Occupation: Office worker (currently unemployed)
Date of Record: December 1988

Research & Arrangement by YANG Nan-Hee

Overview

This is the testimony of KIM Yong-Dae, who was shot and paralyzed from the waist down while fighting to drive the martial law forces out of Gwangju. KIM Yong-Dae, lying face down on his bed, endured pain for more than three hours and testified sincerely. The testimony was arranged by adding “An Injury and Damage Report of the Gwangju Uprising,” a report that he submitted to the Peace Democratic Party of Korea.

May 21, 1980

I fought at the forefront of hundreds of thousands of Gwangju citizens as a reserve officer during the May 18 Gwangju Uprising. I was shot and maimed in the fight against martial law forces who used tanks while committing a premeditated massacre. After being crippled, my dream-like family was broken. I have been living by spending a huge amount of money over the last eight years on treatments for the pain due to the gunshot wounds.

Even to my wife, for whom I feel more sorry than for anyone else in the world, I've never talked about it. I want the people to understand and shed light on the Gwangju Uprising accurately through a truthful description of how I was injured eight years ago. I hope that the terrible slaughter will never repeat itself in this land again. I have not wanted to recall the painful memory of being trampled by ruthless military boots for the last eight years or ever again in my life. But I realized that it was a critical incident that must be revealed. So, I decided to give my testimony.

On May 21, 1980, after an M16 bullet struck my spine in the mass shooting by the martial law forces in front of the Province Hall, I even lost my male function due to a paralysis below the ribs and became disabled, so someone else has to help me defecate and urinate. I once decided to kill myself in desperation and despair, but I felt it was unfair to die like that. Instead of delaying the truth-finding of the May 18 Gwangju Uprising to the next generation, I thought our generation, who experienced it firsthand, should reveal the truth correctly and stay alive until the truth-telling succeeds. So, I personally have been contacting the injured to find out the status of their injuries and collect data. In late 1982, "The May 18 Gwangju Uprising Injured Association" (then known as the Mt. Mudeung Injured Association) was launched at Mujin Church with more than twenty injured people.

The membership screening was made after a person completed a detailed statement on the process and location of the injury at the time of May 18, and submitted a medical certificate, and based on these, it was decided whether a person could join. Until 1987, about eighty members were active, but as compensation issues have been mentioned, there are currently about 450 members (PARK Ok-Jae is the Chairman).

The Gwangju Uprising that fought against the massacre of Gwangju citizens, which was caused by an individual ambition to seize the regime, is a monumental achievement of democracy. Nevertheless, how torn and trampled have we been by the CHUN

Doo-Hwan administration's manipulative politics for the last eight years!

When the first Parliamentary hearing was held, I expected that it would be a great comfort to the May 18 spirits who sacrificed their lives for democratization without a word. Even though the Gwangju Uprising is never just a problem for Gwangju citizens, members of the National Assembly in other regions said, "All we have to do is just compensate the victims and restore their reputations; we don't need to waste any more of our time." I couldn't hide greater mixed feelings than before as I watched the hearing distorted like that.

I am a posthumous child who has never seen my father's face. When I was in my mother's womb, the Korean War broke out, and my father, who was a police officer at the time, was murdered by the North Korean People's Army. Because of this background, I became a thorough anti-communist, and I hated KIM Il-Sung from my childhood. That's why I always thought I should be a professional soldier. In elementary, middle, and high schools, I didn't want to lose to others in anything. And I always served as class president in elementary and middle schools and as a student regiment leader in high school. I had served faithfully as a lieutenant and received many citations from the military until my short-term military service ended in February 1980.

I got a job at Samyang Tire right after my discharge from military service, and went through the May 18 Gwangju Uprising during that time.

On the Historic Site of May

On May 16th, my wife got a checkup at Chonnam National University Hospital. After hearing the result of the checkup that my wife and baby were healthy, I was as happy as if the whole world had been mine. Holding my wife's hand, I walked leisurely around the fountain in front of Province Hall, close to the hospital.

At that time, I witnessed an ardent but orderly discussion and several Korean national flags, *Taegeukgi*, around the fountain. The sight still remains dramatic in my heart. I stepped into a crowd of students. But I just went right back home because I was sorry to see that my pregnant wife was uncomfortable. However, I felt sorry for leaving only the young students behind.

When I went to work on May 19th and 20th, the atmosphere of the company was stirred by rumors such as "The martial law forces killed the citizens and captured students indiscriminately." And those stories were even officially mentioned during the company's morning meeting. At that time, I didn't fully believe the rumors and firmly believed, "even if martial law forces killed citizens, they would have done it by mistake and not on purpose."

On the morning of the 21st, I arrived at the intercity bus stop in front of the Seobu Police Station at around 7:10 to take the bus to work as usual. Commuting buses usually come by then, but it didn't arrive until eight o'clock that day. I waited for the bus, thinking it was strange. A colleague who was leaving work after the night shift said, "Don't go to work because the company is closed." He said, "Last night, the citizen militia came to the company and took discarded tires," adding, "Don't go to work until you get a notification from the company."

Just then, I saw fully armed ordinary infantry trying to enter the city near Korea Electric Power Corporation (KEPCO). In order to prevent soldiers from entering the city, citizens and students sawed down roadside trees and piled four or five trees near the overpass in front of KEPCO. I helped cut down the trees with the other citizens and set up barricades as urgently as possible in two places, one near the intercity bus stop next to the Seobu Police Station, and the other between KEPCO and the Seobu Police Station. Just then, martial law forces attempted to enter the city in jeeps and trucks, and they had a violent clash with the citizen militia. The martial law forces retreated because of the stubborn resistance of the citizens. As I watched these scenes, I thought of many overlapping things: my wife whom I always felt sorry for because I had served as a military officer on the front line for a long time, my little daughter who was just a young toddler learning to walk, and the solemnly protesting students that I saw on the night of the 16th. Suddenly, I missed my wife and daughter, so I ran to my home in Wolsan-dong. After seeing my wife's and daughters' faces, I left home again to participate in the demonstration. My wife grabbed me, but I shook her off and left my home. I just thought I would have been a coward if I looked on with my arms folded on such a sunny day in May when soldiers were stabbing, beating, and arresting citizens and students.

To the Province Hall to Check the Rumors

"No coincidence in human destiny!" I rushed right past Yang-dong toward the Yu-dong Three-way Intersection. I wanted to see the truth of all kinds of rumors with my own eyes. I saw girls who worked at textile factories in Yu-dong clapping and singing in their work uniforms on the bus and demonstrating. When I was on my way to Geumnam-ro 5th Street around 9:00 a.m., I saw two bodies covered with straw bags and carried away in a handcart. I couldn't hide my anger and embarrassment. All the citizens who saw it cried. It was proof that the countless rumors so far were not false. It also disclosed the fabrications of the politicians and the media, who had suppressed the citizens cruelly and said on the air, "Do not be misled by the rumors." I confirmed that there were no lies in the rumors. I suppressed my painful heart and headed toward the Province Hall, the place where it was said that paratroopers were encamping. As I was walking through the streets full of citizens, I remembered the faces of the college students that I saw a few days ago. I couldn't believe that brutal killings were happening in a city of education like Gwangju. And I thought, "Let's go and see what the hell paratroopers that kill people look like!"

The paratroopers, who were completely armed and in military

uniforms, stood five meters apart on the route from the former Young Men's Christian Association (YMCA) to the Gwangju Post Office in front of the Jeonil Building. In front of the troops, lieutenant colonels and captains stood as if they were inspecting them, and after that, the soldiers closed ranks with their backs to the Province Hall, blocking the road. They looked like a few battalions.

I'd like to highlight the situation in front of the Province Hall on May 21. I arrived there around 10:00 a.m., but many citizens heard the street broadcasts and came out there early in the morning. I will never forget the memory of that day. It's not just because of my injury. How can I forget the day when I witnessed the scene from the beginning when the most elite Korean troops fired indiscriminately at the citizens of Gwangju!

The Gwangju citizens who gathered there appealed for broader participation, saying, "We can't just be subjected to this," and shouted slogans such as, "Lift the martial law!" and "Soldiers, apologize to citizens for your offenses of excessive force and go back to your proper responsibilities!" Reportedly, the paratroopers had promised to withdraw from Gwangju at midnight, but that was not clear. But now it was the time when citizens protested against the paratroopers not keeping their promise. Angry young people pushed a tourist bus with more than twenty citizens and slowly moved toward the Province Hall. There was plenty of time for paratroopers to avoid the bus because people just pushed it steadily, instead of speeding it. As the bus moved a little faster in front of the YMCA, getting through the paratroopers, and turned around the fountain toward Sangmugwan, the paratroopers fired at the bus. Then the bullets hit the bus and flashed, and I saw clearly that no one in it could escape. After the tour bus brushed past the paratroopers, two soldiers fixed their backpacks. And I saw one limping off to the side of the road as if he had injured his leg. At that moment, every single paratrooper, who had gathered like a swarm of bees, kneeled down and took a "fight posture" on the side of the road.

I was startled at the sight and ashamed to my wits' end. At that moment, I heard the sound of the ear-splitting gunfire again. It was an LMG machine gun fire, and the branches of street trees near the Tourist Hotel were shot and dropped. It was a warning shot. For a moment, I kept myself close to the wall of the Jeonil Building on the way to the Young Women's Christian Association (YWCA) and looked onto Geumnam-ro where so many citizens scattered now. In the meantime, an armored vehicle drove toward the Province Hall. Then, the vehicle fired at it. As the sound of the gunfire subsided, the citizens began to gather again. Unlike the previous LMG machine gun shooting, the paratroopers shot with M16s, aiming at the citizens who were gathered there. More than ten citizens fell down on Geumnam-ro, and the people who were going out to the road to rescue the injured also fell from the gunfire. Leaning against the wall of the Jeonil Building and coming out to Geumnam-ro, I ran toward the Dong-gu District Office. I heard the sound of the gunfire behind me again.

There were so many people running away that I was slowed down while escaping. I couldn't believe such a situation, while seeing the citizens carrying the injured to the road behind Dong-gu District Office, that not a single soldier was seen on Geumnam-ro. I thought, "Where the hell are they shooting from, and people are falling?" I was so stunned that I looked around for soldiers here and there in front of the Dong-gu District Office. Three soldiers were shooting in a "stand-up position" on the roof of the National Federation of Fisheries Cooperatives.

Paraplegic by Spinal Penetration

It was about thirty minutes after the first sound of the gunfire. In front of the Dong-gu District Office, I also got an M16 bullet in the waist. Maybe I was shot by a bullet from the roof of the National Federation of Fisheries Cooperatives. A citizen took me to Christian Hospital after I was shot down.

Although I became a paraplegic at the scene of the massacre, it is like a dream to think about how I survived and could see my beloved wife and daughter,

I was told that the hospital was able to contact my wife from my work ID in my pocket. She came to the hospital with a heavy body, expecting a baby that month. Doctors pushed me away, saying that it was impossible to resuscitate me even if they performed the surgery. Seeing me being pushed into the corner bleeding, my wife cried, held the doctors, and begged them to let me have surgery. So, I was able to get it. About an hour after the surgery, my wife gave birth to a daughter at that hospital. That's why my daughter was nicknamed "518." After the M16 bullet penetrated my spine, about a hundred shards of the bullet were scattered around my abdomen and sides like grains of sand. Only a few fragments have been removed through surgery, and there are still countless fragments stuck in my body.

Overcoming the Scars of the Day

At that time, there was no neurosurgery at Christian Hospital, so the president of Samyang Tire moved me to Chosun University Hospital at his own expense. So, I received neurosurgery treatments there. But the nerves were not restored, so I've been living with my nerves paralyzed. I can't feel anything under the ribs even if I am pricked with a needle. But the area where I was shot still hurts so much that I can't sleep at night if I skip medicine even for a day, and I become exhausted after struggling with the pain for three or four hours. The doctor said about the reason why I have severe pain though I am a paraplegic: the bullet severed the spinal nerves, which made my lower body numb, and the pain was severe because of the burn shock caused by the bullet searing my spine when I was shot.

After that, I had surgery at Chonnam National University Hospital once and Seoul National University Hospital twice, but they didn't work. And I had electrical procedures to get rid of the bullet fragments, but how can they all be removed? Recently, I visited Suncheonhyang Hospital for medication, but it didn't work much either. I couldn't overcome the pain that continued every day, so my wife brought me a kind of psychotropic drug that could not be sold without the approval of a hospital's director. I got the injection, and the pain subsided. But the price of the drug is extremely expensive, and it is hard to get, so I am treating the pain with other medication now. These days, I'm trying to reduce my medication by even one pill, but it's very difficult.

In 1983, I once visited in a wheelchair with KIM Young-Sam, a party president, who was hospitalized after fasting and collapsing, while I was hospitalized and being treated at Seoul National University Hospital. I introduced myself to him, who was close to death and getting an IV. And I encouraged him, "Let's all cheer up and live hard with no frustration." But I was very worried about how emaciated he was, so I visited him again a few days later. As a result of my visit, various democratic figures were able to visit him. After that, I was discharged from the hospital and came to Gwangju. I don't know how they knew I had visited him, but the staff of the Agency for National Security Planning and the Defense Security Command began to monitor me from in front of my house every day.

They took turns monitoring me twenty-four hours a day, and as it made me feel uncomfortable, I was going crazy. I let them come into my house because personally I felt sorry for them when they were shivering in front of my house every day, whenever it rained or snowed. As a result, my family's privacy was violated. The people who monitored me were KIM Dong-Jin, an employee of the National Security Planning, then JEON Geun-Gan, a planning officer, and JEONG Jung-Kwon, a coordinator. There were a few more people I do not remember. The information department staff who monitored me were mainly at the rank of sergeant, but the ranks were mixed.

The Time after Leaving the Hospital (Supplementary)

For a year and a half after my discharge, I struggled in the belief that I would die if I was shot even by tear gas, protesting on the streets in a wheelchair and falling down, while I was serving as chair and vice-chair of the Injured Association.

Whenever people in high places came from Seoul, or there was an event related to May 18, they tried to keep me away and did not hesitate to drive a wedge between the members of the Injured Association and me. I was slowly dying under the oppression of the shameless CHUN Doo-Hwan regime. However, I thought I could never close my eyes if I died like this. Since I was handicapped, the pain that I physically and mentally suffered from while going back and forth between life and death was so extreme that I couldn't express it in writing. It's not just a day or two that I floundered in despair in desperation. I'm overcoming my mental anguish with only religious belief. Otherwise, I would have turned my back on the world earlier. My wife, who laid our newborn baby on the floor of the hospital on May 21 and wept silently while hugging our crying three-year-old daughter, is filled with tears whenever we recollect the misery of the day as if she were still dismayed. In my life, I believe my wife and I have never committed a crime that should make us suffer such an ordeal...

Completely devoting herself to nursing me, my wife had no choice but to roll up her sleeves and start a stationery store with my severance pay that I received when I was discharged. At first, it seemed to be going well, but my wife, exhausted from housekeeping, taking care of our children, and nursing me, could not endure the stress and quit running the stationery store after nine months. We had to move out at the request of the landlord. We tried hard to find a house to live in, but it was not easy because of my disability. So, we barely managed to move to a store in Yang-dong Market where we could live. After that, my wife learned beauty care services while attending a beauty training institute and opened a beauty salon there. But that wasn't easy, either. Customers who came to get their hair done often just left when they saw me lying down there. After a while, even the hair salon was closed. After that, I thought about what kind of job I could do with my uncomfortable physical conditions. Then, in the end, I started to run an amusement arcade for youth. During the presidential election last year, I was caught while writing and distributing handouts criticizing ROH Tae-Woo[13]. The police officers broke into the amusement arcade, destroyed the machines, and made a mess. Eventually, I quit that job, and now I'm not doing anything.

Unlike other injured people, I had a severe physical disability, and it was difficult for me to do group action. So, during the presidential election last year, I bought a copy machine personally and printed and distributed handouts with two college students to denounce ROH Tae-Woo. I did my best with the determination, "If we can't achieve democratization at this opportunity, there will be no place for me to lie down forever even if I die." Not long after I started the activity, I was arrested by police officers who broke through my door, but I was released relatively easily. At that time, I left my home and worked on opposition activities so as not to harm my family. I didn't get any injections at all and didn't eat much, so my health deteriorated extremely. I was almost dead and even announced my obituary. Since then, I have stopped all activities and have been paying attention to recovering my health by taking medicine that my wife makes.

The Hearing Should be One to Find the Truth

What was the enthusiastic support that Gwangju and Jeolla-do citizens showed to the Peace Democratic Party during the 13th National Assembly election? Who else paid back our support? I

---

[13] A former army general and protégé of CHUN Doo-Hwan, ROH was the president of South Korea from 1988-1993.

saw that members of the National Assembly were helpless even though they certainly knew that the men who ordered the mass firing committed perjury, avoiding responsibility and putting the blame on commanders and soldiers in Gwangju at that time. Even though there is evidence everywhere to show their perjury, it's frustrating to see the members of the National Assembly idling time away while they just exacerbate our painful wounds. Isn't it their job as members of the National Assembly to represent the people and prove clear facts? Although the hearing itself should be an effort to inherit the spirit of the May 18, it only hurt our painful wounds. As I saw the majority of the lawmakers being won over by the government and the ruling party, in referring to May 18 as "an incident," I desperately felt the need to take other measures. If I were to stand to testify, I would go in a wheelchair and draw a diagram to clearly explain the situation at the time, when a volley could not be done without an order to fire. I'm ready to run to the National Assembly and testify at any time when I'm designated as a witness.

If this hearing fails to organize its position properly, I will make a new plan and devote myself to the struggle.

Once again, I would like to emphasize the situation of the mass firing after the noon hour on May 21. As a person who knows the military system better than most other people, I really want to say that it was a pre-planned firing. The most regrettable thing to think about at that time was that while patriotic citizens were collapsing next to me, I, who was a top marksman in the military, fell without even shooting a gun once.

Another thing I want to say is that I believe around 160 people who had a joint funeral on May 29 were killed on May 21. It must be revealed where the people were buried, the people who died on the outskirts or in the Province Hall on the 27th. And then I think the death toll will exceed 2,000 when it is revealed. However, I think the important thing is not the number of the casualties, but the respectful treatment for each and every one of the casualties revealed so far. If compensation and restoration of honor for the bereaved and the injured are properly implemented at the national level, those who are now unable to report for fear of retaliation will also reveal themselves proudly.

Since being shot, I have fainted several times a day because of the pain and struggled with stomachache due to the constipation caused by the lack of exercise. These are the great physical pains I suffer. Needless to say, I'm sorry for my wife's distress, and I'm sorry for the physical condition that means I can never hug my daughters. My personal wish is that the status of the May 18 Gwangju Uprising will be properly established so that when my children grow up, they can recognize me as a righteous person, instead of as a disabled father who is avoided.

Whenever I feel depressed, I visit the spirits who died earlier while fighting for democratization. No one will know my heart-breaking pain when I visit and return from Mangwol-dong with my daughters, bringing one hundred chrysanthemums[14] and offering them to each spirit.

Unlike in the past, I feel the physical limitations that would cause me to collapse if I inhaled even a small amount of tear gas. But I will fight to comfort the innocent souls of May as long as I have life. Failing in the fight with myself sometimes leads to days of despair, but there is a reason I can never give up. At the moment when the brutal gun of dictatorship fired on me and broke my lower body, I planted a flower seed deep in my wound. Until the seed bears fruit, I will never fall back from the front, with the will that I can never give up in the struggles against despotism until the day the rest of my body blows away as red petals.

[14] In Korea, a flower traditionally offered in remembrance of the dead.

2. In Front of the Jeonnam Province Hall

1035. I Opposed the Return of Weapons

Witness: YOO Seung-Kyu (male)
Year of Birth: 1959 (aged 21)
Occupation: College student (currently unemployed)
Date of Record: December 1988

Research & Arrangement by YANG Nan-Hee

Overview

On May 18, 1980, YOO Seung-Kyu, a college student at the time, went to the main gate of Chonnam National University (CNU) on the morning of the 18th on a promise to gather when martial law was expanded. After witnessing the brutal killings by the martial law forces, he struggled hard during the uprising. He made hand-written posters such as "Why Should We Fight?" and took up a gun in confronting the martial law forces. At that time, he firmly realized the vicious reality of dictators and has since been fighting on the front line for the resignation of the dictatorship.

The Vicious Reality of the Dictators that I Have Experienced

I heard that my father attended only the first grade of elementary school, but he still received an elementary school diploma. When he was young, he worked as an elementary school teacher with no certificate and as an employee of the National Federation of Agricultural Cooperatives, but now he is farming in his hometown.

My grandfather had been a farmhand since childhood, and later he farmed about twenty *majigis* as a tenant. And he bought about five *majigis* during the land reform after 1945. After that, my father expanded the field to eight *majigis*. And now he is making a living for his family with the field. I have one older brother and two younger brothers and two younger sisters, and our parents in our family.

In my case, when I was in middle school in the countryside, political interest gradually began to grow within me under the influence of a teacher who was involved in the opposition party.

In high school, I lived with the determination to make every effort for unification of the two Koreas and graduated after receiving a superintendent prize even though I studied in the countryside. I failed the college entrance exam the first time I took it, then studied for another year in Seoul, and got admitted to the Business College at CNU. Until then, I was so naive that I thought I could make a lot of money if I ever get into the business college.

I wanted to participate in the student movement while attending college during the *Yushin*[15] era, but because of the severe suppression of student movement groups, there were few organizations that revealed themselves in public. So, wandering with no connection to any particular group, I just joined protests if there were any.

Spending my college life like that, I got involved in the May Uprising of 1980. Anyone in the Republic of Korea would be shocked after going through May 18, but it was a great opportunity for me to decide how to live the rest of my life. The brutal reality of the dictatorship was quite different from the information about it that I learned from books. That difference made me question how humans could commit such atrocities, and I understood the principles of the world.

[15] Contrary to its original meaning of renewing old conventions, *Yushin* refers to a national emergency act that justified and legitimated the long-term dictatorship of the former president PARK Chung-Hee, which was in effect from 1972 to 1979, when he was assassinated. In taking advantage of the national disorder, CHUN Doo-Hwan seized power by military coup.

From a Student to Citizen Militia

We predicted the school closure order on the morning of the 18th in advance. And I went to the main gate of CNU around 8:00 a.m. in keeping a promise to gather in front of the CNU main gate at that time, Gwangju Station at noon, and Province Hall at 1:00 p.m. There were already three or four students there. Some paratroopers guarding the main gate said, "This is none of your concern, so get back home quickly. It's no use staying here for any longer, and only bad things will happen, so go back." I heard rumors there that the head of the school corps and a professor were beaten by the paratroopers. My legs trembled. At the same time, I was angry because I was wondering, "Why do the paratroopers keep our students from entering our own school while they are inside?" I couldn't stand because my legs were shaking, so I went to one of my friends' place near the school and rested for a while. Then I went out to the front of the school gate with my friend. At that time, about fifty students had gathered. We had a sit-in protest with about forty people on the bridge in front of the main gate. The paratroopers then threatened us with loudspeakers, saying, "If you don't disband yourselves, we'll force you to disband."

A moment later, as a commander gave the order, a squad of the troops took out their clubs and rushed toward us, shouting, "Charge!" We stood up immediately and started running away. On my way back to the main gate, I watched students being indiscriminately beaten, so I threw stones at the forces because I couldn't suppress my anger. Repeatedly, we scattered when the paratroopers chased after us with their clubs. Over time, the number of the students who gathered one by one amounted to almost 200. However, we were forced to retreat due to the vicious suppression of the paratroopers and proceeded to Geumnam-ro via the New Gwangju Station.

At first, confronted by the combat police force on Jungang-ro, we were pushed back again and continued sporadic protests on Geumnam-ro. While we were overwhelmed by the power of the police force and ran away from them as they moved toward Geumnam-ro, marching in lockstep with an ominous beat, we still continued to protest sporadically.

However, we were pushed back by the police force, as they suppressed us by firing tear gas, so we moved close to Yangyeong Academy via Jungang-ro Police Box. There we protested along Dongmyeong-ro back and forth, and I participated with a large *Taegeukgi*.[16] I remember that I went in to Dongmyeong-dong Police Box, took the portrait of CHOI Kyu-Ha[17] from the wall, and smashed it. On our way to the Jang-dong Rotary in the protest procession, we stopped a vehicle of the combat police force and captured the police in it. While moving forward while making them go in front of us, I saw for the first time at the Jang-dong Rotary the paratroopers coming to suppress the protests in the downtown. It was around 4:00 or 5:00 p.m. Hiding in the alleys as the paratroopers rushed toward the protesters, I came out and threw stones repeatedly if the paratroopers seemed to pause. They chased us in a jeep as soon as we ran away, grabbed us, and then, without hesitation, tossed us into a truck. Then, the soldiers on the truck beat us like dogs again.

I went to the university the next morning again because we were supposed to be able go to the school at any time. And if there were nothing special going on at the university, we were to gather at the Intercity Bus Terminal. There I was so afraid when I heard the rumor that the paratroopers would arrest and kill young people or students if they saw them, so I went back home. That afternoon, I went to the City Hall with my uncle who lived with me and participated in the protest. But I cannot remember the details.

---

16) The Korean national flag.

17) The President of Korea at that time.

An Offensive and Defensive Battle against the Martial Law Forces

On the afternoon of the 20th, I hung out with my friends at my house and went out to the Sansu-dong Five-way Intersection. When I heard rumors that "all the Gwangju citizens decided to stand up tonight," my two friends and I began shouting continuously at the top of our voices.

"Dear Gwangju citizens! Let's all join forces and go downtown. All citizens of Gwangju have to stand together to defeat the paratroopers."

After shouting several times, the number of citizens, which was only ten at first, gradually increased to about 100 people. As I kept shouting, my throat hurt, and my voice couldn't be heard well, so I went to the Sansu-dong Administrative Office and asked for a loudspeaker and microphone. One of the employees there insisted that he could not give me them, so I went out and tried elsewhere to get them, but failed. Even after failing, I kept shouting at the top of my voice. After more than an hour of appealing for citizens' participation in the alley, more than 1,000 citizens gathered on the Sansu-dong Five-way Intersection with weapons such as briquette tongs, pipes, and clubs. My friend and I, not in the procession, followed from the sidelines and kept shouting. We went to the Intercity Bus Terminal via MBC Station. Many citizens had already gathered there, so I joined them with the citizens who had been in the procession from Sansu-dong. We went to Gwangju Station with protesters at the Intercity Bus Terminal. There were already paratroopers there. I approached a point about 100 meters away from the paratroopers but couldn't get a closer look because of the thick tear gas. Being chased by the paratroopers, we pulled out a drum full of gasoline from a gas station near the Intercity Bus Terminal and loaded it into a truck and headed to New Gwangju Station. The gasoline caught on fire, lighting up the night like daylight. I wonder what happened to the driver who drove the truck toward the paratroopers? That night, the paratroopers at Gwangju Station fired tear gas and shot intermittently. I don't know the details because I was behind the demonstrators at the time. I went back and forth between Gwangju Station and Geumnam-ro and fought a back-and-forth battle until 3:00 a.m. and went home via the City Hall.

A Young Man with His Broken Neck Dangling

Early on the morning of the next day (the 21st), I heard a street broadcast, "Gwangju citizens! Let's gather at the Province Hall," and went to the Province Hall. Already, Geumnam-ro was packed with citizens who had come out before me. There, I met two female students from Seoul who were said to be from Kyunghee University. They said they had fought against the paratroopers at Gwangju Station until dawn, but they were barefoot. After hearing the news that the paratroopers at Gwangju Station had retreated at dawn, I was very sorry and ashamed that I had gone home before other protesters. At that time, I saw two bodies covered with a *Taegeukgi* on a wagon, but since I was already extremely agitated about the atrocities of the paratroopers, I did not feel much differently just because I witnessed the dead. I approached the martial law forces in front of the Jeonil Building and asked, "How do you think this will turn out?" But they did not answer me at all. I was a little past the Tourist Hotel. As the citizens there shouted, "Let's push forward to the Province Hall," the martial law forces began to shoot blanks. Temporarily scattered by the sound of the gunfire, the citizens gathered again shortly afterwards. As seven or eight of the citizens who gathered again slowly moved toward the Province Hall in a military truck, the martial law forces aimed at the protesters and began to fire live shots. At that time, the people in the car collapsed, and the car ran into the front of the Shinhyup Bank and never moved again. After that, there were two more attempts to drive up to the Province Hall, and those who were not killed or wounded returned to the gathered protestors. At that time, the martial law forces set up three or four large metal drums between the clock tower in front of the Province Hall and the Jeonil Building, and were lying in a prone position behind them.

A young man proceeded toward the Province Hall, standing on the hatch of an armored vehicle, taking his shirt off, tying a band around his head, holding a *Taegeukgi*. He returned with his head tilted back, dangling, after being shot in the neck. That was the scene in front of the Province Hall on the 21st and the miserable image of the young man that are always mentioned when talking about May 18. That scene won't need a long explanation. The person who was fine on his way toward the martial law forces came back with his neck broken and dangling. The martial law forces fired at the armored vehicle, reloaded their ammunition, and began to shoot at civilians. Citizens on Geumnam-ro were shot down by the martial law forces. The person right next to me showed me where the bullet had just ripped through his clothes.

Gun Battles between the Citizen Militia and the Martial Law Forces

Around one o'clock, about 300 citizens and students staged a sit-in protest at the construction site for the underground walkway. When a young man, who appeared to be a student, stood in front of the citizens and encouraged them, we sang songs such as "Arirang," "The Frontier," and "Our Wish Is Unification." Some citizens were hiding between the buildings and watching. While staging a sit-in, we suddenly heard two or three shots. Then a young man standing in the front ran away behind the construction site with one arm holding the other. Those of us sitting there also quickly hid ourselves behind the buildings nearby.

At around 4:00 p.m., a truck appeared near Gwangju Bank. There were about thirty carbines in the truck, but they were absolutely too few for the number of the citizens, so I didn't get one. After that, there was a gunfight between the citizen militia and the martial law forces. The martial law forces fired from the roofs of the buildings but we could not see them. The citizen militia were also hiding between the buildings, coming out for a moment and shooting again. I watched the scene and went home around 6:00 p.m., feeling lonely as if I were walking through ruins.

After thinking about what happened at the Province Hall all night, I decided to fight at the risk of my life, and went out to the road in front of Chungjang Middle School to wait for a protest vehicle. I thought I might die if I went out now, but I decided to fight proudly even if I died. There, I met a citizen with a rifle and said, "Mister, give me that rifle. I'll take it with me and fight." He said he was also an "ace marksman" in the army and refused to give me the rifle. I went to the Gwangju Park with him on a small military vehicle. On the way, he said he couldn't believe our media broadcasts and turned on a North Korean broadcast. Rifles and ammunition were piled up in the park. I was given a carbine and ammunition and got on the truck there and went to the Baekun-dong railway station with about fifteen citizens. We went to the rooftops of tall buildings on the left and right sides and stood guard until dawn. Maybe the code was "cigarette-smoke" then. We informed the Province Hall that we were on guard near the Baekun-dong traffic rotary with the radio that the person next to me had.

At dawn, I slept at an inn near Gwangju Park with three men in their forties who had guarded the rotary together with me. One of them said that he got a rifle because he was upset about his brother's death.

The next morning, we, about forty people with rifles, learned how to use a rifle from a man in his thirties or forties for about twenty minutes at the entrance of the park bridge. We separated into platoon units when commanded to do so. The colleagues in my platoon carried guns in a protest vehicle and spent that night in the Province Hall.

At first the next day, I was on duty next to the bodies put in coffins, and later stood guard in front of the main gate of the Province Hall. Although I was on guard for a short time, I met many citizens who came to check a family member's fate. Meanwhile, five or six people drove to Seobang-dong when they heard that there were some paratroopers hiding in a church there. When the people there wouldn't let them in, they fired one or two shots at the church, saying, "Didn't you hide the paratroopers?" After firing at the church, they tried to go back without searching for the paratroopers. Then, shots rang out one after another from the prison side. On that day, while driving around, I was on guard immediately in any places when I heard that they were dangerous. But I never actually fired a gun in a confrontation with the enemy.

That night, I went back home and made a hand-written poster with the justification of "Why we should fight" on two sheets of drawing paper with my uncle, and put it on the wall of Namdo Arts Center the next morning.

On the morning of the 25th, while I was standing guard in front of the main gate of the Province Hall, my grandmother, who lived with me in Sansu-dong, visited me. She urged me to go back home quickly because my father had come from the countryside. I handed over my rifle to a friend next to me and went home. That day, my grandmother, father, and I walked along a route through the middle of a rice field to Hwasun, away from any roads, and took a bus from Hwasun to the countryside. After that, I didn't come to Gwangju until school started.

My Impromptu Speech When Incensed by the Speeches Advocating Turning in Weapons

After coming to Gwangju, I was distressed by guilt over the fact that I took refuge in the countryside as I heard about the tragic incident at Province Hall on the 27th.

It was probably the day of the "Third Citizens' Rally to Protect Democracy" after the martial law forces retreated from the Province Hall. I made an impromptu speech, enraged when I heard deceptive speeches by someone with white gloves who was allegedly said to have fought for the Korean independence movements, a church minister, Mr. KIM Chang-Gil, and others that weapons should be returned. I remember the point was: "Don't be fooled by their tricks. Patriotic citizens! If we return our weapons now, we will be destined to be shot dead by the martial law forces like flies who don't even know when they are dead. We must all join forces to fight until the day the current administration steps down and we achieve democratization. We can never return the weapons."

I couldn't keep the promise above, but I'm still trying to keep the promise I made to the citizens.

2. In Front of the Jeonnam Province Hall

3084. Thousands of Gunshots Cover Gwangju

Witness: KIM Yong-Taek (male)
Date of Birth: December 22, 1959 (aged 20)
Occupation: College student (currently working in a department store)
Date of Record: November 1988

Research & Arrangement by YANG Nan-Hee

Overview

KIM Yong-Taek participated in the struggle for democratization on campus in 1980 and participated in the torchlight demonstration with other universities on May 16. When the martial law forces fired indiscriminately on the 21st, he was shot and injured his left ankle. A crowd of demonstrators carried him to the hospital, and after a rough surgery, he was treated in several different hospitals.

In 1980, I was in the second year of the Department of Trade at the Seongin Gyeongsang College, the former Honam University.

In line with the rapidly changing situation after the October 26 Incident in 1979,[18] the shouts of democratization soared on the campus, and protests for the resignation of government-patronized professors and employees were in full swing. I also fought hard by joining the protests to eradicate undemocratic problems in the school.

CNU students contacted my school, which had been feverish due to internal problems. They insisted that we demand the abolition of martial law by joining forces with students of each uni-

[18] The day when the former President PARK Chung-Hee was assassinated.

versity and citizens in the city to lead the struggle for democratization, instead of struggling with the domestic problems of my university while the current state of affairs had radically changed.

Many of the students who accepted the request and agreed from that day went out to the fountain in front of the Province Hall. In our school as well, the enthusiasm of the students' struggle was high due to the daily protests, and at the same time, with the persuasion of the leadership, more than 100 students participated in the peaceful torchlight demonstration on the 16th with signs and banners leading the way. In accepting that request, a lot of students went to the fountain in front of the Province Hall from that day. The students' passion for the struggle soared in my school because the protest continued every day. In addition, about 100 students who were persuaded by the student leadership, participated in the peaceful torchlight protest with signs and banners on the 16th.

The Plaza in front of the Province Hall was packed tight with crowd of students and citizens, but everyone participated with a serious attitude. The main slogans that day were "Abolish martial law. SHIN Hyeon-Hwak,[19] Resign. CHUN Doo-Hwan, Resign." The citizens and students who participated in the event held torches and started a peaceful demonstration in groups organized by the leadership. I remember that my group returned to the Province Hall, walking along the Gwangju Stream via Chungjang-ro and Geumnam-ro. Although they marched for a long time, there was no restraint by the police. Rather they took positions to protect the protesters. The torchlight demonstration at the time was a really touching march.

After the emergency martial law was expanded, I went out to the downtown of the city every day from the 18th and naturally joined the protests. Mostly, I fought with stones against the riot police on Chungjang-ro, in front of Wongak Temple and near the

---

[19] The government official who helped the dictatorship.

Intercity Public Bus Terminal. I wandered around the city with my friends and protested. The first time I saw paratroopers was on the side of Gwangju Stream. On my way back from visiting my friend's father, who was hospitalized at Chonnam National University Hospital, I saw about twenty paratroopers in a 4.5-ton dump truck, but I didn't know they were paratroopers at that time and thought they were just regular soldiers.

When I went straight to the front of the Catholic Center with my friends, two or three layers of paratroopers already surrounded it. We approached within twenty to thirty meters of them and threw stones. Unlike the riot police, they had been quelling the protesters with threatening sounds of military boots in groups of about ten soldiers. Even then, citizens were just watching. Then paratroopers followed us with clubs. We scattered and began to flee because once caught, we would be beaten nearly to death with clubs and taken to a truck. I was chased for a long time and hid in a pub in Hwanggeum-dong. It was said that the paratroopers, who persistently followed me there, searched the surroundings and caught the young people who appeared to be students, beating them bloody, and I escape the search and made it home safely.

I came out to the downtown on the 19th and 20th at the appointed time. I vividly remember that I first became angry when I heard that citizens were beaten to death by the paratroopers during the protest on the morning of the 19th. The citizens who were just looking on at the protest on the first day began to join gradually as time went by.

On the 21st, when I was shot, my father, who was doing business at Yang-dong Market, stayed home because the city was chaotic and watched me to prevent me from going out. I was continually looking for opportunities to go out and join while listening to citizens' appeals for participation through loudspeakers. I sneaked out of the house when my father went to the bathroom. I couldn't stay at home because of the memories I had experienced while participating in the protests downtown. I left home at around 10:00 a.m. and walked toward Geumnam-ro. The streets were all littered with tear gas fragments, stones, and broken pieces of Molotov cocktails. As I started to walk from Nongseong-dong and kept walking, I saw a fallen tree burning in front of the Seobu Police Station. The front of Soochang Elementary School began to buzz with citizens.

I had already seen and heard the paratroopers' brutal suppression of the protests from the 18th, but I was astonished to see two bodies covered with a *Taegeukgi* on a wagon in front of Jungang Church on the Geumnam-ro 4th Street. The scene of those who had been stabbed with bayonets and crushed by clubs and boots was so devastating that it was even impossible to distinguish the gender of the bodies. Seeing this scene, I was at a loss because of my rage. "How could they be so cruel to the same race. Oh, God." I was greatly agitated in a raging anger as a person of the same nation.

Because I was a Christian, I was innocent enough to carry the Bible to my chest and participate in the protests. The weapons of other students and citizens were nothing more than stones and pieces of wood. However, my blood surged through me when I thought about the paratroopers brutally killing defenseless citizens and students with clubs and bayonets.

I kept moving toward the Province Hall with an already tangled mind. Many citizens, who became united to drive the paratroopers out of Gwangju, were filling Geumnam-ro in groups.

When I went to the Geumnam-ro 1st Street, the paratroopers were standing in several rows in front of the Jeonil Building across Geumnam-ro, armed with M16s and backed by tanks. I went right in front of them and saw that their ranks were sergeant first class, staff sergeant, and more. I also saw the paratroopers facing citizens in front of the Dong-gu District Office and confirmed that they were red-eyed.

Until then, citizens were not armed, and there were only a few appropriated vehicles. Each car was marked with red paint with slogans such as "Tear SHIN Hyeon-Hwak and CHUN Doo-Hwan to Death." It seemed to me a slogan expressing the resentment of the Gwangju citizens. Among the hijacked vehicles were some armored vehicles. Vehicles and citizens were mixed on Geumnam-ro. The protestors suddenly began to move toward the Province Hall little by little after the armored vehicle was stopped while speeding toward the Province Hall. I was with a crowd in the middle of the road on the Geumnam-ro 3rd Street where Gwangju Bank and Korea Bank were located.

Oh! I Am Shot

I remember it was around noon, and suddenly thousands of shots shook Gwangju City. Those who filled Geumnam-ro divided into two sides like waves and Geumnam-ro was quickly emptied. I ran away to Gwangju Bank, bewildered, and quickly looked back to Geumnam-ro. After confirming that no one had fallen or died there, I began to shout at the citizens who were hiding with anxious faces.

"Citizens! They're warning shots. Don't be frightened. Let's get back together."

Until then, I thought they would only fire blanks. After a while, one or two people who had been hiding here and there began to gather again, and a crowd of protestors gathered together to move toward the Province Hall. Just then, indiscriminate shooting began. At that time, I didn't imagine having been shot but felt just a slight pinch of pain. I was trying to run away without thinking much, but my legs couldn't move, so I fell down on the spot. A lot of people collapsed around me. At the moment, I thought, "Oh! I am shot." I limped over to the sidewalk in severe pain. The banging of the shots stopped suddenly. The streets were as quiet as a tomb. The citizens looked with alarm at those of us who were fallen and groaning. Blood spurted from my left ankle. Seeing me lying down after being shot, a high school classmate of mine in the crowd ran to me and tied up the ankle with a towel to stop the bleeding. After seeing the blood pouring out of my body, I lost my temper and began to cry out.

"Citizens, we can't just stand here. Let's all work together to drive them out."

Like that, I expressed my heartbreak and boiling blood. I went to the hospital with my arms and legs leaning on four students. If you had been hiding near Gwangju Bank on the Geumnam-ro 3rd Street at that time, you would have heard my cry from the heart expressing pain. While searching for a hospital, I was extremely enraged when witnessing a citizen leaning next to the road to the underground shopping mall after being shot straight through his forehead. Even though my friends told me not to say anything, I kept appealing for citizens' participation with a bloody voice on my way to the hospital.

After wandering for a long time, when entering the Hanil Orthopedic Surgery Center on the Chungjang-ro 3rd Street, I saw citizens bringing in a body on a stretcher. As expected, the body was covered with a *Taegeukgi*. When I entered the hospital, hospital officials were very reluctant, saying, "We are under the martial law now, so we cannot receive patients with gunshots." But I was able to receive treatment because of stubborn claims from the citizens there. I was carried into the emergency room and was immediately placed on the operating table. When four colleagues who carried me on a stretcher held my arms and legs at the doctor's instruction, the operation began without anesthesia. It was a penetrating wound from an M16 bullet. It was like sitting in a blazing fire to endure the surgery of sewing raw flesh without anesthesia. It was the most difficult condition in my life. It took only about five to ten minutes, but I, distorted by pain, screamed and felt deep-seated rancor toward the paratroopers. The surgery ended with sewing one stitch on the side where the bullet entered and three on the side where the bullet exited.

There was no ward available after the surgery, so I was lying on spare chairs. The wound on my left leg was bandaged, but the constant pain was indescribable. My body felt so exhausted that I couldn't move an inch, and my left leg swelled up, bruising black from one end to the other. In the meantime, I called my friend's house to tell the story and ask my family to come.

Lying on a waiting chair, I heard loud gunshots again. I saw several people being brought in to the hospital, righteous Gwangju citizens and students who could not stand injustice, fallen down before the enemy's guns and tanks while fighting with stones and clubs.

After a while, I was told from an injured person who was taken to the hospital that citizens and students were given weapons taken from out of town, and that they were fighting against the paratroopers, which gave me strength. The fight was hard to win because the enemy was armed with M16s, but our side with only carbine rifles. But it was still fortunate. In the meantime, gunfire continued to be heard. Suddenly, the sound of helicopters came from close above the Hanil Orthopedic Surgery Center. When I heard the sound of a machine gun, I was scared while lying on the chair. Even in such a terrifying situation, the worries and sighs of "How many citizens would die after those gunshots!" did not disappear from my head. I was lying in the hospital at the time, so I couldn't actually join the protesters and fight, but my heart was already with them. I already thought we were "one" because we prayed for the safety of the citizens with mixed feelings of anger and anxiety, and on the contrary, we hated the paratroopers.

Someone whom I didn't know, either a citizen or a reporter, came into the hospital and wrote down my information in a notebook: school, date of birth, name, address, and etc. When he told me that there were rumors that the paratroopers would go through each hospital and kill the injured in a little while, I was anxious and eagerly waiting for my family to come quickly, but they didn't.

I couldn't stand the pain from the wound, so I begged the doctor to do something for the pain, and he gave me an injection. The pain went away like magic, but after some time, I was suffering from the pain and anxiety again. Then my oldest brother and sister-in-law came. My brother went outside and got a small wagon used on a construction site.

After loading me into the wagon less than half as long as my height, my two friends, more upset to see the gunshot wound I suffered, went back to the protest scene. I left the hospital with my brother pulling the wagon.

Since I went to Nongseong-dong from the hospital with my body crumpled in the small wagon, it is needless to say that the pain of the wound was severe, and the pain from my back and shoulders bouncing in the wagon was also extreme. Citizens on the side of the road applauded for me as I was being carried home after being injured. And a jeep with armed citizen militia stopped on its way. After checking my condition, they told me to take good care of myself and left.

I arrived home around 4:00 p.m. The pastor of Hwajeong Church, where I attended, was called. He looked at my wound and told me not to stay home but to move quickly to the Christian Hospital. With the help of my brother and sister-in-law, I came out to the road and caught a protest vehicle passing by and went to the Christian Hospital.

The Hospital in Pandemonium

The hospital was full of gunshot patients everywhere. Full of disgusting smells and the groaning of patients, the hospital reminded me of Hell. I lay on the concrete floor. About an hour later, I got an X-ray with the help of the pastor. Later, I saw all the bones around my ankle cracked, and the hole through which the bullet had penetrated was clearly visible.

Even that night, gunshots were continually heard, and many injured people and dead bodies were taken in to the Christian Hospital. I heard about the situation outside the hospital through nurses from time to time. In particular, when we were told by a nurse with tears in her voice that a high school girl, attending Chuntae Girl's Commercial High School, donated blood at the Christian Hospital and returned to the hospital as a terrible corpse with the other citizens in the same car due to the indiscriminate shooting from the paratroopers on her way home. And we all cried with despair.

The injured person next to me was a junior in the Department of Economics at Chosun University. He was hiding in the school on the night of the 17th, when the paratroopers were stationed at CNU and Chosun University. He saw his opportunity, and he tried to escape at dawn of the 21st, but was found and shot in the shoulder by the paratroopers. After continuing to flee, he was hospitalized at the Christian Hospital safely with the help of nearby residents.

Minor wounds like mine couldn't be taken care of there. Undoubtedly, mine was considered a minor injury because there were many patients who were more seriously injured than I was and pleading for lifesaving measures.

That night, I prayed countless times and listened to hymns but couldn't fall asleep easily, unlike my usual days. I stayed up all night on the 21st, enduring the fear caused by the continuous gunfire and physical pain.

On the morning of the 22nd, we heard gunshots intermittently. After staying up all night on the concrete floor, I was moved on to a bed. Even then, I could not enter a room. The wound continued to ache, but I had to endure the pain by myself. In the morning, some women made soup for the patients, and blood donors continued to rush in. Wouldn't this show precisely that all the citizens of Gwangju are united as "one"? In the morning, five or six foreigners came to the hospital to videotape the injured people lying down and interviewed some of us who could speak English.

The only treatment I received in the hospital for two days and one night was a few injections and pills. I didn't have to stay any longer because my wound was treated only when I complained that the pain was so severe that I couldn't stand it. At 5:00 p.m., I took three days' worth of medicine and left the hospital.

I went to a hospital nearby to get treatment for my injured leg, which was bleeding through the bandages, because, I conjecture, the wounds got worse while walking on my way home. After that, a nurse had been sent from the hospital run by my father's friend to disinfect and bandage the wound once a day until the 30th.

On the 27th, I heard the news that the martial law forces had occupied the Province Hall and killed and arrested numerous citizens. The next day, I got on the back of a motorcycle and went to Yangmin Clinic, where they pulled out the stiches. On the way from my home in Nongseong-dong to Yangmin Clinic in Yang-dong, I saw a tank in front of the Seobu Police Station and one in front of the Agricultural Products Joint Market.

On June 1st, I was hospitalized at the Christian Hospital again, and they took X-rays. My cracked bone that had been shot was not healed yet, so I put on a cast. From then on, I lived on crutches for five months. While in the hospital, I received treatments and continued physical therapy, and in July, I was able to take a few steps without crutches. I was so happy that day that I even shed tears. When I was in the hospital, we were afraid of retaliation, so all my family moved to Ssangchon-dong.

Even after being discharged from the hospital on July 14, I went to school on crutches and managed to live almost normally in almost everything. I didn't want to talk about getting injured during the Uprising on May 18, so I spent my school life more sincerely than usual. As a result, I even went to Iri Commercial High School for teacher training as a representative of the Department of Trade.

Receiving a Notice of Enlistment

After graduating in 1981, while I was taking care of myself at home due to the severe trauma from the ankle wounds, a notice of enlistment was delivered to me on August 10. I entered Nonsan Training Center with the sore leg. I was very miserable. I felt even more miserable because my mind was full of distrust for and feelings of betrayal by the soldiers. The continuous ankle pain bothered me, and when I went to the military, rumors that the people who were injured during May 18 are nearly beaten to death made me feel depressed.

The waiting period at the training center was much harder than I had expected. But I had a strong determination. Reflecting that I would not be able to stand anywhere if I failed to overcome the trainings that others could do, I struggled to undergo the training. But it was so hard to act like a normal person, so I secretly swallowed my tears. While living in the training center for a few days, I talked to my superior because my leg was swollen and my ankle painful. Fortunately, I was taken to the Integrated Hospital and received medical treatment. And after eleven days of enlistment, I left Nonsan Training Center and returned home. My whole family was pleased with my homecoming.

After that, I often lamented to myself because I could not get a job anywhere because of my damaged leg. Then, after working for a few months at my brother-in-law's construction company, I quit and went to my father's fish market to help and lived like that for about a year and six months.

On April 14, 1983, a notice of re-enlistment was delivered. This time, I went to the 31st Division. I thought I would not have to go to the military because the decision I received for my medical issue at Nonsan Training Center was valid, so I was very frustrated when the notice suddenly came. In the 31st Division, all enlisted trainees received training, and if anyone was ill, they were given a brief treatment at night. After training, my legs were swollen and painful just like the last time, but it was no use explaining the situation to my superiors. I couldn't help but contact my family to send the X-rays I had taken previously to the 31st Division. With the X-rays sent from home, I went to my superior and handed them over to him and explained them in detail. A few days later, he took me to the Integrated Hospital. Three days later, I received a diagnosis from the hospital's orthopedic surgeon that I would have no obstacles to serving in the military, and was trained while persevering through my continued pain with painkillers. I was frustrated and swallowed tears many times due to unbearable hardships.

After the training period, I was deployed to the Reserve Army Training Management Battalion in Chungnam. It was relatively comfortable. But I never neglected my duties there. Since at that time, all Gwangju people were known nationwide as hoodlums and rioters, I had a difficult life while enduring the pain. I was afraid that if I lived my life in a dishonest way, anyone could look at me and think "This is what he is!" In particular, I personally did not want to be criticized as a hoodlum who was shot on May 18, so I made every effort. The Gwangju people were not a mob but strong-willed people, and I determined to show that May 18 was also a righteous struggle. I pride myself on not forgetting this point no matter where I live and how I live.

After being discharged from the military in October 1985, I joined my current workplace and was working hard, and at the beginning of this year (1988), I got married and had a child, and live a harmonious family life.

Even now, when I think about what happened at that time, my

heart beats and I grind my teeth. It must be made clear that May 18 was never a riot of mobs but a bloody struggle of the people for justice. It showed that it was a way for true humans to move toward righteousness by protesting with bare fists against soldiers armed with the latest weapons, while giving their lives without losing courage. Putting everything else aside, how could we overlook, as the same people of a single nation, that the soldiers slaughtered our Gwangju citizens! I am ashamed to still be alive when I think about the patriotic citizens who were killed by the enemy while trying to defend Gwangju and protect our Gwangju citizens.

The X-rays of the ankle with the gunshot wound show that the place where it was pierced is full of flesh now, but a hole remains in the bone. When the weather is bad or it rains, the ankle is cold. And when I overwork, it becomes swollen and painful. The nerve on the left toe is dead and blunt, and the third toe is painful when touched. Also, after the gunshot wound to my left ankle, it resulted in arthritis in the right knee, as I used only my right foot to maintain balance. However, on May 21, I thank God that I was able to survive the bullets pouring from the guns of the paratroopers, and I go to church with a grateful heart.

I received compensation of three million won for the first time ahead of *Chuseok*[20] this year. However, financial rewards will never be able to appease the hearts of patriotic citizens.

Shot, killed, and crushed under the military boots of the paratroopers in May 1980, how could the bitter, traumatized souls of the Gwangju citizens appease their resentment by financial compensation? First of all, Gwangju citizens are the owners of a great spirit, and May 18 was a righteous protest. No other compensation is meaningful if our honor is not restored. The reason that the Gwangju citizens were brave is not only that they had boiling blood, but also that the dismal circumstances made them

[20] The fall harvest holiday in Korea.

boldly confront the soldiers without fear of guns and swords. How could a person without a love for their country stand proudly in front of a gun?

Finally, in memory of the deceased who fought in shared pain for democratization and overthrow of dictatorship, I pray that their wishes will bloom with the Gwangju citizens and give enthusiastic applause to the patriotic citizens who cry out for democracy at the top of their voices.

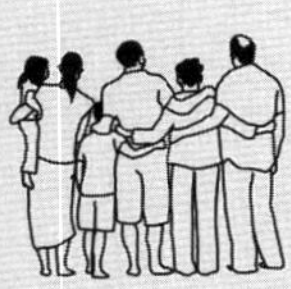

Ⅳ. CRITICAL CONSCIOUSNESS

1. Chonnam National University (CNU)

3029. Witness to Martial Law Forces Stationed at Chonnam National University ___ **AHN Yong-Ho**

3005. I was Going to Join the Military, But Why did They Label Me a Communist? ___ **LEE Sung-Gil**

3027. Chasing Us Down to a Private Study Library, Swinging Clubs ___ **KIM Soo-Young**

3035. A Bus Passenger Taken to CNU ___ **BEOM Jin-Yeom**

2. Gwangju Munhwa Broadcasting Corporation (MBC)

3062. My Spine Injured While Saving My Friend ___ **CHO Young-Bok**

3060. The Flames of Anger that Burned Pro-government Media ___ **SEO Chae-Won**

3. The Fountain Plaza (the Province Hall)

4001. Let's Fight to the End ___ **JEON Young-Ho**

4007. Presiding Over the Citizens' Rally ___ **KIM Tae-Jong**

4. The Province Hall

1007. The Conflict between Settlement and Resistance ___ **SONG Ki-Sook**

1011. The Judgment of the Nation and History ___ **CHO Cheol-Hyeon**

IV CRITICAL CONSCIOUSNESS

1. Chonnam National University (CNU)

3029. Witness to Martial Law Forces Stationed at Chonnam National University

Witness: AHN Yong-Ho (male)
Year of Birth: 1941 (aged 39)
Occupation: Janitor at Chonnam National University
Date of Record: December 1988

Research & Arrangement by PARK Hyeong-Ho

Overview

On May 17th, as a night-duty janitor, he witnessed the arrival of the paratroopers and the arrest of students at the 1st Student Center of Chonnam National University.

Born as a Son of a Peasant

I was born as the eldest son of five children in 1941 in Usan-ri, Songgwang-myeon, Seungju-gun. My family was very poor, farming on only two *majigis* of fields and four *majigis* of tenanted fields. After graduating from elementary school, I continued to farm in the countryside. In the meantime, I decided to enlist in the army with the determination to live away from home and go through hardships, although my parents opposed my decision. At that time, life in the army was difficult, so I had to prepare myself for it. I had a physical examination for joining the army but there were too many applicants, so I couldn't enlist. It was a very difficult time to live, so there were many applicants for the military service. Therefore, some of the applicants were made to wait for enlistment as the first replacements. I was also assigned to the first replacements, so I couldn't join the army and went back to farming in the countryside. After three years, I received the notice of military duty and joined the army. At that time, my parents and myself were not happy with me joining the military because I was used to farming as I got a few years older.

I spent my military service standing guard at the barbed-wire fence of the forefront. And then, because I got older, I got married on the advice of my parents on the lunar New Year's Day, a month before I was discharged from the military. After being discharged from the military, I farmed in my hometown, the countryside, for a year, and then moved to Gwangju with my wife in 1966.

After coming to Gwangju, I worked for ten years as a porter at both the previous train station and the Gwangju Station. However, I couldn't make a good living but only got sick, so I quit the job. As I spent all my money, I had to rent a room in Jisan-dong. I was literally penniless.

I tried various kinds of business such as peddling fruits and vegetables, but the business didn't work out the way I wanted. I thought about going back to my hometown.

Worked as a Janitor at Chonnam National University

In the meantime, with the help of my relative I joined the Consumers' Cooperative Society of Chonnam National University as a temporary employee. Back in 1977, my monthly salary was 30,000 won. I couldn't make a living with that money.

My wife was also making a living by sewing and selling items. My salary was so low that I thought I would quit the job, but my wife persuaded me not to do so.

"You are working at a national university, so let's endure. I will earn the living expenses somehow, so don't think that your salary is low, and let's live life to the full."

That way I endured for about a year, and I got assigned as a full-time employee. Since then, I had been working as a janitor at the 1st Student Center. At that time, my kids were young, so the salary was enough to manage to live.

That's how I lived my life, and the year of 1980 started. At that time, I didn't know that CHUN Doo-Hwan was that bad. Back then, the student president PARK Kwan-Hyeon was leading the demonstrations, saying, "Let's punish CHUN Doo-Hwan, Let's drive him out." I can still see how PARK Kwan-Hyeon wore white rubber shoes during the student president election. At the time, I thought, "They must just study hard" when students demonstrated. Since it was during the dictatorial regime of PARK Chung-Hee, civil servants were not able to say the right thing. I think it's still the same now.

First of all, when students demonstrated, we were annoyed. It was the time when political inspection on campus activities was severe, so detectives kept bothering us, saying, "You didn't tear down the posters" or "You didn't report them to us."

The demonstrations of these days are nothing. At that time, when slogans such as "Let's knock down CHUN Doo-Hwan" were written in the restroom and everywhere, the detectives used to grill us asking, "Did you see it or not?" and "Didn't you even examine it?" We were just easy targets for them. Now I think the world has improved this much because students demonstrated at that time.

Paratroopers Arrived at the School

Around May 1980, the office of welfare service moved to the 1st Student Center and I worked there. I was on night duty on the 17th, and the vice student president of CNU (LEE Seung-Ryong) came in after midnight. He came in and told me not to lock the door. When I asked him why he told me not to do so at that late hour, he said the student president (PARK Kwan-Hyeon) would come soon. At that time, I didn't know much about politics, so I responded to him irritably because his requests were bothersome. I went into the night-duty room without locking the door and just slept. I was sleeping quite a while and heard a lot of noise. I went out, talking to myself, "Sons of bitches, what kind of jerks are doing crazy things?" However, unexpectedly, many paratroopers had gathered inside the entrance of the 1st Student Center. I got angry being awoken from light sleep, and about fifty soldiers were going up to the second floor and breaking or throwing away banners and signs made by students. I believe it was about 2:00 a.m. I stood there, not knowing what to do, and a soldier asked harshly.

"Who are you?"

I answered confidently.

"I am a janitor on night duty."

"Are there students here or not?"

When I replied that I didn't know about it, the soldier asked me to go upstairs with the soldiers. He told me to open the locked door, but I said I couldn't because it was locked by the students. The soldiers couldn't search the student council room or club rooms, but only searched rooms where the doors were open and came down. When I came down, about seven or eight students who had been caught were kneeling in front of the restroom and being beaten cruelly by the paratroopers. I was so frightened that I couldn't bear to watch the scene and went into the night-duty room. At about 4:00 a.m., the students were taken away.

On the morning of the 18th, I saw a military encampment set up in the university stadium. In addition, the area behind the building of the Department of Science (currently College of Home Economics) was a total mess: an outdoor kitchen was installed, and meals were prepared. The soldiers seemed to have treated the captured students ruthlessly at dawn by taking the students off to the conference room at the university headquarters, beating and kicking them in the shins pitilessly. They asked me to bring meals to the students at lunch time, so I took meals from the cafeteria and saw the soldiers keeping their eyes on the students, watching each one individually. The soldiers told the students to eat, but they didn't.

While the martial law forces were stationed at CNU, the building of the College of Home Economics was used as the headquarters of the paratroopers, and I heard that there were many dead bodies in that building. I don't know what was going on in front of the main gate, because I stayed inside the school during the whole day of the 18th. At that time, people had to present passes to enter the school, but employees working at the university were free to move on campus. Commanders of the paratroopers were in the janitor's lodges at the main and back gates of the university, and the soldiers stood guard outside. I worked until Sunday because the shift worker did not show up, and on the afternoon of the 20th I took the shift and left work. On my way home in Jisan-dong, I saw a car burnt in front of the Gwangju Station, and protesters were driving around.

The next day, I came out of my house to go to work, and I heard a female student broadcasting with a microphone. I can't remember what she said. On the roof of the second floor of a house, soldiers (the investigator's note: presumed to be soldiers of the 31st Division) were standing on duty in arms. When I said I was on my way to CNU, they told me not to go there, because I would die if I went there, so I went back home. I was nervous but thought it would be better to go to work, so I left home. At the Seobang Intersection, soldiers with guns wouldn't let me pass. When I said I was on my way to the university as an employee, the soldiers told me to turn around and go another way.

I managed to get to the university and work. In the afternoon, a staff sergeant of the paratroopers came and asked me to fix his watch, saying it was broken. And then, he asked me to buy him a toothbrush, toothpaste, and soap and gave me 5,000 won. When I got his watch repaired off campus and came back, the soldiers had withdrawn, and they were nowhere around. Around the building of the College of Home Economics, stuff abandoned by the paratroopers was scattered here and there, and there were a lot of unpleasant smells. After the paratroopers withdrew, PARK Deok-Jin, a colleague of mine, and LEE Jae-Hwa, currently an assistant at the College of Agriculture (who worked at the headquarters at that time) came back from their hometowns in the countryside. They said they came to school by bicycle because they couldn't make calls and traffic was cut off. After that, I continued to go to school, but there was nothing special to do because students did not come to school.

After May 18, I continued to work at the 1st Student Center, but now I am working at the College of Social Sciences.

I recently bought a house in Duam-dong with fifteen million won I received in compensation for the submerged district of the Juam dam, together with the money my wife had saved. We have three sons who attend high school, middle school, and elementary school, and we manage to make a living educating our children, for I have a benefit from being a civil servant.

1. Chonnam National University (CNU)

3005. I was Going to Join the Military, But Why did They Label Me a Communist?

Witness: LEE Sung-Gil (male)
Date of Birth: July 5, 1957 (aged 22)
Occupation: College student (currently a lecturer at a private academy)
Date of Record: December 1988

Research & Arrangement by YANG Hong-Jin

Overview

In 1980, he was the student president of the College of Law, organizing the Committee for School Democratization and leading demonstrations of the College of Law. Until May 20, he led the demonstration at the main gate of Chonnam National University. He escaped from Gwangju safely when he heard that students leading the demonstration would be arrested. But he was taken into a detention cell on the day he was supposed to join the military after receiving the notification of military duty.

Serving as an Executive of the Committee for School Autonomy

Back in 1980, I was a junior majoring in law at CNU. At that time, the Committee for School Autonomy was organized to eradicate anti-democratic elements on campus and to support struggles for democracy taking place in each sector of society. In addition, the complete dissolution of the Students' League to Defend the Country was enforced to get rid of anti-democratic elements such as Students' League to Defend the Country, government-patronized professors, and student military training. As a student representative of the College of Law, I served on the Committee for Campus Autonomy. I informed the students of the legitimacy of the revival of the student council and the schedule for democratization on campus by distributing leaflets in order to establish a democratic independent student body with a guarantee of the free creation and activities of school clubs.

After PARK Kwan-Hyeon was elected as the president of the student council and I was elected as the student president of the College of Law on April 9, we started activities to democratize the campus by making an issue of the resignation of government-patronized professors. The student council created public opinion on democratization through a ceremony to commemorate the 20th anniversary of the April 19 Revolution and a ceremony to express hope for the revival of the student council. We encouraged students to inform the local residents of the inauguration ceremony of the student council by holding a recreational event next to the main building of the College of Medicine.

After April 19, on-campus issues developed into off-campus ones. The student council issued a statement condemning the cabinet of CHOI Kyu-Ha, which included eradicating remnants of the *Yushin* dictatorship and denouncing the extension of their martial law. And the student council demanded "the schedule for democratization of the interim government, the lifting of martial law, the refusal of constitutional amendment led by the government, the release of democratic figures, and the prohibition of arrest and oppression of workers." In addition, the student council made it clear that it would carry out a vigorous struggle to achieve these things. Under these guidelines, each college decided to carry out street demonstrations in order to inform the citizens of their intention to implement the struggle, and to gain favorable response from them. As a preparatory step, the College of Law decided to go downtown with a rented school bus. The College of Law was the first in the university to go on a street demonstration. We went out of the back gate of the university after having a discussion in which we agreed to go to the downtown first and engage in a street demonstration while chanting slogans and distributing leaflets. We mainly chanted the slogans such as "Abolish martial law," "Resign CHUN Doo-Hwan and SHIN Hyeon-Hwak," and "Reveal the Political Schedule for Democratization."

At this time, a police car came to the protesters of the College of Law and told them not to hang a funeral streamer and not to distribute leaflets. Student representatives of the College of Law asked the police to escort them, telling the police that they would go to the CNU College of Medicine by bus. As the police continued to block the street demonstration, we got off near Honam Electric, formed a scrum and chanted slogans. Then the police no longer stopped us from going downtown and told us to get on the bus. We went downtown, chanted slogans, distributed leaflets out from the bus. And we tried to contact the CNU student council to ask for solidarity. However, we couldn't contact them, so we had a sit-in protest at the College of Medicine, got on the bus, and returned to school. It's hard to remember exactly what day it was, but it must have been around May 10. Universities across the country decided to raise the flag of national struggle to fight, and grand rallies for the nation and democracy were also held in each college of CNU. The campus was filled with students' shouts for struggle, and the students decided on an off-campus demonstration.

On May 13, we dispersed after throwing stones at the riot police at the school gate.

Breaking Through the School Gate

On the 14th, we held a rally at the university stadium with plans for strategies and tactics necessary for fighting, and then we advanced along the stream toward the school gate. The police confronting us at the school gate fired tear gas and pepper fog by volleys. Despite this, the students quickly broke through the front and rear gates and ran toward the plaza in front of the Province Hall, rearranging their lines by college amid shouts and slogans. The demonstrators who gathered in the plaza in front of the Province Hall assembled around the fountain and were seized by the excitement and passion for holding "the Grand Rallies for the Nation and Democracy." The president of the student council rose to the fountain to announce the start of the Grand Rallies for the Nation and Democracy and a declaration of the current situation. Students chanted slogans, "Proposal of the Schedule for Democratization, Suspension of the Interim Government's Leadership in Constitutional Amendment, Immediate Lifting of Emergency Martial Law, Eradication of Remnants of the *Yushin* Dictatorship, and Suspension of Oppression of Democratic Opinions of College Students." The student council president returned to school with a fervent response from citizens after giving a speech, where he said he would take responsibility for peaceful demonstrations and actions.

On May 15 there was the same protest as the one of the previous day. On this day, as students were confronting the riot police and some of them were injured, citizens participated in the students' demonstrations and sat together with the students at the fountain.

Around 2:00 p.m. on May 16, all universities in Gwangju, including community colleges, Chosun University, Chonnam National University, and Gwangju National University of Education, attended "the Torchlight Rally for the Grand Rallies for the Nation and Democracy" in the plaza of the Province Hall. Citizens welcomed them on the street with applause and cheers. Representatives of each university went up to the fountain and read a declaration of the current situation, and a student from Chonnam High School received enthusiastic responses from citizens when he spoke at the fountain that he would devote his life to democracy. The students chanted slogans after reading out their statements. The rally for democracy ended with the same slogans as the previous day, and then we held a night torchlight protest with the citizens. Students from CNU were divided into two groups and came to the Province Hall passing through Geumnam-ro, Gyerim Five-way Intersection, the intersection in front of the City Hall, Sansu Five-way Intersection, and Nongjang Bridge. Although the police were on guard, we decided to hold peaceful demonstrations and student representatives watched their fellow students closely for fear of any possible incidents from the torchlight protesters. So we were able to end the protest in an orderly manner. In other words, we confirmed the citizens' demand and aspiration for democratization with the response that we showed during the demonstration.

After returning to the campus, the student leadership checked what happened that day and agreed that if the university was not going to be closed, we would attend classes from the next week. We thought that the demands of the students were well delivered to the citizens through that day's demonstration. However, we agreed to gather on the campus if the order of closure or martial law was expanded. That evening, we had a get-together with representatives of the student council and discussed the direction of the struggle.

On the evening of the 17th, I met with representatives of the student council of the College of Law at a restaurant near the school and discussed the direction of the struggle of the College of Law. That time, we talked about taking classes as usual unless there were any problems.

Because I was tired from the continual protests lasting for days, I was exhausted after drinking a little. That evening, I went to the house of the student in charge of general affairs and slept there. At that time, I was studying for the bar examinations with the bar examinations research team, so I mainly ate and slept on campus. Sometimes, I stopped by my eldest sister's house to get food and change clothes, but around that time, I had no time to pay attention to studies due to continual protests, and I stayed up all night in the student council room.

On the evening of the 17th, my friend and I slept soundly with a radio on, and I woke up at dawn when I heard from the radio that universities across the country had been closed and emergency martial law had been expanded. I woke my friend who was sleeping next to me and urged him to listen to the radio. After waking up from a catnap, we arrived at the main gate of CNU at around 8:00 a.m., worrying about what to do.

Entering the School through a Doghole[21)]

At the main gate, martial law forces stood fully armed. I tried to enter the school, but they blocked me from entering it, and they told me to go home because the school was closed. At this time, professors told them they had to go in because they convened a faculty meeting, but they did not let them in. When the professors complained by demanding why they could not enter, the soldiers blocked them and even beat them with clubs. We did not disperse but waited for more students to come in front of the main gate when the armament and tyranny of the martial law forces became more brutal than ever before. I was most curious about what would have happened to the friends at the bar examination research team if martial law forces had already taken control of the university. According to students who gathered at the school gate, those who were on campus on the evening of the 17th were dragged to the conference room on the third floor of the university headquarters. I thought I couldn't stand it, so I walked out in front of the soldiers. I asked them politely to let me in, saying that we had to go in to bring books for our studies, but they still refused. A friend of mine who was the student representative of general affairs of the College of Law, another friend who was a deputy student representative of general affairs, and I sought a way to enter the school. There were

---

21) A doghole is the idiom for a narrow secret passage that people use to sneak in and out of a place.

martial law forces at the front and back gates, so we decided to enter through the back of the College of Agriculture Sciences. After checking there were no martial law forces behind the College of Agriculture Sciences, we went through the woods behind the College of Law by going through a doghole of water pipes, which were piled up in an area of woods. When we went to the front door of the College of Law, it was a total mess. The hand-written posters and banners on the wall had been torn down and were trampled with footprints.

A janitor found us and spoke quickly.

"Seong-Gil, did you come in to be killed? If you get caught by the martial law forces, you would get into trouble, so get out of here right now."

"It's okay. Everyone gets caught. I don't care. I'm just curious, so don't worry too much."

I answered with nonchalance and went to the bar examination research team, but the janitor grabbed and stopped us.

"I was also beaten by them last night and passed out, and only came around at dawn. No matter how much I said I was a janitor, they hit me without mercy. When I came to my senses, I found that I was at the conference room on the third floor of the headquarters, and I begged them to let the staff members out at least, and I finally could come here."

I wondered what happened to the student president who must have been on the campus.

"What happened to the student president?"

"Well, I don't know. Anyway, everyone who was on the campus last night was caught and held in the university headquarters."

The three of us decided to go to the student council office first. The two friends decided to go first, because we were afraid that we would have been in danger of being caught if all of us had gone there together. We agreed to meet at the back of the central library and parted. I went to the back of the graduate school, passed by the College of Commerce, and got to the back of the central library. My friends didn't come, so I hesitated a little and then went into the room of the bar examination research team, taking my backpack, and getting to the 1st Student Center. Two soldiers shouted, "Raise your hands!" pointing their guns at my back. Annoyed, they aggressively pressured me with their Gyeongsang dialect.

"Who are you? What brought you to the school?"

"We also attended university before joining the military, and now are having such a hard time like this. Why are you students demonstrating, not studying?"

Although I was nervous, I was interested to hear that they attended university before joining the military. I thought that if I explained the students' point of view, they would understand us well enough because they were also college students.

"It's serious that college students give themselves up to demonstration when they need to study. But have you ever thought about the fundamental reason why they protest?"

I asked them this question with a humble tone. I even tried to enlighten them about the reason. But the soldiers didn't care about what I said and asked me again why I come to the school.

"I came to study, but the campus was closed, so I came here to buy a book."

"There is no bookstore here. That's nonsense."

They suspected I was saying things that didn't even make sense. I pointed to where the campus bookstore was.

"There it is."

But they still looked at me suspiciously,

"You! How did you come here?"

"I came in through the back of the College of Agriculture

Sciences."

"If you go this way, you will die. Get out of here quick."

They said, pointing to the front gate. After I got out of there, I turned back the way I came from and went to the main gate.

In Front of the Main Gate of CNU

At the front gate, I met the two friends who had gone to the student council room and asked what happened. They said that when they went to the student council room, they found that the equipment was broken and the room was a total mess.

The friends said that the president of the student council seemed to have gotten out of school. They also said that they got out of the student council room and then came out toward the College of Agriculture Sciences by sliding down a water pipe through a hill because they had no time to go to the central library.

The number of students gathered at the main gate gradually increased, and those who had been fighting on the 14th, 15th, and 16th, three days in a row, insisted that they should enter the school instead of staying outside. And students gradually and naturally started to sing and chant, saying that they had to fight the martial law forces. At this time, there was a truck at the university stadium, and soldiers were at close-order drills with tents set up and were looking at the situation outside the school. As the students went out chanting slogans toward the main gate and perhaps someone contacted the barracks of the martial law forces, a platoon of soldiers was immediately dispatched and came out in front of the main gate. The soldier with a megaphone said, "The school has been ordered to close, so go home. If you don't disband within five minutes, we'll take compulsory measures, so go home and study at home," he repeated. Paying no attention to this, the students raised stones and began throwing them, ready to fight.

However, unlike their usual behavior, the martial law forces aimed guns forward at the order of the commander, counted to five, and began to charge at the students. A platoon of troops continued to charge, swinging clubs ruthlessly at the students. They chased them to the alley, dragged them out, and stomped them with their military boots. At that time, construction was underway in the current residential area in front of the main gate, so 200 to 300 students fought back for about an hour. However, seeing the students taken away, I thought that we should not fight like this. I suggested that we go out to the downtown and fight there in order to inform citizens of the atrocities of the paratroopers. However, the subsequent events were not the result of any certain student suggested joining citizens to fight, or that the student leadership suggested fighting according to some plan.

Going Downtown

Like the street demonstration the previous day, we stood in four columns and confronted riot police at Geumnam-ro Underground Shopping Center. We threw stones at the riot police. While students and riot police were pushing and shoving each other, the riot police began to be pushed to Taepyeoungyang Chemical in Geumnam-ro 5th Street. However, as some instructions seemed to have been given to the riot police, the martial law forces came up to the protesters in pairs from Yu-dong and trampled on them with clubs and military boots mercilessly when they were caught. I always went with KIM Kyung-Seok and PARK Ki-Soo, but I get separated from PARK Ki-Soo in the downtown. KIM Kyung-Seok and I went to the front of Gyerim Police Box to throw stones, went to Ki-Soo's house at around 8:00 p.m., and discussed further plans. It was difficult to contact the student representatives because they were wanted by the authorities. However, we thought if we fought in the way we had been fighting so far, we could not overcome the brutality of the martial law forces. We were in despair, thinking how long we would continue to lose this fight to them. When I gave a call to my eldest sister, she said soldiers had come into her house in their military boots. She told me to hide myself because they were looking for me. However, I thought that it would be unacceptable for students to start fighting and not to see it through until it was settled, and that we should not leave the situation irresponsibly.

Flight

On the next morning, the 19th, we fought the martial law forces by throwing stones at them at the Intercity Public Bus Terminal. Being dispersed and pushed back to the Jang-dong rotary and the CNU College of Medicine, we had a push-and-pull battle all day long. Now even citizens were joining the demonstration. That evening, PARK Ki-Soo said, "The suppression by the martial law forces is gradually turning into slaughter, and it will be difficult to survive if we continue like this." He added, "PARK Kwan-Hyeon seems to have left Gwangju, so you should leave Gwangju, too." He also said that the student representatives were now wanted, so I should go somewhere safe. After much thought, I thought of my homeroom teacher when I was in the fifth grade in elementary school. I liked him, calling him an uncle. I called him like that because he was close to one of my older sisters. I went first to Jisan-dong, where he lived. The uncle also told me to leave Gwangju because I would not survive if I were caught. On the morning of the 20th, after deciding to go to Wando Island, I went to the bus terminal and took a local bus toward Maryang, Gangjin. If I sat right behind the driver, I would not be caught because inspectors checked people toward the back. There were two inspections, but fortunately I arrived in Gangjin without being caught. When I gave a call to my parents, they told me not to come home, so I went to the house of my grandparents on my mother's side in Gogeum Island and started staying in an underground room. I hid myself there listening to the radio without contacting people at all, and my second oldest sister's husband sometimes visited me and told me the news of Gwangju and my family, so I stayed there until the 26th.

I thought I should return to Gwangju when the uprising ended, so I went to downtown Wando and to Hanryeosudo on the 27th. I went to Seoul via Busan and came back to Gwangju, but there was nowhere to go, so I visited the uncle in Jisan-dong. There, I heard how brutally the martial law forces trampled on Gwangju citizens. I regretted leaving Gwangju because if I had only accurately anticipated the situation at the time, I would not have escaped like that no matter how much people around me worried about and tried to convince me.

But because I was still wanted, I wasn't safe in Gwangju either. The uncle contacted my sister and said I would better stay in a quiet temple in the mountains. Just at that time, a friend of mine from high school called my sister to ask her about how I had been doing because he was curious about the situation in Gwangju, and he suggested that I should stay at a place where he was studying for a state exam. After the suppression of the martial law forces, some people tried to persuade me to turn myself in, because some of the wanted student representatives had already done so. However, I had no intention of turning myself in at all. I decided to go to Gapyeong, where the friend was studying for the exam, and I took a train with him at Gwangju Station. Students in a *gosichon*[22] had a lot of interest in the Gwangju People's Uprising, but they wouldn't believe the actual truth. I stayed quiet first and then told them about the May 18 People's Uprising as I witnessed it. I couldn't just let them regard Gwangju citizens as rioters, as the media had gabbled. I talked about the situation in Gwangju that they were mistaken about, after saying that the reason why

[22] It refers to a residential area where people stay to prepare for state examinations. The space is usually narrow and crowded.

I was there was to escape the bloody oppression of Gwangju citizens. Later, they were convinced and would comfort me and sympathize with my situation. While I was in Gapyeong for about six months, my cousin in Seoul paid for my rent. The students preparing for state exams came to me in their spare time and begged me to tell the story of Gwangju. I told people from other regions that the Gwangju People's Uprising was currently distorted by the mainstream media and the truth had not been revealed, that Gwangju citizens were by no means rioters, and that these things were what I had witnessed myself. And then, they gradually got to understand the real situation.

Notice of the Physical Examination for Enlistment

In 1981, when the public notice was announced for those who had not gotten a physical examination for military enlistment, my younger brother visited me in Gapyeong in early January and told me that an order for my physical examination for the military had been issued. He came with the news that I had to go down to Gwangju because of the physical examination. It was not the time for the physical examination to be issued, but I got to know their intention clearly. But I had no choice but to accept it. I only thought that my required enlistment in the military had been moved up in time. I can't remember the exact date, but as soon as I had the physical examination in January, the draft notice came shortly after. The draft notice was issued the day before CHUN Doo-Hwan came to Gwangju to open a national youth athletic competition. I went down to Mokpo with my friends to have a small farewell party and then prepared to join the military. I thought that if enlisting in the military was my duty, I should accept it as my life and do my best for independence and national reunification in a positive manner.

"A Bastard Like You Is Not Allowed to Join the Military"

The next day, I was scheduled to arrive at Yudal Elementary School at 8:30 a.m. I parted from my friends in front of Yudal Elementary School and arrived five minutes late, and I got punished for being late. After the punishment was over, I presented the draft notice and told my name, and suddenly someone seized my arms. The intelligence division staff had been there in advance preparing to take me with them. I desperately cried out,

"Why are you doing this? I'm going to join the military, but why do you prevent me from doing that?"

I cried shaking off their arms. A detective from the intelligence division said, "If a bastard like you joins the military, all the other recruits will turn into communists. So we cannot send you to the military."

And then he put handcuffs on me. At that moment, I was humiliated and felt a blast of rage.

Being conscious of the gaze of so many people there, I did not know how to appeal. I pleaded. However, the draft notice was not sent to the Ministry of National Defense but sent back to the Military Manpower Administration. While I was taken from Mokpo to Wando, I pleaded with the detective, complaining that he was going to end my life in that way. I appealed that I had my hair cut short to join the military, and pleaded with him to leave me alone, but the detective was merciless. The detective said to me that I should go to the Intelligence Division first because it was a matter of the interests of the unexamined, wanted people. Then, he took me to Wando Police Station and put me in a detention room. When I questioned him why he wouldn't send me to Gwangju, he told me not to say anything and keep quiet. Because it was the day CHUN Doo-Hwan came to Gwangju, he left me in Wando to avoid that day. The next day, I was handed over from Wando to Gwangju Seobu Police Station and was put in a detention room without any appropriate procedures. Even though martial law had been lifted and the announcement order for the unexamined was issued, I was imprisoned for about four months without the government taking legal steps because the standard of arrest was not announced. Torture and interrogation were not that severe at the time. Later, by the time I was released, the director of student affairs of the College of Law and a professor visited me and said they would stand guarantee for me and comforted me. I was indicted without detention and did not receive a trial. And I was sentenced to probation for causing a disturbance and violating the martial law declaration order.

I returned to school in 1983 and graduated in September, 1984. Before returning to school, I worked as a lecturer at Sangatap Academy to teach school qualification exams during the vacation in 1982. And after graduating from school, I worked as a lecturer at a private cram school.

Ashamed When I Think of May 1980

Now when I think of May 1980, I feel shameful and disgraced about being alive. I feel guilty for not remaining in Gwangju and not fighting with all my body at the scene between May 22nd and 27th. I just feel guilty for not being able to continue until the conclusion of the fight that the students started. Honoring the wishes of the fallen who died during the uprising, I am doing my best to live without shame until the day when democratization and unification of our country are achieved by taking the lead in carrying out democratization in my workplace. I believe treatment of teachers at private academies will be an indicator of true human education, only when the teachers first do their best with responsibility and good work ethic while human labor is not measured as a mere product. Currently, I have an aspiration to create workers' unions by workplace not only for teachers at private cram schools, but also teachers at foreign language academies, state examination academies, and even teachers at nursery schools.

In addition, I have joined a gathering mainly comprised of friends who had served as executives of the student council in 1980. And we discuss what to do in the current situation. During the 1987 presidential election, we let people know the horrors of May by organizing a group of 30 volunteers to distribute scraps of papers with reports of the protests made by the Justice and Peace Committee to each region. Furthermore, during the election of the National Assembly, we visited places for election campaigns to let citizens know the tragedy of May 1980 by showing videos. Above all, we will have to take the lead in awakening the spirit of citizenship in the future, and we give greater significance to uniting for the end of military dictatorship.

This year (1988) we held a memorial service for the 6th anniversary of the death of PARK Kwan-Hyeon by organizing the Commemoration Service Association of PARK Kwan-Hyeon. The only thing I should do to wash away dishonor is to honor his soul, who died fighting for democratization of Gwangju citizens and to do my best as a living person in this era without overlooking contemporary continuing, undemocratic treatment.

1. Chonnam National University (CNU)

3027. Chasing Us Down to a Private Study Library, Swinging Clubs

Witness: KIM Soo-Young (male)
Date of Birth: August 4, 1963 (aged 16)
Occupation: High school student (currently a college student)
Date of Record: September 1988

Research & Arrangement by KIM Hye-Hyeong

Overview

Kim Soo-Young, then a sophomore of Jeonnam High School in 1980, witnessed by chance a protest in front of the main gate of Chonnam National University on May 18th. After that, he continually joined the protesters and fought against the martial law forces. He was never injured or taken away.

In Front of the Main Gate of Chonnam National University on May 18th

I was born in 1963 in a neighborhood that is now the site of CNU. According to my mother, her father lived in Bonhyang-myeon, Songjeong-ri during the Korean War, and he was quite rich. She said that the police killed her mother because her father helped communist partisans.

At the time of May 18, I was a sophomore at Jeonnam High School. Living in Sinan-dong, I used to go to a private study library located in front of the main gate of CNU to study for the midterm exams in May. On May 18th, the weather was nice, and I didn't want to study, so I went to CNU for fun by bike. However, the main gate was closed with only the left side door open, and paratroopers were there. One of them who appeared to be an officer was outside walking back and forth doing something, one soldier was at each side door, and seven soldiers stood inside the large gate with clubs in their hands in a "Sling, arms" posture. When I reached the bridge in front of the main gate, three or four college students came and went back. In front of the Seogi Supermarket nearby, twenty to thirty students gathered and talked, but after a while, the number increased to about fifty. At the front gate, some students carrying books said, "We are going to the library because we are students who have nothing to do with the demonstration."

But the soldiers didn't let them in.

As the number of students increased, a platoon leader of the paratroopers spoke through a megaphone, "The school is closed. Go home."

"Boo"

When a student threw a stone at the main gate, fifty other students began to throw stones at the same time, and two soldiers standing at the side gate withdrew into the main gate, and the door was closed. The platoon leader told the students to go home again, but the students kept throwing stones. About two or three minutes later, about twenty soldiers lined up in a zigzag formation inside the school gate.

The platoon leader urged the students to disband within five minutes, saying if the students continued to throw stones, the troops would disperse them by suppression. However, the number of students continued to increase, and students in small groups reached to the front of Yongbong Supermarket. As they continued to throw stones, the front door opened and the paratroopers were arranged in a semicircle blocking the side door. They threw the stones more violently, but the paratroopers did not dodge them and got hit. Suddenly, we heard a command,

"Charge!"

The paratroopers quickly ran toward the students and began to suppress them by beating them with clubs and kicking them with their military boots. The students ran toward the CNU Intersection, but the paratroopers overtook them, and the situation became a mess.

I was standing across the street from Yongbong Supermarket and saw a college student running away and tripping over a bicycle. The following paratrooper kicked the student's head, picked up the bicycle, and threw it at the student, and his stomach was pierced by the pedal of the bicycle. In the meantime, I ran past them and fled from the scene. The students fled in all directions, but I heard that the paratroopers continued to pursue students who ran toward Yongbong Supermarket and caught three of them.

I went up to the study library on the third floor. When the owner lowered the shutter, several high school students rushed under it. When four paratroopers followed them up to the study library, the owner protested to them.

"This is a study library where students study. How could you do this here?"

"Bullshit, a study library? What nonsense are you talking about?"

And then they started rummaging through the place. One of the paratroopers in pairs saw my school badge and moved past me because he saw number two on my badge, but he grabbed PARK Young-Shin by the collar, a third-year student at Kumho High School, who was studying next to me, and raised him up,

"You bastard stand up!"

"Why are you doing this?"

In an instant, another paratrooper next to him smashed Young-Shin on the top of his head with a club. He immediately collapsed and lost consciousness, and blood splattered across his notebook and book. They looked around for a moment without any expression and then left.

Students around Young-Shin helped him to go outside, and I tore up his bloody notebook and threw it in the trash can and followed them, but they still couldn't get a taxi by then and stood there outside. Then, a college student (around twenty-seven or twenty-eight years old) came up to us and asked what had happened. Young-Shin was holding his head unconsciously. When someone flagged down a taxi by Ilshin Supermarket, the college student gave him 10,000 won and told him to use it for the fare and medical expenses. It was said that Young-Shin had twelve stitches in his head.

A college student asked me where a pay phone was, and I guided him to Ilshin Supermarket. I handed him change for the phone, borrowing it from the supermarket, and listened to the telephone conversation:

"Something urgent has happened. Call them to come quickly."

After the call, he stroked my hair and thanked me.

Forming a Scrum and Heading for the Province Hall

I went back to the study library, packed my bag, left it at home, and then got back out on my bike. About 250 students went back and forth singing in groups at the CNU Intersection for about half an hour and then ran toward downtown forming a scrum. They threw stones at the Gwangju Station Police Box, went out to Gyerim-dong through the City Hall, and destroyed the Gyerim Police Box. The demonstrators ran so fast that girls gradually began to fall behind. The demonstrators were stopped and forced to disband in front of the Community Hall, and about 10 to 20 people were caught. The demonstrators were divided into two groups moving toward the Bus Terminal and Chonnam Girls' High School. They were disbanded.

"Let's gather in front of the Province Hall."

I went to the front of the Catholic Center around 3:00 p.m., and the road from the Catholic Center to the Province Hall was quiet without protesters. Broken objects such as flowerpots, sidewalk blocks, and trash cans were scattered, and there were no cars. I looked at Jeil High School from the intersection of the Intercity Public Bus Terminal, and there were ten trucks with paratroopers. Some paratroopers were on guard in a jeep. Watching that sight, I returned home that day.

I went to the MBC building on the afternoon of the 20th. Citizens asked to open the door where the shutter was closed. But the door didn't open. Just then a young man came in a military truck and crashed into the shutter with the truck. As the shutter was crushed and went up halfway, college students entered the building with Molotovs, and fire broke out immediately after that.

Attacking Gwangju Station on the Evening of the 20th

On the evening of the 20th, I was standing between the Gwangju Express Terminal and Intercity Public Bus Terminal, and smelled the spicy tang of tear gas exploding somewhere. In the parking lot in front of the Gwangju Express Terminal, citizens clattered to open the closed wire door, and then two people who appeared to be mechanics came out. When the citizens said they would break the door if the mechanics did not give them buses, the mechanics talked to them for five minutes, saying they had no authority over the buses and should ask someone in charge. They went inside and came out in just two minutes and said, "Do as you please."

Just then, the citizens crowded in and brought out seven express buses.

When the buses full of citizens ran toward Gwangju Station to break through, people on the bus with me ripped down the curtains and covered their mouths with them. The paratroopers were standing along the streets at the Five-way Intersection of Gwangju Station while leaving the road open. They threw stones and tear gas canisters when the buses came. At first, the windows cracked; and the second time, tear gas canisters came inside the buses as the windows were broken. On the bus where I was, a tear gas canister from the opposite side of the driver's seat fell on the front of the driver's seat. The bus made a sharp turn toward the Jungang Express Terminal and stopped when it hit a telephone pole. I jumped out of the window and went to the front of Korea Express through the back of the current North Gwangju Telephone Station.

A man was sitting on a barrel, smoking, and a woman was holding his arm and begging him to go in.

"No, people are all dying. What am I going to do when I get home? I'm going to kill all those bastards."

When he said this, everyone there cried. The man persuaded the woman to go home. Watching the scene, we applauded with shouts. That kind of situation was happening here and there. When cargo trucks from local areas came to the road in front of Korea Express, citizens asked the drivers for the trucks. They all handed over their trucks easily, and one of them who was carrying radishes from Yeosu City said, "Ill crush these guys down." And he rushed toward Gwangju Station.

At Gwangju Station, signal flares fired by the soldiers flew with the sound of "da-da-da-da" and red flames. This situation continued all night, and I was able to get home at 3:00 a.m.

Shooting in Front of the Province Hall on May 21st

At around 8:00 a.m. on the 21st, when I went to Gwangju Station, there were no soldiers but only eight vehicles that had been smashed and burned and turned upside down. Most of the vehicles that had crashed into the fountain and roadside trees were trucks and military jeeps. And slogans saying "Gather together at 2:00 p.m. on Buddha's Birthday" were written on telephone booths everywhere.

In front of the Province Hall, a corpse covered with a *Taegeukgi* was carried out in a handcart. People said that was "a man who was beaten to death by a soldier's buttstock." I went by a protest vehicle to Lotte Confectionery Company near Mudeung Stadium, and people were making noise in front of the company asking to open the door. Someone came out and asked what they wanted, and they asked him to give out all the food inside the building. They wrangled with each other for about 30 minutes, and then he opened the door. Bread, eggs, and Coke inside the company were distributed little by little for each passing car. There was a truck loaded with eggs, so when people tried to take the truck whole, the company staff dissuaded them and handed out the eggs.

I went out to Geumnam-ro and saw citizens sharing foods such as *gimbap*,[23] milk, and bread. I also received two rolls of *gimbap*, one pack of milk, and two bottles of Coke for my share and ate them in front of the Gwangju Bank headquarters, and then I met my uncle on my way to the front of Jeonil Building. He scolded me, saying that he was on the verge of death several times while looking for me.

At that time, the paratroopers were inside the Province Hall, and citizens kept pushing in, so my uncle and I were pushed to the front of the Province Hall. There was a sudden sound of gunfire.

"It's a blank"

Someone shouted. Without knowing the situation, the demonstrators in the back kept pushing forward. As my uncle and I grabbed a person in front of us and walked toward the American Cultural Center, a young man who followed us shouted.

---

[23] Korean rice rolls.

"Sir, sir, I am shot."

However, we couldn't do anything for him right away, so it was not until we got out of the demonstrators that we moved him to a nearby hospital. The hospital only disinfected him and told us to take him to a larger hospital.

Two or three people were lying dead in front of the Province Hall. When someone brave approached and brought the bodies back, people applauded.

In front of CHOI Hee-Cheon's ENT Clinic on the other side of Gwangju Bank, a young man distributed guns, so I also received five rounds of live ammunition and a carbine. In front of Gwangju Bank, a high school student was shot dead in the shoulder because of an accidental shot while a gun was manipulated. After that, people shouted the slogan, "Point a gun to the sky." But another accident occurred on the passing jeep and a student in the jeep was shot in the shoulder. After I fired two shots of blanks into the sky, a man announced through a megaphone that those who couldn't shoot or hadn't been to the military should return their guns. Then I returned the gun. I went to the vicinity of Yagwang Cabaret next to the current Dong-gu District Office. A bullet from somewhere hit the leg of a young man who was three to five meters away from me. The young man grabbed his leg and rolled over. Another young man was shot in the stomach, and a pregnant woman was shot in the chest and killed instantly. People carried the corpses through the aisle of the mall and laid them side by side under the wall of a restaurant near the back gate. However, paratroopers came from the back alley of the Jeonil Building and beat the people who stopped them from taking the corpses, and pulled them away. I went up to the roof (4th and 5th floor) of a coffee shop next to the Dong-gu District Office. And when the paratroopers withdrew, I came down and found two corpses missing. A tin door was covered in that place. When I lifted the tin door, blood pooled in a radius of one meter in all directions where the corpses were laid, and the blood was clotted in the size of two pieces of tofu with the overwhelming smell of blood. People gathered again and were enraged, saying, "There is no one worse than those thugs."

At the CNU Main Gate on the Afternoon of the 21st, Too

That afternoon, when I went to the CNU main gate, there was about a battalion of soldiers standing guard along the wall. Protesters were asking them to open the gate. When a civilian (he said that he was a journalist) with a large camera in a military jeep came in, the protesters cleared the way. While he was filming in the middle of the bridge, someone shouted from behind.

"He is a spy."

"Pull him down!"

"No. I am not a spy."

But people pulled him down. A man at the forefront of the protesters asked the paratroopers to call a truce and dragged off the man, grabbing him by the neck, and then a soldier opened the side gate on the left and took him in. When a paratrooper and a civilian shook hands, the protesters applauded. The man was dragged behind the guard office.

The demonstration began again, and people shouted chants such as "Let's tear CHUN Doo-Hwan to death," "Lift martial law," "Release KIM Dae-Jung," and "Murderers, Step Down." The paratroopers fired tear gas again, but people did not run away. Instead, they broke the wall to the left and ran into the school. I looked down at the main gate in front of the graduate school located at the site of the College of Social Sciences building. I saw the paratroopers retreating backwards, forming an S formation toward the rear gate. The soldiers rallied again and launched a fierce counterattack. The citizens cried out.

"Let's go to the Province Hall."

I quickly got home.

Listening to the Gunshots at Dawn on the 27th

On the afternoon of the 22nd, I went to the CNU stadium. There were still traces of the soldiers who had withdrawn. There was a mark showing where a rice cooker hung, metal barrels were half full of gasoline (four barrels), and tents were taken down and burned.

About fifty to two-hundred people came from each *dong* to participate in a rally in front of the Province Hall. When they had a flag with the name of their dongs on it, vehicles came and picked them up to the front of the Province Hall. Anyone was allowed to speak freely at the fountain.

On one occasion when I was on the way from Baekun-dong to Naju by jeep, someone pointed to a rice paddy and said, "There they are, too."

We went there and found eight men shot dead with their faces blackened.

I went with my father to find my uncle to the morgues of CNU, Chosun University, and Red Cross Hospital, and the corpses at CNU Hospital were piled up one by one with their faces painted so they could not be recognized.

On the early morning of the 27th, I woke up to the sound of a helicopter, went up to the rooftop, and heard, "If you surrender your guns and yourselves, we will guarantee your lives."

And leaflets were spread around. I heard loud gunshots from the Province Hall for about half an hour, and the television was out for a long time.

After May 18, people with no certain residence, such as ragpickers and shoeshine boys, were not seen, and the rehabilitation centers were almost all closed. No matter how much the truth is revealed, it will be difficult to know the exact number of deaths.

1. Chonnam National University (CNU)

3035. A Bus Passenger Taken to CNU

Name: BEOM Jin-Yeom (male)
Date of Birth: September 20, 1959 (aged 20)
Occupation: Unemployed
Date of Record: January 1989

Research & Arrangement by KIM Jeong-Gi

Overview

At around 10:00 a.m. on May 18th, he was dragged to Chonnam National University when paratroopers searched for demonstrators in the bus No. 10, in which he was passing by the rear gate of CNU. He was mercilessly beaten and immediately released after insisting that he was not a college student. Currently, he has lost the use of his left eardrum and cannot find a job because of the violence and a spinal injury.

I was born in Saengyong-dong, Buk-gu, Gwangju, as the eldest son among three sons and two daughters. My family had twenty *majigis* of rice paddies and some farming fields, so we managed to live an average life.

After graduating from vocational high school in 1978, I immediately started working at Daejin Synthetic Fiber Co., Ltd. in Incheon, and then worked at Hanbo Industrial Co., Ltd. in Seoul until September 1979.

In 1980, I joined the military but became the subject of *Soonbang*[24] so I waited for another time to enlist, helping my

[24] Kim misused the term, "Soonbang," which means formal visiting. Probably, he meant to use the term, "Hoonbang," which means release after a simple warning from authorities like a police station. It is alleged that Kim meant temporary discharge for reenlisting in the military.

family farm at home.

At around 10:00 a.m. on May 18th, I left home by bus No. 10 to go on an errand for my father to buy pesticides at a gardening shop in Seobang Market. The bus stopped at the rear gate of CNU, and passengers who seemed to be college students got off. Simultaneously, paratroopers who were hiding behind the CNU wall approached the bus and told everyone on the bus to get off. Everyone was scared and no one got off. Then they boarded the bus and started to beat the passengers indiscriminately. I, too, was suddenly beaten with their clubs.

After that, they dragged those who looked young out of the bus. About twenty passengers including me were taken to the wall near the rear gate. We stood in front of the wall and were beaten again by their buttstocks. We didn't know what wrong we had done to be beaten up.

Frightened by their force, we couldn't say anything but were beaten in silence.

While being dragged into the CNU campus, about seven people attempted to run away and got caught and beaten indiscriminately again by the paratroopers. A female student broke her leg and couldn't even walk, but they dragged her over anyway.

Brought into the CNU campus, we were kneeling under the wall of the rear gate and keeping our heads down on the ground. I was so beaten up that I was panicked and just kept my head down on the ground. After a while, the military commander seemed to have asked if there were anyone who was not a college student and asked them to come forward. While I was lost and couldn't understand, the person sitting next to me saw my short hair and helped me step forward. Since I was about to join the military, my hair was short. The commander took another look at those who came forward and told those who weren't college students to return to where they had come from. I got out of there with a few other people.

When we came out from the rear gate of CNU, soldiers who stood there said, "What are you doing here?" and beat us up again, who were already in a mess. They fastened bayonets and acted like they would stab us with them if we showed any sign of defiance. So I kept being beaten as they beat me.

After they beat us up, the soldiers shouted, "Get out of here." I immediately left the campus and tried to take a bus, but the buses did not appear, so I had to go on foot. But after I walked a little, I felt like vomiting, so I threw up seriously once.

There were a lot of people coming and going, but no one looked at me. After barely recovering, I thought I should go to buy the pesticides and walked to Seobang Market although I vomited more.

When I finally arrived at the gardening shop in Seobang Market, I can't remember what I said, but I did purchase the pesticides and took a bus. Because I thought I would not be able to be treated right even in the hospital, and for some reason, I thought I was going to die and I would like to die at home.

I almost lay down on the bus and arrived home. My family looked at me and asked, "What happened?" As soon as I got home, I almost fainted.

After that, I took oriental medicine and treated the wound at home. However, the after-effects of the injury have become too serious disabilities in my life. My elbow was crushed, so I couldn't write properly. And I couldn't do anything hard because I hurt my spine. My cheekbones were distorted, and my left eardrum was destroyed. Even now, when I get a little angry, my head gets hot all over; and I suffer so much that I am panicked. Even if I got a job, I had to quit within ten days due to a spinal injury. I once gave up on my life and even thought of committing suicide because I didn't really want to live. I was exempted from the military because of the injuries at the time. I thought I should do something rather than wandering around. So, I entered

Seogang College in 1983. However, I spent my college years meaninglessly, feeling unwell all the time. And I graduated.

My family urged me to marry because I was the eldest son in my family, so I got married in 1986.

After some time, I heard that those who had been wounded were to report but I hesitated to do so because of rumors that people who reported had bad consequences, such as going to jail. I reported it quite late in 1988. After that, I received a three-million-won loan from the government as a living stabilization fund. Even now, I am sick and unable to get a job. I help my family with farming and sometimes go to the Injured Association to help its operation.

Watching the hearings that are being aired on television these days makes me so angry as one of the wounded during May 18. Maybe it is better for me to ignore how the people in charge of the Gwangju massacre can be so shameless. It is because I can't control myself and my body hurts even more when I feel even a little bit of anger.

Ⅳ CRITICAL CONSCIOUSNESS

2. Gwangju Munhwa Broadcasting Corporation (MBC)

3062. My Spine Injured While Saving My Friend

Witness: CHO Young-Bok (male)
Year of Birth: 1943 (aged 37)
Occupation: Wholesale and retail bedding business
Date of Record: January 1989

Research & Arrangement by HEO Hye-Ja

Overview

On May 22nd, while trying to save his friend in front of the Wolsan-dong Police Box, he was hit by a vehicle driven by the citizen militia, which lost its balance and ran onto the sidewalk. He injured his spine.

Lonely Childhood

I was born as the eldest son in Jinwon-myeon, Jangseong-gun in 1943, two years before liberation from Japanese colonial rule.

After my parents, who farmed about ten *majigis*, passed away during the Korean War, I lived with my grandparents. Like all the parentless, I also had days of loneliness and solitude. I graduated from Jinwon Elementary School under the guidance of my grandparents.

I left my hometown when I was eighteen. I went to Seoul with no plan and worked at a sewing factory for about four years.

However, life in Seoul without close relatives and friends was boring, so I came to Gwangju, close to Jangseong. In Gwangju, I went back and forth between bedding factories and shops. In 1980, I set up a bedding shop in Daein Market and engaged in the wholesale and retail business as well as manufacturing bedding.

On May 17th, I went to Busan for business.

On May 18th, I heard the news about the extension of emergency martial law on the way to Daegu from Busan by car.

Burning the MBC Station

On May 19th, I took a bus from Daegu to Gwangju at 3:00 p.m. But the situation in Gwangju changed so rapidly that the bus was the last one to go to Gwangju. As I entered Gwangju and arrived at the Gwangju Express Bus Terminal, there was no noticeable change. I arrived in Gwangju around 8:00 p.m. The city seen from the Gwangju Express Bus Terminal was dark and eerie. Looking around, I saw flames rising from the Intercity Public Bus Terminal.

I tried to take a bus, but they weren't running, and I couldn't even take a taxi. Reluctantly, I walked all the way to Daein-dong.

Arriving home, I heard about the brutality of the paratroopers, which was beyond imagination. I couldn't believe that soldiers who were supposed to guard the country were beating and stabbing unarmed citizens and students. At that time, there were about ten employees in the store, but they did not go home because they were afraid of walking down the street at night.

The next day, on May 20th, I went downtown with four or five friends to check the situation with my own eyes because I couldn't believe the stories that I heard the night before. In the morning, there was little movement between the martial law forces, citizens, and students, but the situation began to change in the afternoon. On one part of the street, citizens and students were driving, shouting slogans such as "Lift Martial Law," "Release KIM Dae-Jung," and "CHUN Doo-Hwan, Resign." On the other hand, the martial law forces were roaming the city.

Around 8:00 p.m., I arrived in front of the MBC station with my friends. I was standing right in front of the station. From the station to the Labor Center, the street was filled with citizens, but there seemed to be few students, and most of them were ordinary citizens. Citizens were outraged as they saw the broadcast of distorted reports depicting the situation in Gwangju as a riot caused by rebellious figures, KIM Dae-Jung's manipulation, and rioters.

At this time, several students tried to open the station's gate, but the tightly closed door did not open. A citizen in the crowd brought a ladder from somewhere. At this time, flames rose from behind the station. I found it strange. The citizens were gathering in front of the station, trying to open the door, then how come the fire started from behind? Even now, I wonder why when I think about that time.

I wandered around downtown. It was past 10:00 p.m. when I got home.

I went out to Geumnam-ro with my friends early in the morning on May 21st. I was standing near the Catholic Center, and Id never seen so many people gathering in my whole life. Like the previous day, citizens and students were on one side, and the martial law forces were on the other side of the road, driving around.

It must have been 1:00 p.m. A gun went off somewhere and a citizen in a vehicle collapsed. The crowd was surprised to hear the gunfire, but they retreated just a few steps but did not step back. And then they moved forward again.

I also heard the gunfire and saw people fall, but I didn't feel scared. And I didn't feel like going home. I just wanted to watch the scene of history with my own eyes.

At that moment, citizens from somewhere appeared carrying two bodies in a handcart. There were so many people that I couldn't look closely, but I saw the bodies covered with blood.

Around 4:00 p.m., I noticed some citizens were holding guns. I was not scared when I saw the martial law forces carrying guns. But when I saw citizens holding guns, I suddenly felt afraid. So I went to the Hanseong Building in Daein Market, where my friends often met. On the way to the market, young students were holding guns, so I taught them how to shoot. That evening, we talked about what was going on in Gwangju until late at night. Since my house was in the market, I met and talked to many people, and I heard that the martial law forces had retreated to the outskirts of Gwangju in that late afternoon.

A Unified Heart to Defend Gwangju

On the 22nd, I went out to downtown early in the morning. When I went through Geumnam-ro to the Gwangju Police Station, people in white robes were carrying two bodies from a nearby building. There were a lot of people in front of the police station as well, and a young man who looked like a college student said there were a lot of weapons and asked to go inside the police station.

A little later, a man in a police uniform tried to break the door of the police station. Some of the citizens who were in front of the police station stopped him saying, there are already many weapons, so there's no need to break in. At this time, there was a beautiful scene where citizens arrived with a handcart full of food. But even the children refused to eat it and gave it up for the protesters. All Gwangju citizens were united with one heart and one mind.

I was able to understand the situation in the downtown to some extent, but I was curious about the outskirts of the city. So I got on a dump truck in front of Geumnam-ro 5th Street with about twenty people and looked around the area near the entrance to the prison, the West Roundabout, the highway entrance, the entrance to the industrial complex, and Hak-dong.

Like the downtown, the outskirts were not much different. The prices of daily necessities such as cigarettes, alcohol, groceries, and ramen remained unchanged from before May 18th. And there was so much to eat such as *gimbap* in the vehicle that we had to give it to others.

Wherever we went, whoever we met, all Gwangju citizens renounced their selfhood for so long, and we united with a strong heart to defend Gwangju, our town.

When people were hurt, citizens immediately took the injured to hospital and took care of them with as much care as their own family.

Injury

I got off at Daein Market and met some friends and talked about what I had seen on the truck. And I left home with four of my friends around 5:00 p.m. to meet a friend who lived in Wolsan-dong. Among my friends, BAEK Dong-Gi, who was from Daegu and was running a shop at Daein Market, was suffering from anxiety after being dragged out and beaten up by the martial law forces on May 18th.

Walking in front of the Wolsan-dong Police Box, we saw students and citizens driving vehicles. It is said that they were on their way to Songjeong-ri after hearing that the martial law forces were coming in from Songjeong-ri. Seeing this, BAEK Dong-Gi started to run because of the anxiety provoked after being beaten by the martial law forces. He ran toward the road and shouted that he had to go home.

I was worried about him, so I went to BAEK Dong-Gi to take him. At that moment, a jeep that lost its balance rushed toward the sidewalk from behind and hit me. Later, I found that people from a beauty salon beside the road pulled BAEK in while he was running toward the jeep. So he was safe.

I was hit by the jeep in which four students were riding and taken to the Red Cross Hospital without losing consciousness. I hurt my lumbar vertebrae No. 2 and 3, and vertebra No. 12 (compression fracture). From then on, my life in the hospital began. In the mortuary, there were constant cries of the families of the deceased, and there were no more wards, so extra beds were made. And the corridors were filled with the injured. As the wounded continued to come in, there was a shortage of doctors and nurses, so ordinary students who did not study medicine acted in the place of doctors and nurses.

I was in a special room.

When I was in the room with my wife at dawn on May 27th, I heard gunshots from somewhere else. Shortly thereafter, a woman broadcast in an urgent voice, "The martial law forces are coming into the city shooting early in the morning to suppress the citizens and students who are defending the Province Hall."

I also became anxious lying in the hospital room. So I told my wife.

"Our children are alone at home. So call and tell them not to worry and keep the door locked."

My wife went out to make a phone call, and after a while, she rushed into the room trembling with fear.

She said, "The martial law forces have come into the hospital."

I was more concerned about the children at home.

"Go to the nurse's office and call."

At that moment, the door burst open, and the martial law forces with guns came in, looked all over the room, and just left. My body trembled and I felt like my heart stopped.

I'm not sure if it was May 28th or 29th, but the head of the nurses came and said that a joint investigation team would examine the injured. She told me to think about what to do when they came.

A little later, I was examined in the hospital director's office in the presence of the joint investigation members in military and plain clothes. They asked me how I had been injured, and I answered them that I had been injured by a car that students were driving when I was out in the downtown to do business. After that, the grade of my injury was determined according to the condition, and it was grade 3.

Staying in the hospital, I had a lot of thoughts. For the first time in my life, I pondered over how I should live in the future while reflecting on the way I had lived so far. Before May 18th, I did not think about other people and was only concerned with making money while living a petit bourgeoisie's life, following my feelings. However, while I was living in the hospital, religious groups and ordinary citizens whom I did not know came to visit me and had conversations with me, and my life began to change. I decided that I would live a religious life and work hard for others when I would be discharged from the hospital.

May 18 as a Voluntary Struggle of Citizens

I was discharged from the hospital, but I felt awkward when moving due to the spinal injury. I couldn't even manage my business properly. The situation of the store gradually became difficult. And I was sick and tired of everything, so I could not find peace of mind.

In the end, my wife ran the large store by herself and went bankrupt with huge debt in 1984. In the midst of this, I began to have religion and started learning calligraphy.

Life became difficult and annoying. But worse than that, police officers and staff of the National Security Agency came and bothered me on May 18th every year or when there was a big event in Gwangju.

After 1984, I ran a private philosophy office for over a year with the philosophy I had learned while attending a calligraphy academy because I couldn't just be idle as the head of the family. After that, my friends who found our family felt so bad for us that they helped me to set up a bedding factory in Yangdong Market. Taking that as the beginning, the factory is still running.

Even now, my back hurts when the weather is bad. Also, I can't stand up for a long time.

May 18 was neither controlled by someone behind the scenes nor a riot of rebellious figures. Watching the soldiers, who were obligated to protect the safety of the people, killing citizens and committing atrocities, which was unimaginable for humans, the citizens were infuriated and rose up spontaneously.

Even now, the government's ruling party is concealing the truth of May 18 and branding the citizens of Gwangju as rioters. May 18 should be considered in the same context as the March 1 Independence Movement and the April 19 Revolution.

The government should not try to solve the problem in a lukewarm response by giving money to the families of the deceased or to the injured. But they should establish a life plan in the form of a pension system for those who have lost their ability to make a living.

Currently, I am working hard in my own way, serving as the vice president of the May 18 Gwangju People's Uprising Injured Association, of which LEE Ji-Hyun is the president.

2. Gwangju Munhwa Broadcasting Corporation (MBC)

3060. The Flames of Anger that Burned Pro-government Media

Name: SEO Chae-Won (male)
Date of Birth: October 28, 1961 (aged 18)
Occupation: Unemployed (currently a clinical pathologist)
Date of Record: November 1988

Research & Arrangement by CHOI Jeong-Sook

Overview

In 1980, Mr. SEO was preparing for an examination to be a civil servant after graduating from high school because his family was in a bad financial situation. He was in front of the MBC station when it was burning on May 20th. Around noon on May 21st, he carried a man shot by paratroopers in front of the Labor Office to hospital. On May 24th, while going down to the countryside with his relatives after hearing that the martial law forces would come back to Gwangju, he was shot and injured by paratroopers

A Poor but Outgoing Boy

I attended Gyesan Elementary School in my hometown, Gangjin. When I was in the first grade of elementary school, one *majigi* of rice paddy was all that our family owned.

In my elementary school years, when my family had a hard time, I didn't have a school bag, so I packed books in wrapping cloth. I've never worn sneakers and only worn black rubber shoes. On a rainy day, I didn't have an umbrella, so I cut chemical fertilizer bags and wore them with my neck and arms out of the holes. My parents were particularly enthusiastic about education. They had all my siblings study in high school despite our difficult circumstances. Among them, I received more educational benefits than other siblings, as I even studied at a university that no one in my family would dare to want, considering my family's circumstances.

Because of the economic difficulty, my mother encouraged me to go to an agricultural high school in the countryside when I graduated from middle school. But I was stubborn in order to take the high school entrance examination to enter a high school in Gwangju. After that, I passed the exam and was assigned to Chonnam High School.

When I came to Gwangju, I got a room in Seoseok-dong. I wasn't the only one who came to Gwangju as my father and my younger sister came with me. My father had so much bad luck as he lost three million won after he vouched for another person's debts, so he came to Gwangju to overcome the situation by opening a real estate agency. My mother and youngest sister were left in our hometown. My family was forced to separate due to our financial difficulty.

At that time, there was no desk for me to use for study in the rented studio where my three family members lived together. So, I had to use the meal table as a desk.

It took me quite a while to adjust to life in Gwangju, even though I confidently came up to Gwangju from the countryside. The psychological complex that I'm from the countryside and the fact that my family had financial difficulty made me discouraged. But thanks to my outgoing personality, I got along amicably with my friends.

In my high school years, the ethics teacher and homeroom teacher influenced me significantly, and they taught me to live my life right.

At the end of my high school days, I heard the news on a city bus that the strong hold of President PARK Chung-Hee's eighteen-year dictatorship had collapsed. I realized that we had to harvest the consequences of what we sow in the great wheel of history. I couldn't even think of going to college after graduating high school and decided to prepare for the civil service exam early. I was fortunate to graduate high school considering my family's condition. I thought I could go to college when my family got a little better off. My father and sister went back down to our hometown after I graduated high school. So I rented a studio beside the railroad right next to Nongjang Bridge and lived there with my cousins. I usually studied at the library or home because the registration fee for a private academy was expensive. Then it was May 1980.

Stabbed by a Bayonet

I felt something moving in my heart as I saw college students' demonstrations become more agitated in May of that year. On May 16th, there was a torch march in front of the Jeonnam Province Hall with countless citizens and students, and I participated in it, too. The march got highly enthusiastic. After returning home that day, I struggled to calm myself down, recalling my position as a test taker.

On May 18th, I was sitting at my desk to study, but I could feel the noisy atmosphere outside. I was curious and wanted to know what was happening. I couldn't sit any longer, so I kicked the door open and went out to the street.

The atmosphere was quite brutal, with paratroopers standing all over Geumnam-ro. I was walking back home scared when I encountered paratroopers in front of the Catholic Center. As four paratroopers rushed to the Catholic Center, people ran about in confusion to escape. At that moment, something hit me hard enough to drop my shoulder. I consciously and quickly dodged but felt a sting in my back. I couldn't stand it. So, I kicked the paratrooper next to me. Then I ran away with all my might.

Since childhood, I had exercised. I had the official 1st grade in Taekwondo and 4th in Kung Fu. I must have been seriously injured if I hadn't trained in those martial arts. When I got home, I took off my clothes and looked at the wound. I found my shoulder, which had been clubbed, was swollen and my back was bleeding from being stabbed by a bayonet. Fortunately, the bayonet was deflected right next to the spine, leaving it unharmed.

While treating myself with medicine I bought from the pharmacy, anger boiled inside me. Why should I have got beaten like this for no reason?

Preparation for the civil service examination was no longer important to me. Newspapers and broadcasting stations simply dismissed the harsh stories circulating in downtown Gwangju as groundless rumors and aired them casually as if they were trivial. Hearing the news made me even angrier.

From the next day on, I acted as one with others as a member of the Gwangju citizenry.

On the evening of May 20th, the MBC station was ablaze and I was in front of it. When I went to the station, the door was tightly closed and 400 citizens were gathered in front of it. Citizens urged the MBC station to report fairly, as the station was reporting false and distorted news when innocent citizens of Gwangju were brutally killed by guns and military boots of the paratroopers.

But MBC still gave a distorted broadcast. The citizens started to get enraged. Some of them brought a large wooden pillar from a lumber yard. Fifty to sixty citizens joined forces to slam the station's closed door with the wooden pillar. The door started to break. At that moment, flames suddenly began to flare up in the broadcasting station. Was any of the citizens an electrician? Anyway, I think he was the one who knew well about an electric installation since the station was on fire after he controlled the voltmeter next to the station. Almost simultaneously, paratroopers standing by the Labor Office drove up in armored vehicles.

Ttadada Ttadada... The armored vehicles running straight with the lights on were like monsters. The street in front of the station was absolutely in shambles with people fleeing. I got out of there and went back home.

The next day (May 21st), I went out to the Labor Office at about 11:00 a.m. In front of the Labor Office building, two vehicles were turned over and on fire. Citizens drove fire engines and pumped water into the burning vehicles. Roads from the Labor Office to the Province Hall were almost blocked because paratroopers went on shooting indiscriminately. Nevertheless, some people were moving toward the Province Hall. At that moment, two men right in front of me collapsed to the ground with the sound of gunshots. I carried one of them on my back and ran to the hospital nearby. In the hospital, I found that the bullet had penetrated the left side of the man's abdomen and his bowels were coming out of his back. It was a sight too agonizing to see. I came out of the hospital covered in blood he had shed. Even now, I wonder if he survived or not. Probably not.

Around 12:30 p.m., an armored vehicle of protesters came from Yu-dong toward the Province Hall. In front of the armored vehicle, a young man who appeared to be a high school student stood holding a *Taegeukgi*. The eyes of all citizens turned to the armored vehicle. When the armored vehicle approached the Gwangju Tourist Hotel, gunfire speared the air. At that moment, the young man who was standing with a *Taegeukgi* collapsed, his blood spurting from his head. I still remember the scene I saw then, the red blood spurting like a fountain. It should not have happened, and I can't believe it could have happened. All the citizens who saw it couldn't help but cry.

The citizens began to arm themselves. I didn't receive a gun because I didn't know how to use it. I was mostly in protest vehicles every day after the paratroopers retreated. And I was overwhelmed by the passion and orderly manners of the citizens. At that time, Gwangju was all thrilled, and all citizens became one.

I could not remember the exact time and date during the days in May. But after the paratroopers retreated, I visited Chosun University Hospital and CNU Hospital and found countless bodies there.

To Be Shot at While Fleeing

On May 24th, rumors that the martial law forces were coming in soon were spreading, and I stopped by my cousin's house nearby. My cousin, the son of my uncle, was forty-eight years old at the time, about the age of my father.

He said that we should get out of Gwangju quickly. I heard from a woman who rented my parents' house that her son was an officer of the paratroopers and he called his mother. Her son had told her to leave Gwangju immediately because they were planning to ruin the city on the evening of May 24th. My brother said that we should get out of Gwangju because of the story I told him.

I hesitated to leave because I remembered the citizens who fought with me. I wasn't willing to run away to live a coward. However, at the suggestion of my brother, I roughly packed my luggage, and we left together. There were about twenty people in total, including my brother's family and those who rented his house. The destination was my hometown, Gangjin. To get to Gangjin, we had to take the outer road to Baekun-dong. But as we heard that the martial law forces were guarding there, we went to Jiwon-dong. As the sun set and the night deepened, we stayed in a guest house.

The next day (May 25th), we woke up early in the morning, had breakfast, and hit the road again. We had no choice but to take an outer road near Baekun-dong. We walked hard. It was when we were about to get out of Gwangju. We were shot on the highway to Songam-dong after passing Baekun-dong. Bang, Bang. It was an attack from the martial law forces lurking in the mountains. They fired in a row on the road right next to our feet.

For a moment, we quickly jumped into the rice paddy by the road. Only then did I realized that I was shot. I was bleeding from the knee. Then another person was shot in the ankle.

The martial law forces descended from the mountains as we were lying in the rice paddy as if we were dead. Then they told us all to come out quickly. They had all of us kneel down when we got out of the rice paddy with muddy water all over us. My cousin came forward and begged.

"We've done nothing wrong. We didn't do anything. We were just going down to our hometown because we were too scared to stay. So please let us go."

The martial law forces, gabbling for a while, let us go.

We hastened our steps again, feeling like our lives had been reduced by ten years. I tore my clothes and tied up my bleeding knee with it. Fortunately, the bullet deflected near the bone and only slightly cut the flesh. I can say I was lucky. Then we reached the entrance of Pochung Temple. We saw a military truck with hive-like bullet marks rolled over on the side. It seemed to have been shot by the martial law forces. We walked for a long time, wondering what had happened to the people in the truck when it ended up like that. I suppose it was Kwangsin Drivers' Restaurant, standing on the side of the road. There stood a passenger vehicle with hive-like bullet marks like the previous one.

We had terrible thoughts, so we walked fast and arrived at the crossroads between Nampyeong and Naju. There was a bridge guarded by the martial law forces. They were fully armed with bayonets, helmets, and clubs. My heart sank at the moment I saw them. It was too late to choose another path.

While walking, I had picked up about ten empty M16 shells. At that time, the guns that the citizen militia had were M1s and carbines. The empty M16 shells must have been from the gunfire by the martial law forces. So, I had picked them up, thinking they would be evidence later. However, when I saw the martial law forces, I quickly hid them next to a stone on the side of the road because I thought I would be in danger when they frisked me. I did so because I wanted to take them later.

We hesitatingly moved up to the bridge. The martial law forces dragged three or four young men, including me, down the bridge. They made us sit down, put clubs between our knees, and began stomping on our thighs with military boots. The pain was literally unbearable. I clenched my teeth, but a groan came out of my mouth. My cousin on the bridge began to beg again. But it was in vain. It was only when our legs were almost paralyzed beyond the ability to walk that we could get out of there. We usually took arterial roads and walked. Sometimes, while taking a shortcut, we could go to a pharmacy on the side of the road and get painkillers. We slept in civilians' houses. Most of the people treated us warmly. When sleeping in Yeongam, the owner cooked warm rice and warmed up the room we were staying in. I was so touched that I was about to cry with gratitude.

We finally arrived in Gangjin on May 28th. We were done with the tough evacuation journey of four nights and five days. We looked terrible and exhausted.

I treated my injured leg by taking medicine at a pharmacy run by a brother of my mother. I also took oriental medicine my mother brought. She said the poison had to be extracted. In August of that year, when the wound began to heal, I came back to Gwangju.

Life as a Civil Servant

Gwangju looked as if nothing had happened. I continued to prepare for the civil servant exam. On September 21st of that year, I took the exam at Chosun University Engineering College. I applied for the Grade 5 administrative civil service examination and was lucky to pass.

The place where I was appointed was the Hayang-myeon Office in Yeocheon-gun. I got a room with a colleague and lived there. My base salary was 89,000 won, but it totaled about 120,000 won including the family allowance. I saved 40,000 won from it.

As someone from a rural area, I knew the plight of farmers better than anyone else and tried to be a true partner to them. As time went by, however, I was filled with conflict and anger over the life of a government official. The atmosphere at the time was so brutal that I could not speak even a word about May 18. Media was condemning May 18 as the deed of rioters.

Whenever I had a chance, I tried to tell my colleagues and residents there about Gwangju in May as it really was. But the more I did, the more I was shunned. I was also secretly under surveillance. I could not continue my public life to earn a living while ignoring my conscience. So, I quit the job after only a year and seven months of working.

A New Start

My family members were disturbed when they found that I quit the job. They considered me completely strange beyond comprehension. I was greatly distressed, too. Although I acted according to my conscience, I felt deeply sorry for my family. But no regrets.

In August 1982, I was enlisted in the military as a replacement force and started to work in Gangjin. I wanted to talk to my colleagues about the May 18 that I experienced. While speaking about it, I got beaten with a club a lot. But the more I got oppressed, the more I obstinately felt that the truth of May 18 must be revealed.

After my discharge from the military on October 28th, 1983, I took the college entrance exam. I applied for the Department of Clinical Laboratory Science at Gwangju Health College. My parents did not readily consent to my plan for attending college.

"Pay for just the enrollment fee, please. Then Ill take care of the rest."

So I managed to enroll in the college.

In May 1984, my first year in college, I was given a suspension for being an organizer of a demonstration at school. There were five of us who planned it. We first planned on holding a rally, at which we were supposed to deal primarily with campus issues. After writing a leaflet hurriedly, we made copies of it all night long in front of CNU College of Medicine in Hak-dong.

The next morning, we handed out copies to the students coming to school. And I gathered them in the park behind the Yangrim Police Box located in front of the college. Up to that time, there had been no occasion like that in my college. Without knowing the reason, all the students who took the leaflets gathered at the park and boycotted classes of that day.

Standing in front of those students, who were mostly four or five years younger than me, two of us explained everything. Everything that I had seen, heard, and felt on May 18th.

That event threw the college into utter confusion. No one would have thought that such a thing would happen in Gwangju Health College. Also, there was a slogan, "Ch, Step Down." Ch was the first sound of the problematic dean's name, but it was interpreted as CHUN Doo-Hwan, which made the matter even more serious. The school tried to expel us. Then the head of the Department stepped in and tried to ease the disciplinary action. In addition, all students protested against such an unfair action, turning in letters of voluntary resignation. Thanks to that, we only received a suspension. I couldn't go to school for a month. I had nothing to say to my parents.

"Wouldn't it be better to be born without my parents?" I was distressed to know that I made my parents suffer.

After that, I returned to school and became the focus of public attention.

Upon graduation, I obtained a professional certificate of medical technologists. After working in Seoul for about a year, I am now working in Gwangju. I got married and my wife gave birth to a son.

I reported myself as an injured person in the spring of 1988. For the past eight years, Gwangju citizens have been defined as rioters, and now politicians are talking about compensation without finding the truth of May 18. I think these attempts are killing Gwangju citizens once again. No historical evaluation or compensation can be made without finding out the truth. If May in Gwangju was a riot caused by mobs, how can we be compensated?

Historical evaluation of May 18 will be made possible by clearly finding the truth. Then the compensation problem will also be solved. In addition, when the truth is found, those involved should be punished within the legal boundaries to prevent the same thing as May 18 from happening again. Historical facts cannot be eliminated or erased by any force. May 1980 will remain in our history forever.

IV CRITICAL CONSCIOUSNESS

3. The Fountain Plaza (the Province Hall)

4001. Let's Fight to the End

Witness: JEON Yong-Ho (male)
Date of Birth: August 10, 1958 (aged 22)
Occupation: College student (currently working in publishing)
Date of Record: September 1988

Research & Arrangement by KIM Myeong-Soo

Overview

Active in a mask-dance club at Chonnam National University, JEON Yong-Ho wrote leaflets and distributed them from May 18th. He also organized a team for *The Fighters' Newsletter* and dedicated himself to propaganda activities. He organized a rally in front of the Province Hall after May 22nd.

The Life of the Deulbul Night School

In my family, my father was an education official, so I grew up in a strict family environment. The economic status of my family was middle-class. After attending South Boseong Elementary School, I was transferred to Gwangju Gyerim Elementary School, and then I went to Chungjang Middle School and Gwangju Jeil High School. After studying for the university entrance exam two more years, I entered the Department of Economics at Chonnam National University. At school, I was a member of the Folk Culture

Research Society (a mask-dance club). Since I was an economics major, I created a club called the Society for Research on Social Studies in Underdeveloped Countries (The Economics of Underdeveloped Countries Society) and participated in it in the 1980s. From the second half of 1978 to the first half of 1979, I taught Chinese characters as a lecturer at the Deulbul Night School. I joined the Deulbul Night School because the people who founded the School were my high school alumni, and I was interested in social sciences, so I was easily accepted into the group. In the Deulbul Night School, we educated first graders in the doctrinal education room of the Catholic Church in Gwangcheon-dong, and the second and third graders in the Citizen's Apartment in Gwangcheon-dong next to the Catholic Church. We also got a room in the residential area across the street and started living a Deulbul Night school life.

At that time in 1980, on-campus circles for social sciences burgeoned along with the contemporaneous political vacuum: the Economics of Underdeveloped Countries Society formed primarily by the members of the College of Commerce, the Labor Research Society by the most important and active members such as NA Sang-Jin and LIM Nak-Pyeong, the Social Research Study Group by SHIN Young-Il, PARK Kwan-Hyeon, AHN Jin, and others, the BM (Bible and Music), the former organization of the Christian Students Association, the Women's Issues Research Group led by KIM Kyung-Hee, the National Literature Research Group led by SONG Seon-Tae, the Korean Rural Issues Research Group, and the Folk Culture Research Group (the mask-dance club).

Before 1980, there had not been very many social science circles as clubs for cultural activities, such as *Eolsaem* (the club that developed into a humanities research club) and the mask-dance club. In 1980, the necessity of ideological associations was urgently demanded. So, students changed the contents of the existing circles and formed the Association of Labor Issues and the Association of Peasant Issues Research to study peasant and labor issues, which were the most crucial issues in Korean society. And in order to do so, various social research study groups were established to investigate and examine social phenomena in greater depth. Since the South Korean economic status was still that of an underdeveloped country, there had been a demand for the establishment of a club that studied the economy of underdeveloped countries. Hence came the social science circles at Chonnam National University.

It was a period of suppression before 1980, so there were few legal activities on campus. Detectives kept control over all the functions of the school, so we could hold an event only after submitting an event application form to the counseling director's office and obtaining permission. The introduction of a club was also made possible only by a poster with the seal of the counselor, so there was very little space for students to meet. If there is authentic democracy, there must be a left and a right, so that the left and right are shown to the public, and the public can choose. I believe it would be true democracy to do what the majority chooses. But the authorities even blocked the application to introduce the mask-dance club and the Economics of Underdeveloped Countries Association, so legitimate activities were impossible. That situation continued until 1979.

In the 1980s, a little bit of autonomy was granted to universities, and more and more students were able to come into contact with each other. In April 1980, when the student council was organized as a so-called democratic student council, the democratization movement was being carried out. Around the end of April, a senior student in my same department, LEE Jae-Eui, suggested that we make an underground newspaper that could deal with the issues that the current student council could not. So, LEE Jae-Eui decided to take charge of the financing and planning of the underground newspaper, and the organization was formed by me, PARK Young-Hwan (Department of Administration, College of Law), KIM Dong-Gyu (Department of Mathematics,

College of Natural Sciences), OH Byeong-Hak (College of Agriculture), and two students from the Department of Education, College of Education, and the seven of us decided to lead the team. We named the underground newspaper "Voice of the University." Since KIM Dong-Gyu, a student of the Department of Mathematics at the College of Natural Sciences, was living on his own at the back gate of CNU, he prepared mimeograph and copying equipment in his room, and we discussed the issues of the student council there. Although the student council was working as a legal organization, it had a limitation in not being able to deal with all issues. So, we agreed to address the issues that could not be dealt with by the council through the underground newspaper.

In the meantime, it was May. I was also working hard on the mask-dance club. From the beginning of May, we began to hold meetings by Colleges. I joined the College of Commerce and held the mic to moderate the meetings. From May 14th on, CNU students started going out on to the streets. After breaking through the school gate, we held three public rallies at the Province Hall.

On May 17th, the Grand Rallies for the Nation and Democracy were over, and all the active leadership took time off. So, I went to a friend of mine in Hwasun to take a break with him, with whom I had become acquainted. That night on television, we heard the news that martial law had been expanded. Seeing that news, I thought there was something wrong.

Let's Make Leaflets

Early on the morning of the 18th, I came to Gwangju with my friends. We were supposed to meet in front of the main gate of CNU at 10:00 a.m. in case of an urgent situation, but I couldn't come on time because my friend's house was in Hwasun. When I arrived in Gwangju, it was a little before 11:00 a.m. I got off in front of the Province Hall to find out what had happened in downtown, and then I wanted to go to the university. As I was going toward the Jeonil Building, 200 to 300 students were rushing toward Geumnam-ro, making a collective sound of struggle. I thought that we the people were all the leaders of the student movement, so I looked carefully around to find out who was leading, whether they were the people I knew, students of Chonnam National University or Chosun University. But there was no one I knew. So, I realized that they were students who had spontaneously joined the protest. After watching for a while, I left my bag with my friends to join the ranks of the people. And I saw PARK Mong-Goo, a student senior to me, walking in the back of the procession. I found that other acquaintances were passing by beside the protest procession. At that time, a man named KIM Dong-Gyu, who was working on the "Voice of the University," was leading the ranks walking parallel to the main procession.

I quickly greeted him and followed the protest procession, chatting with him about what was going on. The procession headed toward the Province Hall, and there was no one to stop them. I tried to go to the Plaza in front of the Province Hall but turned right toward the Gwangju Post Office. We passed the Samyang Department Store next to the Tourist Hotel and went toward the Gwangju Post Office. As we went from the Gwangju Post Office to the Chungjang-ro Police Box, we threw stones and damaged some property. From that moment, the riot police began to be deployed. They blocked the way toward Geumnam-ro and started to block the front of the Chungjang-ro Police Box as well. The procession split into two near the Police Box: one moved toward the park and the other toward Geumnam-ro in joining the people on the sidewalk. I also went to the sidewalk and stayed in the crowd.

When I came back to Geumnam-ro and tried to look around the streets, there was a huge crowd of people on the sidewalk. On my way down to Chonnam Girls' High School, I met the people who were active in the student council of the College of Humanities.

We promised to meet at Namseon Coffee Shop at 3:00 p.m. When we met any classmates we knew, we told them to meet at Namseon Coffee Shop.

At that time, I met many fellow students, and we decided to inquire about the whereabouts of the student council and discuss how to deal with the situation. While coming down from Geumnam-ro, I met my fellows in the mask-dance club near the back wall of Jung-ang Elementary School. We talked about what to do right then in that situation and agreed that the most important thing was to inform the citizens of the current situation. And we decided to create and distribute leaflets right away. That was meant to be a propaganda campaign.

So, I decided to use the mimeograph and copying tools that I had used for the "Voice of the University" and took a taxi to KIM Dong-Gyu's near the back gate of CNU. I brought the tools to his room, discussed the text, and printed more than 500 copies. We continued printing the leaflets until 3:00 p.m. In the meantime, we were working on it without knowing the situation downtown.

"Martial Law was ordered. What does Martial Law mean? People are getting hurt because of it. We citizens must stand tall."

We wrote the leaflets, completely unaware of the situation downtown. I put about 500 leaflets and the mimeograph and copying tools, just in case, in a large rice bag, and returned to the downtown. I took a taxi because we were supposed to meet at the Namseon Coffee Shop at 3:00 p.m., and I wanted to check out the situation downtown.

"Let's go downtown."

"You can't go downtown."

"Why can't we go downtown?"

"It is a mess downtown."

"Then let's go as far as we can."

"I'll drive you all the way, but it's a mess downtown right now because the paratroopers have come."

After Distributing Leaflets

To get to the downtown from the back gate of CNU, we had to pass by the Intercity Public Bus Terminal. But the taxi didn't even reach the Intercity Public Bus Terminal before the driver dropped us off. I was very curious about the situation downtown. To obtain information about the situation, two of us were drinking *makgeolli*[25)] at a *makgeolli* pub and waiting with the mimeographs. The other person and I decided to check the situation downtown. I first gave a call to Namseon Coffee Shop. The owner of the Namseon Coffee Shop screamed as soon as he answered the phone.

"You are out of your mind, aren't you? There's no one in the coffee shop right now. There are only tear gas bombs."

"I was supposed to meet someone at 3:00 p.m., but did you ever get a phone call?"

"I got a call or two looking for someone like that, but now there is no one here. Geumnam-ro is in an uproar now."

"Ah! The situation is changing very urgently," I thought. I hung up the phone and went to the Intercity Public Bus Terminal. However, there was not even a human shadow in the Bus Terminal, where there usually were so many people. It looked just gloomy.

It was right after the paratroopers had passed. The place where the girls of Daein-dong bars normally stood in a row was also empty. I could only see young men wearing disheveled clothes here and there occasionally. I had not fully grasped the situation because only a few hours had passed. We entered the Intercity Public Bus Terminal.

25) Korean traditional alcohol made of fermented rice.

It was the same there. As I was about to go out the other side of the entrance, three or four military vehicles were passing by. At first glance, I noticed something (like people lying face down) in the cargo box. But I didn't know what it was at the time. However, I thought it was so strange that I turned around and went back to the *makgeolli* pub. The two friends who were there also seemed to have heard about the situation to some extent from the owner of the bar. My friends told me the stories they had heard when I entered the pub. They said that citizens were chased from Geumnam-ro to the Intercity Bus Terminal and were beaten by the paratroopers, and then the paratroopers swept through the Intercity Bus Terminal again.

We thought it would have been dangerous if we had continued to the downtown, so we divided the leaflets between two teams and distributed them. One team went up to Sansu-dong, and the other through the back gate of Jungang Elementary School. And we decided to regroup afterwards. I belonged to the Sansu-dong team and walked toward Sansu-dong, distributing the leaflets from house to house. After all the leaflets were distributed in Sansu-dong, we were able to gather again in Hak-dong at 7:00 in the evening.

At that time, we heard from the radio broadcast that the curfew was moved up earlier because of martial law. We gathered together in Hak-dong to get feedback about the leaflets that we had distributed. And we gathered up the stories that each of us had heard about and drafted leaflets for the next day. We bought 2,000 sheets of cheap test paper for printing and printed them all night.

On the morning of the 19th, I gave calls to each of my junior colleagues to meet together. We met and regrouped into our teams. We decided to meet at IM Nak-Pyeong's and parted. Each of us went to Bangrim-dong, scattering the leaflets on the streets. But IM Nak-Pyeong didn't show up. It was then about 2:00 p.m. He was living in a rented house in a mountainous neighborhood, from which we could look down at the downtown. We saw black smoke rising from three or four places in the downtown. It was probably pepper fog. After spending a little more time distributing the remaining leaflets, we decided to gather around the Sansu Five-way Intersection again. But the other group didn't come. We went to a junior colleague's, who was active in a theater club. And we had dinner there and rested. But that night, when we heard the rumor that the paratroopers were searching houses in Sansu-dong, we were terrified and had to stay up all night.

It started to rain on the morning of the 20th. We split up with the junior colleague after promising to meet again if we survived. I had no place to go. I put the remaining thirty leaflets in my bag and thought about where to go. All my communication with my friends had been cut off. I was left in complete isolation. Then I took a taxi and headed to the Gwangcheon-dong Deulbul Night School. To get to Gwangcheon-dong, I had to cross a bridge, so I was very worried that there might be a checkpoint. I hid the leaflets under the seat. Fortunately, there were no checkpoints that morning. When I went to Gwangcheon-dong Catholic Church Night School, I saw many teachers who were my senior and junior colleagues at the Night School. When I saw them, I felt as if my body had been re-energized. However, when I recalled that we had written and distributed the leaflets urgently, I was deeply upset, thinking that they had been lingering leisurely around here. So, I asked, "What are you guys doing here?" They said that they also went around distributing leaflets. It seemed that they produced the leaflets by using the copy machine that they had bought for the night school materials. That day, everyone looked exhausted after two days of continuous stressful activity. We were all relieved. I spent the whole day in Gwangcheon-dong meeting with senior colleagues YOON Sang-Won and KIM Young-Cheol, asking them what we should do.

A Touching Moment

I came out of Gwangcheon-dong and came to the intersection in front of CNU. Near the intersection, about 200 soldiers holding their rifles at trail arms were slowly moving at two arms-length distance. However, there were no signs of protest, and the citizens were just watching. The military announced through a street broadcast,

"Citizens, this is the local 31st Division. We have no intention to harm you, and we are retreating now."

Seeing that, my friends and I walked toward Geumnam-ro. It was about nine in the evening and getting dark. I was lying down to get some sleep in the warehouse in front of the rice shop at the Jeonnam Textile Factory Intersection in Im-dong. Then, I suddenly heard a shout of protest outside. We quickly changed clothes and went out. That was a very touching moment. At the Mudeung Stadium, young people were riding various vehicles like a procession of refugees and holding makeshift wooden clubs. The procession of vehicles was long enough that I could not see its end.

I recall that it was the first vehicle protest. All the vehicles had their headlights on and were moving forward, singing the reservist and unification songs, and the national anthem. Part of the vehicle protest procession proceeded to Geumnam-ro, and part to the Jungang Express Bus Terminal. I followed them with my friends. The procession parted at the Jungang Express Bus Terminal Intersection, one going toward the Gwangju Station and another toward Gwangju Express. Those who went to the Gwangju Station targeted the KBS.[26] I followed them. It was so dark that I couldn't see anything, but I sensed that white powder was being sprinkled around. It was definitely tear gas powder. Because of this, I suspected that soldiers were present. After a while, I suddenly heard gunshots, bang, bang, bang, and people

26) Korean Broadcasting System.

ran away in confusion. The gunshots were blanks, and no one appeared to be injured. From there, I went to the MBC[27] station and found that it was on fire. I went to Cheongsan Academy with the protesters. There were also soldiers there. And I heard gunshots; whether they were blanks or not I did not know. And armored vehicles were moving quickly back and forth to the front of the neighborhood Citizens' Hall. We were also chased, so we climbed over the wall of Chonnam Girls' High School.

Escaping over the wall and the main gate of Chonnam Girls' High School, I came out toward Gyerim-dong and found that young people were gradually moving barrels, filling them with oil and rolling them to prepare to fight. After watching the scene, we went to the Im-dong warehouse and slept. It was around two in the morning. I heard later that there had been a fight in which people risked their lives that night in Gyerim-dong, and the paratroopers opened fire.

Organizing a Team for *The Fighters' Newsletter*

I went to Nokdu Bookstore on the morning of the 21st. Professors and senior student colleagues gathered. They were writing a placard at the Tax Office in front of the Nokdu Bookstore. Not only that, they also were making Molotov cocktails and were protesting at the Province Hall. That day, I saw eight corpses behind the Dong-gu District Office. Among them, a corpse was carried in a wagon by citizens. Geumnam-ro was full of citizens. Soldiers were stationed around the fountain in front of the Jeonnam Province Hall. I went back to Nokdu Bookstore. At that time, my senior colleague YOON Sang-Won, after a meeting at the night school, told me, "We of the Deulbul Night School are in charge of an assignment. We are publishing a fighters' newsletter."

[27] Munhwa Broadcasting Corporation.

We decided to get on a passing truck and go to Gwangcheon-dong to gather people and publish the fighters' newsletter. The name of *The Fighters' Newsletter* was given by Sang-Won, who told us to do so, and the organization was divided into four groups: a procurement group, a text writing group, a writing and copying group, and a distribution group. We were ten in total. However, the distribution group was practically pointless. The situation at that time was that when we left the newsletter on the roadside in the city, vehicles would take and distribute them. Hence came the teams of *The Fighters' Newsletter*.

Around 5:00 p.m. on the 22nd, a citizens' rally was held spontaneously in front of the Province Hall. At that time, a man named JANG Hui-Dong, the head of Hanil Theater, made a remark for the government. He said that the citizens of Gwangju should surrender. At that time, a person named KIM Jong-Bae (a senior of Chosun University, the chairperson of the Settlement Committee) took the microphone away from him. So, a minor tussle broke out at the fountain.

The citizen militia that stood guard at the Tourist Hotel and watched the scene fired blanks. Hearing the gunshots, citizens thought the martial law forces were coming, and the atmosphere went wild. I went to the YWCA. There, we discussed the civic rally. There I met my fellow students, senior colleagues from the National Democratic Youth and Students Association, and the friends with whom I had distributed the leaflets the first time we did it. We promised to meet at Boseong Enterprise in front of Gwangju Park the next day, which one of my senior colleagues was running, and I went back home and slept.

Preparation for a Rally

On the morning of the 23rd, as I was supposed to meet them at Boseong Enterprises at 9:30 a.m., I walked there. Boseong Enterprises was completely empty. At that time, I did not know what had happened there. But I heard later that they had gathered at Boseong Enterprises and then scattered immediately. I turned to the YWCA. A few young people, including PARK Hyo-Sun (in the troupe Clown), and YOON Sang-Won, gathered together to form a temporary propaganda team. The team decided to hold a rally at the Province Hall. The theater club of CNU initiated the propaganda team and invited speakers for the rally. We decided to write the contents and install microphones. Because the rally had been disorganized the previous day, we were thinking about how to organize the rally in an orderly manner. On the first day, the rally was held in the order of opening remarks, silent tribute, a report of progress, and the sharing of feelings about the Gwangju incident. Housewives' representatives, citizens' representatives, and laborers' representatives were selected to give speeches. The team of *The Fighters' Newsletter* was in charge of publicizing the citizen rally. After that, we produced and distributed *The Fighters' Newsletter* and promoted the citizen rally, installing microphones and loudspeakers on the vehicles of CNU and traveling around the outskirts. In this way, we were able to hold the first citizens' rally. At this time, the propaganda team for the citizens' rally moved naturally to the YWCA. The copied the newsletter in the main room of the YWCA, and the propaganda team used the external auditorium. I served on the propaganda team. I rode around in a street-broadcasting vehicle and at times distributed leaflets and put up posters. When other people were busy, I took the microphone myself and gave speeches from the podium and installed microphones and loudspeakers. We did the same things on the 24th as the day before. From the 24th or 25th, the college students were asked to come to the YWCA, which became the college students' gathering place. We persuaded the college students to fight all together in explaining to them what to do at that present moment. And we organized them into teams and sent them into the Province Hall. We held the second rally on the 24th and the third on the 25th.

Let's Fight to the End

On the morning of the 26th, I received a call that the martial law forces were entering the city. At that time, the people in the Settlement Committee told the soldiers they would have to go through them if they wanted to pass, and the citizens finally stopped the soldiers. The martial law forces came all the way to the front of the Rural Development Agency but didn't come any further. Perhaps they came in at that location in order to secure an outer road as a supply route. On the 26th, we immediately called an emergency meeting. On the 26th, the fourth rally was held in the morning, unlike the previous rallies held at 5:00 p.m. And the fifth was held again that afternoon. The reason was that there were rumors that the martial law forces were coming in the early morning of the 27th. It sounded plausible because someone I knew received a call on the afternoon of the 26th from the wife of a soldier living in Sangmudae. The message was that the martial law forces would push into the Province Hall at dawn the next morning, and that the wife asked my acquaintance to stay and hide at home.

There was also a rumor that the martial law forces were going to have a pork barbeque party that night. We had obtained that news already, too. So, after contemplating whether or not to inform the citizens of the news, we decided we would and announced to the citizens the news at the end of the rally.

"Citizens! We have heard that the martial law forces are finally coming in early tomorrow morning. But let us fight to the end."

After the rally, we marched to the Rural Development Agency with raised placards. On our way back, I spoke, "If you want to defend our city to the end, please stay," and about 500 people remained. I placed them near the YWCA and the Province Hall. On the 26th, I got a message from the Province Hall that the people at the Province Hall would keep an eye on the state of affairs and give me a call when trouble came at the YWCA and the Province Hall. So I got some sleep. Around fifty people, including *The Fighters' Newsletter* team and the propaganda team, slept in the YWCA, and young high school students took turns keeping the night watch.

At around 3:00 a.m. on the 27th, I heard a woman's voice (PARK Young-Soon).

"Citizens! Fellow citizens! The martial law forces are forcing their way into the city."

We were wide-awake. First, we helped the women escape to Sansu-dong through the back door. Then, about twenty men remained. Senior colleague KIM Sang-Jip and I decided to go to the Province Hall and headed there. On the way, we expected that there would be a lot of people in front of the Province Hall, but we could not find any. I was so scared that I also went into the Nokdu Bookstore. After a while, I heard gunshots and helicopters. After being stuck in the bookstore, I got up around 8:00 a.m. to wash my face.

At about 9:00 a.m., I saw one or two people passing by. I also came out of the Nokdu Bookstore carrying the protest manifesto that I had read at the rally. I heard that the Nokdu Bookstore was also occupied by the martial law forces as soon as I left.

What I felt while going through the Gwangju Uprising was the importance of social class in the process of revolution. Those who took up arms at that time were the deprived and exploited. And they desperately longed for social change. However, the wealthy people were hiding at home.

3. The Fountain Plaza (the Province Hall)

4007. Presiding Over the Citizens' Rally

Witness: KIM Tae-Jong (male)
Date of Birth: December 14, 1957 (aged 22)
Occupation: College student (currently a private academy teacher)
Date of Record: October 1988

Research & Arrangement by KIM In-Sook, KIM Yang-Hyeon

Protests Against the Transitional Cabinet

I was born in Jindo as the oldest son of four sons and two daughters. Since my father was a police officer, his workplace was subject to change. I spent all of my elementary school years and two years of middle school in Hampyeon, well-known for its beautiful mountains and clean water. I transferred to Chosun University Middle School in Gwangju when I was in the third year of middle school because of my father's change of workplace. I studied harder when I came to this middle school because I had a strong desire for learning. So, I got accepted easily to Gwangju Jeil High School, which was difficult to get into. I had a lot of complaints about society during my high school years, probably because I maintained emotions fostered by the financial difficulties of my family that I had experienced since childhood, and because I had new perspectives on things at that age. The students of Gwangju Jeil High School often held protests, inheriting the spirit of the Student Tower smeared with the blood shed by our senior students during the April 19 Revolution.[28] When I was a sophomore, I protested against the *Yushin* regime and broke through the school gate with other students, arm in arm, to the

28) 1960 protests against the corrupt President RHEE Syng-Man, which led to his resignation and exile.

front of the Province Hall. But soon we were dispersed. A large number of students were arrested by plain-clothes detectives. The students who were not caught by the detectives ran back to the school with all their might. We climbed over the back wall of the school, but all of us were caught by teachers guarding the other side of the wall. We were sent to the auditorium and punished by the teachers. During my junior year, we tried to protest, which was provoked by the incident of patriotic martyr KIM Sang-Jin, who committed suicide by disembowelment. However, only about twenty friends were expelled for the conspiracy to launch a protest. In this situation, I naturally began to neglect my studies in high school. I also used to see reality in a slightly distorted way in my attitude toward life.

I graduated from high school in 1976. I got into the Department of Languages of the College of Humanities and Social Sciences without any romantic feelings or expectations for university life. Even though I didn't have much interest in college life, I joined SALT (a volunteer circle) with KIM Yoon-Gi and KIM Seon-Chul. I managed to become good friends with them by reading and discussing books designated by the club.

I joined a drama club near the end of my first semester, recommended by a student who was my senior in SALT. I practiced performing works in the club but couldn't participate in it actively and quit it in the middle of the practice because of an inner conflict. In the second semester, I decided to take a leave of absence from school because of my parents' expectations for me as their oldest son and skepticism about my university life. Despite my parents' opposition, I finally applied for a leave of absence in September. After taking a leave of absence from school, I went down to my parents' house in the countryside because I had nothing to do in Gwangju and wanted to restore my mind. Staying there, I spent my time reading books I wanted to read, including the poetry of LEE Sang, whom I admired. And I thought a lot about life and how to live. I did not take a definite stance on the problems I was contemplating in the first semester of 1977, but I returned to the university. I participated in the activities of the drama club again. There were ten members in the drama club, where we got along well, feeling attached to each other in a family-like atmosphere.

In 1978, serving as president of the drama club, I established an organizing system for the club and guided learning until 1979 when I was a junior. My student-colleagues KIM Seon-Chul and KIM Yoon-Gi, who started studying social science after they had participated in the activities of the SALT club, were on the run because they were involved in the "June 29 Educational Manifesto" incident. I usually had a lot of conversations with SHIN Young-Il. After the incident, there were few protests in CNU, and the situation in the university was serious as many students involved in movements were arrested or wanted by the authorities. It was difficult to even produce leaflets. Beginning in 1978, the CNU activist organization had gradually established its system, and I participated in the core group in 1979. There was no self-study in the group, but each team was in charge of its own learning. Just before the Bu-Ma Democratic Uprising,[29] we discussed the current situation in the core group. As a result, PARK Yoo-Soon and KIM Jung-Hee set fire to the student counselor's office. All of them were arrested. As the CHOI Kyu-Ha transitional government came to power after October 26, JEON Yong-Ho and KIM Jung-Hee led protests. The slogan was "Opposition to the Transitional Cabinet." At that time, I tried to occupy the broadcasting room and to broadcast the contents of the opposition to the transitional cabinet of CHOI Kyu-Ha, but I failed. We gathered again in front of the central library after failing to mount a protest at the back of the First Student Center.

---

29) Busan-Masan, October 16th-20th, 1979.

Lecture on *Doeji-Puri*[30)]

There were a lot of students, but no one was willing to step up and inspire a protest. Then I shouted, "Everyone! Let's sing with all our hearts 'We Will Win!'" And I began to sing. As soon as the roar of a powerful song rang out, tear gas burst. Immediately, the police ran to arrest the students, and the protesters were all scattered. I was caught by a cop and beaten mercilessly while being taken from the front of the central library to the headquarters. I had been active in resistance without revealing myself that much, but I was taken to the Gwangju Police Station. I was stigmatized as a very radical student because I led the protest and tried to occupy the university broadcasting office, and because I swore badly at the police and resisted them while I was being taken to the station. After staying in the Gwangju Police Station's protection room, I was taken to Defense Security Command, and then to Sangmudae Combat Arms Command. I was handed back over to the police station because I wrote out a plausible statement at Sangmudae Command. And I received five days of immediate detention. The drama club tried to form a meeting with the mask-dance club as a cultural movement, but the meeting was disbanded because KIM Seon-Chul was on the run in connection with the Educational Manifesto Incident. After that, around December 1979, KIM Yoon-Gi and KIM Seon-Chul, former members of the drama club, founded the theater company "Clown." This company was established to perform drama within a cultural movement. At that time, younger students became the leadership within the school, and older students assisted the leadership. In the early 1980s, the student movement, which had been exterminated through emergency measures and the *Yushin* Law, began to actively develop under the slogan of democratization within the school. In March, the "CNU Committee to Facilitate School Autonomy," which had been formed in January, began to estab-

30) Exorcising pigs' spirits.

lish a system for an autonomous democratic student organization. In April, the CNU Student Council was formed with the chairman PARK Kwan-Hyeon. I gave a supporting speech for PARK Kwan-Hyeon during the presidential election of the student association. The drama club put on a performance called *Doeji-puri* at the YWCA under the theme of the pig crisis, which emerged as a serious problem in rural areas at the time.

By May 1980, the goal of our struggle had rapidly shifted from the school democratization movement to the struggles to reject dual governance of the university,[31] to gain democratic rights, and to call for the abolishment of martial law. We were in a chaotic atmosphere but gathered at the YWCA every day, and continued to read *The Chronicles of Han* written by HWANG Seok-Young.

On May 17th, there was an invited lecture by Professor PARK Hyeon-Chae at the YWCA. After the lecture, I stayed with PARK Seok-Myeon, who had been on leave from the military service, and I slept at his house.

On May 18th, the next morning, I was told by Mr. PARK Seok-Mu (he was a teacher of the Daedonggyo Movement at the time) that my senior colleagues who had been involved in the Incident of the Democratic Young Men and Students Association[32] had been arrested, and that martial law had been expanded nationwide. After breakfast, I left the house because I was supposed to practice a play at the YWCA around 10:00 a.m. I arrived at the YWCA and tried to practice, but I couldn't because of the unusual atmosphere. We went to the Catholic Center in pairs to find out what was going on. There, in the downtown area, the police were suppressing people by force with pepper fog

---

31) Split between government authorities and the university's institutional administrative structures.

32) It was an incident in which around 180 people were imprisoned in April 1974 when they were charged with attempting to overthrow the nation and establish a communist government under PARK Chung-Hee's regime founded on the Yushin Constitution.

vehicles. Looking at the situation, I suddenly suspected that the military had seized power. In the afternoon, I met a younger student-colleague who lived near CNU at a coffee shop near Choheung Bank. I heard from him about the situation in front of the main gate of CNU in the morning and thought that I should let citizens know about it. We decided to work in two teams.

JEON Yong-Ho first informed the citizens of the situation, and the others got a mimeograph in Sinan-dong and wrote leaflets on the spot. We distributed the leaflets in front of the main gate of CNU and tried to get to the Intercity Bus Terminal. However, people kept us from going there, saying that it was now a mess near the terminal. So, I went toward Seobang-dong and distributed the leaflets to passers-by and high school students who had just left school early. After the distribution, I was passing by a store where I saw a television screen, which showed the curfew in Gwangju would be moved up from 9:00 p.m. to 8:00 p.m. With KIM Yoon-Gi, KIM Seon-Chul, and JEON Yong-Ho, I went to the Mudeung Nursery near the Hungry Bridge. LEE Hyun-Cheol was living there. He was using a room with a kitchen a little way from the nursery by himself. We discussed there what to do from now on. And we decided to divide our team into two, a patrol team and a leaflet team.

Write and Distribute Leaflets

On May 19th, we still stayed in the nursery and published leaflets in the names of the Student Revolution Committee and the Chosun University Student Council. I wrote mainly about the situation that the patrol team had seen. I also wrote about rumors circulating at the time. The leaflets were distributed to Bangrim-dong and Hak-dong as soon as they were copied, and also delivered to protesters' vehicles. It was dark, and I left the nursery not knowing what time it was exactly. Around 6:00 p.m., thousands of citizens gathered at Gwangju Park, shouting "Overthrow the dictatorship" and protesting for democratization. Vehicles began to emerge, and each vehicle was driven to the downtown. I watched this scene until dawn and went back to the nursery. From this day on, the park seemed to have become the base for the struggle.

The next day, on the morning of May 20th, we also published and distributed leaflets. When we left the nursery near evening, we saw the Hak-dong Police Box burnt down. At the CNU medical school, protesters sprayed water from fire trucks they stole to wash away tear gas. Protesters were confronting police and soldiers with fire engines in front of them, even though it was getting darker everywhere. Though protesters were angry, they did not explode emotionally. Some citizens even held sickles or stones in their hands. Protesters were about one hundred meters to the left of the Province Hall. A mixture of riot police and paratroopers were deployed in the Province Hall area. At the time, all the nearby shops were closed. I went to a mountain-climbing equipment store near the Province Hall with a junior colleague. We knocked on the closed door, but nobody responded. So, we broke the window and went into the store. When the owner came out, we asked him for gas, and he refused it at first. As we continued to beg, the owner put gas in a climbing gas can. We were going to use the gas tank when given a chance. We followed the protesters and came through Chungjang-ro when we saw several police officers and soldiers standing around the post office. As we went toward Hwanggeum-dong, we heard a citizen talking agitatedly. He said, "There are about one hundred students trapped in the underground shopping center, and construction workers at the underground construction site are injured. Let's go rescue them together." As we went there, the riot police were shooting pepper fog, and the protesters were pushed to the front of the Veterans' Administration Office because they couldn't break through the cordon. When one of the protesters threw a stone, saying, "Let's burn down the Tax Office in front of the Veterans'

Administration Office," stones began to fly from all over the place. Then, one citizen spoke convincingly, "This building is our property. Let's not burn our property recklessly." But on the other side, some people were crying out, "Let's burn it up." I went into the building to the back wall. I poured the gas from the tank I had carried around onto the curtains and lit it. But when I looked from the outside, the flame only flared up the curtains for a moment and soon went out. On this day, I went to HWANG Seok-Young's house and stayed there with a junior colleague of mine.

On the morning of May 21st, I woke up late, and the people I had been with the day before were already gone. I left the house with the junior colleague to contact people around 11:00 a.m. When we were just out of the house and in the phone booth, we saw a military jeep coming and soldiers raiding HWANG Seok-young's house. We might have been caught if we had left one step later. We went straight to the Province Hall. There I was very shocked to see soldiers being officially ordered to fire at unarmed civilians near the Labor Office. I went to the park around noon. There were quite a few people in the park. There, CHUN Ok-Ju held the microphone and kept saying something I couldn't hear. Some people were talking noisily. So, I went there to check the situation and found that citizens had caught a man wearing only an undershirt, claiming that he was a paratrooper. It was not clear whether he was a paratrooper or a riot police officer, but the citizens were poised to pounce on the man in a simmering rage. The man trembled and pleaded that he was not a paratrooper, but few people believed him. Then people calmed down when CHUN Ok-Ju, who was holding the microphone and speaking, made it clear that he was not a paratrooper. I was in the park that day and went to my uncle's house in Gwangcheon-dong with the junior colleague. I heard gunshots continually while I was sleeping there.

I had breakfast late at my uncle's on May 22nd. I found a

protest vehicle and got on it to the Province Hall. At 5:00 p.m., the Settlement Committee held a negotiation report in the Plaza in front of the Province Hall, which outlined the agreement made with the martial law forces during the day. While the citizen representative was reporting on the result of visiting the martial law authorities, JANG Hyu-Dong came out and said, "If we act this way, we are nothing but a mob after all. Let's quickly surrender all the weapons and return them to the Martial Law Command, and hand over control of city security to the police." When he made these remarks, there was a commotion all around. KIM Jong-Bae immediately jumped up to the podium, taking the microphone that JANG Hyu-Dong was holding, and said "As a politician, JANG Hyu-Dong is not speaking from a citizen's perspective. With so many Gwangju citizens dead, we shouldn't just talk about the settlement of the situation. We should present concrete measures to deal with it." When the rally was over, I went home for the first time in a long while. My mother had been extremely worried about me.

On May 23rd, I resisted my mother's dissuasion and left the house. I went straight to Nokdu Bookstore. Several people were gathered there. At that time, YOON Sang-Won was working at the bookstore. YOON Sang-Won suggested that we should work together by dividing roles because no students were in the Province Hall. He was in charge of connecting the Student Settlement Committee and the Citizen Settlement Committee. We discussed the current situation that was changing rapidly. We concluded our discussion by saying that we should not surrender the weapons in the way suggested and should achieve democratization by energizing the atmosphere. As a practical plan, we decided to hold a "Citizens' Rally." We prepared the items needed for the rally at the YWCA (amplifiers, microphone equipment, etc.). While riding a school bus, we promoted the rally, and people voluntarily gathered to attend the rally.

Presiding over the Rally

At 3:00 p.m., "The First Citizens' Rally to Protect Democracy" was held in the Plaza in front of the Province Hall. The ceremony of the rally was conducted in the following order: silent tribute to the victims, singing the national anthem, announcing notices from the Settlement Committee, and giving three cheers for democracy. On that day, statements were announced by representatives from all walks of life, including laborers, farmers, citizens, and students. KIM Young-Chul as the representative of the laborers and YOON Ki-Hyun as that of the farmers expressed their feelings. In addition, the extent of the damages to citizens and students was reported: more than 500 people had died, more than 500 people were injured, and about 1,000 people were arrested. When I presided over the rally, the reaction of the citizens was the strongest when I said, "This country's democracy is not just given, but achieved only by blood and fighting." The citizens cheered and applauded. Since the start of the rally, a helicopter had hovered in the sky and spread leaflets. The rally on that day ended amidst an enthusiastic response from the citizens. After the rally, we decided to hold a more effective rally the next day by burning an effigy of CHUN Doo-Hwan. A group of people, including me, gathered next to the current Hansem Academy building and made the effigy. When we were arrested later, we were severely questioned about the burning. We conducted independent activities apart from the Settlement Committee of the Province Hall at that time. On that day, there was a rumor that the U.S. had sent an aircraft carrier to support the citizens of Gwangju, and hand-written posters about the rumor were put up. Those posters expressed an anti-American sentiment, not a self-imposed illusion of trust and dependence on the U.S.

From the morning of May 24th, hand-written posters that criticized the attitudes of the Settlement Committee at the Province Hall as well as those of the government officials of the Province Hall were posted in the downtown area. As a follow-up to the previous day, "The Second Citizens' Rally to Protect Democracy" was held at the Plaza in front of the Province Hall. Prior to the rally, we took a moment to condemn the Settlement Committee for being non-cooperative and surrendering. We met to express our outrage, and we burned the effigy of CHUN Doo-Hwan. The enthusiasm of the citizens was heightened. Even in the rain, more than 50,000 people filled the Plaza. It was noisy because of the rain, but when I said, "This rain is tears shed by the victims of May 18, so let's all close our umbrellas," all citizens readily complied with my request. I continued to preside over the rally because there were no students to do the job, and I had experience in speaking in support of PARK Kwan-Hyeon during the elections for the student president of CNU. My voice was pretty good and loud. On this day as well, the rally was held in the order of silent tribute, national anthem, progress report, democratic poetry recitation by CHOI In-Seon, a member of Clown, and a statement announcement by each representative. At the rally, SHIN Young-Il's mother, who came to find her son, came out with her son and gave a speech. SHIN Young-Il said, "I don't know how to solve this situation, but we should never surrender the weapons. The only way is to fight. There will be a great deal of repression if weapons are surrendered, and that would be so unjust." At the end of the ceremony, college students gathered in front of the Namdo Arts Center, and citizens were also prompted to gather by each district. From that day on, college students gathered in front of the Namdo Arts Center. At the end of the rally, we circled the downtown, marching on the streets by spontaneously forming a protest line, all the way to Hwajeong-dong, which was a point of confrontation with the paratroopers, and passing through the New Gwangju Station. After the rally, forty to fifty people gathered at the YWCA for evaluation, reflection, and discussion for future work. We assessed the rally of the day to be effective, but from then on we determined we should divide the work and have an organized system. We divided the work into the planning team (YOON Sang-Won), the rally team (the Clown Team), the street broadcasting team (PARK Jung-Yeol), the hand-written poster team, and the leaflet team (most of the leaflets were written by PARK Yong-Jun at the time). Female students were mainly in charge of the cooking or the hand-written poster teams. At that time, we were at a loss as to how to address the necessary issues, but we managed it efficiently by systematically dividing the work. After finishing the work, a few pivotal people went to Boseong Enterprises. There, we had a discussion with our senior colleagues, such as JEONG Sang-Yong and LEE Yang-Hyeon, both related to the National Federation of Democratic Young Men and Students, and YOON Kang-Ok and AHN Gil-Jung, who was in the leadership of the Province Hall. We shared opinions like "Let's continue to hold the rallies. We need to take control of the Settlement Committee of the Province Hall. Currently, the Settlement Committee consists of people who joined the Province Hall on the day the Province Hall was taken over, and an orderly system has not been well established. So, we should take control."

On that day, I went home by taking a protest vehicle. The protestors were singing in a friendly mood. There were people wearing armbands with the words "Settlement Committee" and standing guard all over the streets.

Looking at Gwangju Citizens' Active Participation in the Rally

At around 8:00 a.m. on May 25th, because of the so-called poisoned needle attack incident, the situation got complicated. YOON Sang-Won explained in detail that the incident was fabricated. A doctor at CNU Hospital said the wound was not a puncture but a tear. And a biopsy showed that it was normal, not poisoned. On the same day, "The Third Citizens Rally to Protect Democracy" was held. I had to prepare for the rally, so I went back and forth several times between the YWCA and the

Province Hall. It was very chaotic inside the Hall. PARK Nam-Sun, dressed in a white gown, took command of the chaotic situation. He was in charge of interrogation, since there were also a number of intelligence agents in the Province Hall. And only foreign journalists could come into the Province Hall. At that time, there was a lot of distrust of the local media, so domestic journalists who came into the Province Hall were beaten. But foreign journalists were treated favorably because they were thought to report the actual situation in Gwangju as it was. YOON Sang-Won would brief them on the situation. High school girls prepared meals in the Province Hall. From this day, the confrontation lasted for a long time, and the military withdrew. So, many students gathered. At the rally, "An Article to the Families of the Victims, Religious People, and Democratic Students across the Country" was adopted. And the representative of the citizen militias read aloud "Why We Had No Choice But to Take Up Arms?" In addition, "The Gwangju Citizens' Resolution" was adopted.

Around 5:00 a.m. on May 26th, it was reported to the Province Hall that the martial law forces were entering the downtown with tanks from Nongseong-dong. Citizen Settlement Committee members suggested that the martial law forces return to their original positions while the Committee would first calm down the center of the city. As the news spread that the martial law forces were entering, "The Fourth Citizens Rally to Protect Democracy" was hastily organized around 8:30 a.m. And at 3:00 p.m., "The Fifth Citizens Rally to Protect Democracy" took place. Also, 5,000 citizens who insisted on continuing to fight went to the Hwajeong-dong confrontation point to protest and returned to the Province Hall. At the rally, the citizens' code of conduct was adopted with the idea that we should arouse ordinary citizens' consciousness by taking this opportunity, instead of continually issuing statements. And a lot of citizens came out and spoke. They talked about a wide range of issues such as politics and the economy from the national emancipation to the present. A woman, whose family members were all killed by the martial law forces around the prison, was so traumatized that she could hardly speak without tearfully crying. The code of conduct was announced by the Settlement Committee. People also told the Settlement Committee that they should understand the situation correctly. One female teacher asked what she should do in such a situation as ours. A middle-aged woman who visited the Province Hall for the first time said that she had seen news reports on television showing rioters and gangs shooting recklessly with guns, but the real situation was completely different from what she saw on TV. She even asked us to come to remote areas of the city to promote the actual situation. And an old lady said that people were not killed this way even during the Korean War. At the end of the rally, a young high school teacher in his early thirties stepped onto the podium and spoke coherently and logically. On this day, I lost my voice while presiding over the rally. And around 5:00 p.m., we had information that the martial law forces would enter the next day. We inferred the information from the news, received from a defense soldier working at Sangmudae, that a pork barbeque party was held to boost military strength and morale, and a military officer's wife had been contacted by her husband and told that he would not come home for several days. About 200 people who decided to defend the Province Hall waited at the YMCA under the direction of the Chief of the Situation Center. People were exhausted by the continued protests, and we knew that only Gwangju was isolated. The number of protestors decreased significantly, and the number of students was very small. Most of the protesters were people of lower economic and social status, including laborers, employees, and the unemployed. The Settlement Committee began to clash with some hardliners. Since the internal conflict could not be allowed to cause confusion in that urgent situation, PARK Nam-Sun said that from that time on those who insisted on surrendering guns would be considered spies, so those who wanted to leave were required to leave immediately. It was not until the afternoon that we resolved to fight vigorously against the martial law forces.

On the afternoon of May 26th, we finally agreed to fight. We told young students to go back home because we didn't know when the martial law forces would come. About seventy college students gathered at the YMCA. And we were determined to enter the Province Hall and fight it out. PARK Nam-Sun, who was wearing a military uniform, taught people how to shoot and deployed them. I came back to the YWCA. I cooked a lot of rice because people were tired and hungry. Everyone ate their fill, but there was still rice left. And guns were distributed to us. At that time, I didn't think I would die even if the martial law forces came. I prepared the leaflets that would be distributed the next day and gave JEON Yong-Ho other leaflets and declarations that I had gathered at each citizens' rally. I was so tired and ate so much food that I fell soundly asleep around midnight. Around 2:00 a.m., an urgent street broadcast with a young woman's voice saying, "The martial law forces are entering," passed through the early morning air. I was so tired that I only wanted to sleep more. KIM Jung-Hee (currently my wife), a member of Clown, who was next to me, kept waking me up. I came to my senses. I got out of the YMCA on a ladder that had been prepared in advance because there was information that martial law forces would come in at dawn. I heard incessant gunfire and bombing sounds, too. The martial law forces were coming in from the Sanjang area, Hak-dong, Baekun-dong, Hwajeong-dong, and everywhere while firing. In this urgent situation, I left the YMCA and went to a house in Sansu-dong where a senior colleague lived. There I contacted my home with a note. I managed to get out of Gwangju and went to a very small island near Mokpo. After staying for about fifteen days on this island, I came to Mokpo and found myself on the wanted list while reading the newspaper. So, I went to Seoul and Gwangju, and lived on the run. In Gwangju, I disguised myself as a tenant of my sister-in-law's house. But I couldn't stay there any longer. I thought the tenant in the next room looked at me with suspicious eyes because I seldom went out and just wandered around at night, and I had moved in at night. I went back to Mokpo. I pretended to be a student of Mokpo University and got a room and lived there for a few months.

After Spending One Year and Six Months on the Run

I came to Gwangju to meet my wife. I got a room in Dongmyeong-dong. I went to a grocery store to buy *makgeolli* to refresh myself. I had a strange feeling when I came back home with the *makgeolli*. A stranger approached me. As I got closer to the house, my wife beckoned me to run away. But I didn't want to run away, so I was taken. When I got caught, I felt rather calm. I was taken to the Air Force Security Command. Basically, I denied everything. I was brought back to the Sangmudae guardhouse, then to Combat Arms Command, and was handed over to the police. I was charged with the participation in a rebellion as a ringleader. In the course of the investigation, they severely interrogated me on burning the effigy of CHUN Doo-Hwan. When I asked them how I got caught, I was informed that the tenant who lived at my sister-in-law's house mistook me for a spy from North Korea and reported me to them. I had a hard time while spending a long period of one year and six months on the run, but I was much better off than those who were caught at the time of the uprising. I shed tears when I thought about the hardships that my senior colleagues went through.

I was detained in the Gwangju Police Station for about a month. I was tried without imprisonment because I had no previous criminal record. I admitted all the facts the judge read. At the next trial, I was sentenced to two years and six months in prison and three years of probation, and released in September 1981. I was finally freed from a year and six months of fugitive life that made me feel anxious and nervous and just hope that time would pass quickly. Also, I was finally freed from a sickening memory of being caught, beaten and interrogated, which I hated to even remember. After my release, I stayed at home because I was expelled from the university. At that time, the financial situation of my family was very difficult, and as the oldest son, I felt sorry for my parents and decided to get a job. I saw job advertisements in the newspaper and sent thirty resumes, but I didn't hear from any of the companies. Then, in March 1982, when I saw a job advertisement for a Korean language instructor at Dongyang Academy (a GED Academy), I submitted my resume. At that time, there was an absolute shortage of teachers at that academy, so I got a job there and was in charge of teaching the Korean language for the high school qualification examination. After about a month, I quit Dongyang Academy due to the low pay. And that winter, I got married to my wife in a difficult situation without a regular job.

In 1984, I was readmitted to the Department of Korean Language and Literature of CNU, owing to the measure of reinstating the expelled students. With permission of my professor, I took lectures in the morning and worked at an academy in the afternoon. After graduating in 1985, I worked at several academies before finally settling in Yangyeong Academy. Academy teaching is not a stable job, but I feel rewarded because I am able to have open conversations with students and think I am cut out for teaching.

And finally, while presiding over the citizens' rallies during the May Uprising, I considered propaganda and instigation to be part of the cultural movement, so I took it for granted to participate in those activities. At that time, the uprising leadership at the Province Hall was led by Deulbul Night School and Team Clown. At that time, intellectuals spared themselves even when they had to take the lead. Even though it is called a people's uprising, many souls who fell under the wheel of history while namelessly protesting still lie in their silent graves. I confirm their boundless love for their fellow human beings. Currently, I am a founding member of "Jeonnam Democratic Youth Association" and active in "May People's Uprising Comrade Association."

Ⅳ CRITICAL CONSCIOUSNESS

4. The Province Hall

1007. The Conflict between Settlement and Resistance
Witness: SONG Ki-Sook (male)
Year of Birth: 1935 (aged 45)
Occupation: Discharged professor (currently professor)
Date of Record: December 1989

Research & Arrangement by SONG Ki-Sook

Before the May 18 Democratic Uprising

I attended elementary, middle, and high school in Jangheung. In 1956 I was admitted to the Department of Korean Language and Literature in the College of Humanities and Science at Chonnam National University.

The following year, I enlisted in the army as a student soldier. After one and a half years, I was discharged from the military and returned to my studies. In August, 1961, I graduated from university and was accepted as a graduate student of Korean literature at the same university, and finished graduate school in 1964.

In 1964, I taught the course titled "Theory of the Novel" for two semesters. In March, 1965, I became a full-time lecturer at Mokpo National University and taught there until the end of February, 1972. I started teaching at Chonnam National University in March, 1972.

In September 1964 and 1965, two of my critical essays were chosen for and published in *Modern Literature*, and I officially became a literary critic. After that I began to write a novel. I have now written eight works including novels such as *An Elegy of Jaratgol* and *Amtaedo*. I am currently working on another novel, *Mung-bean General*.

On June 27, 1978, I announced the declaration of educational democracy under the title of "Our Educational Manifesto" with ten other professors of the same university, including Professor MYEONG Noh-Geun. I was arrested for violation of section 9 of the Emergency Law, was sentenced to four years in prison, and was imprisoned for one year and one month. I was released on special amnesty on the Constitution Day (July 17th) of the next year.

I was dismissed by the disciplinary committee of the school and had not yet been reinstated when the May 18 Democratic Movement took place.

Spring of Democracy in 1980

I was waiting to be reinstated at the university, as I had been dismissed due to the case of the "Educational Manifesto." This happened in 1978, when eleven professors at Chonnam National University issued a statement titled "Our Educational Manifesto," which is a declaration of educational democracy, and they were all dismissed. At the beginning of the next semester, all professors except me were reinstated. However, I was allowed to teach as a lecturer. The administration of the university expressed their apologies for the lack of reinstatement and called me an adjunct professor, an unofficial position at that time. I also used this title during the investigation by the police in order to show that I was a professor.

I was in an ambiguous position, and professors and students had such an eager desire for democracy that I did not need to involve myself directly in the faculty council activities and the movement of school democratization. I had other important things to do: research and writing. Watching the development of the situation, I gave unofficial comments if asked.

From the beginning of the semester, the resignation of government-patronized professors was the primary issue for the students. The times were more troubled due to the publication of the white paper on government-patronized professors. But the government-patronized professors would not resign, and students became more violent. No wonder that the student movement was in a stalemate. I was of the opinion that students' claims could have practically no effect other than a warning since there was no institutional law forcing these professors to resign. I advised them to backtrack on their claims. Some students reacted strongly against my advice, but there was no alternative, unless the government-patronized professors repented and resigned of their own accord. My opinion turned out to be true, because they held out to the last, and there were no other means available for the students.

Students who were concerned about the problem began to become nervous, and they began to turn the direction of the movement to political affairs such as lifting martial law, along with the formation of the student council. Students who had been tied to inner-campus problems so far began street protests in May, shouting higher levels of political slogans. Students who were attempting sporadic street demonstrations collided with riot police at the CNU school gate on May 14th, breaking through the police line and successfully entering the city. The students went out sporadically and occupied the fountain in front of the Province Hall. About 8,000 students gathered there, and they rallied against the government. It was the first grand assembly named the "democratic assembly." I was looking around in front of the Law School and came out downtown with some professors shortly after the students broke through the school gate. The students sat around the fountain, and the professors sat in a circle on a low bank under the fountain. The number of professors was about 200. Outside where the students sat, citizens surrounded them.

The police gave up blocking the students and stood at distance from them, just watching them. The police who gave up blocking the rally looked so powerless.

The fountain became a podium, and student council executives gave speeches to denounce the government and resolve future struggles. It started to rain around 4:00 p.m. As the rain gradually thickened, several female professors escaped the rain and went into a dry spot under the fountain, but no more professors followed them. The female professors who went in there were embarrassed when the other professors sat in the rain, and they came out again, and we were all standing in the rain together.

Professors and Students Demonstrate at Geumnam-ro

By the time it was dark, the students prepared to go back to the CNU campus. The office of student affairs of CNU asked the professors walking along with the demonstrating students, who would march along Geumnam-ro in several rows, to prevent citizens from joining them. However, some professors said it would be better for professors to walk in front and lead the student demonstrators. I decided to do that. A large *Taegeukgi*, the Korean national flag, nobody knew where it came from, led the procession at the front of the line. Six female students took the national flag at the front, rear, left, and right of it, and took the lead, followed by more than 200 professors. After that, the students stood in eight rows and marched along Geumnam-ro shouting slogans or singing songs. The rain got thicker and thicker, and when I had marched halfway down Geumnam-ro, I got soaked to my underwear. Along the sidewalk, numerous citizens flocked in the rain to watch the procession.

The faces of the citizens watching the procession were all

terrified. Martial law was still in effect, and it was impossible to predict how the political situation would change. But professors were protesting in cooperation with students, so citizens along the sidewalk seemed to be worried about what would happen to the students and professors.

I looked closely at the reactions of citizens as I walked along in the middle of the faculty line. While the demonstration procession marched onto Geumnam-ro, there were only three people who clapped in support. A girl clapped from a coffee shop on the second floor of the Hanil building across the street; after the procession progressed a little further, a man in his 40s clapped; and a little later, another man clapped in the middle of the crowed. Meanwhile the watching citizens were confused and scared.

The rain poured all the way while we marched some three kilometers to the school. It was dark when we arrived at the school; since our shoes as well as our clothes got entirely drenched in rain, we had to take our shoes off to pour the water out. Nonetheless, the professors all looked pleased. Waiting for the school commuter bus, they were excited, as if they had accomplished something great. It was wonderful to see them laughing while sharing cigarettes together.

At that time there were a group of CNU professors, who, having suffered dismissal for their participation in the incident of "Our Educational Manifesto," had recently been reinstituted to their jobs. Naturally they drew the students' attention in the midst of the fierce call for democratization, while the other professors felt pressured. Therefore, the latter felt good, for they too could make some contributions to the democratization movement by their voluntary participation in the demonstration procession with a bunch of the students, all soaked in the rain.

The incident made a decisive impact on the Gwangju citizens' perception of the current political situation, as they saw it as a collective movement of students and professors. I believe the incident inspired many citizens, who then eagerly participated in the May 18 Uprising later.

I was told later by the lawyer HONG Nam-Soon that after the demonstration procession many people came to ask him what the world ahead would be like. They must have felt frustrated with no clear idea about the current situation in which even the professors joined the protest when the future of the political scene was bleak. After all, in the eyes of the citizens, the demonstration procession led by the professors was seen as a huge incident as significant as the past professor-led demonstration that ended the April 19 Student Uprising.

The Torchlight Demonstration, the Festival of Democratization

On May 15th, the same as the day before, the students gathered around the fountain and held a "Democratization Rally" to discuss the current political situation. The previous day, they had marched out into the street, breaking through the police who had tried to stop them at the school gate, but that day, the police gave it up at the beginning. Pushing through with force, the students expanded the democratization space from the ground of the school campus to the streets of the city. The number of the participants that day seemed to be more than twice that of the previous day, for the Chosun University students, some other college students, and even some high school students joined the demonstration. It could be said that the demonstration spread all over to all the students of Gwangju. The number of citizen participants increased much more than that of the previous day, and they grew more active. The police stepped aside to the corner of the street and helplessly looked on again.

The professors, unlike the previous day, did not sit together near the fountain but remained scattered in groups and just watched the rally. They were a little more relaxed after their demonstration march through the rain the previous day, for which they received encouragement from many citizens.

May 16th was the day of the torchlight demonstration. Professors and police officers were nervous. I was concerned that the torches would become offensive weapons if the students clashed with the police, and I was also concerned that even if it did not develop that far, they might cause a fire by mistake. However, after hearing about the protest plan, I felt somewhat relieved. It was not that all the students carried torches, but that they marched with torches at intervals of three or four meters in the middle row of the seven in the procession.

On one side of the plaza near the fountain in front of the Province Hall, students were eating bread distributed by the student council while they were preparing for the demonstration, preparations that included torches with cotton balls and oil-soaked cloth attached by wires. The view of the riot police watching the scene from the other side seemed even more helpless. I felt sorry that only students were eating, so I proposed to the professors to raise some money. The intention was to give the riot police at least milk to drink. In an instant, some 90,000 won was collected. I handed it over to the Dean of Student Affairs, and he said that he handed over 100,000 won to the police after contributing some more money. Later, when I was under investigation, something funny happened because of the source of this money.

As it got dark, the torches were lit. The student council paid careful attention to the torch management two or three times, and asked the professors for their cooperation.

The torchlight procession consisted of two processions, led by Chonnam National University and Chosun University. These two processions were planning to make their way through the main streets of Gwangju. One by one, the gas-soaked torches began to catch fire. More than a thousand torches lit up the night sky. The torchlight procession began to move. The students sang songs while they marched. The torches stretched far away to Geumnam-ro. It was spectacular. Because there were no police blocking the procession, the students felt more secure, and because it was a festival that concluded the assembly of the last three days, they felt more relaxed.

The torches that ignited the cotton balls and burnt were a sacred flame that lit the dawn of democracy in the dark and painful land of *Yushin*. Each of those torches represented the joy of celebrating democracy that will unfold over this land, where everyone lives as one, and it was a cry of a strong will to reject oppression and expropriation, and it was an active volcano that burned the chains of the heinous dictatorship. The long torch-bearing procession was roaming the streets of Gwangju like the Janggang River, dancing to the roaring sounds of young people. Citizens pouring out from every street applauded and cheered, and shouted out their emotions and support. It was a dramatic festival of empathy that made us overjoyed when students and citizens harmonized as one.

The torchlight demonstration was very orderly, and it was a spectacular sight which was reminiscent of an art. It was a beautiful combination of movement and art.

The professors were amazed at the meticulous preparation of the students and the orderly execution of the event. Students had planned and conducted various events as well as kept a certain cooperative relationship with the school from the beginning of the new school year to the birth of the student council. And the professors at the university headquarters also admired the maturity of the students acting all in unity. The professors followed the torchlight procession in case of an unexpected accident. However, the march ended without a single incident. The torchlight demonstration marked the grand finale of the three-day pro-democracy assembly.

The idea of the students ending the three-day pro-democracy

assembly with such a festival was surprising, given that the students had previously shouted and demonstrated only on the campus. The peaceful and beautiful torchlight festival has firmly engraved the students' will and conviction for democracy into the hearts of Gwangju citizens. A few days later, all citizens were outraged by the atrocities of the paratroopers and fought to the death against the ruthless airborne. The sense of unity that had been formed between the students and the citizens through the festival became the basis for the citizens' resistance. Moreover, since Gwangju is a place that has the history of the Gwangju Student Movement, it is no wonder that the affection and trust of the citizens toward the students is exceptionally high.

Meanwhile, the students ended the three-day "Democratization Assembly" and they decided to watch for a change in the government's attitude and departed. The professors were relaxed and drank in a good mood or returned home safely.

I think that CHUN Doo-Hwan and his party should be punished for a long time in history, given the sheer fact that they trampled on the students' peaceful democratization movement and maliciously branded it as a riot that disturbed the country.

May 18th, Dark Morning of Rebellion

On the night of the 17th, I had a late night chat with my friends about the current situation and returned home in a hurry to meet the midnight curfew. Just as I arrived at my house near the back gate of Chonnam National University in Jungheung-dong, the phone rang. While I was untying my tie, I left it hanging around my neck and picked up the handset to answer the phone. It was the wife of KIM Sang-Yoon, who was at the time the representative of the students who had been suspended for previous political activity and then readmitted. KIM Sang-Yoon, along with YOON Han-Bong, were two pillars of the CNU student movement. Mr. YOON did not return to school after readmission in his efforts to protest outside the campus, while Mr. KIM returned to school and was practically guiding the student movement of CNU. They were both given heavy sentences for being masterminds behind the infamous Incident of the National Federation of Democratic Young Men and Students in 1974, but were still active in the student movement while their sentences were suspended.

"The boy's father was taken away just a while ago."

It was an urgent message that seemed to come out of nowhere.

"What?"

"I think the people who arrested him are from the National Security Command. He was caught just before I called. You should hide quickly, too."

I re-fastened the tie I had loosened and then just stopped. I plopped down on the sofa in a desperate mood. It was a kind of desperate hostility. Are these guys going to come down so hard on protesters after all? I was sitting there in despair. The image of the peaceful and beautiful torchlight march, which danced with the students' cheerful music, was flickering before my eyes. It looked like the authorities were about to break into my house any time, but I didn't want to avoid it. At this point, whether guilty or not, it was wise to stay away from the situation. However, there was no place to hide. If I had avoided the situation, I could have been misunderstood as being guilty, even though I had done nothing wrong.

While calling around, I came to realize that the emergency martial law had been expanded nationwide, and thus it was suggested that I had better stay away from the situation that seemed desperate for the time being. However, I decided that I wouldn't run away from trouble. In the meantime, no one came to arrest me that night. In the morning of the following day, I was told that paratroopers had occupied Chonnam National University and Chosun University as well. The circumstance I faced was quite serious. Later on, I overheard that the persons subject to arrest were readmitted students and leaders of the student body. The paratroopers seemed to be standing by at their houses to arrest them at midnight when the expanded martial law took effect; therefore, many of the readmitted students and the leaders of the student body such as KIM Sang-Yoon, JEONG Dong-Nyeon, and others were arrested.

I received many calls from different people: the paratroopers had brutally beaten the students. Besides, even the students sleeping in campus labs had been indiscriminately captured, and the students bound for the library had been ruthlessly rounded up, stripped to their underwear, and made to bend at the waist while balancing with only their heads and feet touching the ground and keeping their hands behind their backs. I heard that even the female students had been inhumanely stripped and beaten. Stepping out of my house, I went to see what was actually happening at the back gate of CNU. At the main gate of the university, the troops arrested the students without knowing what was going on, asking few questions and thrusting clubs into their stomachs. I observed that male students wearing only their underwear inside the university fence were lined up into rows and forced to balance on their heads and feet. Since it was Sunday, most of the students had been heading for the library. Glancing at the fence, I could not see any female students. Later on, I found it was an exaggeration that even female students had been stripped and beaten, but it was true that the troops were brutal enough to deserve such a rumor.

First of all, I figured out the situation while meeting professor MYEONG Noh-Geun and his colleagues: it seemed that the paratroopers did not advance on downtown Gwangju, and they abused the students as I mentioned above. Assuming that the readmitted students and leaders of the student body were arrested, we as reinstated professors should be cautious and well aware of the possibility of being arrested. As is widely known, the brutality of the troops that day would be notorious. That night, Professor

MYEONG and I hid ourselves in my friend's house.

The Face of an Airborne Officer on May 19th

On the morning of 19th, we were heading for school by bus. Because we were not allowed to walk through the main gate, we entered the university on the commuter bus. Looking out the window, we could see the arrested students being beaten while balancing on their heads and feet under the fence by the gate. Moreover, there was an appalling rumor that a young professor in law school had an argument with the paratroopers and was beaten up on the way to school the previous day.

Military tents were installed in the university stadium. I heard that the military headquarters were on the third floor of the university headquarters, so I went up but discovered that their headquarters were not there. A lieutenant colonel, who appeared to be the leader of the troops that were stationed at CNU, was hanging around with an irritated look. I finally met the leader of the fearsome paratroopers that, until then, I had only heard of. His face was tanned to a deep copper, and he had a coarse beard on his chin. He looked like he had just returned from war. Later, rumors spread that the paratroopers had been trained to suppress protests for a month before they stormed in and stationed themselves at the university. When I heard that rumor, it brought to my mind the lieutenant colonel as I had seen him in that moment. It is now well-known that CHUN Doo-Hwan's party did not expand martial law merely in response to the intensification of the student protests. In fact, they had made plans to do so at least a month earlier and had been preparing martial law very carefully.

I think the lieutenant colonel spoke to us first, but I don't remember what he said. We were terrified by his flushed face and could not protest forcefully. We only said a few words because we were aware of the students who were being caught at the gate and having their heads forced to the ground.

"Yesterday was Sunday, so most of the students who came to school yesterday must be those who are preparing for tests to get jobs – those who are not interested in demonstrations at all. Most of those who slept at school the previous day are those same students. Moreover, they came to school with their school bags on a day like today, even though they knew that martial law had been extended. Isn't it obvious what kind of students they are?"

It was frightening to say even this much in such a threatening situation. However, the lieutenant colonel appeared to half-heartedly admit that we were right.

He was Colonel KWON Song-Man — the commander of the army stationed at CNU who later testified at the Gwangju hearing that he had suppressed the protests. I remembered his name because I saw his name tag at that time. It was perplexing to see him testifying shamelessly at the hearing. Because we wondered for about a decade where these troops had been and what they had been doing, we were perplexed as we saw his face on the TV screen. I also felt more perplexed because his confident attitude with his eloquence represented how they considered their deeds at that time. It was obvious that this attitude was not his own alone — it clearly reflected the government's attitude toward the Gwangju uprising. The government says it is a democratization movement or something, but this is nothing but a pretense. The true position of this government is probably illustrated most honestly by those like the lieutenant colonel.

Like a Frog Hit by a Stick

My fellow professors seemed anxious about seeing Professor MYEONG, me, and others who had been dismissed from the university. They went so far as to advise me that it would be good to stay away from the campus. My colleagues and I had intended to do so, but we couldn't stand by and watch innocent students being beaten within the university campus. We tried to meet with President MIN Jun-Sik. However, we heard that the president had been lying at home ill for a few days. After some discussion, we decided to visit the president's house. As far as I remember, Professor MYEONG Noh-Geun, Professor KIM Dong-Won, Professor LEE Hong-Gil, and three or four more professors accompanied me.

We appealed to the president that he should go to campus and fulfill his duties even if he was not feeling well. We asserted that no matter how ruthless the paratroopers were, they are subject to the authority of state institutions such as CNU. If he held a position as a national university president and delivered a message to the paratroopers, we argued, they would not be able to wield such merciless violence against our students, at least on campus. The president promised to go to school even though he was not feeling well.

After leaving the president's house, some went to other places, and some of us, including Professor MYEONG and me, went out to the city for lunch. After lunch, we went out near Jungang-ro, where the underpass was under construction at that time. Protesters were swarming around, pushing and pulling. Around that time, we heard from a reporter from *Jeonnam Maeil Newspaper* that an arrest order had been issued for us as well. So we were overwhelmed with the feeling that someone would come out and arrest us at any moment.

Around this time, rumors were circulating on the streets that soldiers from Gyeongsang Province were publicly saying that they had come to kill the people of Jeolla Province. The soldiers allegedly said that in Mudeung Mansion Apartment. It was said that a paratrooper from Gyeongsang Province said, "I will kill you all, bastards." However, it seemed that the very unusual Gyeongsang dialect of the paratrooper, compounded by regional rivalries, caused his words to grow into the rumor.

We went up to the rooftop of Hwani Department Store and

watched with a crowd of others the protests that were taking place on Geumnam-ro. The protesters confronting the paratroopers were retreating toward Jungang Church. The street emptied out instantly.

At that time, a young man neatly dressed in a suit walked from the current Hyundai Wedding Hall toward Geumnam-ro. Two paratroopers went over to him. The young man stood tall, not running away. He seemed to have thought that his attire would plainly prove to them that he was not a protester. But it was a miscalculation. One of the paratroopers right in front of the young man, struck him straight in the head with a club.

"Ohmea"

The people standing next to us screamed simultaneously. At the blow of the club, the young man fell forward helplessly like a piece of wood. The paratroopers went straight to Jungang Church. We were all looking down on the fallen young man from the rooftop. He seemed to move a little, and then his hands trembled, spread apart. He looked like a frog that quivers its four feet and dies when mischievous boys hit it with a stick for fun. Recalling the frog dying, I thought that the young man also stopped breathing. Even those who had no such experience with frogs seemed to think the young man was dead as they saw him trembling. The sight of his hands trembling seemed like death throes to everyone there. But after a while the young man seemed to be moving. The crowd on the roof held its collective breath. The young man moved a little further and then stood up. It appeared almost as if a corpse had risen. He looked around on both sides and then stood up straight. His white shirt was reddened with blood. The young man staggered and disappeared from our sight. We breathed a sigh of relief. It seemed that human life is surprisingly tough.

"He Is Not Airborne"

Again, Geumnam-ro began to fill with protesters. It was a huge crowd. The crowd, which had been invisible as if they had been hiding, came rushing out. We went down to the street. Protesters were rushing into the Catholic Center building. They were entering the building because some paratroopers had entered the building after being pursued by the protesters. It was possible to tell from the outside to which floor they were running. This was because every time they went upstairs, they searched the rooms, opening the doors and shouting as if to inform those outside of the search situation; someone smashed a window in anger. It was about halfway up the seven-story building. With the sound of tear gas canisters being fired from the Province Hall, the crowds on the street rushed toward Jungang Church. At that time, Professor NOH Hee-Gwan and I ran around the main branch of Gwangju Bank and ran to the back of the Catholic Center building.

There we saw a strange sight. On the top floor of the Catholic Center building, a soldier stood on the window sill, pressing his body against the window, and holding the window sill with both hands. Certainly, it seemed that he was escaping from somebody who threatened to kill him. From below people shouted to kill him. His gun was strapped across his back. The gun was not an M16 but a carbine. Also, the military uniform was not paratrooper's but a common soldier's.

"He is not Airborne," someone cried, and then, the people below shouted all at once to not kill him.

"He is not Airborne. Do not kill him."

They shouted loudly from below, but the sound could not be heard up on the 8th floor. But after a while the soldier climbed down from the window sill into the building. It seemed that he could be saved not because of the screams from below, but because it turned out that he wasn't a paratrooper. Later, I was informed that it was a soldier of the 31st Division who was guarding the Christian Broadcasting Station there.

It was right after the soldier was gone. A crowd swarmed from the police station. Paratroopers were chasing them! We ran away. I went right down Jungang-ro and went under the half-closed shutter door of a shop. As soon as I entered, the shopkeeper slammed the shutter door down from both sides. Professor NOH was following me but he was slow: he was lying flat caught under the shutter door and couldn't move at all. I shouted and raised the shutter door to save him. Everything was so urgent that I couldn't blame the shopkeeper for that unkindness.

In the meantime, there was a terrible slaughter going on at the Catholic Center. When the paratroopers understood that their comrades had been trapped at the Center, the soldiers desperately defeated the protesters on the street, and then went up, smashing them from below, just as the protesters had done a while ago. That horrible situation was the same as what many people have testified.

After wandering the streets, we met again late in the afternoon and slept together at Professor NOH Hee-Gwan's home in the Sajik Apartments in Sadong. There were eight of us, including Professors MYEONG Noh-Geun, KIM Dong-Won, and AHN Jin-Oh.

The apartment overlooked the city, and there was a roar of protests early in the evening, but later it was gone. Then, flames rose from the train station. I heard later that it was from a cargo truck with a Gyeongsang-do license plate.

It was raining outside. We discussed what we should do the next day; because of the paratroopers' brutal suppression, the protests were unlikely to be escalating further. If they did, the paratroopers would be in a rage to arrest us. We thought we should get out of Gwangju and escape to Seoul and come back after everything calmed down. We were agreed on this, and we decided to escape to Seoul the next day. We contacted our friends who had cars here and there and asked them to take us out of town early the next morning. We asked three people, and no one refused. That meant that, even though some of us eight professors did not have to escape, everyone felt victimized, and they would go with those of us who did have to go to help protect us.

Looking back, it was a too-hasty decision to flee at that time, but because we could not predict what would happen at all, all we could judge at that time was that we thought there would be no more protests.

May 20th, Fear of Arrest

Around 8:00 a.m. on the 20th, all the people who promised brought their cars. The eight of us split up into three cars and left Gwangju on the side road toward Bia-dong. We did not know what would happen in Gwangju, so we decided to spend the night at Daejeon and went to the home of KIM Byeong-Wook, a professor at Chungnam National University who had graduated from Gwangju High School.

There, we made a phone call to Professor NOH Hee-Gwan's home, and his wife told us about the horrible scenes of that day in an agitated voice. We felt depressed, but we decided to go to Seoul anyway, as we were on our way out.

After arriving in Seoul on the 21st, all eight people stayed at an inn near the Jung-gu District Office. Mr. KIM's office was around there, and he had taken great care of us when we were suspended from the university. Whenever I went to Seoul, I stopped by and stayed there, so I visited him again this time, and he led us to the inn.

After contacting several places here and there, I borrowed a desk and sat down at it. I was going to write about the situation in Gwangju in detail and spread the word in Seoul. At 5:00 or 7:00 p.m., I turned on the television because it was news time.

A huge announcement came out. It was broadcasting the government's policy of hardline suppression, and I don't clearly remember whether it was the anchor who said it, or whether it was LEE Hee-Seong, Martial Law Commander, who made the announcement himself, but it was a report that they would destroy Gwangju. It was even more frustrating because I couldn't hear any actual news about Gwangju because the phone lines to Gwangju had already been cut off. I called back here and there and heard that all the people in Gwangju seemed to be dying now.

"What happens if we're here like this at this stage?"

I stopped writing and suggested going back to Gwangju.

"It seems like all the people in Gwangju are dying right now, and if we run away, sleep under a blanket, and survive like that, how can we live with any self-respect? Let's go down there. Let's go down and die together. The reason we decided to take refuge was to avoid a bad situation for a while because we thought the protests would decrease, and the soldiers would be in a hurry to arrest us. I didn't know things would go this far. But now that we're at this point, we've become cowardly fugitives."

I strongly argued in a furious voice, crumpling the writing paper. Not all the people who came with me were there. There were three people who had gone to meet people they knew, and five or so remained. There was no objection from anyone. I called Mr. KIM to say I would go down to Gwangju again, and he came running. First, he was worried whether or not it would be okay when we explained the reasons for returning, but he did not try to stop us because he felt that our resolution was firm.

Among the people who were there, some decided to come the next day because they had made appointments to meet friends, and only three of us, including Professor MYEONG Noh-Geun, Professor KIM Dong-Won, and I, decided to go down first. However, the express bus had already been cut off. Then we decided to head to Seoul Station to take the train. Mr. KIM took us to Seoul Station in his car.

However, trains on the Honam line had already been cut off. We were perplexed. Looking at the notice board, the line to Yeosu via Jeonju was not cut off. It was just five minutes before departure. We hurried to get tickets to Gokseong.

As we were running like crazy to catch the train, Mr. KIM gave us quite a lot of money with tears in his eyes. It was like sending someone off to war. The train departed as soon as we got on it with the farewell of Mr. KIM. It was as dramatic as a scene from a movie. Later, I heard that the line had been cut off after that train, so we would have had a hard time leaving if we hadn't left then. On the other hand, if we had not been able to catch the train, we might not have been accused of being the masterminds of the Gwangju uprising, so life is a mystery.

We switched to a sleeping compartment with the money that Mr. KIM had given me but couldn't fall asleep. We couldn't sleep thinking about the terrible scene in the Gwangju streets and got off at Gokseong Station around 4:00 a.m. A taxi had its light on in front of the quiet station where only three of us got off. The taxi seemed to be waiting like that for us, too.

Silence of the Defeated Soldiers.

"Gwangju, please."

"Gwangju?"

The driver had a look on his face like he thought we were people who woke up in some other world and didn't know anything about Gwangju.

"We understand the situation. We'll give you whatever fare you ask, so please just give us a ride as far as you can."

The driver was unwilling to accept our offer, but after an extended effort, we talked him into it, and he began to agree and got moving. We were planning to pass around Gwangju Lake from Changpyeong, and cross over Jat-gogae Pass in the direction of Mudeung Mountain.

Just as we were about to take a byway to Changpyeong, soldiers barricading the way with roadblocks stopped us. We said we were business people in Seoul, and we were going to Gwangju because we were worried about our families in Gwangju. They allowed us through without further questioning. Later, they turned out to be soldiers of the 31st Division.

As we got close to Ji-sil Village near Sigyeongjeong Pavilion on the upper side of Gwangju Lake, the driver stopped the taxi and said he couldn't go any further. We paid a lot of money for the taxi because we were thankful to him for driving us even that far.

It was still before dawn. We have an acquaintance in Ji-sil Village, so we went to his house and called him. There was no answer. Everyone in the village seemed to be awake, but they didn't answer our calls. That's because they were all scared. The door didn't open until we called out our names. As soon as we heard the general news of Gwangju, we walked toward Chunghyo-ri, where Chungjangsa Shrine was located. When we stopped for breakfast and ate ramen at the inn on the way, we asked about the news of Gwangju. They didn't know the details, but they said they had been just astonished at the news of the terrible scenes in Gwangju.

The sun rose as we got close to Chungjangsa Shrine. Not a single ant was seen on the road. Then a lady was following us with a basket on her head, and one girl who looked to be thirteen or fourteen years old cried and hung on to her mother's skirt. The mother tried to say something and soothe her, but the child cried and did not listen to her mother. I went up close and heard the girl's crying words. The girl told her mother she would die if she went to Gwangju, but the mother comforted her child, saying that she had to sell those things in her basket and she could buy food with that money. There seemed to be some wild greens including bracken in the basket, and they seemed to be a family that made a living by selling wild greens. The mother finally shook off her crying daughter and walked down the road, and the daughter still followed her mother with a whimpering sound. We seemed to have seen a fragment of miserable country life. The daughter followed for a long time and stopped and cried. Professor KIM, who couldn't bear to see the scene, asked us to buy all the vegetables from them. But the lady was already moving away from us.

The moment we crossed over the hill near Chungjangsa Shrine, we stopped at a sudden sight. About ten strong men showed up somewhere in front of us. The only people on the road were our party and the wild-greens woman, and we were surprised to see such an unexpected group of people. Besides, they looked strange in their clothes. Most of them wore training suits or shirts, but they didn't wear matching tops and bottoms like a full training suit. Some of them wore jackets on training pants, and others even wore training pants and suit jackets. The way they dressed was a total mess. And every one of them was carrying a small bag. At first glance, it seemed that they were manual workers.

"How is Gwangju now?"

By appearances, they looked like ordinary men so I asked what I wanted to know. But as if they hadn't heard us, they passed us by and went their own way. Although I asked the people at the end of the line the same question again, they did not respond, either. Wondering what their problem was, we stood for a while watching them walking away.

Feeling weird, we went a little further. Then there was another group of people like the first. There were about twenty people wearing mismatched outfits similar to those of the group we met before. They looked nervous as well. We asked the same question again. However, all of them held their tongues and just kept going. We couldn't figure out what was going on. We were completely baffled. After letting them go, another group of such people went by. Again, we asked them the same question.

"How do I get to Boseong from here?"

A man asked without answering our question. We gave him rough directions and asked who they were. However, he left without answering. It was after passing by four or five groups that we found out who they were. One of them was wearing military trousers. Based on that, we inferred they must have been police officers who had been called out from the provinces to suppress the protests. They were getting out of Gwangju, covering up their identity with sweat suits they wore as pajamas or casual clothes they obtained from private houses. The reason they kept their mouths completely closed must have been that they worried about the troubles they would face if their identity was exposed. From their attitude, we could guess at the horrific things that had happened in Gwangju while we were gone. Considering they had seen the most horrendous killings committed by the paratroopers, they would have thought that they too would face retribution for being on the same side as the paratroopers.

From Namdong Catholic Church to the Province Hall

While we talked to them, the woman carrying the wild greens had already gone and was nowhere to be seen. On Jat-gogae Pass I looked down at Gwangju. We could hear gunshots here and there. However, as it turned out, it was gunfire by young people who were shooting for amusement on the outskirts of Gwangju. It was because by then the paratroopers had already been defeated. As we came down to Duam-dong, middle school students were walking around carrying carbine rifles as if they were sticks.

Arriving at Professor KIM's house around ten, I made a call to my family and found that they were safe. But there were several urgent messages from the Province Hall and YWCA asking me to come. After having breakfast, Professor MYEONG and I went to lawyer HONG Nam-Soon's house to figure things out first.

On entering the house, before we said anything, lawyer HONG got up and walked out the gate. It turned out that he thought we had come to pick him up to handle the situation. He had also fled to Seoul in a similar situation as ours and returned to Gwangju with a similar feeling; and, before even catching his breath, he received a call from both the Province Hall and Namdong Catholic Church to come there. When we showed up, he felt leery with doubt at some names of the people gathered in the Province Hall. We went to Namdong Catholic Church. More than ten people were gathered there, including parish priest KIM Seong-Yong, Elder JO Ah-Ra, YWCA General Secretary LEE Ae-Shin, Elder LEE Sung-Hak, Mr. LEE Young-Saeng, and lawyer LEE Ki-Hong.

Having arrived at the cathedral, we first discussed whether we would join the people in the Province Hall, who already had been discussing a settlement, or whether we would handle things on our own. This is because it was difficult to trust some people gathered in the Province Hall as being representative of the citizens. Since most people at Namdong Catholic Church had the experiences of fighting in defense of democracy during the *Yushin* regime, it was inevitable that we would scrutinize the inclinations of the people in the Province Hall. At that time, Father KIM Seong-Yong suggested listening to what was going on in the Province Hall first and making a decision on how to handle things after Father JO Pius, who was out at the Province Hall, returned. After some time, Father JO Pius came back. He roughly described the atmosphere of the Province Hall and outlined the settlement conditions being discussed there. With those settlement conditions, we agreed to join the people at the Province Hall and went to the Province Hall all together. When we arrived at the office, seven terms of the settlement conditions had reached the final stage of discussion. Although the conditions were not fully satisfactory, there were opinions that we had no choice but to accept such conditions for the time being, so we agreed on them. The people who already had been discussing the settlement in the Province Hall were supposed to contact the martial law enforcement headquarters with the settlement conditions. We agreed to meet again when they returned from the martial law enforcement headquarters and parted. This means that the members of the Settlement Committee at that time were neither elected representative of citizens nor delegated in any way; rather, they were volunteers. Although the people at Namdong Catholic Church were volunteers, too, they had the obvious experience of fighting against the *Yushin* regime and gathered all the time for discussing democracy. These members were the so-called Settlement Committee of Namdong Catholic Church, and the martial law headquarters later attempted to charge them with the whole responsibility for the uprising.

Professor MYEONG and I went to Professor LEE Seok-Yeon's house, Gongmuwon apartment in Sansu-dong, and we were able to hear the details of the uprising on the 20th and 21st, when we were not in Gwangju, for the first time. We were absent from Gwangju for those two days when the citizens fought most fiercely.

A Choice Foreshadowing Death

After getting some rest at Professor LEE's home, Professor MYEONG and I went to the Province Hall again around 6:00. Citizens gathered around the fountain in the middle of a rally, but the crowd was not that large. Upon our arrival, though, we were asked to gather the students, to create a leadership authority in the absence of a citizen's command structure, and to lead the practical process of the settlement. They expressed strong suspicions in identifying several members of the Citizens' Settlement Committee and other people, and revealing concern about their past careers.

Professor MYEONG immediately agreed to form a student settlement committee. But I disagreed with us taking a very active role in and doing such a thing. I could not explain the reason for my disagreement right away, so I only expressed my strong opposition, but Professor MYEONG did not listen. He suddenly took over a portable megaphone that a student had and told all the college students to gather there. I tried to stop Professor MYEONG, saying it would be a big problem, but he wouldn't listen.

I was at a loss. I disagreed with him for the following reasons.

First, there was no Citizens' Army central command yet, and if we took the lead and organized the central command, both of us would risk taking responsibility for the whole situation. That responsibility meant death. Although the Airborne brigades had now retreated to the outskirts of Gwangju for a while, if negotiations between the military and the Settlement Committee failed, it was only a matter of time for Gwangju to be retaken by them again because the citizens of Gwangju were now fighting against virtually 600,000 troops. And at that time, it was obvious that the military would force Gwangju citizens to take responsibility, as much as they themselves had committed such brutal slaughter. If so, it was too obvious that we would be the primary targets because we both had past opposition records. Even if the Committee settled the situation, we would be targeted. But if the Airborne brigades carried out a recapture operation, the Committee would naturally turn into an organization of struggle and leaders of the struggle. So there was no need to ask for how much more responsibility it would be held to account. We decided to die with the Gwangju citizens when we came back from Seoul, but we didn't mean to step forward and die that way.

Second, we could not rule out the possibility that the actual leadership had gone underground and would not reveal itself, even thought that meant they would be less influential. Moreover, if the leadership was an invisible force, we could be targeted for death as soon as we entered Province Hall. The possibility was extremely low, but I thought that we could not risk our lives. Even if we would not be targeted, the atmosphere after the battle was extremely heated at that time, so opinions would naturally differ in various ways, and even a small disagreement could trigger emotions and provoke people to use their guns. Then it would be a dog's death. That my idea about the underground leadership was not hypersensitive could be understood from the fact that the direction of the initial investigation of the Joint Investigation HQ was just like I suspected it would be. Of course, such an underground leadership was not found even though the HQ made a thorough investigation. Anyway, the attempt to discover underground leadership was the initial direction of the investigation.

Third, the uprising was initiated by the students at first, but citizens armed themselves to drive out the paratroopers. And it was doubtful whether it would be right to form a leadership with college students who were not the actual subjects of the uprising in the stage of the armed struggle. Most of the students had already left Gwangju on the 19th, and the people who actually fought with guns were the citizens from the less-privileged classes. Moreover, we professors couldn't join that rally and just looked around and chose to leave the spot. We had an assumed reputation for participating in the democratization movement, but that was in the past. What would happen if people like us, who had an assumed reputation for participating in the democratization movement in the past, took a leadership role? I thought even if demonstrators did not have a leadership role right now, there would probably have been people who led small units during the battle. And so it would be better for them to gather together and form their own leadership, even if there was some conflict or delay. It seemed to me that only then would the logic of the demonstration be justified properly. The third reason was actually the most crucial for me to oppose Professor MYEONG forming a student settlement committee. Also this was a matter of responsibility that would be remembered in history for a long time.

Forming a student settlement committee was a matter of immediate life and death and also of historical responsibility. However, students were already gathering in front of Professor MYEONG. I knew very well who Professor MYEONG was and saw that I couldn't stop him anymore. I guessed we shared the same opinion, but one thing was different. Once he made up his mind, he pushed ahead whatever the result may be. I've always admired his great courage and determination, but I couldn't act with him here. I decided to leave alone and turned around. Actually, I turned away reluctantly because I couldn't accompany him to death. I looked back several times and soon reached the Labor office. But I couldn't go any further. Because of my self-consciousness I couldn't run away alone leaving Professor MYEONG. Moreover, it was me who had strongly persuaded him to go back to Gwangju from Seoul, so it was the same as if I had cornered Professor MYEONG into a deadly situation and then left him alone. What would happen to me if Professor MYEONG died alone? I fell into serious mental agony. In my affinity with Professor MYEONG, I had never resented him like this. I went back to see what was happening. There were already more than 100 students there.

"Please gather students from Chonnam University and Chosun University separately and pick five representatives from each university."

Professor MYEONG's voice rang loudly on a megaphone. Five representatives were chosen. Everything was going well. I had no choice but to go to his side.

"We've driven out the Airborne, but without leadership, the Citizens' Army is unsure how to proceed. As you know, the Citizens' Settlement Committee has already been formed and they went to Sangmudae for negotiations, but I think they do not command the Citizens' Army. Everything has been triggered by students, so students should be at the forefront. Let's go into the Province Hall and form a student settlement committee."

Professor MYEONG explained why they had to form a student settlement committee and took the lead toward the Province Hall. I had no choice but to follow him. I took that unwilling step as if I were going to a slaughterhouse. It was around 7:00 p.m.

"I'm a High School Teacher"

At the main gate of the Province Hall, the Citizens' Army wearing helmets of the riot police, which gave them the nickname Admiral YI Sun-Sin at that time, were holding guns and controlling those who walked in and out with a combative demeanor. The helmets had been taken away from the riot police. The soldiers were called Admiral YI Sun-Sin because, wearing the helmets with the wire mesh turned to the back, they looked exactly like the statue of Admiral YI Sun-Sin located at Gwanghwamun Plaza in Seoul.

We took ten students through the front of the Admiral YI Sun-Sins and entered the Province Hall. We were about to enter the General Affairs Department, where the Settlement Committee had met in the morning. Right at that moment, JEONG Si-Chae, then the Lieutenant Governor of the Province, came down and saw us and said there was something we needed to discuss. Professor MYEONG went up to the second floor with Mr. JEONG.

I alone took the students to the General Affairs Department. Inside, the department was a shambles. More than a hundred people were in chaos. On one side, some people sat other people in front of them and yelled at them, and it seemed like they were doing some kind of investigation. They were trying to interrogate people who had been caught because they were suspected of being spies of government agencies. This kind of investigation was not something that anyone there had the authority to conduct, so they were just yelling. On another side, *gimbap* was piled up, and gunshots were heard here and there. People were shooting either for fun or by accident. What was more frightening was the sight of people with grenades strung across their bodies. They had connected the grenades in a row by attaching them through the pull rings of the safety pins, not realizing that the rings were not meant to be used like that. If the rings had been pulled out, a lot of people would have died like flies. Also, it was disconcerting to see them stirring guns like sticks because they didn't know how to hold them.

I thought I'd retrieve all the grenades and teach them how to hold a gun. However, everything was in such a mess that I didn't think anyone would gather around me and listen to what I had to say.

I thought that the people in the room first needed to be organized in order to have a meeting. So, I told the students to organize the people inside.

I was bothered by the people who were running the interrogations, so I went over to them to check how the investigation was going. There I saw that most of the people who had been caught were drunk, talking nonsensically or violently.

"Don't lie. Tell me the truth."

"I'm telling you, I'm a high school teacher."

"Then show me your ID."

"Shit! Would anyone who came out to see the demonstration carry an ID card?"

"This is driving me crazy. You may go now."

Most of the investigation was done like this.

When I tried to gather people and talk a little bit, people suddenly appeared and yelled absurdly.

"Corpses are rotting right now. What are you doing, not trying to get coffins?"

The red-eyed people shouted loudly while pointing their guns. They were making such demands because they thought a leadership had already been formed in the Province Hall. After I barely succeeded in appeasing them, other unexpected people appeared and shouted, "What are you waiting for without preparing for the paratroopers' attack?"

"What the Hell is a Settlement? You Want a Grenade?"

Ups and downs of such absurdity continued for a while when a young man with a different attitude appeared. When he heard about establishing the Student Settlement Committee, he opposed it head-on.

"What the hell is a settlement? You want a grenade?"

He threatened us with a grenade in his hand.

"Then what do you want us to do?"

"What are those students, coming up this late and insisting this and that?"

It was kind of expected. But his question pricked my conscience.

"Then tell us your opinion."

"We need a combat command, not a settlement committee."

"Yeah, we have to create an organization either of combat leadership or the settlement committee. What if the paratroopers attack again while we are messing around like this? We should try to get things in order and prepare in case we have no choice but to fight if the military will not comply with our request, shouldn't we?"

However, he objected to the students taking the lead in the end.

"You're right, but who will stand in front of us while we do not know who is who? If anyone takes the lead simply because he took up arms to fight, the citizen militia members will not just believe him since even those who took up arms do not know each other well. Then how can the leader hold the leadership? Students can be trusted by everyone and are the only available option for us, right?"

He did not argue with me any further, but he did not seem to agree with me either. This young man named KIM, who had been identified as someone studying to retake the college entrance exam, seemed to have exercised power among the people. It was difficult to cope with the disagreements since such dissenting opinions did not appear at one time but burst out sparsely and abruptly. Even though it would take time, however, convincing everyone who had objections before establishing the committee seemed the right thing to do.

Another young man with bloodshot eyes and a bandage on his shoulder appeared with an M16 rifle. We could tell immediately that he had fought in a fierce battle. All the young men there looked at him with frightened eyes.

"What is happening here?"

"We are about to set up a settlement committee."

Student representatives explained the circumstances.

"A settlement committee? What kind of settlement? We must fight until we die. What is to be settled? Now, the paratroopers are in the mountains preparing to attack again. Who are you?"

Suddenly he put his gun to my neck. He placed the gun with force right on the sunken part under my chin and shouted. It seemed like he was quite offended by the word "settlement." If he pulled the trigger, my head would be blown apart. Judging by those eyes, he could pull the trigger without blinking an eye. Since he was pushing my chin up with the gun, the muzzle followed whenever I turned my head to the side. I tried to turn away a few times, but it was in vain.

"You bastard! Move your gun away from me! Two thousand have already died! We have to live! You bastard!"

I screamed, raising my head against the muzzle of the gun and looking him in the eye.

When one of the student representatives told him about my past activities, including as a professor at Chonnam National University, he reluctantly turned the gun away.

"You seem to be offended by the word 'settlement,' but shouldn't we be able to establish order somehow? If the paratroopers attack us, how will this disorderly crowd fight them?"

He insisted that we should attack and clear away the paratroopers on the outskirts of the city. As I had explained earlier to the young man studying to retake the college entrance exam, I suggested to him a compromise by which the student settlement committee could serve as the combat command when the paratroopers would attack us. He became calm as naturally as he had been forceful.

In the process of convincing others, I became more confident in my logic. So many had died; I thought that was enough lives lost. What's more, I thought, what would happen if all these young people died? I did not hate those who opposed me so vigorously; rather, I thought that these were precious young talents who could risk their lives in times of crisis like this. Just as we can see that a pine tree is beautifully green only in winter, we are able to see that these young people are truly human when it comes to times like this; they become people who, during peaceful times, we could not know they could be.

I thought that the excitement of the battle had not yet subsided, and so they should be dissuaded from starting another fight with the soldiers. A tragic romance story gives those in it an anxiety so desperate that their blood seems to dry up, but it is a beautiful thing to watch from the outside. Even death at this time may be heroic and glamorous to the spectator, but the person involved is giving up his one and only life; moreover, these young men are precious talents with a unique sense of justice. About 2,000 people died, and that was enough in terms of the movement. Even if there were one or two thousand more deaths, the meaning would not increase in proportion to the number of deaths.

The sad thing is that I haven't been able to see again the young man who pointed the gun at me so forcefully back then. Judging from his personality, if he were alive, he would definitely have appeared as a member of the Injured Association or some other group, but he was never caught and taken to Sangmudae afterward, and we have no news of him so far. I do not know his name or identity, but his face is as vivid in my memory as in a photograph. I think he died during the operation to retake the Province Hall, but I asked around, describing what he looked like to the young people who were in the Province Hall at that time, and no one knew. I just hope that he is alive somewhere.

Mr. KIM, who threatened me with a grenade, still meets me and smiles every time we talk about the past. "Even now, seeing you is terrifying. When I saw your expression at that time, I felt like you were really going to explode the grenade." When I joke like this, he smiles and laughs, saying that I was also as bad. After that joke, I am reminded of that young man with the M16. He was about thirty years old, of average height, and gave the impression of being a worker, and he had a fairly large bandage on his left shoulder as if he had been injured. When he first came in, he was holding the gun in the air, gripping it by the bolt action. His eyes were bloodshot as if he had been fighting quite fiercely, and he was full of energy.

Birth of the Student Settlement Committee

It seems that it took three or four hours to persuade everyone broadly and arrange the chairs. Since no one else expressed any other opinions, the meeting began. However, not knowing when opposing people would appear again, we made sure that the meeting would proceed quickly and efficiently.

Chonnam National University students and Chosun University students sat on both sides of the long desks.

"Who would you like to be chairperson?"

When I asked, someone pointed to KIM Chang-Gil, a third-year student at Chonnam National University.

"Since KIM Chang-Gil had been back and forth to the Martial Law Command as a student representative all day, I agreed that he should be the chairperson."

"Any other opinions?"

"No"

"Then you will be the chairperson. Who is going to be the vice-chair? Since the chairperson came from Chonnam National University, would it be better for the vice-chairperson to come from Chosun University?"

Then, a student at Chosun University recommended KIM Jong-Bae.

"No. I'll take care of the funerals."

He said that he was a Christian and had been to each hospital for a few days taking care of funerals.

"All right, you serve as both the vice-chairperson and the commissioner for the funerals."

There was no objection.

"Now, what else do we need?"

They decided they needed a gun recovery team, a vehicle control team, and a public relations team, and the head and assistant head of each of those teams were selected.

In addition, there were reportedly resistance bases in such places like Sajik Park and the Sansu-dong Five-way Intersection, and some organizations might appear from those places, and, perhaps the next day, the student organizations that had gone into hiding might reappear.

"This student committee, which we have organized here, is a temporary one because there is no leadership to control the citizen militia members right now. If the student organization or any other representative organization appears tomorrow, it will have to hand over the initiative. Looking at the present situation, I think many students will gather tomorrow morning. So, we will act temporarily until tomorrow morning and call this organization a provisional student committee."

Subsequently a provisional student committee was set up under the condition that it would be temporary until the following morning. What made this so easy was that among the students gathered there, they already felt the need for such an organization. Even though some of them suggested organizing a provisional student committee, they had not yet reached a conclusion until we appeared; therefore, they came to agree with us. In other words, they had an idea about organizing a committee, but there was no way to gain representation from citizens or students, whereas we were professors and gave them representation on account of our contributions to the democratization movement in the past.

We met with a group of the citizen militia in the Province Hall to inform them of the formation of a provisional student committee and ask for cooperation. It was past 11:00 p.m. After discussing the settlement plan with the Lieutenant Governor of the Province, Professor MYEONG attended the Citizens' Settlement Committee to discuss the settlement and finally came down to the administration office. It was Professor MYEONG who started the work, and I carried it out.

Seeing the students start their activities, I suddenly felt fatigued. I told them that I would like to go home, sleep a little, and come back in the morning, and that I needed transportation. The head of the vehicle control team went out to arrange it and shortly returned, saying that a vehicle was ready and that he would take me home. That's how quickly we took control of the citizen militia. I went out and saw an express bus with all the windows broken, on which rough slogans such as "Kill CHUN Doo-Hwan," "Free KIM Dae-Jung," and "Lift Martial Law" were scribbled. When I looked into the bus, I saw about twenty YI Sun-Sin-like gunmen sitting in the dark. It seemed they came to escort us; however, it was so alarming to look at them in such a posture in the dark that I did not feel like getting on the bus right away.

"The bus is too big!"

I protested a little, and the head of the vehicle control team called in a jeep at once. On both sides of the driver's seat, two citizen militia members, holding the body of the car with one hand and a gun in the air with the other hand, escorted us. I laughed bitterly as if I were being treated like a commander. Anyhow, riding downtown in the dark under such an escort, I felt like I was a real commander.

When I arrived at home and took off my clothes, I saw my underclothes soaked in sweat. It seemed I shed cold sweat when I had to deal with the armed citizens. I was surprised that I had sweated so much in such a situation.

The Rise of the Citizen Militia Leadership

I called the university president early on the morning of the 23rd to explain in detail how the provisional student committee was formed the previous day and ask for a general faculty meeting, in which the school authorities could confirm the formation of the provisional student committee. I thought it was necessary to take measures to ease my responsibility if I were questioned in the future. Around 9:00 a.m., professors gathered at the Boy Scout building next to the Province Hall. There were about sixty people. At the meeting, Professor MYEONG and I explained how the provisional student committee was formed and asked for approval. The faculty meeting confirmed it without discussion, and even made a resolution to delegate everything in the student matters to the two of us in the future. However, later in the investigation process, these measures were not taken into consideration at all.

When the faculty meeting was over around 10:00 a.m., I went to the Province Hall. Professor MYEONG went to the Citizens' Settlement Committee, and Professor KIM Dong-Won and I came together to the General Affairs office, which was used as the headquarters of the provisional student committee on the previous day. It is said that a total of 1,500 guns or so were collected overnight. Almost all were voluntarily returned. Many in the citizen militia remained armed to the end, hoping to oppose the paratroopers that had mercilessly killed their fellow citizens in front of their eyes. When the paratroopers retreated and the people thought things looked like they would go well in the future, it felt burdensome to them to have guns, so many people were looking for a way to return them. There were even people who left their guns lying on the road.

The next day, however, the student council executives did not appear, and also the other leaders did not appear. Then the condition of the provisional student settlement committee couldn't help but be a problem. When I asked if there was a quiet place to discuss the matter, I was told that the basement of the Province Hall building annex was good. It was the place of a ridiculous rumor that the protesters had stockpiled explosives. I went there with the executives of the Student Settlement Committee. Professor KIM Dong-Won also went with us. It was dark there, so the explosives could not be seen clearly and only looked like a large pile. The amount seemed to be about two truckloads.

The "provisional" issue was simply resolved. Someone asked what would happen if we removed the "provisional" tag and continued to promote the committee, so I told them to do so.

"But there is one problem. Last night, a man named PARK Nam-Sun set up a separate command center, but he doesn't listen to us, so please convince him to accept our leadership."

I had thought something like this was going to happen. It seemed that the forces that actually held the guns had risen to leadership. At that moment, I realized it was not my business to intervene.

"What kind of person is he?"

"He has fought quite hard, but it seems that his younger brother died in this fight."

"What is his job?"

"I don't know exactly. He didn't go far in school, but he's running all over the place with a pistol."

"How many people follow him?"

"I don't know for sure, but there are several people."

"Though I will meet him, it will be difficult for me to get deeply involved. But I think it would be better not to clash and work together while discussing what to do."

My somewhat vague response seemed to surprise the students, as if they expected more from me, but I had a fundamental skepticism about students taking over the leadership of the militia, so I had to hope for an organic development of cooperation between the students and militia. Even if there might be some clashes, it seemed that they had to somehow coordinate among themselves. My thought was that the right leadership would be born according to the basic flow of the movement, and it would be better that way. If the people like me with no specific leadership position tried to intervene, it could not work out as I hoped, and the natural adjustment would likely take longer. The previous day, despite the opposition of some, the committee was formed because there was no clear organization and people just expressed their individual complaints. If they had an organization, there would be no need to rush so much. To the last, I couldn't shake the self-consciousness that I had not been a subject of the armed struggle.

I wanted to meet PARK Nam-Sun and find out his various intentions, and I wanted to help coordinate the relationship with the students to some extent, but he had gone somewhere, so I couldn't meet him at that time.

That day, I finished the job by removing the word "provisional" and attended the Citizen Settlement Committee. And from the next day, I decided not to attend any more meetings. After that, the Student Settlement Committee called me whenever there was a problem, but I only told them to discuss it for themselves. It might have seemed irresponsible for me to withdraw from the discussions after organizing the Student Settlement Committee, but I thought that it was right to entrust the work to the parties who had fought directly, and those who were around me also advised me that such a course of action would be reasonable. It was not the fear of the responsibility, but the thought that it was proper that everything should be left to the will of the militia itself, the active subjects in the struggle.

A Tragic Turn to the Struggle

Early on the morning of May 25th, I got a call from the Settlement Committee members in Nam-dong asking me to come out to the YWCA. There was something important to discuss. It was raining a lot, and I couldn't find any taxis on the street. There were no taxis or people to be seen. Not a single person appeared while I was walking the two kilometers to the vicinity of the Gyerim Theater. It was as if the whole city was empty.

As I passed the Gyerim Theater, a man was smoking a cigarette and fixing the shutter door. Cigarettes had already been cut off in the city, so I had not been able to smoke since the previous day. It was the same for daily necessities such as vegetables, but for a cigarette-lover like me, the craving for cigarettes was the most painfully intense. Shamelessly, I asked him to hand me one. He took out a pack of cigarettes and pulled out one cigarette, then pulled out another cigarette and gave me two cigarettes. Guessing from the look of the pack, it seemed that there were only two or three cigarettes left for him.

I always tell this story whenever I talk about the potential of the people; I was able to confirm the fact again that such a great morality emerges when the people reach a voluntary agreement. Even during the Donghak Peasant War, if you look at the testimony of Confucian scholars such as Maecheon and KIM Yun-Sik, you will see that although they criticized the Donghak movement, they nevertheless praised the participants for their morality as evidenced by their considerate acts like not trampling a single field of barley. The infinite potential of the people can be seen here, and the optimism of the *Minjung*[33] view of history starts from this.

When we reached the YMCA, several people had gathered. Among them there were attorney HONG Nam-Soon, Elder LEE Seong-Hak, attorney LEE Ki-Hong, Professor MYEONG Noh-Geun, YOON Young-Gyu, PARK Seong-Mu, JANG Du-Seok, and others. JEONG Sang-Yong, whom I had never seen before, was also there. I had heard about JEONG Sang-Yong, but I met him for the first time that day.

This was a very important meeting that would determine whether our course of action should be shifted from settlement to uprising. JEONG Sang-Yong explained that given the situation we had no choice but to choose uprising and began to try and persuade the non-government independent political figures to support his position. Except for Elder LEE Seong-Hak, no one

[33] *Minjung* refers to the people, especially the common people, the folk, the oppressed masses. The historiography of *Minjung* describes the progress of history made possible by the people, the subjects of history.

readily agreed. We were scared because the memories of the ruthless devastation that had continued until the previous days were so vivid.

The records of that meeting appear in detail in various places. Regardless of the positions of the people gathered there, the fact that they attended the meeting itself was later used as a decisive criterion for investigators to determine a person's tendency. The investigators believed that the political sentiments of the people at the meeting were obvious since they had been invited to a meeting at which those who later formed the leadership of the uprising asked them to support a shift from settlement to uprising. None of the people who attended the meeting were exempted from being given a sentence.

We were asked to issue a statement supporting the protest, but we concluded that we could not do it. When I entered the Province Hall, a violent temper was already in the air. The day before was the day of the Songam-dong massacre, and unlike the initial favorable attitude taken by the Martial Law Command, none of the conditions for settling the case that we sincerely offered to the Martial Law Command were properly met. We couldn't figure out the attitude of the Martial Law Command itself. It was later found out that the Martial Law Command and the Airborne had different command lines and were functioning separately. Since we were unable to get the inside story in depth, all such capricious attitudes could only be taken as their military tactics, and thus we had no choice but weighing only two options, shifting to a hardline stance or waiting longer.

At that time, KIM Chang-Gil, who visited the Martial Law Command four times as a representative of the Student Settlement Committee and met with the deputy commander Major General KIM Ki-Seok, maintained his trust in the military to the end. That was because of the sincere attitude that Major General KIM was showing. However, since the real power was already on the Airborne side, it seems that he was no longer in command. When

Professor MYEONG went to Sangmudae as the negotiating representative, he witnessed a scene where a one-star general cursed at Major General KIM Ki-Seok and pointed a pistol at him. This scene represents a typical case revealing the conflict within the military. Their conflict seems to have been so serious that such a disturbing scene was exposed to even the representatives of the citizens on our side. If the disagreement within the military over the Gwangju Uprising was serious enough for someone to pull out a pistol, I believe that this is a critical event that tells how the operational order for the Gwangju Uprising was decided. To me, it is still a puzzle that Major General KIM Ki-Seok was not called as a witness at the hearing about the Gwangju Uprising, given that he must be a far more decisive witness than CHUN Doo-Hwan just by the fact that he resigned from office after that incident.

At that time, it was inevitable that the positions taken by the citizen militia made up of students and citizen settlement committee members were divided into two. It would be reasonable to categorize the Citizen Settlement Committee members into a moderate surrender group and a hardline non-surrender group and divide the militia into the resistance and non-resistance groups. Among the Citizen Settlement Committee members, the moderate surrender group wanted to surrender their weapons unconditionally and wait for the authorities' mercy, while the hardline non-surrender group did not want to hand over their weapons until it was guaranteed that, as a minimum condition, they at least would not be punished for having taken up arms as a means of justifiable resistance against the paratroopers' indiscriminate slaughter of citizens. The hardline group believed that all responsibility lay with the Airborne. They made substantial concessions on the settlement conditions. However, the military did not accept the minimum condition. The so-called Namdong Catholic Church Group all refused to surrender themselves to the military.

Among the students, the moderate non-resistance group argued that their resistance with M1s or carbine rifles would be meaningless, more like committing suicide; therefore, they thought everyone had better retreat from the Province Hall. In contrast, the resistance group believed that the military would kill all those who had carried weapons as long as the military did not accept the condition of the exemption for the armed citizens, the condition that the Citizen Settlement Committee had proposed as the very last one.

As the overall atmosphere leaned toward the opinion of resistance, KIM Chang-Gil expressed his intention to step down as chair of the Student Settlement Committee, and his colleagues had already left the Province Hall. I tried to find KIM Chang-Gil but failed. After a while, however, I was able to meet him.

"Sir, what shall we do? Some people want to fight against the military; however, the military seems to want to kill all of us without mercy, as I have understood the attitude in the room of the Martial Law Command while going back and forth between here and there. The military has not put us down until today because some conscientious members in the military have held out, but they seem to be at the breaking point."

Mr. KIM Chang-Gil had been through sleepless nights since the 22nd, as his bloodshot eyes attested. As the Settlement Committee chair, he was quite overwhelmed and frustrated at his responsibility for the current situation.

He said, "I cannot agree to fight against the military at the expense of the people's lives."

"There is no room for argument about this issue, and each side deserves to be reasonably respected. Nobody can be forced to choose a side; the choice is totally up to each individual person," I said with sadness.

Long Nights on the Run

On the 26th, in the early morning, I received a call from a friend living in Hwajeong-dong, informing me that the operation seemed to be up and running, and tanks were entering the town. The progress of an event is evident only after the event is over; however, although no one could anticipate exactly what would happen at that time, I couldn't help but suspect that, if tanks had entered the downtown, an operation to put down the Province Hall had surely commenced. We couldn't even think about getting to the Province Hall because the Province Hall was the target of the operation.

I made a call to Professor MYEONG. I urged him that now was the right time to leave Gwangju; otherwise, the outskirts of the city would be blockaded right after the military put down the resistance in Province Hall.

We, four persons including Professor KIM Dong-Won, who came along from Seoul, and Professor LEE Hong-Gil, got out of Gwangju city, passing by a prison. There were a lot of people like us, and Titan trucks were delivering people to Damyang by charging one thousand won. We took a taxi from Damyang to Jangseong and headed for Seoul by train. From that moment, a wearisome one-month escape effort had begun.

In the meantime, we learned about the situation of Gwangju by newspaper and word-of-mouth, as we moved around to three or four places. On the basis of newspaper accounts of the ongoing investigation, the lawyer HONG Nam-Soon seemed to be targeted as a ringleader, which was completely ridiculous.

Moving around four or five places, I came to realize that Professor MYEONG and I were on the wanted list. At the beginning, that information was not open to the public. Later on, it was made public, with a reward of three million won and a special promotion by one rank offered for our capture. More specifically, our photos were televised and posted on walls. The situation we faced was becoming desperate, and it was too difficult to find shelter because possible providers were warned that they could be charged with harboring a criminal. We were at bay as they chased us down. We could realize how hard it was to be on the run while on the wanted list. Moreover, our relatives and friends who could potentially provide shelter were constantly monitored and watched, so we could not be near such places at all. Then we had to hide in places other than those, but we could not find them, and we could not even ask for a hiding place because we felt sorry for the providers. Because asking anyone to hide us meant risking imprisonment for the providers, we could not ask such a selfish favor. We were driven into a corner.

At the end of that time, it was Mrs. KANG Kwang-Pa, a graduate of Chonnam National University, who hid Professor MYEONG, Professor LEE Hong-Gil, and me. I still remember Mrs. KANG's generosity to us. Although her husband worked in a government office, she took great care of us because she thought that we might feel sorry for burdening them. Later, the couple almost got severely punished, but, fortunately, measures had been taken to protect them. In the early days, the aforementioned Mr. KIM had found two places for us to hide – at the houses of friends of his. Without these people, I don't think I could have held out mentally. However, such gratitude can be so easily forgotten. With bitter self-mockery, I sometimes repeat the proverb that says, "Don't take in animals with black hair."[34)]

Even while we were living a miserable life on the run, we occasionally had a laugh. One occasion was when people who had seen our wanted posters told us about them. They said that at the bottom of my picture, "handsome-man type" was written as one of my characteristics. In the wanted posters that I had seen on TV a few days earlier, expressions like "thief type" and "farmhand type" were used for the physical characteristics of wanted persons. A little bit better than those expressions was "handsome-man type at first glance" which was used to describe

---

34) Meaning, "Don't rescue and take in humans because they will betray you in the end."

LEE Byung-Joo, who was the chairman of Dong-A Committee for a Free Press at that time.

It cheered me up, even in such a situation, when I heard that I was described as a "handsome-man type."

"I think CHUN Doo-Hwan's administration will last a long time," I said with a serious look on my face.

"Why?"

My unexpected comment made the others open their eyes wide with astonishment.

"These guys know how to identify people. Think about it. Personal opinions may be involved in judging things like the Miss Korea Competition. But you have to be much stricter when judging the physical characteristics of political prisoners who threaten national security. These people observed my characteristics and described me with pinpoint accuracy as 'handsome-man type.' Don't you think they hit the nail on the head? 'Handsome-man type at first glance' means that he may look like a handsome guy at first, but he is not handsome if you look at him carefully, so you need to look carefully. But I was just described as 'handsome-man type,' period, without any additional words. So how accurately would you say these guys see people?"

They burst into laughter.

"You know the KS (Korean Industrial Standards) mark? It means that the government guarantees the quality of a product. Since these guys saw my face like that, I am a 'KS-certified handsome man' who is approved by the government."

They burst into laughter again.

Although we laughed like this, our painful reality was crushing us like torture.

A few professors hidden in Seoul had kept in touch with one another. After about a month had passed, we began to discuss whether or not we should continue hiding. It was painful to put such a huge burden on the people who hid us. The distress of our families at home was also enormous. We heard that our children could not even go home because people from four government organizations visited and bothered them every day. In the meantime, I contacted the president of CNU. He said that he was in a position to act as a kind of mediator between us and the authorities and that he had been promised that, at least, we would not be tortured. He told us to come out of hiding if we could, and most of us leaned toward doing that. However, each of us had played a different role, and so each was in a different position. It was expected that Professor MYEONG and I would be treated roughly. I didn't want to come out of hiding, so I met Mr. BAEK Nak-Cheong, with whom I had kept in touch throughout, and we discussed it. He told me to stay in hiding. He said that he would take the responsibility of getting a place for me to hide, even though that was difficult to do for all of the professors from CNU. It seemed that he had already found such a place.

The CNU professors, including MYEONG Noh-Geun, LEE Hong-Gil, KIM Dong-Won, and I, had a final discussion that evening. Most of the professors agreed to come out of hiding. I struggled to come to a decision. However, after much consideration, I also decided to come out. Considering how the police dragnet was closing in, it seemed that it was just a matter of time before we got caught. If we decided to give ourselves up, it would be better to emerge all together at once. Moreover, since as a mediator the CNU president had given us a kind of guarantee, we thought that if we came out then, we would be able to get that "benefit" —if it could be called a "benefit."

We decided to give ourselves up voluntarily, and we contacted Officer OH, the policeman who had been giving us news of the authorities through a friend. However, later we found out that we were reported to have been arrested — not to have given ourselves up voluntarily. This must have been a measure to win the reward. Of course, money is money, but it seemed that some would also do anything to get a special promotion within the police force. I realized the cruelty of human beings. After that, judging from the fact that the circumstances of our arrest were never mentioned at all, I suspect that there must have been a tacit agreement among them.

A Lost Child in the Basement

On June 27th, we were taken to the basement of the Defense Security Command. Starting from that first day, we were interrogated and were told to write affidavits. The other professors were assigned to the academic section, but Professor MYEONG and I were assigned to the dissidents section. At that time, the Joint Investigation HQ, which consisted of four agencies, including the Defense Security Command, the National Security Agency, the Military Police, and the Police, had four parts: the wiretapping section, the dissidents section, the academic section, and the local section. I was investigated mainly for my relationship with the Student Settlement Committee. That was the only involvement I had, so the investigation had no choice but to focus there. They seemed to expect something huge from me, so they seemed to be very disappointed when there was nothing else. The investigation continued on the third and fourth days, and no further interrogation was conducted. I thought things would be quite easy. The interrogation started again in about three days, I guess. During those three days, they might have conducted an extensive investigation into everything about me after finding that nothing special came out of me. Police Officer LEE was in charge of my investigation: he seemed to have met officials of the university and people of various classes during the investigation. He was not harsh to me, and told me I had gotten good character references from other people. He seemed to be talking about his impressions from the people he had met.

It was a few days later. He appeared with a quite nervous look and asked if I had ever met somebody whom KIM Dae-Jung had sent to me early in that year. I said no because no such thing had happened. But he held persistently to that line of questioning. At first, I didn't think much of it. But if I had any relationship with KIM Dae-Jung in that way, it was bound to be something tremendous. This is because they had written the scenario that the Gwangju Uprising was controlled by KIM Dae-Jung and focused all investigations on that. However, what he asked did not seem to be mere conjecture or a completely absurd thing: it seemed to be based on some kind of information. It was said that I met the person sent by KIM Dae-Jung at Mido Motel. When I said that there was no such fact at all, he did not investigate further.

Whenever Mr. LEE went to his superiors to report on the investigation, he told me he was going crazy. He seemed to have been severely rebuked for not being able to find out anything. But he continued to treat me favorably, and after a while he didn't show up anymore. Later, it turned out that he had quit the police at that time. That might be because he was kicked out of the Joint Investigation HQ. It was said that the policemen who had been called up to the Joint Investigation Department had special promotions one by one, but unfortunately, he was fired, though I'm not sure if it was solely because of me or something else.

It was a few days after such a back-and-forth dispute over my connection to KIM Dae-Jung. It was on June 27th that I voluntarily turned myself in. And I remember it must have been around July 4th when they seemed to clear out the entire basement. I guess that they moved out desks, cleaned the rooms, and moved everyone in the rooms to some other place. Lawyer HONG Nam-Soon, who was in the next room, was also moved out, and it seemed that everyone in the seven basement rooms had left. I thought they were going to let everyone go now, and I was waiting for my turn to leave, but there was no sign. The basement was quiet. I thought I might be the only one left, so I cleared my throat to see if there was anyone else outside in case they had forgotten about me. But there was no sign until dark. It seemed strange that a meal was delivered, which meant I'd not been forgotten.

"This Bastard is in Good Shape"

It was around midnight. I was called to the next room. That room was the largest room in the basement, three times the size of the room I had been in: it was a room where three or four teams were investigating at once. The room was cleared, and there were three desks next to each other, on which three investigators I had never seen before were seated in a row. At first glance, their faces were very tense. I looked around the room. Five or six long wooden sticks leaned in the corner of the room. It looked like they might have just been cut from a willow right before. I noticed that because a twig still had leaves on it. The sticks and the investigators' hard faces made me feel deadly despair. They did not look bloodthirsty or malicious but nervous, so I was able to see they were doing what they had been ordered to do. My sixth sense at such a moment was like that of an animal that feels harm that is coming to it.

The first thing they told me was to take off my clothes. I took them off. I took everything off except my underwear and shoes. I was placed in front of the desk in the middle of the three investigators sitting there, and then interrogated. The interrogation was focused on inquiring who was sent from KIM Dae-Jung. For that interrogation, they started asking the same questions from the beginning of the investigation. They asked about my activities from the early spring of that year. They pressed me carefully, double checking everything that was slightly different from the previous interrogations. That is, unlike the previous interrogations, they brought up my previous answers, examining them in detail one by one. However, unlike the earlier terrifying atmosphere, they did not beat or insult me but used honorifics. They questioned me continuously around the clock for three days in three shifts of three people each. In other words, nine people were divided into three teams of three people and interrogated me, just one person, for eight hours in three shifts for three days. For three nights and three days, I sat motionless in a chair and was questioned. The interrogation continued except for time to eat and time to go to the bathroom. Of course, not only could I not sleep, but I couldn't even turn my head to the side, not even once. The time I was in the bathroom couldn't have been more comfortable. That time I was in the cramped bathroom sealed with four walls was the only time I was free. I wondered how face-to-face contact between humans could be this painful.

It was early evening on the third day. Even then, the frustrating and tedious questioning continued, and it seemed like someone was coming in. At first glance, I could see a club in his hand. It was a short club as thick as someone's ankle. The guy touched my naked back all of a sudden.

"Hey, this bastard is in good shape!"

At that moment, he smacked me without mercy on the back with the club. There was a thump on my back. It was so sudden, but I dared not look back at the guy's face because I was so terrified and was expecting more frightening torture. What he was doing at that time was like the prank of a gangster who saw a pretty woman on the road and tried to fool around. It was a foreshadowing of the dreadful thrashing to come. It was because even though you were in such a place like that, you could not have done such a thing to anyone. From the sound of his words, he seemed a bit drunk, but it turned out later that he was Staff Sergeant KIM of the military police, and giving such beatings was his job there. So, he was brought there as one who professionally beats people up. He seemed to have drunk in advance because he knew he would torture me that day. That's why he smacked me like that in advance as a foretaste.

Judging from the three days of the interrogation and the fact that he drank, I expected that there would be torture that day, but the investigators in charge of me showed no sign of that. The day passed safely.

An Interrogation Specialist, A Torture Specialist

It was the next day, that is, the fourth day after moving to that room. The night was deep. It was around midnight. Police Officer KIM, the chief of Section Two, that is, the dissident section, to which I belonged, came in. The interrogators tensed up and gave him a middle seat. Not only the interrogators whose turn it was in the room but also those who had gone off duty came and watched with frightened eyes. The investigation into me seemed to have been of great interest to them.

"Hey, you asshole. Who told you to let him put his shoes on?!"

He was angry that I was wearing my shoes. I took off my shoes and socks.

"Put the club between his legs!"

Staff Sergeant KIM who smacked me on the back the previous day told me to kneel on the ground. He made me lift my hips and put the club that he had hit me with the previous day between my knees under my calves. So, the day before, the club was not just carried around in vain, but it must have been for that purpose. After putting the club in, he ordered me to lower my hips and raise my hands. I had never heard of this form of torture, but at first glance it seemed bearable. But as time went by, that was not the case. In less than five minutes, sweat flowed down, and the ground under my knees was soaked. What was more unbearable was the coarse sand stuck under my knees. If a cement floor is swept with a broom, coarse sand is usually swept away, but the Defense Security Command building was a new building at the time and had a lot of coarse sand, probably because of shoddy construction. And I felt like I was going crazy because the sand was stuck under the bare skin at the tip of the bone.

Staff Sergeant KIM was standing on one side, holding a willow club that had been placed in the corner in advance, and the interrogators next to him looked frightened. In that state, KIM's ferocious interrogation began. It wasn't about KIM Dae-Jung, but about all sorts of petty things. He did that kind of interrogation for about thirty minutes. I later found out that such an interrogation was a preliminary one to intimidate me. The hatred on his face during the interrogation was truly terrifying. It showed a murderous spirit as if he held a personal grudge against the one who killed his parents. I wondered if such an expression could be made otherwise. Some describe the expression as that of the Grim Reaper, and I had an impression that he could have come from the other world, not from this world. I didn't feel any human emotions or reason at all from him. All I could feel from him was a monstrous bloodthirstiness. It seemed that a ghost who had died with some kind of resentment to all humans in the world had survived the grave. His face was pale, making him seem even more inhumane. Every word he uttered was not a word, but a knife that digs into a person's flesh. Every time he spoke, he seemed to be pouring poisonous gas out of his mouth.

I still get goosebumps when I think of that face. Perhaps he is an extremely excellent investigator, and he is an extremely suitable person for such a job. As a person, it was not a job to have. It is for an interrogation and torture machine such as LEE Geun-Ahn.

The Precipitous Cliff of Despair

After thirty minutes of interrogation, he asked something and I said "No," and he suddenly shouted and jumped onto the desk at once. There was a porcelain bowl next to him, and he was about to hit me right away with the bowl. It was not Staff Sergeant KIM's club, but the bowl that would come running to me.

"Hey, you punk. Do you know where you are? There's no one in here right now. Even if I kill you here, the Gwangju incident death toll will only increase by one. Say the right thing!"

He continued to shout while threatening me with the bowl. Now I don't remember what he asked, but I answered at once what he wanted me to answer. If someone observed this in a normal state of mind, they might hear these threats as just intimidation, but that was not how I reacted in my condition. I believed he was ready to kill me right there. While under investigation for four days, I guessed that their script was to hold me responsible for the entire Gwangju Uprising.

What led me to such a judgment was not only the content but the atmosphere of the interrogation. The fact that they emptied the entire basement, even sent out all the soldiers guarding the hallway, and interrogated me all together, though the interrogation could have been done by each interrogator in turn, as well as the fact that they all seemed very nervous, pointed to that conclusion. I also knew that HONG Nam-Soon, a lawyer who seemed to have been pointed out as the ringleader of this incident by an interim report made public in the newspaper, was released from this room, and they were interrogating me in this way.

Lawyer HONG was investigated with several people, and when I overheard their investigation from the next room, though the interrogation was the last step, they were asking petty details, and he thoroughly denied even very obvious facts about himself. Therefore, I thought that lawyer HONG, who spent his entire life under the law, couldn't be manipulated to appear as the ringleader, and they chose me instead to invent as the head of this incident. At the same time, at first I was suspicious, but I thought it must be because I saw the chief of the department himself come and question me so mercilessly. The chief directs the entire investigation, but there had never before been such a direct interrogation by the chief of a department.

Then I thought that it is meaningless being beaten and enduring such violence. Already, I was in despair of not being able to survive. As he said, there was no one in the cellar except for the investigators since all other people had been sent out. In the past, armed guards were in the hallway, but even they were sent out, too.

When I obediently answered his question in the affirmative, he put down the bowl and sat back into place. He was looking down at me. There was a long silence.

"If you don't want to die here, speak correctly. You met the man KIM Dae-Jung sent, right?"

Finally, something came out of my mouth. I, who was already in despair, replied "Yes" as soon as he asked, as if I was ready for the question. If I said no, the bowl would fly at once and destroy my face. If he had decided to extract the sound from my mouth, no matter what, I thought it was meaningless to endure their violence and become crippled. So, rather than suffering such torture and dying from it, I was already choosing to have a rope wrapped around my neck and to be formally executed with a death penalty.

The moment I answered without any resistance, I heard a light sigh from the investigators who stood next to me. For the last three days, I had wrangled with them and persistently refused to confess, but now I confessed immediately. They seemed to feel betrayed by me. At that moment, they may have felt skeptical about their more polite method of questioning. When I listened to their sigh, a lot of thoughts about manipulation crossed my mind, and I thought this was how to manipulate someone. They made me say the exact words they wanted from my mouth. Their manipulation was so skillful that even their gang was fooled by it.

"Mmm, I knew it. Where did you meet that person?"

He looked satisfied and asked me in a very low voice.

"I met him at Mido Motel."

I had no choice but to answer as they said.

"On which floor?"

"The second floor"

"The second floor. The room number?"

"I can't remember that."

"Which side on the second floor?"

"West side on the second floor."

I answered whatever came out of my mouth because I had been to Mido Motel before.

"So, what is his name?"

That was a hard question to answer. If I hesitated to answer, the bowl would fly at me. But I couldn't say some name randomly. They had to give the name to me in order to manipulate my answer because there was no such fact from the beginning. In other words, if they intended to manipulate the situation to make it appear as if I revealed the fact, they had to ask a question of me by mentioning the real name.

"I don't know the name."

Even if the bowl flew at me and hit me, I couldn't help it.

"Mmm, by the way, what message did KIM Dae-Jung send to you?"

Here again, the only question was what answer he wanted. When I hesitated for a moment, Staff Sergeant KIM's club flew across my back. He smacked my back with a two-meter club the thickness of his forearm. For a moment, the thought that crossed my mind was not the pain. I thought that my liver or lungs might have been dislocated. I tried to breathe and I was sure that I could breathe normally. My lungs were safe. I was reassured., There is a saying that "My liver dropped."[35] But it was surprising that my lungs didn't get hurt even after being hit so hard with such a long, thick club. The moment I got hit with the club, I thought my liver or lungs were ruptured. That's because the ruthless-looking Staff Sergeant KIM swung the thick, long, and raw willow club with all his might and smashed me in the back. In order for him to swing the club freely, it seemed that unnecessary items such as a desk had been removed from the large room. It was only during the interrogation of me that the room was cleared. Based on this, I guessed that they had never given a beating like that to any of the others interrogated before me.

"He told me to instigate and elevate an atmosphere of protest among students."

He was satisfied with my answer.

My Mind Is as Clear as a Mountain Stream

"You received money from KIM Dae-Jung, didn't you?"

When I heard that, I fell into despair again. They would accept my answer if I said that I got a large sum, such as ten million won or more, on KIM Dae-Jung's orders. But then it was obvious that they would ask me to whom I had given the money. If they did, I would have to lie to them by telling some people's names. Even though I had been interrogated in one seat for four full days, and I couldn't sleep for three nights, my mind was as clear as a stream in a deep mountain valley. At that time, I had nothing but an animal instinct to avoid getting beaten and to survive. But I was disconcerted when I had to fake the name of someone who had nothing to do with it. However, I realized that if it would happen anyway, it was best to give them as few names as possible.

I understood that bad things had already happened to me and it had been unavoidable. Now the amount of money was the important issue because it would determine not only the number

---

35) The idiom means to be extremely startled, scared out of one's wits, or scared to death. Professor SONG plays on the figurative language as he continues.

of people involved but the scope of the case. Namely, it was a major turning point in the investigation. How much money would I have to say for them to accept my words? Twenty million won? No! Would it be better if I said ten million won no matter how many times I got hit by the club? No! Five million won? I decided five million won at the risk of my liver being dislodged by a blow from the club. Actually, it didn't take long to think about the sum. I didn't have much time because if I hesitated just a bit, the club would fly at me. This complicated thought process ran through my head before the next blow by the club.

"I got five million won from him"

"Mmm, five million won. Cash or check?"

Unexpectedly, they took my word for the five million won. I could breathe a sigh of relief for a moment.

"It was cash"

"Five bundles of one million won, right?"

"Yes."

"Was it new or old?"

"It was new money."

"Where did you put it?"

"One bundle was in this pocket, the other one was in this pocket."

I chose not to be beaten to death right away, but to extend my life a little bit and to be hung without so much pain. I was a beast that only had an animal desire to avoid the ruthless club.

He asked me if I took a taxi or walked home with the money, and asked me where I put the money while I was sleeping.

The Language of Betrayal Is Like Chewing Iron

"Who did you give that money to?"

Finally, the expected question came out. Several faces had

already come to mind. They were KIM Sang-Yoon, JEONG Dong-Nyeon, HAN Sang-Seok, Professor MYEONG Noh-Geun, and others. Judging from their investigation of or preemptive arrest of KIM Sang-Yoon and JEONG Dong-Nyeon, they seemed to have drawn up a scenario based on Chonnam National University. Then, distinct people such as KIM Sang-Yoon were inevitable subjects of attention, anyway, according to this scenario. I thought it was very fortunate that the money was minimized to five million won. I gave out the names above except for Professor MYEONG, insisting I distributed about 500,000 won evenly. My heart was torn by the painful betrayal as if my mouth, naming my students, was chewing iron.

However, in the case of Professor MYEONG, there was a problem. Readmitted students had been active since the beginning of the semester, but professors had never been active. If I told him that I gave 500,000 won to Professor MYEONG Noh-Geun, Professor MYEONG would have to drag other people in or pretend that he had taken a role large enough to be commensurate to the amount of money, and to do so would be difficult in many ways. So with a slight reduction, I said I gave 300,000 won to Professor MYEONG. I named about six people and said I spent the remaining two million won. I said I paid off my debts, paid off my bar tab, and stood some people to drinks. In light of the purpose of the money, I had committed a kind of breach of trust.

The interrogation was going on when an embarrassing thing happened. Suddenly, Professor MYEONG Noh-Geun came in wearing only underwear like me. Come to think of it, not only I but also Professor MYEONG had been locked up in the other room in the basement. The torturer who beat me was bored because he didn't have a chance to beat me. Then when I said Professor MYEONG Noh-Geun's name, he went to the other room and beat Professor MYEONG, asking how much money he received from a man called SONG something. Even Professor MYEONG, who was stubborn, couldn't help it in the face of the beating.

"He also confessed that he received the money."

Staff Sergeant KIM spoke proudly.

"How much did you get from SONG Ki-Sook?"

"I've got 500,000 won."

Already, our words did not match each other. It would have been a disaster if I had said that I had given 500,000 won to Professor MYEONG as well. Mr. KIM was ordered to take Professor MYEONG back.

Although it was the feeling of a cruel heart, I felt relieved that Professor MYEONG was in the basement together with me. I thought I could understand the harsh hearts of leprosy patients who hoped that everyone in the world would become leprosy patients.

It turned out that Professor LEE Hong-Gil also remained there. Staff Sergeant KIM went to the other room alone and beat Professor LEE when the opportunity to beat me didn't come soon enough. Professor LEE was beaten mercilessly. The room was so small that it seemed he was beaten with a short club, but I heard thudding noises and some grim screams. Later, a scream that almost seemed as if he were dying burst out. I thought he might die.

After interrogating me about the source of the money, the chief moved on to more important issues. Then again, it came to the point of identifying the name of the person sent by KIM Dae-Jung. When I said I didn't know, he yelled at me to tell the truth. At that moment, the torturer's club pounded on my back. However, there was no way I could manipulate the answer. The club kept falling. Whenever I was hit, I tried to breathe reflexively. No matter how much I hoped otherwise, it seemed that not muscles but the liver or lungs would be damaged by such a tremendous clubbing. I endured three or four blows that hit one after another, but I couldn't bear it anymore and rolled on the cement floor. Even though I was beaten so mercilessly, I only breathed reflexively every time I was hit to make sure my lungs were okay. It was almost an instinctive animal reaction. I acknowledged all the claims that implicated me to save my life for the time being and not to be disabled; it was an unconscious response like the animal instinct for life. Although it sounds unbelievable, I barely felt pain while being beaten. I was only scared of whether there might be something wrong with my liver or lungs. A miserable animal was rolling around in pain just like that, only to confirm whether or not its lungs were okay when the club was falling.

My Choice as Pre-determined Death

I was rolling around in pain for a while; then, the thrashing stopped. The chief made me kneel down again. At that moment, one of the investigators who had shown some favor to me said something to the chief and took me to the next room. He was not a cop. It was the room where I had been a few days ago.

"What was happened? If you already revealed your guilt, why are you letting yourself get such a hard time by not telling his name? Does it make sense that you do not know his name whose task is as important as that? Your pain here is meaningless."

Although he was not the investigator who was in charge of me, he had sometimes dropped by my room and shown favor to me ever since I had been brought there. Since I felt like all of the favors were part of the interrogation scheme, I was somewhat wary of him. For this reason, when he inquired what happened to me before moving to this room, I replied that nothing I confessed had actually happened. He asked again whether he could trust me, and I said that he could bet on my character; he tilted his head, saying it was strange. This made me vaguely think that they might not have set up the whole thing; rather, they might have some information about the man whom they believed KIM Dae-Jung had sent to me.

Since he came over to me and earnestly inquired about the

matter again, in spite of such a tough situation, I began to think what he showed to me could be a pure favor rather than a scheme for the investigation.

"To be honest, I have never met such a man."

I told the truth.

"What? Then, why did you say that you met him?"

He seemed to be baffled.

"How could I endure without saying yes during such a brutal beating?"

"Heh heh, don't you know how important this is right now? It is a matter of whether you live or die. You would be a ringleader who is supposed to take the whole responsibility for the Gwangju Incident. The ringleader! If you are considered to be the ringleader, you will die. Die! If there wasn't any meeting, tell the truth from now on."

He took me back to the room.

"To be honest, I never met the man."

"What?"

Mr. KIM contorted his face at once.

"You bastard, you still need more beating."

The club came down again in a moment as if it had been waiting for a time when Mr. KIM spoke the word. In thinking that I had been mocking his clubbing by lying to him, Mr. KIM became even more angry, and he swung the club with all his force, more malignantly clenching his teeth. I rolled over again. This time I was rolling around on the wooden floor without any moment to breathe.

"I met him. I met him."

The beating stopped. If I were beaten like that, I could be seriously injured and might not be able to live a normal life, even if I were able to stay alive.

"What's his name, then?"

"I really don't know his name."

"You bastard, you are making fun of me!"

Overjoyed at the Thought of Survival because of a Broken Shoulder

The club came down again. I rolled over again. I was beaten that way for a while. At that moment, there was cracking sound from my left shoulder. It was the sound of breaking bones from the club hitting my shoulder. It was the left arm. There was no doubt about the sound of breaking bones, since it was a brief cracking sound. I felt like I could survive. That is because, if my shoulder was broken and my arm dangled, such a state might not allow them to hit me more. They, too, seemed perplexed by the sound. I tried to move my left arm. But what on earth is this? My arm was lifted. It was not broken. I found out later that my arm was not completely broken, but it was about four-fifths broken with some parts still attached.

Then, he covered my head with a black cloth. As if the cloth had been made for such a purpose, it was just the right size to fit over my head; and it even had a string that he could tighten around my neck like a pants string.

I felt like I was going crazy when he covered my face in cloth. At other times, I could sense the club coming and its direction. But after they covered me with the cloth, there was only black despair. It was a series of fears because I didn't know when and where the club would hit me. I had never thought this would make such a big difference.

"We met."

The club stopped.

"What's his name?"

"Actually, I've never met such a person."

"You bastard!"

The beating began again. I was knocked down again.

"I met him."

The beating stopped. What's his name; I don't know. You bastard. I met him. I didn't meet him. A sequence of arguing and beating continued. The investigator who interrogated me shortly before took me to the next room again. The same words were said. He looked really frustrated. The investigator advised me not to change my words if he wasn't present. But I couldn't be sure I would be able because I was really afraid of the beating.

I came back and the beating continued. It was a repetition of "I met him" and "I didn't meet him." After some time, the beating stopped and the cloth was removed. It was getting bright outside the basement window. This meant the day had dawned. I guessed I was beaten from around midnight to dawn. It was so harsh. I'd been struck more than a hundred times.

The most ruthless beating I've ever heard of was about people involved in the YWCA counterfeit wedding around the end of 1979. From what I heard from those who suffered at the time, such as BAEK Ki-Wan, LIM Chae-Jung, and KIM Byung-Gul, the beating at that time was not just a beating as torture, but a tremendous retaliation which resulted in them being disabled. It was said that they had been beaten indiscriminately on their backs and legs. Fortunately, the beating I got was still better than what they got. Although the beating was harsh, I usually got hit on the back, and it was not fatally dangerous. There would be a difference between professional torturers and those who are not.

Hell Is on the Edge of Hellfire

Mr. KIM (the section chief not the sergeant) ordered me to write everything I told him and went out. For about half a day, the investigators examined the records I wrote down again, and it seemed that the investigation was over. For the next three days, I was imprisoned in another room, and I seemed to have been moved to another place again. A car carrying me left the Defense Security Command. I guessed I was headed for the military prison in Sangmudae. I felt like I had just escaped the slaughterhouse. But the car went somewhere else. It was a small room of the Defense Security Command in Sangmudae. It was a small Japanese-style wooden building next to the catholic church, and it was used by an American military advisory group. Just a couple of soldiers were working in this small building, but they locked me in a room, and I was kept under their armed guard. Their strictest vigilance made me helpless. The hope that I might live was shattered in the blink of an eye.

Meanwhile, there was a long desk, so I was able to lie down and sleep for the first time in days. It was really the first time since I had been interrogated. I was lucky because I didn't have to see the investigators, but it was obvious what this strict imprisonment and constant vigilance meant. Without knowing what would happen to me, I was imprisoned there for about twenty days. Once, I had a chance to talk about hell with a pastor. At that time, I said hell is not hellfire in a boiling kiln, but on the periphery of such a kiln. It's because if I fell in a kiln, that would be all, but the possibility of falling made me crazy.

One day, I heard a piano melody from the catholic church. It was John Howard Payne's "Home Sweet Home," with the lyrics, "Be it ever so humble, there's no place like home." This familiar melody made me feel disharmony. How can such a peaceful song be sung in the world without regard of my desperate crisis while I was wandering near death?

I guess it was on the third day that something unusual happened. I had been reading the Bible there, but suddenly I couldn't read it that morning. I could only see the big letters but couldn't see the small letters at all. There is an old story that a person who was chased by a tiger barely escaped death by climbing a tree. Next morning when he woke up, he found his hair had turned white because of the previous day's distress. My agony at that time was close to his.

I later found out that Professor MYEONG Noh-Geun was also in the room next to mine. I realized he was there only about three days after he had arrived because the security was very tight. There was a not-so-funny reason that Professor MYEONG came there so late. At that time when the investigation of my case was finished, I was confined to a terrible place. The place was where cleaning tools were kept by blocking the space beneath the stairs going up. The space was so narrow that I couldn't even stand properly. Around the middle of the night, there was a sound of urgent footsteps coming down the stairs. It was an investigator who came to interrogate me. He looked for me from room to room and asked the guard on the stairs where I was. When I told him I was here, he muttered, "Who locked you up in such a place?" and ordered the guard to open the iron door. He took me to another room.

"Hey, you. It is said that you gave money to the riot police on May 16th. Where did you get the money?"

"This was already investigated before. The students were eating bread, but the riot police were just watching them eat. I felt sorry for them, so I raised money from the professors. Over 90,000 won was raised, and the money was handed over to the Dean of Student Affairs. I heard that the Dean made it 100,000 won and gave it to the riot police."

"Damn, it's nothing."

He stopped writing in the investigation record.

"Why do you lock me up in such a place? Let me just stay here."

"Okay, you stay here."

That was how I got out of the terrible place, but the next day, as there were not enough investigation rooms, they took Professor MYEONG to that place. So, he was locked up in that stifling small room for a week and then came to the branch office of Sangmudae. After that, I laughed at the story, saying that if you do good, you will be blessed like that.

Natural Healing of Broken Shoulders

Professor MYEONG and I were transferred from there to the military police guardhouse after twenty days. It seemed that I avoided being wrongly accused as a ringleader. In order to be accused as a ringleader, being connected with KIM Dae-Jung was a prerequisite in their scenario, but it seemed that they gave up on accusing me as a ringleader since the allegation that I met someone sent by KIM Dae-Jung did not turn out to be true. I assumed that they gave up because other things could be fabricated with more possibility of success, but if they had fabricated such a crucial part of their story without any evidence, and then an alibi was established or the crucial part was revealed as a lie, the whole scheme could go completely wrong. If that had turned out to be true, I would have suffered to the point of being physically disabled if I had been accused as a ringleader, and they would have fabricated other incidents. In the case of JEONG Dong-Nyeon, he had visited KIM Dae-Jung's house once before, and this fact met the prerequisite of their scenario, so he was wrongly accused as a ringleader.

While I was imprisoned, the bruises spread down both of my shoulders. I only got hit on the back, but the bruising was so deep that it spread to both shoulders and gradually went down. Later, it went down to my fingertips and then slowly lifted up at the same speed it had descended. When I came to Sangmudae, I asked for treatment, saying my shoulders were broken, but my request was repeatedly rejected. Even my request for having X-rays taken was rejected. I guess they rejected my pleas because they were afraid that rumors would get out that a professor had been beaten and his bones broken. But my shoulders were healing naturally.

After a while, I could feel coarse lines running along the bones of my shoulders. The lines were about half the thickness of a finger and wrapped around the length of the shoulders. They wrapped around the shoulder blades in an oblique angle, a bit off from the spine. The lines naturally revealed the ways my shoulders were broken when I was beaten by the club. The cracked parts became their own casts. It was a mystery of the human body.

At that time, we didn't know, but it would have been the same time that the investigation of JEONG Dong-Nyeon's case was concluded by wrongly accusing him as a ringleader that we were moved to the guardhouse of the military police. A few days later, an investigator came back. Having observed the investigation process, I could guess that the investigation was in its final stage. He only asked me trivial questions such as what I thought of KIM Dae-Jung and how I escaped to Seoul. I was tired of arguing because he forced me to say things, so I told him that I would just sign a blank paper and he could write anything he wanted. The investigator would think, "What a windfall!" I signed by pressing my thumb print on about twenty blank sheets of paper. I did so because I thought I must have escaped the death penalty. I had the courage that it wouldn't matter if I was sentenced to life in prison or twenty years as long as I was exempted from the death penalty. This was because for political criminals there was not much difference between a sentence of life or a year in prison if they were exempted from the death penalty. In fact, in the case of the Gwangju Uprising, even JEONG Dong-Nyeon, who received the death penalty, was released after being imprisoned a little longer than a year.

The second trial ended after I was transferred to six places; first to a prison, then back to the Air Force guardhouse, and moved back to a prison, and so on. The prosecutor demanded ten years, and the court sentenced me to five years in prison. After the Supreme Court confirmed that sentence of five years in prison on April 3rd of the following year, I was released from prison after receiving a reprieve in the course of the cross-examination by a judicial office.

The Airborne Should Be Disgusted by Their Own Deeds

Ten years have passed since the Gwangju Uprising. During that time, the Gwangju People's Uprising seemed to have sublimated politically to a higher level with the June 29 Uprising[36)], but today's political reality shows that the June 29 Declaration is nothing more than a deceptive political tactic. What is the Gwangju Uprising? It is a cry for the democratization of this country from the beginning to the end, and it was a murderous suppression that crushed the earnest yearning for democracy with guns and bayonets. The military brazenly justified their brutality in the name of both-sides-ism[37)], but this is no different from a robber who is caught by the police arguing that the responsibility should be equally shared as he was beaten in the course of the arrest.

Just by looking at the massacre that took place in Songam-dong, on the outskirts of Gwangju, we can see how shameless their claims are. They seriously wounded a peasant by shooting him while he was picking weeds in a rice field, killed a first-year middle school student bathing in a reservoir as if they were duck hunting, killed a woman hiding under a drainpipe by shooting her six times, and killed a fourth-year elementary school boy who tried to pick up his rubber shoes that had come off while running away from the soldiers by shooting him ten times and literally tearing apart his body. They also shot cages of domestic fowl and

36) The witness refers to the June Democratic Struggle, a nationwide pro- democracy movement that took place from June 10th to June 29th, 1987. The 6.29 Declaration was announced as a response from the government to this widespread public uprising.

37) "Yang-si-ron" (兩是論) refers to a tendency to justify both sides of an issue equally, and in this context, the witness might have meant bilateral responsibility which falsely exempts the accountability of the martial law forces.

killed more than 200 animals as well as shot cows to death. This slaughter took place entirely in Songam-dong. It wasn't because of the excitement caused by the battle. But it was done while they were moving troops on May 24th after retreating to the outskirts of the city on May 22nd and taking a break from the conflict for two days.

With weapons paid for by taxpayers for the purpose of protecting their country, they brutally murdered their own people, not their enemies, including innocent children. That is something that hardly happens even to enemies. If this was not done according to the commander's intent, the person in charge should have killed himself. But there was no such commander. All of them have given up on being human. Or, rather, they were not human beings in the first place as they crushed the people and took power by using the fear of ruthless slaughter.

The people, freed from their fears, rose again. It was the June Uprising of 1987. Those in power conceded in the nationwide struggle at last and declared democracy, and the people chose politics without shedding blood, believing their words. However, in the meantime, they have betrayed the people. During the ten years after 1980, they betrayed the wishes made by the bloody outcries of Gwangju and the people.

Setting aside everything else, there can be no place for justice in this country without punishment for the person in charge of the random shooting at the little hands of the elementary-school fourth-grader who tried to retrieve his rubber shoes that came off while he was running away. How can a murderous robber or a thief be punished, and, moreover, those who accidentally strike someone in a car accident, without punishment for that person? After August 15,[38] the history of this land that for forty-five years did not punish the pro-Japanese national traitors has been a

---

38) August 15th, 1945, the date on which Korea was liberated from thirty-five years of Japanese colonial rule.

history of nihilism that denies justice. Our struggles had all been in vain. Take examples from the Japanese colonial period. The descendants of those who stood up for independence all ended up being uneducated or beggars, didn't they?

Just as those who wielded great power during the Japanese colonial period took power again and lived on the fat of the land, there will be no justice in this land even if forty-five or even 450 years have passed, unless there is due punishment of those people. People are pre-occupied with material well-being, making a fuss about economic development, but, unless we punish such people and establish justice, our children will be left in a defenseless state in the face of the guns of such ruthless power zealots that will appear again and again in the future.

But we have to be sober in dealing with our pursuit of justice. The Nazis, who were infected with Hitler's madness and slaughtered six million Jews, trembled at Hitler when waking up from their madness. The penitence of Germans for such ruthless crimes is the moral pillar of Germany today.

A human being cannot shoot a child bathing in a reservoir or a fourth-grader reaching for his shoe. Their leaders had driven their men into such madness as Hitler did his people. They destroyed their human personality and turned them into demons that harm people. There were rumors the soldiers were on drugs. That was because their deeds were something human beings cannot commit. Whether it was due to drugs or some sort of hypnosis, it is an undeniable fact that they did something that real humans could not do, and those who are in charge were not held responsible for the cause or the effect, and only rose to power.

Here we realize that the soldiers who shot the Gwangju citizens mercilessly at that time were nothing more than victims themselves who had become automatons manipulated by the military leaders. That is, the soldiers were victims who committed a crime that was unimaginable for a human being because their humanity had already been damaged. We can neither blame them nor the guns during the Gwangju Uprising. Rather, we need to console them as the victims, because they will also be trembling like the Nazis in Germany under Hitler's control.

Shortly after I was released from prison, Professor LEE Hong-Gil said that he met the torturer Staff Sergeant KIM in a public bathhouse, and that seeing him was terrifying. But when he saw that the staff sergeant had brought his son there to bathe, he felt that the staff sergeant was such a caring father. We discussed how we should treat him if we happened to meet him in the future. After long discussion, we concluded that we should pat him in the back, saying "You must have had a hard time doing what you hated to do at that time." We decided to do that. This is not meant to be hypocritical. The staff sergeant would think that we will surely be hostile to him, but if we act unexpectedly in this way, he will feel a great internal conflict, and he might be enlightened by comparing us with the people who made him do such inhumane acts. This, of course, is based on the idea that he is only a beating machine, a functionary who does whatever he is ordered to do.

Where Has Politics Gone?

Politics has consistently betrayed the spirit of the Gwangju Uprising for the last ten years. As a result, the 10th anniversary of this uprising was celebrated without even the enactment of a compensation law. Moreover, in the process of discussing the enactment of the law, even the spirit of the protest was distorted. When the Peace and Democracy Party suggested a compensation of 300 million won to the deceased, the former Republican Party called for a compensation of 350 million won, adding 50 million won. They acted irresponsibly as if bidding at an auction. It gave the impression that the greater the compensation for the dead or injured, the more satisfactorily the question of Gwangju would be resolved. The Gwangju Uprising was diminished to the level of such a thing as a traffic accident that could be settled with a lot of money.

While the politicians were talking only about money in this way, the bereaved and the wounded were building luxurious houses in their imaginations with their 300 or 350 million. At the same time, even the citizens who had been arrested assumed monetary compensation as a matter of course and had the illusion of building an expensive tile-roofed house soon. Unlike some dead or wounded people, the arrested citizens are those who participated in the protest voluntarily, at least running the risk of a certain level of sacrifice. Therefore, since the price for their sacrifice has been paid with the democratic development of this country, for them to demand monetary compensation is a contradiction in which they deny their voluntary involvement. What is the restoration of honor, and what is monetary compensation for them? Politics is responsible for this confusing situation.

In addition, since the politicians, even those in the opposition party, discussed compensation only on an individual level, the Gwangju Uprising has become individualized and limited as if it were a struggle of only those who suffered visible damages. This alienated other citizens and residents of Gwangju and Jeollanam-do, who were the actual subjects of the uprising. It is true that the dead and wounded individually suffered the most, but their damage is only a fraction of what was suffered by all the citizens and residents of Gwangju and Jeollanam-do. Moreover, many of the dead or wounded involuntarily participated, and they were not only people who took part in the struggle. In short, the main body of the uprising was all the citizens of Gwangju and Jeollanam-do.

If the compensation is for damages, it should be made in some way to the vast majority of citizens of the province and city, even if they suffered minor damage individually.

Some citizens claim that it is reasonable to make indirect compensation by introducing the concept of collective compensation here, because there is a technical problem of objectifying any individual's damage. Turning the Sangmudae site into a commemorative park, as the Peace and Democracy Party insists, could be a good example. For translating this view into action, the Uprising Foundation that will lead these projects must be legally organized, and the operating funds must be secured as compensation. Therefore, the emphasis of political negotiation should be put on this point rather than monetary compensation for individual victims. In the current political system, efforts toward this direction will be best.

In that the Gwangju People's Uprising is one of the fundamental starting points of our country's democratization movement, the legal organization of an Uprising Foundation which will inherit and nurture this spirit, and the procurement of the funds as collective compensation have the following multiple meanings.

(1) Since the Gwangju People's Uprising is a great milestone in the progress of democratization in Korea, the settlement of the Uprising acquires historical significance by nailing down a tangible inheritance that will pass on and amplify the Uprising spirit instead of compensating for individual damages. This is because the Gwangju Uprising is not something to be resolved with financial compensation like a traffic accident, but a great event for which the compensation is to entrust its spirit to history.

(2) Securing the operating funds for the Commemorative Association in the cause of collective compensation for the damage of all Gwangju citizens and Jeonnam provincial residents results in correcting the false perception that only those who suffered visible damage, such as deaths, injuries, and detention, have been the subjects of the Gwangju Uprising. Rather, the practical subject of the Gwangju Uprising was the entirety of the people who lived in the area of Gwangju city and Jeollanam-do Province.

(3) The plan to turn Sangmudae into a memorial park, which

the Peace and Democracy Party claims, is also meaningful as a fruit of the protest when it is proudly demanded in terms of compensation for damage to Gwangju citizens and Jeollanam-do provincial residents, not in terms of a benefit granted by the government. It is pretty obvious that the park will have proper significance as a memorial park only when it is argued and enforced as a concept of rights.

(4) If the Commemorative Association becomes a legal organization, the Association can prevent political distortion or abuse of the spirit of the Gwangju Uprising by directly managing all elements of the memorial project such as commemorative events, the monuments, memorial towers, memorial parks, and memorial cemeteries. Even when a memorial tower is to be built, the Association must lead the project so that the inscription on the tower can suit the consciousness and senses of Gwangju citizens and Jeollanam-do residents. Seeing that the government used to distort and exploit the spirit of the March 1st Independence Movement and the April 19th Democratic Struggle at the convenience of the regime, an independent organization like the Commemorative Association must manage all the events concerning the Gwangju Democratic Movement by itself.

(5) Because the Gwangju Uprising is a democracy movement in its nature, legitimate activities of the Commemorative Association will not be suppressed even when an undemocratic regime is established. That way, the Commemorative Association will be able to carry out a permanent democratization movement in a legitimate space.

If the Commemorative Association is established as a foundation, and if the board members are appointed by the National Assembly or the city council, or the provincial council, the Association will be able to maintain its objectivity in practicing its business. It is not right if only the victims such as bereaved families, injured people, and detainees should participate in this. If such an organization is legally established, the agents of the project will be able to receive a grant of park sites and exclude outside political influences in putting the projects into practice with designated funding, and so will be able to do it objectively.

I visited KIM Dae-Jung, leader of the Peace and Democracy Party, together with some professors, and we strongly insisted on the establishment of this Commemorative Association. We also tried to get the project included in the political agenda of the Peace and Democracy Party. We even visited the senior members of the Democratic Liberal Party to elicit a promise of cooperation. However, the Peace and Democracy Party has something to repent of as a political party in even approaching the matter of the compensation law. None of the members of National Assembly representing the Peace and Democracy Party would have been elected to the National Assembly without selling the name and values of the Gwangju Uprising in the election campaign. Nevertheless, their attitude of dealing with it has been too insincere. In discussing the compensation law, which is a tangible expression of a political resolution to the Gwangju Uprising, they just made noises about the cost being practically unfeasible. They revealed their shortsightedness in neglecting to strengthen the spirit of the Uprising.

4. The Province Hall

1011. The Judgment of the Nation and History

The Witness: CHO Cheol-Hyeon (Baptismal name: Pius, male)
Year of Birth: 1936 (aged 44)
Occupation: Catholic Priest
Date of Record: December 1989

Research & Arrangement by YANG Nan-Hee

Notes: What follows here is based on a direct interview as well as the book entitled *Resistance and Meditation* written by Father CHO Pius, who served on the Citizen Settlement Committee.

"The Gwangju People's Uprising is an incident in which political military thugs put all the blame on Gwangju citizens in the process of plotting and carrying out a rebellion to usurp the regime. Now, nine years have passed since the Gwangju People's Uprising, and we have an opportunity to reverse the history of stigma and misjudgment and to be justly judged in front of the nation."

I was working at the Catholic Church in Gyerim-dong in 1980 when the Gwangju People's Uprising took place.

Around 11:00 p.m. on May 17th when martial law was announced and extended, five of my acquaintances, including poet MOON Byeong-Ran and Mr. HWANG Il-Bong came to my rectory. They wanted to "take refuge because preemptive arrest was carried out in other places." I told them that if they were subject to preemptive arrest, my rectory would not be safe, for the intelligence agency usually watched my actions. They agreed with me and left for somewhere else, urging me to "be careful." Every minute, I felt that something ominous was under way.

I even wondered whether democratization, for which countless young people had fought, risking their lives to escape from the yoke of oppression, was about to evaporate like a bubble again.

At midnight May 18th, emergency martial law was extended throughout the country. No news about Gwangju was heard when the weekend Mass was dedicated, and believers had no special reports. After the Mass, I was supposed to go to the Little Flowers Sisters in Mudeung Mountain for another mass there with the members of the church's *Legio Mariae* (a religious organization, translated as the Legion of Mary) and the members of the Church of St. Mary's. When I returned to the church in the afternoon after the Mass, I discovered the whole city was in a great uproar. I thought that students, who had been waiting for the government to show a sincere attitude as they had stopped months of protests, were protesting against an unexpected crackdown under the nationwide extension of martial law.

I got a lot of calls early on May 19th. Half of the people who called me were believers, and the other half were ordinary citizens. Citizens called me to complain, saying, "What are the religious people doing when soldiers are committing atrocities in the city?" The believers called to send their regards, saying, "Now that the soldiers are committing terrible atrocities, stabbing young people and beating them with clubs, Father, you should be careful."

I couldn't just sit back at home when I heard that. I had happened to catch a cold, so I went to Wolsan Pharmacy, where I used to buy medicine, and the pharmacy was closed. As I turned to the bus stop to return to the church, I saw five or six martial law soldiers stopping a city bus and getting on the bus, dragging young people out of the bus, and kicking them and beating them with their clubs. I gave up on taking a bus and walked back to Gyerim-dong.

I got a call around 1:00 p.m., and heard that the Catholic Center was thrown into chaos. When I went straight to the Catholic Center, there were many citizens near it, and martial law forces were flocking in groups of five or six in every alley. The inside of the Catholic Center got littered with broken glass pieces as citizens seemed to storm in, breaking the doors and windows of the building. Father PARK Sang-Soo and Father LEE Young-Soo, who live at the Catholic Center, explained to me, "Citizens found the soldiers of the 31st Division, who were dispatched to the 7th floor of the Christian Broadcasting Station, mistook them for the cruel martial law forces, and they stormed in the Catholic Center." They added that the citizens disarmed the captured soldiers and let them go, and that afterwards they also returned the weapons they had taken from the soldiers.

While staying at the Catholic Center for a while, I could look out the window and see the barbaric behaviors of the paratroopers on Geumnam-ro. They took young people who seemed to be students, as if dragging them away, their faces and chests covered with blood. Sometimes they dragged two or three people. On the sidewalk of Geumnam-ro, about twenty to thirty young people were naked except for their underwear and were forced to stand on their heads (i.e. a military penalty in which you hold your hands behind your back with only your head and feet on the ground); if they moved a little, the paratroopers kicked them with their military boots and beat them with clubs.

When I got out of the Catholic Center and went to Gyerim-dong, near the Dongmun Bridge, I heard a loud noise from Daein Market. A military truck was waiting nearby, and the paratroopers chased the protesting students and turned over the market in the name of searching for the protesters. They beat young people unconditionally, dragged and loaded them onto the truck. I trembled all over my body as I saw the bloody young men being loaded onto the truck. Having witnessed the indiscriminate atrocities of the paratroopers even though I was forty-five years old and was not young, I did not have the courage to watch them anymore, let alone stop them, because of my fear that I could be beaten. I was afraid that the clubs of the paratroopers would fly toward me, so I hurried back to the church.

On the 20th, I was resting in the rectory in the morning because I had a bad cold and didn't want to go outside, but I got a lot of phone calls. Most of the calls were about shops and coffee shops in the city being attacked by the paratroopers. Many people said that many civilians were injured and killed and that they were being dragged away.

The department manager of the regional defense force in the Dong-gu District Office came along with two other people and asked the clergy, "Whom can the citizens trust to take care of the difficult situation because the city of Gwangju has deteriorated out of control?" Even though I knew that the situation was getting worse and worse, inasmuch as the city officials asked for a settlement, I felt more pressure than remorse as a priest, recognizing my limitations in not being able to do anything. To come up to their expectations, what can priests do? I went to the Catholic Center under tremendous pressure in that helpless situation. I talked to the priests at the Catholic Center, but they also couldn't come up with a special solution other than worrying about the situation. At around 5:00 p.m., the lights of vehicles started to appear from the direction of Soochang Elementary School, and then they approached the Province Hall. Dozens of the vehicles turned on their headlights and they began to move head-on, challenging the fully armed martial law forces. The situation gradually made me feel a sense of crisis and extreme tension, as if a wide and deep valley were laid between the two sides lined up.

After leaving the Catholic Center, returning to Gyerim-dong and arriving at the Gyerim Five-way Intersection, citizens gathered in front of a lumber shop, opened the door locked with a wire, took out hundreds of wooden clubs and headed toward Geumnam-ro. I was swept away by the crowd and followed, but the crowd moving toward Geumnam-ro suddenly turned toward Jungang Elementary School and went to the Gwangju MBC station. Many people had already gathered in front of the MBC station. The front of the procession seemed to be trying to set the MBC station on fire. Around 8:00 p.m., the MBC building suddenly caught fire. Among the citizens, some said that they set the MBC on fire because of its distorted and biased reporting, and others said that the martial law forces set fire to provoke citizens. I was praying in my heart all the time: "Oh! This dark street and this wretched world, burning bright! When will the world of light come out of darkness? Lord, save us."

From May 18th to 20th, innocent citizens were unilaterally killed by the atrocities of the paratroopers. On the 20th, the citizens, who saw the bloody scenes of their parents and children, husbands and wives, brothers and sisters, seniors and juniors, and friends being brutally slaughtered without any wrongdoing, rose up to fight to the death. They would rather fight and die than be killed, believing that they would be killed either way. With wooden clubs, tongs, iron pipes, staffs, and other things in hand, they resisted by risking their lives, win or lose. Now, in the city of darkness, which cannot trust in the authorities or armed forces, I got calls from many unknown citizens and believers demanding that the clergy should step forward. But as I witnessed the scene of the terrifying horror, I was afraid and did not have the courage to go out.

Just in time, I got a call that priests in Gwangju were going to gather at the rectory of the Honam-dong Church, and I joined them. It was probably around 11:00 a.m. on the 21st. Citizens who could not stand their resentment and the martial law forces (paratroopers) were facing an imminent crisis in which it seemed they must collide head-on at the fountain of the Plaza in front of the Province Hall. If the troops fired, we would end up drowning in a sea of blood. But how could we who dedicated ourselves to God and the people just stand still? What could we do as priests? Couldn't we just stand still like this? I was regretful and frustrated because of the helpless situation. Eight of us, the priests, discussed how we could act as mediators to find a way to settle the situation peacefully without provoking the two sides. The eight priests who gathered there made a solemn decision to go out, dressed in albs, holding banners, to the front of the fountain where the citizens and the martial law forces were confronting each other.

We made banners like "No Violence, No Weapons," "Let's Talk It Out for a Peaceful and Honorable Settlement," and "Release Students and Democratic Figures." We took great care not to use the provocative red color but to use blue or black in writing the messages. Father JANG Ok-Seok, who was the head of the Honam-dong parish and vice-bishop, called General YOON Heung-Jeong (then the head of a branch office of the martial law forces), with whom Father JANG was acquainted at that time. He gave a call to convey our intention of peaceful settlement to the martial law forces. The call was made in almost twenty minutes, but it seemed that General YOON was not present and the deputy chief in the secretary's office was answering the phone. Father JANG asked him that the military should not open fire as the priests would go out in front of the fountain in white albs to try to mediate for a peaceful settlement. In response, the military expressed its refusal, saying, "We cannot be held responsible for any emergency." We didn't have the courage to go out without a firm guarantee that the military would not fire on us. The meeting stagnated, and our good intentions seemed to be denied. So I had a heavy heart and felt distressed.

At that time, I went out to check the atmosphere in front of the Province Hall. It was just when I left the rectory and had just reached the iron main gate of the church. A helicopter was heading toward Gwangju Park. I heard the sound of machine-gun fire three times, "rat-tat-tat, rat-tat-tat, rat-tat-tat," the muzzle flashes stretching from 50 centimeters to almost a meter in the sky above the Bulo-dong Bridge across the Gwangju Stream. Confused and horrified, I reflexively stood close to the wall and stared at the helicopter. In an instant, the helicopter crossed the park and disappeared toward Wolsan-dong. I was so alarmed that my heart was pounding and my legs were shaking. I could not leave the church and went back to the rectory. Other priests were very startled by the sound of the machine gun, so they came out and asked with a frightened look what the sound was all about. I said it was the sound of machine-gun fire from a helicopter. The priests, who had not given up on the peaceful mediation role we had planned, and had not parted until then, completely abandoned the peaceful mediation plan and all parted after they heard the machine-gun fire from the helicopter. Unable to do anything in such a chaotic situation, we had to feel nothing but helplessness and disappointment.

Later, I testified that I witnessed the machine gun shooting from a helicopter in the MBC documentary film *A Mother's Song* and at the National Assembly hearings, and that this was not an act of self-defense that the military had insisted on, but an outright murder. As a result, I was accused of defamation by those involved, and I was threatened by the Democratic Justice Party to file a lawsuit of perjury.

"Whether it is right in the sight of God for us to obey you rather than God, you be the judges. It is impossible for us not to speak about what we have seen and heard" (Acts 4:19-20). Like the testimony of the apostles at the Sanhedrin, I didn't mean to damage the honor of the military authorities or anyone involved. I was merely testifying what I saw and experienced while standing on the witness stand of the people and history that demanded to find out and reveal the truth. When it was reported that I had been sued, I received concrete reports from people who witnessed the scene of the helicopter shooting or from people who experienced moments of fear and trembling at the point of fire. Thankfully, they have volunteered to testify in court, at parliamentary hearings or in public forums, giving their names, addresses, and phone numbers. I felt very heart-broken and sad that I had to testify to the story on the witness stand of the hearing, which was neither honorable nor shameful in my life. The story I had to tell was the one that the whole nation should suffer from and cry over together. Why should I be interrupted and threatened when telling the truth? The dead and other victims demand repentance and apology from the perpetrators, but why are the perpetrators still not repenting and apologizing before God and the people? "For there is nothing hidden that will not become visible, and nothing secret that will not be known and come to light" (Luke 8:17). I sincerely hope that the perpetrators who are cowardly distorting and concealing the truth and shifting the responsibility to someone else will stop rejecting God's mercy and grace.

On the night of May 21st, the citizens who took over the Province Hall asked people of all walks of life to gather for a settlement. The situation outside was so volatile and chaotic that I couldn't even dare to enter the Province Hall.

From the morning of May 22nd, phone calls from citizens started pouring in. I went to a Settlement Committee meeting arranged in the Lieutenant Governor's office. Dozens of legal, media, and religious figures, students, and professors gathered together. Initially, the meeting did not go well, and many different opinions for settlement were randomly expressed. At this time, Archbishop YOON suggested, "What role can we play in such a distracted state? We should select representatives from all walks of life and organize the committee systematically." And the representatives from various fields were selected. On the side of the Catholic Church, Archbishop YOON, Father JEONG Gyu-Wan of Buk-dong, and Father LEE Young-Soo of the parish office were in attendance, so we discussed it together, and Archbishop YOON ordered that "Father CHO should represent the Catholic Church." From that time on, I had been a member of the Settlement

Committee, forming a deep relationship with May 18. Archbishop YOON returned to the parish office with Father LEE Young-Soo.

After the representatives were chosen, we discussed choosing the chair of the Committee: "Who shall we appoint as the chair?" Lawyer LEE Jong-Ki volunteered to serve as the chair. The Settlement Committee consisted of eleven members: two pastors as representatives of Protestant churches, national independence movement activist CHOI Han-Young, and businessman JANG Hyu-Dong, and so on.

The Settlement Committee members discussed requirements for the negotiation of a settlement with martial law authorities. The majority of the members agreed that martial law troops were fully responsible for the indiscriminate massacre that suppressed the people's peaceful demonstration and democracy. Besides that, the Settlement Committee members came up with specific requirements: the lifting of emergency martial law, the prompt establishment of a democratic government, the dissolution of the *Yushin* party, the release of the arrested students and figures in the democratization movement, the return of the military to its position of national defense, the prohibition of military attacks on peaceful street demonstrations, and so on. With these concrete requirements, they decided to adopt their stance on settlement.

Assuming that the Uprising was caused by the paratroopers' violent suppression of the citizens' peaceful demonstration, the Settlement Committee offered seven requirements as follows: (1) admission of the martial law forces' excessive suppression, (2) release of the arrested students and figures in the democratization movement, (3) compensation for the loss of citizens' lives and properties, (4) punishment for the person responsible for the order to open fire and an apology from the head of state, (5) arrangement of citizen funeral services for the deceased, (6) a peaceful settlement and prohibition of paratroopers' violent suppression, (7) no revenge against the citizens and students after the settlement. Then the eleven committee members went to the branch office of the martial law forces in Sangmudae.

When we arrived at Sangmudae, the head of a branch office of the martial law forces, General YOON Heung-Jeong was dismissed but still stayed, and General SO Jun-Yeol was appointed as his replacement. General SO Jun-Yeol told us, "I have no idea about Gwangju since I've come here very recently; you had better speak with the deputy commander Major General KIM Ki-Seok." Therefore, Major General KIM, three Brigadier Generals, the Defense Security Commander (Colonel), and the Military Police Commander (Lieutenant Colonel) began to talk with the Settlement Committee members.

The Settlement Committee members explained the seven requirements one by one and tried to negotiate with them. First, the settlement members required them to admit the martial law forces' (paratroopers') excessive use of force; the branch office of the martial law forces made an excuse that they just aggressively put down the aggressive protest. Again, the members argued that it was not plausible to say that the citizens with their bare hands aggressively protested against the armed martial law forces. The members explained the context of the protest that since the martial law forces had exerted excessive violence, the citizens reacted in an uncontrollable resentment to their violence. But the martial law officials would not listen to our explanation. Both sides disagreed on this issue and thus they agreed to discuss it later and brought up the other requirements.

Upon the issue concerning release of the arrested students and figures in the democratization movement, the martial law officials answered, "Most of them will be released selectively." But the settlement members opposed this position and insisted that all of them should be immediately released without any conditions. And the martial law officials opposed us with "release selectively."

On the topic of compensation for the loss of citizens' lives and properties, the martial law officials irresponsibly responded that the loss would be reimbursed selectively in consultation with their superiors. At this point, all of sudden, I hit upon something to offer: "Such an important negotiation between both sides like this should be recorded or officially written down with participants' signatures, and then the documents should be exchanged. We should keep a record of this historic settlement meeting; otherwise it would be problematic later without any record." Despite my strong suggestion, I could not get any agreement from both sides. The atmosphere of the branch office of the martial law forces was so tense that I was baffled when even the settlement members did not agree to my suggestion.

The settlement members suggested the fourth requirement: "Punish the one responsible for the order to open fire, and the President must apologize for it publicly." Then they answered, "We will talk about it with our superiors."

As to the fifth requirement, "The funeral of the deceased should be held as a citizen funeral," they responded, "Let's hold off discussion of this point because a citizen funeral may provoke the citizens."

They agreed on the sixth requirement, "The citizens voluntarily surrender the weapons; the martial law forces are strictly prohibited from violently suppressing citizens and shall settle the situation peacefully." The martial law forces agreed to this, but they also demanded the weapons be quickly surrendered and returned unconditionally.

The martial law forces also agreed on the seventh requirement, "The martial law forces guarantee no revenge after the settlement."

However, no promises were kept during the whole period of the May 18 Gwangju People's Uprising. The settlement meeting was in vain.

Nothing was gained through the negotiation but selective release. It was disappointing, but we had to tell the citizens about the negotiation results. When JANG Heu-Dong, one of the Settlement

Committee members, reported the results at the Fountain Plaza, the citizens booed loudly. "What in the world did you negotiate?" Professor MYEONG Noh-Geun stepped forward, grabbed the microphone, and calmed the citizens. As the citizens' anger subsided, we retrieved weapons and stored them next to the main gate of the Province Hall. We then attended the second settlement meeting at Sangmudae and brought about 150 retrieved weapons with us. Martial law officials found fault with us for "bringing so few weapons" to the meeting. We demanded, "We will retrieve weapons again, so release the citizens." The Martial Law Command released some citizens, excluding dissidents, figures in the democratization movement, or student council members, and we brought them back with us. About 800 people were released that day (researcher's note: 848 people were released on the 22nd, and thirty-four people on the 23rd.) When we returned and reported the news to the citizens, they protested fiercely because those who were expected to be released had not been released.

On the evening of the 22nd, I received a call that people from Namdong Catholic Church were looking for me. Dissidents gathered at the church to discuss how to settle the situation, and they asked me to tell them about the progress so far. So I talked about things that had taken place, including our going to Sangmudae for settlement. The people at the church talked about the citizens' reaction to the activities of the Settlement Committee earlier that day. They said that the Settlement Committee members were suspected of being pro-government or the like. I suggested that the people in the democratization movement at the church should join the Settlement Committee to cooperate and steer it in the right direction because the citizens were unlikely to trust the Settlement Committee members of the Province Hall because of the unsatisfactory negotiation results at Sangmudae. The dissidents who had discussed the settlement measures at Namdong Church joined the Settlement Committee of the Province Hall and began full-fledged settlement activities.

Starting on the 23rd, dozens of corpses that had been transported to the Province Hall were sorted and organized. All identified bodies were shrouded and moved to Sangmugwan, and unidentified bodies were moved to a corner of the Province Hall to be identified by citizens who were looking for their family members. In about ten cases, the faces were ruined and unidentifiable, which brought the citizens indescribable despair. The armed citizen militia members guarding the Province Hall lined up hundreds of the families and instructed them to check the bodies in an orderly manner. If a corpse's face was too damaged to be identified, the family members moved the body around and looked for other identifying marks of a person who they raised and hoped to find. Family members who identified their loved one's bodies sometimes passed out from weeping, and those who could not find their loved one's bodies cried out in despair. The area for identifying the corpses became a sea of tears. The bodies identified were shrouded, and then they were transferred to Sangmugwan. As a member of the Settlement Committee, I was tasked with guiding the families. I shed tears endlessly and felt pain in my heart. Why had they pointed a gun at the chest of their own kin? Was shooting and killing people the best way to settle the situation? What was the reason and purpose of such an inhuman slaughter? I felt endless indignation and grief at the sad reality that the dawn of the democratic era, which we had hoped for and trusted in, had disappeared into the darkness of frustration once again because of the political army obsessed with the delusion of power. This murderous deed that was caused by a few people's ambition to rule and trampled on the people's aspirations for democracy is an indelible sin against the nation and its history.

The weapons recovery team was part of the Settlement Committees, and I actively participated in it. I ran around to retrieve the weapons when I had time while guiding citizens to identify the bodies. The students retrieved weapons independently and managed them in one place. More than 3,500 firearms were recovered by May 22nd from the time we started recovering weapons right after we took over the Province Hall in the afternoon of May 21st. Many young people, however, still carried weapons and insisted, "We should defend Gwangju."

When I went to the branch office of the Martial Law Command at Sangmudae to negotiate the second settlement, the deputy commander Major General KIM Ki-Seok told the Settlement Committee members: "We have armed helicopters and tanks ready, so if we try to subdue Gwangju, we can do it in a few minutes. However, the soldiers are waiting patiently in order not to kill the people, so you should retrieve and surrender the weapons of the citizen militias immediately." The committee members believed that they should resolve the situation by quickly retrieving the weapons. But they had a hard time persuading the deputy commander and making him understand that "it is impossible to retrieve the weapons unless the Martial Law Command carries an investigation into the cause of the incident and the locus of responsibility, and provides measures and guarantees for the safety of the citizens." The committee members affirmed to the Martial Law Command that they would "retrieve the weapons at risk to our lives if the Martial Law Command guarantees the safety of the citizens, although we have no authority to command and lead them." However, the Martial Law Command showed a high-handed attitude, demanding the surrender of the weapons. I felt a shivering fear in the bloody atmosphere, recalling the helicopter from the large courtyard at Sangmudae when I went for the negotiation.

I felt frustrated and desperate when I intuited that it was a difficult task to persuade the Martial Law Command as if "getting meat from a tree." Citizens were harmed, but I found myself that I had no choice but to convince the citizens to find the last possibility of avoiding an armed conflict.

When I went for the negotiation with the Martial Law Command on the 23rd, Professor MYEONG Noh-Geun also went with me. As the requirements were not met, he remained there to continue negotiations, and we returned to the Province Hall with released citizens.

We went to retrieve the weapons around the outskirts arrayed by the citizen militias from the dawn of the 24th. Pastor JANG Sye-Kyun, Attorney LEE Jong-Ki, Father NAM Jae-Hee, and I traveled around the outskirts, including near the Baekun-dong railroad, both sides of the Hakun-dong bridge, Sansu-dong, Geyrim-dong, the west side of the prison, near the Mudeung Stadium, and the entrance of the Hwajeong-dong Industrial Complex. The citizen militia was deployed in a force the size of a company. I got around from 3:00 a.m. on an appropriated bus and couldn't turn on the headlights because, if I turned them on, we were likely to come under a fusillade by the martial law forces.

When the committee members tried to persuade the citizen militias to retrieve the weapons, they asked, "Who do you think you are? We are the Settlement Committee, the representatives of the people."

We answered, "Then, who authorized you?"

They then asked, "And do you think the Martial Law Command guarantees the price of the blood and the lives of Gwangju citizens when we surrender the weapons?"

We had no choice but to answer, "We have no idea."

The citizen militia members firmly refused to surrender the weapons, saying, "We won't put down our weapons until we receive the price of the blood and the lives of Gwangju citizens." That was a very reasonable argument. Our group, who went to retrieve the weapons without providing any guarantees or alternatives for the post-settlement problem, was rather ashamed. But the only way to a peaceful settlement was to get help from the citizens.

We tried to persuade them with a precondition for a peaceful settlement: "The martial law forces have set a deadline and are trying to forcefully suppress us. If the retrieval of the weapons is delayed, not only the militias in arms with loyalty and passion to defend Gwangju, but also the general citizens will suffer enormous casualties. So, in order to prevent casualties and further tragedy and misfortune, the weapons must be retrieved."

The militia members protested, pointing their guns at my chest and saying, "Who the hell are you to make me surrender the weapons without any guarantees or countermeasures?" The last thing I could do was try to convince them to believe me because I am a religious person and a Catholic priest. I told them I also risked my life to appeal to them to minimize the damage to the properties and lives of the citizens of Gwangju, and then, some of them surrendered their weapons.

I wandered around trying to retrieve the weapons until after midnight on the 24th. When we went to Sansu-dong, citizen militia members shouted, "What are these bastards?" and pointed their guns at us.

"Who would compensate us for the cost of the lives and blood of our brothers, sisters, and friends in retrieving the weapons? And how could the cost be compensated?"

"The Settlement Committee members are negotiating with the government and the martial law authorities about compensation on condition that we surrender our weapons. We, too, are sad and angry just like you. However, to minimize the number of casualties of Gwangju citizens, we cannot but seek a peaceful settlement measure though it's regrettable."

"Is your life so precious? My brothers are dead, but what are we going to do while we survive?"

While I was talking with them, I was proud of them, on one hand; and the situation made my blood boil and my tears well up in my eyes, on the other hand. We patted them on the back, and they said they were hungry. The citizen militia headquarters at the Province Hall was supposed to deliver supplies, but it did not.

After moving around to retrieve the weapons, we went to the Province Hall, loaded up bread and drinks, and left again. We toured the outskirts one after another, giving citizen militia members bread and drinks and trying to persuade them again. It was because of the sense of duty to save even one more person's life.

At that time, the citizen militia members in Sansu-dong handed over ten to fifteen weapons, and all the weapons were retrieved at the prison area and the highway entrance.

I went around all night to retrieve the weapons, but I did not get a good response from the citizen militia members who were stationed at the entrance of the industrial complex, the park, and on the sides of the Hakun-dong Bridge.

On the morning of the 25th, I went around to the areas where the weapons had not yet been retrieved for the third time. The first place I visited was the Hakun-dong Bridge that leads to Hwasun. On that side, the martial law forces were stationed in Junam Village, so the citizen militias were building a defense. When our group arrived at the scene, the militia members were exhausted without having breakfast. A citizen reported that there were corpses in Junam Village, so militia members with a white flag and wearing Red Cross armbands approached the martial law forces along the pavement in a jeep, but they were fired on and retreated. Unlike the atmosphere of the strong objection to the idea of surrendering the weapons the night before, the militia members at the Hakun-dong Bridge, in size a bit larger than a platoon, argued among themselves about the appeals of the Settlement Committee members. After days of tension with their guns, they finally decided to surrender their weapons. And they withdrew from Hakun-dong before noon.

And then, at around 10:00 a.m., I went to the citizen militia defending Gwangju at the entrance of the industrial complex. There, about a company of the citizen militia was hiding in an empty bus; and the martial law forces at the general hospital were ready to charge at any time with tanks. I could see with the naked eye that the soldiers, who had been trained by the people's taxes, were pointing their guns at the citizens' chest, not at an enemy's. That scene further fueled my tenacity and eagerness for a peaceful settlement.

The commander of the citizen militia at the entrance to the industrial complex was a veteran, and most of the militia members were young ragmen or shoeshine boys. Their attitude was determined.

"We'll die one way or the other. But we will never surrender our weapons. If it is settled, we'll be dragged to death," they claimed anxiously.

We, the Settlement Committee members, knelt down and begged, comforting them, "Let's die together even if we die, and live together even if we live."

Because of the mournful appeals of the committee members, the citizen militia members got on a truck and returned to the Province Hall, saying, "We are withdrawing, but we will not surrender our weapons."

Even when they came to the Province Hall, they held their guns to their chests and did not let go. Elder LEE Seong-Hak (now deceased), one of the Settlement Committee members, suggested that because the weather was chilly, we should buy the citizen militia members underwear with donations from the committee members and the people in the Province Hall. Although the money that Mr. YOON Young-Gyu collected in his hat was not that much, we handed it to the citizen militia members who had withdrawn from the entrance of the industrial complex. After they filled their hungry stomachs with warm rice prepared by female volunteers at the Province Hall cafeteria, they surrendered their weapons.

Some of the citizen militia went out of the Province Hall, and about seventy to eighty joined the defense forces at the Province Hall. But they would have gone to the park later because there were mainly college students in the building. There were many citizen militia members guarding the outskirts of the city before they surrendered their weapons. About 150 to 200 people were stationed in Gwangju Park, fifty to sixty people in Seobang, and about a company was stationed on each of the Baekun-dong railroad, the Hakun-dong Bridge, the road to the prison, and the side of the highway. I remember those places in more detail because I provided them with meals.

More than 4,000 firearms were retrieved by the 25th. The retrieval of the weapons in the outskirts ended that way. But the Province Hall and the park were the places where the largest number of the citizen militia stayed to defend Gwangju. Now that the withdrawal from the outskirts was completed, negotiations had to be made, using the retrieved weapons, at least to restore the honor of Gwangju and free the detainees. Until that time, the honor of Gwangju was seriously damaged due to the distorted reports of the media, and the uprising was propagated as a riot caused by the maneuvers of communist dissidents.

After retrieving weapons until midday on the 24th, I got exhausted, and I went back to the parish church late in the afternoon to celebrate an evening mass. The members of Gyerim-dong Church prayed hard, saying the rosary, together with the nuns in front of the Eucharist every day. After I came out of the Province Hall and told them what had happened, everyone burst into tears. After the evening mass, I felt so tired that I fell asleep in the nave. Because I had been walking and standing most of the time, I was exhausted, and my feet were so swollen and blistered that I could not walk properly.

After I walked into the Province Hall as a member of the Citizens' Settlement Committee on the 22nd, I ate and slept inside the building with citizens for three days. During that period, I also witnessed the fabricated "poison needle incident." After a while, when a martial law trooper was captured, some of the enraged citizen militia members became angry with him, but the leadership of the citizen militia did not allow any harassment. All I saw was the martial law force was slapped on the cheek by a very infuriated young man. The Settlement Committee members requested that the captured martial law soldier be released, and later the citizen militia dressed him in civilian clothes and told him to go out safely.

When I was in the Province Hall, college students misunderstood the situation and said that the U.S. naval ship, *Coral Sea*, had come to hold the military forces in check and help the citizens of Gwangju. They even printed this on a big wall poster for a while. I told them "Why do you think the U.S. military force would support citizens instead of the Korean military? Don't be crazy. And do not put your hopes in useless things."

One time, one of the citizen militia members claimed to me that I was a pro-government committee member. I scolded him, saying "If I were patronized, by whom would I be patronized? We have been committed to protecting the property and lives of our citizens. What do you mean by 'patronized'?"

The citizen militia maintained order autonomously by holding those who acted suspiciously after entering the Province Hall or incited others with violent language. They conducted investigation activities while blocking them from contacting others, and releasing them after background checks. As the conflict progressed, suspicious people captured by citizens were handed over to the martial law forces. This strict control was maintained because while all communication to and from Gwangju was shut down, the mass media, which conspired with the military dictatorship, reported that Gwangju became riotous by being instigated by the subversive or mischievous and following the leadership of a small number of radical gangsters. Thus, the citizen leadership judged that there should be no riots by disruptive people and warned itself against any disturbance.

It was a celebration day for Pentecost. The number of the believers attending Mass had significantly decreased. I read the ministry letter for Pentecost sent by Archbishop YOON Gong-Hee and gave a sermon. I prayed with tears that "If it is not resolved peacefully, the martial law forces will be ready to enter Gwangju by force. Let us pray earnestly for a peaceful and honorable settlement. I am risking my life as a member of the Settlement Committee and trying to go beyond my capacity to reach a peaceful resolution."

I hurried to Nam-dong after Mass as I was informed that Archbishop YOON Gong-Hee was looking for me in Nam-dong. Archbishop YOON said that Cardinal KIM Soo-Hwan had sent a charity donation for the victims of Gwangju. Archbishop YOON said that a military priest had arrived at Sangmudae by helicopter with the check for the donation, not knowing how to deliver it. Archbishop YOON would like me to take it over from him at some place because my status as a member of the Settlement Committee would make me free to travel.

Upon leaving Nam-dong, I explained the situation to Professor OH Byung-Moon, my school mate, who had also been participating in the Settlement Committee. When I asked him to go with me, he agreed without hesitation. I arranged a meeting at the Integrated Military Hospital with Father JANG Yong-Bok, a military priest at Sangmudae. Professor OH Byung-Moon and I walked to Nongseong-dong, rode bicycles borrowed from a nearby bicycle shop, and arrived at the Integrated Military Hospital where we met the military priest Father JANG Yong-Bok.

I was about to return after receiving the Cardinal's message and check from Father JANG, but I met Colonel KIM, the head of the Integrated Hospital. I asked if I could see the actual situation inside the hospital, and he gave showed me around himself. Within the hospital, there was a militia ward and a martial-law-forces ward. There were many wounded soldiers of the martial law forces because the Sangmudae soldiers and the martial law forces mistook each other for the citizen militia and engaged in a fierce battle. In one place, there were two unconscious patients with severe burns, swelling like a barrel. When I asked who they were, he replied, "They are rogues captured around the prison." I looked around the hospital and asked, "I heard rumors that there are a lot of corpses in the Integrated Hospital. Is that true?" He denied, "There is no such thing." However, unfortunately, he said that a young man with a name tag of a school for deaf mutes was hit in the head with a club and was the first to enter the hospital as a dead body. People weren't interested in the first death because so many people had died, but, for heaven's sake, what did the deaf man do to be beaten so severely with a club that he died? Once again, the scene of the gruesome reality was revived. I left the Integrated Hospital immediately and returned to Nam-dong to deliver Cardinal KIM's donation check to Archbishop YOON.

In the afternoon I went to the Province Hall. The leadership of the Province Hall had changed a lot from the previous day. In the meantime, many members of the leadership were replaced with CNU students, and many dissidents joined the Settlement Committee. On the night of the 25th, I stayed up almost all night in the Province Hall. When I slept, there was no bedding, so I squatted on a chair or slept on my side on the sofa.

The Settlement Committee members discussed the explosives in the basement of the Province Hall. "If an eight-ton truck's worth of explosives were to be blown up by rioters, all Gwangju citizens would die. However, the people who currently guard the explosives do not know each other and have no command structure, so it cannot be left as it is. There are many priests and pastors among the Settlement Committee members, so let's bring in believers and replace the guards." We agreed and scattered immediately.

There were also a few pastors and priests, including Father

KIM Seong-Yong, Father JEONG Kyu-Wan, and me. It was around 10:10 p.m. when I left the Province Hall.

It was a dark, moonless night. I heard gunshots intermittently, so I arrived at the Gyerim-dong Church with fear. After asking around, I gathered twelve young men who had been in the military. As I was walking toward the Province Hall with them, gunshots sounded more often. We hid in the building and came to the Province Hall. I was the first to arrive, and Father KIM Seong-Yong brought three others around midnight. Father JEONG Gyu-Wan couldn't come because he had a stomachache, so he sent a young man. No matter how long we waited, the pastors did not come. The priests and pastors made a strong oath to guard the explosives no matter when we were in danger, but they didn't show up.

I thought we should replace the guards with just the number of the young believers, so I found the person in charge. When I met him, he said that they had already been replaced by CNU students. Then, thinking that it had been worked out, I brought the believers to the governor's office so they could sleep. I stopped the believers who tried to go out to guard the explosives, and then sent them all out at dawn.

However, this event would have serious effects on the investigation into me at the Defense Security Command later.

At dawn on 26th, we received an urgent message from a citizen that tanks and martial law forces were entering the city from the outskirts of Gwangju. "Isn't this a sign that the martial law forces will suppress Gwangju by force, despite our initial agreement?" The Settlement Committee members of Nam-dong took the lead and decided, "Seventeen people should go out as human shields and block tanks to prevent the martial law forces from entering the city, at least temporarily." When the group of the seventeen left the Province Hall in the early morning and reached the front of the Rural Development Agency in Nongseong-dong, the martial law forces and tanks already were being stationed there. With blistered feet, I barely managed to follow the members to the Rural Development Agency. In front of the Agency, I met a Major of the martial law forces and asked, "Since I came here as a citizen representative for a peaceful settlement, please guide me to the branch office of the Martial Law Command."

He seemed to be contacting someone with a walkie-talkie, and soon after, a Major General appeared in a military jeep. Among the Settlement Committee members, Father KIM Seong-Yong went as a spokesman for the Committee because lawyers HONG Nam-Soon and LEE Ki-Hong and I could not go for our badly swollen feet. Seeing our members had left for the branch office, we were anxiously waiting for them as if a quarter hour were three years. We noticed that soldiers were building positions with sandbags, and machine guns were installed and aimed at the downtown. And the martial law forces took over all the tall buildings by the road leading to the downtown and pointed their guns toward the downtown as well. Even though we stayed there and waited nervously for quite a long time, there was no news of those who went to the branch office of the Martial Law Command. We couldn't wait with uncertainty, so we went back to the Province Hall from Nongseong-dong.

Around 3:00 p.m., Father KIM Seong-Yong who had visited the branch office of the Martial Law Command stopped by the Province Hall. Without particular explanation about the situation, Father KIM said, "I found out the atmosphere of the branch office was serious, and tension was increasing. I should inform the outside world of the situation in Gwangju." And he asked me to keep it a secret that he had departed. In the evening, the citizen militia inside the Province Hall was overwhelmed by a very depressing atmosphere with anxiety that "the martial law forces will come in tonight." The citizen militia was divided into two groups. The one was the moderates who insisted that they would surrender the weapons first to reduce the number of victims. The other was the hardliners who argued that they would "surrender weapons only when the martial law forces would admit their wrongdoing and would restore Gwangju citizens' honor." Because these two opinions were in a fierce standoff, Lawyer LEE Jong-Ki and I decided to mediate between the two groups. I planned to meet both groups together around 6:00 p.m., but it was not easy to gather them in one place because they were busy.

Around 8:00 p.m., believers from the Gyerim-dong Church came to see me. That day was a feast day of Philip Neri, the patron saint for Gyerim-dong Church, and it was a day of the parish church as well. Many believers gathered in the church to wait for me, the parish priest. A priest was supposed to give mass at a fixed time. But I thought mediating between the leadership in the Province Hall had priority because many people's lives depended on the results of the mediation. So I contact the church and ask the members to wait for me while praying the rosary. Then I joined the meeting where the two sides shared their opinions.

The meeting was held at the governor's office. Of the Settlement Committee members, lawyer LEE Jong-Ki and I attended the meeting. KIM Chang-Gil and Hwang Geum-Sun, who held moderate views, insisted, "There is no chance of winning even if we resist as we have done so far. So, surrendering weapons and disbanding the leadership of the Province Hall will reduce the number of victims." They argued that the right way was to prevent the sacrifice of citizens rather than to defend them with weapons. KIM Jong-Bae, JEONG Sang-Yong, LEE Yang-Hyun, and HEO Kyu-Jung, and others who had a hardline view, strongly asserted, "How can the sacrifice of innocent citizens' lives be compensated? If nothing is guaranteed, we're going to die one way or the other. Moreover, without a guarantee of a peaceful settlement, we cannot make a meaningless and disgraceful surrender. But we won't hold you if you abandon your weapons and leave the Province Hall. Feel free to choose."

As a priest, my opinion was frankly close to that of the moderates. I had thought that the damage that citizens would suffer should be reduced as much as possible because it was obvious that everyone would fight to the death. I implied that even if we replenished our forces, we would not be able to compete with the elite special forces armed with great firepower, but I couldn't change their strong stance.

The argument of the hardliners was basically right. It was a resolution to confront the fate that was sure to lead to tragedy rather than avoid it. It was indeed a brave, magnificent, youthful spirit of Gwangju. In the midst of tension and fear, opinions of both sides were directly opposed, but there was no fight. During the meeting, they tried to persuade each other while controlling their emotions and thinking rationally because they were all comrades and brothers for the sake of their citizens and country. The moderates, who judged that there was no chance to win the battle, left the Province Hall that night. The Province Hall was now controlled by citizen militia members who resolved to take a hardline action. As more than 200 remaining militia members were lining up for battle with guns, I got a message from believers of Gyerim-dong Church who had been waiting for me at the entrance of the Province Hall. I told the people around me that I had to go to the church and left the Province Hall. It was around 8:45 p.m.

When I left the main gate of the Province Hall, I began to shed tears because I felt like I was cowardly as the only one escaping to live, on one hand; and I thought it might be a night for many young men to lose their lives, on the other hand. The tears kept falling out of control.

At Gyerim-dong Church, more than 300 believers were waiting for me, praying the rosary. Coming into the church with tears all the way from the Province Hall, I began to hold a mass. And I sobbed, saying, "The citizens of Gwangju may face another miserable situation tonight." Then all the people broke down in tears, and the church was full of tears. While preaching a sermon, I cried out "Because of Abel's innocent blood, the sinner got God's punishment and had to wander in the desert. The tragedy of a fratricidal conflict in which soldiers trained and supported by taxes killed innocent citizens does not simply end miserably. The lives of citizens who died not knowing anything and the blood of young men who protested against injustice will be righteous blood that can save not only Gwangju but also our history from distress. The unjust, sorrowful deaths of the righteous and their blood will be lifted to God's heart, and God will surely grant our wishes."

During mass, I received the Eucharist in sincerity of heart. There was a request from the depths of my heart that "there are only young people in the Province Hall, and I have to go there." I repeated, "Jesus, I would go to the Province Hall after mass. Give me courage and strength." When the mass was over, I was so exhausted that I couldn't keep myself steady. It was probably because of the tension, fear, and fatigue piled up for a long time. Being supported by believers, I sat down on the sofa in the rectory.

I might have had a short sleep; then, suddenly I heard a gunshot. They were gunshots from the Province Hall and the park. The suppression operation had begun. The fact that our brave young men were being killed by those bullets broke my heart. All I could do for them was pray.

"God, save our young men."

It was at the moment when I heard a loud knock on the door of the rectory. When I stood up to open the door on the second booming knock, four martial law soldiers kicked the door, broke the lock, and rushed in with their bayonets attached to their rifles. When I asked them, "Why are you kicking the door of this rectory without any notice in advance? It is where a Catholic priest lives," the soldier who seemed to be a commander replied that his unit received an order to search in Gyerim-dong Church, Gwangju High School, and Gyerim Elementary School, as they got a report that rioters were hiding in the church; so they broke in. The soldiers were so rude that I came to think that I should not leave them with that attitude. I complained, "Why are you so rude? Where did you get that education to enter into the rectory in military boots?"

"We did it because we heard there were rioters," the soldiers responded with unease. They said that they would check and search the rectory; and, then, they entered the kitchen, bedroom, and office in their military boots, checked every detail, stabbed the ceiling with their bayonets, and were about to leave.

I protested to the martial law soldiers who replied they came to arrest rioters. I asked, "What is a rioter? Gwangju citizens are not rioters, but the democratic citizens," and suggested to them, "Listen to me for a moment and go"; but they did not sit down at first. As they sat down at my urging, I gave a brief account of the cause and circumstances of what had happened so far. I explained that, as the paratroopers violently suppressed the peaceful protests of the students and massacred the innocent civilians, citizens resisted with wooden clubs or pokers as a means of self-defense. And the situation was exacerbated into a gunfight. They asked me to open the church door in order to search the church. The soldiers thoroughly searched the ritual room, the confession box, the altar, and even the choir room on the second floor. Then they said they should search the convent. Although I persuaded them not to go to the convent, as the convent was off-limits to men, they insisted that all places where rioters might be hiding should be checked. Since I was worried that the nuns would be startled, I asked the soldiers to search after I let the nuns know and made them keep calm first. After confirming that there were no rioters in the convent, the martial law forces proceeded to Gwangju High School by crawling in battle formation.

As the soldiers approached Gwangju High School in a military crawl, a First Sergeant ordered them, "If anyone tries to run away, shoot him right away. Not a single person can escape!"

I was astounded and grabbed the First Sergeant's hand and said, "Why are you going to kill them? Gwangju citizens are not rioters but good people, patriotic citizens just like you. So please don't shoot them." But the First Sergeant gave the same order again. A few shots rang out shortly after the soldiers entered Gwangju High School. How on earth was such a military discipline formed that orders were given to shoot at the back of civilians running for their lives? The act that pointed a gun at the heart of the same race was heartless enough. I thought that shooting the fleeing brothers from behind meant that soldiers reacted emotionally to the resistance of the Gwangju citizens.

It seemed that the operation was over. Reserve forces and Province Hall officials were asked to go to work early in the morning through radio broadcasts. Firefighters and government officials of Province Hall affiliated institutes also went to work and were mobilized to clean up the Province Hall. One of them who was working at the Province Hall said that he piled up corpses one by one in two heaps.

After Gwangju citizens' resistance to dictatorship was forcibly suppressed by the martial law forces, the joint investigation headquarters started to search for me from May 29th. They had difficulties finding me. They even searched for me right in front of me because they didn't know what I look like. For example, they had no choice but to turn back when the young members of the church or the executives of the priests' association properly made excuses for my absence. After a few days like this, I thought it would be better to move to another place, and so I did.

Soon after, Father KIM Seong-Yong and I were on the wanted list with a 500,000 won reward. They searched for us desperately but couldn't find us. In early June, I discussed this problem with Archbishop YOON. We concluded, "As Fathers, we are ashamed to run away even though many people are being arrested and are struggling. We will talk about our activities thoroughly and forcefully reveal the atrocities committed against innocent people in Gwangju." After that, I contacted Father KIM Seong-Yong, who was in Seoul, and we appeared together at the Defense Security Command.

As soon as we entered the Defense Security Command, we had to take off all our clothes, and the belongings in our pockets were also confiscated. Immediately, we were detained and interrogated in a solitary cell in the basement. An investigator forced me to write everything in my life from my childhood up until the present moment. Actually, he forced me to write the same statement three times in a row. After completing an eighty-two-page long statement, I was then required to write its summary. When my personal statement was over, he began to conduct a full-scale investigation. The investigator led the investigation in the following direction: "You planned a second April 19 and urged students and citizens to overthrow CHOI Kyu-Ha's regime. You started a riot and plotted rebellion in order to set up KIM Dae-Jung as president of the nation."

He also took issue with the fact that twelve believers were brought in to guard the TNT in the basement of the Province Hall on the night of 25th. The investigator claimed that I gave an order to replace the existing forces with the ones discharged from military and then defend Province Hall to the death. I explained that I had them stand guard with acquaintances on the explosives because the explosives were dangerous. But the investigator would not listen to me.

I wasn't assaulted but was made to kneel down with only my underwear on while a guard was watching me to keep me awake.

Avoiding the eyes of the guard who prevented me from sleeping, I dozed off sitting on a chair and fell asleep on my stomach at a desk used for the interrogation. The guard sometimes let me doze off. The investigator visited every day around 1:00 or 2:00 a.m. to interrogate me.

The investigator told me to testify to as much as I knew about lawyers HONG Nam-Soon and LEE Ki-Hong, but I didn't want to testify against them as fellow members of the Settlement Committee. When nothing unusual was found in my statement that could lead to an indictment, the investigator tortured Lawyer LEE severely and made him testify that "Father CHO had incited people to replenish forces and not surrender weapons." However, they themselves seemed to know better than me that I had worked hard for a peaceful settlement as a member of the Settlement Committee. As no criminal act worthy of leading to an indictment was found in my statement, I was investigated around the fact that Father KIM Seong-Yong's testimony (titled "Sorrow Rather than Anger") includes my remark made during a rally held in front of the fountain at the Province Hall: "If I had a gun, I'd like to shoot the paratroopers who committed murderous atrocities at will." The investigator was full of confidence at first, but as the investigation progressed, he looked discouraged. This was because my words expressed my feelings as they were, and not only did I not put them into action myself, but also the phrase of "the paratroopers who committed murderous atrocities at will" was seen as nothing but an expression of anger against the ghastly killings of the paratroopers. In the end, the investigator who was in charge of me tipped me off that he had submitted a release proposal to the head of the investigation department. However, it was said that after receiving the release proposal, the head of the investigation department threw it into the investigator's face, saying in anger "Don't you know what kind of person he is! Tie up that person," and the investigator asked me to cooperate in the investigation.

During the investigation, I happened to see the organizational chart of the leadership of the Gwangju Uprising, where the Defense Security Command wrote me down right below Lawyer

HONG Nam-Soon. The investigator had suggested releasing me, who was made such an important figure, so there was no way they would just let me alone. As the investigation progressed, there had been some changes in the organizational chart, where Father KIM Seong-Yong took my place, and I was placed in KIM Seong-Yong's position.

After this, Investigator Mr. KIM at the Defense Security Command who was in charge of me, grumbled, "I was unlucky enough to meet a priest and became an incompetent investigator." This was because during the Gwangju Uprising I served as a member of the Settlement Committee to achieve a peaceful settlement, not only persuading armed citizens and retrieving weapons from them, but also visiting the Martial Law Command branch office as a citizen representative to present a peaceful solution, and mediating a conflict of opinion within the citizen militia leadership in the Province Hall. This alone did not meet the requirements and was insufficient for accusing me of being an important figure in a rebellion.

The investigator who used to come to interrogate me at 1:00 a.m. every day unexpectedly did not appear for two days, so I was rather anxious and waited for him. Two days later, the investigator appeared with a seven- or eight-page-long statement in his hands. He confidently said that this was a statement written by citizen militia leadership officials, saying, "Father CHO ordered that Gwangju should be absolutely defended, and we cannot yield and should not surrender until the price of the blood of Gwangju citizens is guaranteed." Included in the list of names of the witnesses shown by the investigator were lawyers LEE Ki-Hong, HEO Gyu-Jeong, LEE Yang-Hyeon, and KIM Jong-Bae, who were being interrogated in the next room. I doubted my eyes. The young people who were all supposed to have died at the Province Hall were still alive!

It was really nice and surprising. I did not care that the contents of the statement were disadvantageous to me. I stopped the investigator and asked again. "Are they really alive?" The investigator was speechless and puzzled by my excitement, and a glow appeared on my face. It was because he had never seen a person who was excited by the fact that people who testified against him were alive.

While staying in the basement of the Defense Security Command, I could not hear any news about those whose lives were saved after the Gwangju Uprising ended disastrously with the military's violent suppression. The only thing I knew was that a lot of people had died at the Province Hall and those who were alive were taken somewhere unknown. I had affection for the young people who led the citizen militia in the Province Hall because of their strong will for democracy, courage, and loyalty. I was also grieved at the wretched reality of having to take up arms in front of the political army faction, who used force to unjustly satisfy its political ambitions on young men who would lead the country. However, I decided that peaceful settlement was the better option since no matter how righteous the young people's claims may be, it would be impossible to persist in the face of the physical force of the soldiers with formidable weapons.

After the Province Hall was suppressed, the faces of young militia leaders would flash through my head. I thought they were all killed on May 27th. Even so, it was regrettable that I left the place alone and stayed in the rectory that night. Someone should have been there with them, but a sense of guilt for not being able to do that always lingered in the corner of my heart. Therefore, the fact that they were all alive was a source of great joy to me.

The investigation report was rewritten several times. At first, it included statements such as, "If I had a gun, I'd like to shoot the paratroopers who committed murderous atrocities." But due to the possibility that the brutality of the soldiers could be admitted, the investigator deleted it from the report. Next, they wanted to include the seditious contents from the lecture I gave in April 1980 to students at Chosun University and Chonnam

National University on the subject of "April 19 and Democracy." It was also deleted, as I argued that if it had violated martial law, it should have been problematic when the entire text of the lecture was published in the university newspaper since the Martial Law Command thoroughly inspected even university newspapers at that time. Later, they tried to include in the report the content of a mass sermon of mine at the Namdong Catholic Church and a lecture on the state of affairs as criminal facts and even the fact that Father JEONG Kyu-Wan and I were stopped at the Intercity Bus Terminal on our way to Seoul to attend the March 1st prayer meeting and failed to get there.

When I asked the investigator to delete the statement that I ordered to replace the guards at the Province Hall with people who could handle guns, he said, "Even if you insist that you didn't do it, it's already an established fact, so don't waste your time meaninglessly and put your thumbprint on it." Then, he threatened me to get my cooperation, saying, "Because you are a priest, I treat you gently. Otherwise, you could have been beaten up." In fact, moans and beating could be heard intermittently from the next room. Part of me wished I would rather sign with my thumbprint and be transferred to the military police out of this disgusting Defense Security Command basement.

When the investigator threatened and forced me to sign, I quickly grabbed his hand and argued, "Your beloved children who are sleeping like angels now don't know the fact that their father has done such a bad thing to a Catholic priest and is accusing him wrongly. And your wife probably doesn't even know you're doing this. If your mother found out about this, she wouldn't believe it." He shouted that he was fed up with the investigation and left. While being interrogated for a long time, I indirectly asked and got to know about the investigator as a Protestant Christian and his family background.

Two days later, the investigation started again, but the "replacement of forces" section was deleted and the statements made by the leadership at the Province Hall were included in the report. When he came to make the investigation report, I signed with my thumbprint. After the twenty-three-day investigation was over, I was quarantined in the Military Police Battalion of the 31st Division. Father JEONG Kyu-Wan was already there. A few days later, lawyer HONG Nam-Soon also came to the Military Police Battalion of the 31st Division. Seeing Father JEONG Kyu-Wan being released after about a month, I had mixed emotions, wondering when I would be released. I stayed with common criminals for about a month, and then was transferred to the Air Force Military Police Battalion of Songjeong-ri.

I met lawyer HONG Nam-Soon, lawyer LEE Ki-Hong, Father KIM Seong-Yong, and Professor SONG Ki-Sook there. It was very nice to meet them. Under the investigation by the military prosecution, I denied all the points wrongly reported in the investigation report for three days. I was working with Professor SONG Ki-Sook to prepare a response to the final draft of the prosecutor's final report. The prosecutor threatened in tears that if Professor SONG or I denied the crime, he would take us back to the Defense Security Command and investigate all over again. In the middle of the investigation, I saw Professor SONG, and he signaled that he would sign with his thumbprint. I said no but soon realized that denial was meaningless. So I signed with my thumbprint.

Disheartened, I entered the guardhouse of the Air Force; everyone asked about our decision. We chuckled and made a gesture of signing. Lawyer HONG scolded us, saying, "You shouldn't have signed it even if you were beheaded. But you did." However, Father KIM Seong-Yong and lawyer HONG Nam-Soon also came in disheartened on the third day of the prosecutor's interrogation. They had no other choice but to sign.

On the day the interrogation was over, lawyer HONG Nam-Soon complained to me, "Father CHO, where is God! If God existed, how could all this happen?" He expressed his anger in a loud voice and protested. I calmed him down saying, "Sir, take it easy," and explained the "parable of the wheat and the weeds" from the Bible. The investigation report was typed and delivered to me.

The prosecutor demanded seven years in prison, and the judge sentenced me to three years in prison in the General Military Court. I was released on October 30th, 1980, exempted from execution of the sentence. Waiting for the truth about Gwangju to be revealed even in court, I appealed to the High Military Tribunal and to the Supreme Court, but all the appeals were dismissed.

I gave my final testimony in the General Military Court: "Although they accused me of rebellion by distorting and manipulating the truth, surely the day will come when those who are judging me now and I are judged before the people, history, and justice." Now is the time not to curse and hate anyone, not to distort history, not to repeat tragedies, but to tell the truth.

It was said that a Province Hall executive official visited my church when I was being investigated at the Defense Security Command, and he said, "Father CHO had a hard time retrieving the weapons, so I will recommend him to the government awards for a citation."

The church believers told me that they had found my name in the roll of honor. It was so ridiculous that they told him, "Are you out of your mind? The Father was taken to the Defense Security Command and is not even allowed visitors. What is the use of awarding him a citation?" He felt sorry and left.

What a contradiction this is: The martial law forces took me and accused me of rebellion; and the administrative authorities would grant me a citation?

I have two pieces of evidence to reverse the martial law forces' claim to the Gwangju People's Uprising. They denied that they had ever given an order to open fire, I clearly remember that a First Sergeant gave a shoot-to-kill order at around 4:20 a.m. on the 27th.

The other is the very strafing that occurred from helicopters on the 21st. They claim that they shot in self-defense, but that is an outright lie. They are deceiving history and the people in saying that shooting from a helicopter is self-defense.

Who should be responsible for the Gwangju Tragedy? Needless to say, the tyrants who were involved in causing the innocent to bleed, seizing power by trampling on the wounds of Gwangju, receiving medals, and enjoying prosperity, should be held accountable. It is an inevitable command demanded by history, conscience, justice, and the people. Therefore, in the name of the people, we strongly urge those involved in the suppression to step down from power and make atonement to mark a milestone for genuine democratization, restoration of public trust, and social stability, and to usher in a new era. Even if we should forget the tragedy now, it still haunts us; even if we should forgive them, our heart remains hardened; even if we should reconcile, our hearts are not relieved. The reason is that, until the present, they have been giving us a prescription that is nothing more than a stopgap measure without healing the fundamental wound. If we all hope for a democratic society and genuine national reconciliation, the government should 1. Tell the truth, and admit and apologize for the faults; 2. Realize true democracy; 3. Have the people involved step down from the political frontlines and power; 4. Restore the honor of Gwangju; 5. Compensate for damages; 6. Build memorials; and 7. Consecrate the cemeteries.

V. FIERCE BATTLES

1. The Gwangju Station

3068. I was Shot by the Martial Law Forces on the Night of the 20th
__ **JEONG Hyeon-Taek**

2. Gwangju Park

2025. Firearm Training and Command of Local Defense at Gwangju Park
__ **MOON Jang-Woo**

3. The Province Hall

3107. Both Legs Cut Off __ **PARK Byeong-Jun**

2014. An Attack on the Province Hall by a Middle School Commando
__ **CHOI Dong-Buk**

4. Gwangju Young Women's Christian Association (YWCA)

3109. To Take Up Arms for Democratization __ **CHEON Young-Jin**

V FIERCE BATTLES

1. The Gwangju Station

3068. I was Shot by the Martial Law Forces on the Night of the 20th

Witness: JEONG Hyeon-Taek (male)
Date of Birth: June 19, 1956 (aged 24)
Occupation: Office Worker
Date of Record: November 1988

Research & Arrangement by PARK Hyeon-Sook

Taking Evening Classes in Community College While Working

I was born in Jangseong and grew up there until I graduated from elementary school. My father ran a small business, but it did not go as well as he planned, so he stayed home. My mother was a school teacher. Because my father failed in business, my family had serious financial problems when I attended middle school. It was difficult for a family to sustain life on only the salary of a public school teacher, without extra income from farming. Because of the family circumstances, I gave up going to a general high school, although I attended East Middle School in Gwangju. I thought I had to make money after graduating from a vocational high school because my family had a hard time. While attending middle school, I commuted from Jangseong to Gwangju and sometimes lived with my younger brother in Gwangju. And sometimes I also stayed in my relative's house.

After graduating from a commerce high school, I applied to a bank but failed. I believed that I could be accepted because I had kept my grades moderate. I guess I failed because the bank reduced the number of employees due to the recession. So, I prepared for the civil service examination. After a while, I applied to the riot police, thinking that the situation of the job market would be better when I completed military service. I was trained in Nonsan and served at the Yeonggwang Police Station. Also, I served with the coast guard in Gangjin and Wando. For this reason, I feel close to and familiar with the riot police. Even when I was shot, I suspected that soldiers would not shoot me.

Discharged from the military service in March, 1979, I got a job at Samyangsa in April that year. Until I was shot, I had rented a room in Im-dong and stayed with my younger brother who attended high school. I worked hard.

The October 26th Incident happened while I was in the military. I had no interest in politics at the time. But I sometimes cursed PARK Chung-Hee. In particular, my senior soldiers swore a lot at him because they thought he was too much. There was a lot of controversy about him. I got to know about the October 26th Incident from the radio and clapped my hands, thinking "Well done." I thought it was good that the evil one died.

I was taking an evening class in college ("Tax Accounting 1" at Seongin Gyeongsang Community College) while I worked during the day in 1980. I happened to see demonstrations, going back and forth between my office and the downtown in May. I watched the demonstrations out of curiosity and believed that the students did that for something meaningful. I thought I should support them by standing by them though I could not join them as they protested for an important purpose, not just for staying away from their studies, even in those hot days. I had no special interest in a civil movement but had an implicit antigovernment tendency.

At First, Looking on at the Protest

I saw the torchlight protest in the downtown on May 16th. I saw it on my way to the downtown to have a dinner with my senior colleagues. It was great to see students singing in a row while the riot police stood around them and watched.

I went downtown the next day, too. At first, I looked on at the protest but then joined it. Following the rear of the protest procession, I sang together with the others. Citizens were confronting the soldiers standing in front of the Province Hall as the citizens tried to advance to the Province Hall while occupying Geumnam-ro. Then, suddenly, soldiers marched down from the Veterans' Administration Office. The citizens dispersed in groups in all directions. I also ran away. It was unimaginable for me to join a protest because I was an old college student and working for a company. Moreover, I had no time to leisurely linger in the downtown because my company was located in the outskirts. I used to go downtown to visit a bank on the Geumnam-ro 2nd Street for business even though I understood what was going on there. But I should not have joined the protest. I remember students in my community college discussed whether to join the protest at the Province Hall or not. On the 18th, I went to Gwangju to see my old friend who had stayed close to me during the military service. When I tried to go to Gwangju in the afternoon that day, he dissuaded me, saying that Gwangju was quarantined. But I insisted on going to Gwangju for my work the next day. But I couldn't get there because all public transportation had stopped. After looking for a way to Gwangju for a while, I was able get there with the help of people who had come from Seoul to go fishing.

I walked home from the Intercity Public Bus Terminal around 9:00 p.m. I didn't expect the streets toward Im-dong would be closed to traffic. When I stepped toward Geumnam-ro, I couldn't see anyone. I could see about ten military trucks pulled over near

Soochang Elementary School. Without knowing what was happening, I walked across the street. The soldiers didn't have any reaction to me at all. Later, I heard that soldiers had beaten and taken people, but they let me pass by at the time. Judging from that, I guess that the soldiers had just arrived. But I thought that it was strange to see the military trucks pulled over, not knowing whether they were paratroopers or not. I didn't know the seriousness of the situation until I heard stories from the people in Im-dong.

I went straight home that evening and slept. The next day, I came out for work. My office was in front of the St. John of God Hospital. Ladies out in the street told me to run away. They also told me that the soldiers stopped vehicles and ordered those who looked like college students to get off, beat them up, and took them somewhere. I was twenty-five at the time, so I looked like a college student. I told them I would just go to work and walked into an alley toward my work. I worked all day. But all my concern was with the downtown.

I went downtown on the 19th, too. Students went up the stairs of the Catholic Center to catch the paratroopers who were reportedly hiding and radioing. Knowing that, other soldiers rushed into the building. Many students were arrested, and I saw people running away leaving the students behind. I felt so bad at that moment.

I went downtown on the 20th, too. But I don't remember anything special. Stuck in the crowd, I moved toward the Gwangju Station via Yu-dong and the Intercity Public Bus Terminal. I remember soldiers were guarding the Gwangju Station area. And I heard they shot blanks that evening.

I went back to work after finishing my task in the downtown on the afternoon of the 20th. I think nothing special happened like the previous day. I didn't complete my work but left the office earlier than usual around 7:00 p.m., thinking I would continue my work the next day. I left earlier because I thought I would not be able to work because of the commotion outside.

After leaving, I went straight home. I lived in Im-dong with my younger brother, who was in his second year at Dongsin High School. I told him not to go outside because it was noisy and dangerous. And we went to bed early.

Maybe it was around midnight. I felt into a deep sleep but suddenly heard an uproar outside. My house was on one side of the street in front of Seorim Elementary School. I woke up to the noisy sound of citizens. To the sound of the citizens singing the national anthem, I looked out from the second floor, wondering what was happening. Many people occupied the streets and sang the national anthem, moving from St. John of God Hospital to Mudeung Stadium. I was touched by the scene of the citizens surrounded by the vigorously resounding national anthem. I left home in a sweat suit, earnestly telling my bother not to go outside. I began to find out the current situation in joining the citizens and singing the national anthem. The citizens were crowded along the way from Mudeung Stadium to the Yu-dong Three-way Intersection. Some citizens walked, and some road in cars. I saw an overturned eight-ton truck reportedly from the Gyeongsang Province. And I moved toward the Gwangju Station via the Yu-dong Three-way Intersection. Then, I moved to the area near the MBC station, passing the Intercity Public Bus Terminal. I was standing there, watching the MBC station burn from a fire set by citizens because it had reported false information and biases on Gwangju issues. While moving around, the number of the people continued to remain the same. I moved from the Public Bus Terminal to the Gwangju Station as the citizens suggested burning down the KBS station that engaged in distorting Gwangju along with MBC. But we could not advance any more when confronting paratroopers near the fruit and vegetable market near the Gwangju Station.

Shot at the Gwangju Station

I was trying to grasp the situation, following the rear of the procession instead of leading in the front. Watching the protesters confronting the paratroopers on their way to the KBS station, I thought I should go home then. It was about 1:00 a.m. Alleys were dark, and it was said that soldiers were standing guard here and there, so I was too scared to go home. I gave up going home and followed the protestors, thinking that I would tell my colleagues at work the next morning and at school in detail about what I had seen. I am not sure what time it was but the citizens sometimes rolled down metal barrels filled with gas toward the Gwangju Station. Bullets were flying among about a thousand of the crowd. I guessed the bullets flying toward the sky above Im-dong Catholic Church and the Intercity Public Bus Terminal were blanks. I thought they were tracer bullets or blanks because they were shot toward the sky. And because it was not long after I was discharged from the military, I was sure that they were blanks.

However, people began to run with all their might toward the fruit and vegetable market behind the procession. I moved to the front from behind and stopped them from running away, shouting at them that they were just blanks. Keeping moving forward in that situation, I found myself standing in the very front of the procession. While standing in the front, I was seriously concerned that they might really shoot me. At the time, a metal barrel was ablaze in the front of the procession across from the fruit and vegetable market.

At that very moment I suddenly heard a bang in front of me, and something brushed past me, who was just standing there, and I felt as if I had been hit by a hammer. I didn't know whether I was shot or not. But I realized that I was when I touched my back and saw the blood. Even at that moment, I said, "I am shot," falling down. I guess that I was shot because I was exposed by the light of the burning metal barrel in front of me to the paratroopers stationed at the Gwangju Station, who aimed at my heart and fired. There were dozens of people around me. I am not sure how many people were hurt but I saw the person behind me get shot and fall down.

People supported and carried me to the rear of the procession, telling me to stay with them. They wrapped my wound with a towel. Three people beside me tried to carry me on one's back to hospital. We got out of the procession but stayed where we were for a while. Fortunately, a Gwangju Express Bus came from between the Public Bus Terminal and the Gwangju Station and got me. I sat in the back supported by the people sitting in the front seats. A moment later, another wounded person got on, but I saw him collapsing as soon as he stepped in. In fact, the man was shot, and the people helped him get on the bus. But, unfortunately, he was shot on the bus again by a bullet from outside the bus. I kept myself up so I would not lose consciousness after I was shot, and the bus ran looking for a hospital, slipping toward Yang-dong.

Arriving at a general hospital, the people knocked on the door. But as no one answered, they broke the window in an angry uproar. But the door stayed closed in the end. The bus we were riding wandered quite a while. In the bus, some people stayed with the wounded to care for them. The bus stopped at a doctor's office in front of the Hanmi Shopping Center in Daein-dong. I am not sure whether the office was Kim's Orthopedics or not, but we got emergency treatment there. We headed to a medical center for special treatment as the doctor told us he could not treat the wounds there.

I thought, "It's unfair. I don't think it's time to die. I should have protested more." I also wondered if I would be shot dead like that or hospitalized. I don't remember where and how the bus moved, but we finally arrived at the Red Cross Hospital. I got emergency treatment there again. Giving me a dextrose solution, they said I needed special treatment. They also told me to go to CNU Hospital, but we were worried because a rumor circulated that the CNU Hospital was closed. Just in time, an ambulance driver suggested trying the CNU Hospital. So, I was supported by four people, and the ambulance sped off carrying us to the CNU Hospital. It was probably between 2:00 and 3:00 a.m. The people who were supporting me in the ambulance gave me words of comfort, "You shall not die. You were brave."

Hospitalization for Nine Months

I found that many people were lying on the floor in the CNU Hospital. The people who had supported me returned to their places, and I was left alone on a bed in the emergency room. The next morning, a doctor asked me about my contacts. I told him that if he contacted my company, people from the company would come. When my colleagues came to the hospital around 10:00 a.m. and signed a consent form for a surgery, I lost consciousness. When I came to my senses, I found myself lying in the intensive care ward. I regained consciousness between 2:00 and 3:00 p.m. on the 21st. Later, I heard that a bullet had pierced through my left chest, grazed the pericardium, and stuck in my back. Because of that, my diaphragm, lung, and large intestine were ruptured, and my pancreas was gone. The first surgery was successful, and I was sent to a room on the tenth floor a week later. However, a month later, an infection formed around the wound and pus burst out, so I had to have surgery again. After the first surgery, I was able to move soon since I was very healthy. But the pus formed around the wound because the surgery staff were too busy to sterilize the surgical instruments completely. Ten days after the second surgery, pus formed again, so the wound broke. Feces came out from my large intestine into my abdomen. I lost consciousness when I heard that the next surgery would be my last chance.

For ten days, I didn't know who came to visit me or how I was treated. When I regained consciousness, the doctor told me that he tried surgery again because I was young and healthy. As I was in that situation, my parents came from Jangseong to take care of me on the 21st. They couldn't sleep while caring for me. My mother stopped teaching for me. I had surgery four times in three months. Domestic medicine didn't work, so I relied on imported medicine. At first, the hospital told me that they couldn't afford the imported medicine because it was too expensive, so my family paid for it. Because of that, my family was in enormous financial difficulty. My parents sold the house in Jangseong to pay for my hospital bill. And they served me dog meat and beef a lot. However, I suffered many times because when I ate something, my stomach ripped, and food leaked into my abdomen.

After having surgery on the morning of the 21st, I heard from my friend about the stories outside. He said that soldiers shot at the protestors and that the citizens took up arms to confront the soldiers.

On the morning of the 26th, I guess, I heard gunfire, so I looked out. I was on the tenth floor, and bullets flew into the hospital room, broke the window, and stuck in the ceiling. Because of that accident, a nurse hurt her hand.

While sleeping on the dawn of the 27th, I suddenly heard a loud sound of gunfire outside. A plaintive female voice echoed through the speaker from Hak-dong, saying, "Dear, citizens." The message was that death was near.

I looked out around 6:00 p.m. and saw the soldiers coming in from Hak-dong with tanks in front of them. Behind the several tanks, they were moving along the street on each side toward the Province Hall.

I was questioned just once while in the hospital. When I was lying in the recovery room around on the 27th, which was three or four days after the surgery, the military and police joint investigation team came to question me. I suspect that the man who investigated me was a police officer instead of someone working in the Defense Security Command or an intelligence agency. And I cannot remember his position and rank, but he was in plain clothes. Other patients in the same room were also investigated by the man. He asked me how I had been hurt, and I answered him with the truth. He defined me as a rioter and categorized me as grade C. At the time, I didn't know anything but told the truth. In fact, I couldn't lie. Later, I heard that those who lied to him and the leaders, except students who had actively participated in the protest were taken to the Integrated Hospital and beaten up. I didn't say I was a student. But when I found my record later, it was written that I was a student. And I learned later that they came to my college for the investigation. I was accused of being a rioter because I told the truth. It was said that other people, that is the ones who were injured accidently, received compensation of two or three million won. However, I was accused of being a rioter, so I didn't receive compensation at all.

In February 1981, I was discharged from the hospital after nine months. I was not fully recovered, but I was frustrated and could not endure life in the hospital. In addition, not only my parents had a hard time in the hospital, but also we could not cook food good for my recovery. So, I chose to be discharged. The hospital official said that I could receive regular outpatient treatment. And I decided to go home and receive the outpatient treatment. I was not forced to leave the hospital.

The suffering in the hospital for nine months was indescribable. In addition to the rotting smell, whenever I ate something, excrement leaked out. And I was washed every morning and evening, getting dressing treatment twice a day. As I got the dextrose solution continuously, it became difficult to find a place to insert the IV. Since I was first hospitalized, I stayed with six other patients, and later with three. However, other patients complained about the bad smell from my body, so I was transferred to a private room. After two months, when I got the third surgery, something began to decay inside my body. Feces leaked out, and the smell was so terrible that I could not stay with other patients. That is how I used a private room as the hospital took special measures for me. As I got better, I stayed in a room for two people. At first when I used the private room, I didn't have to pay for it. But as I got better, the hospital told me that they could not pay for it forever. But I could not move to a room for three people, so I stayed in the room for two people for over five months. Then, my family had to pay for the difference between the room for two and the room for three. The cost of hospitalization and medicine was affordable. I could manage to pay for the cost with the money that I had saved.

However, when I was discharged in February, I spent a lot of money because I had to eat good food. I rested in Jangseong for a year but had a relapse. Whenever I got a cold, I coughed up phlegm, so I got treatment in the hospital. My company tended to give me favors. They allowed me to work in the morning and to have an injection in the hospital in the afternoon. After that I went back home to Jangseong. I would rather say I went to work as nothing more than a formality to get paid. In the winter that year, I might have overworked myself, got a cold with high fever, and had a relapse. It was sometime in December when my lungs began to decompose. It smelled bad, and I had expectoration of blood. I was hospitalized at the CNU Hospital for the second time. However, I heard that my organs became so hardened and complexly entangled that they could not perform an operation. I felt hopeless. We decided to take medication, but it didn't work well. I went to Wonkwang University Hospital and had surgery. I went there because my physician at the time of 1980 became a medical specialist and transferred to the Wonkwang University Hospital. I was on medication and got surgery there until March. But after twenty days, I had a relapse. My stomach ripped, and

I got a second surgery. The doctor told me the operation went well, so I was relieved. However, I had to have surgery again because pus formed. In this way, I got surgery seven times. I cannot describe my struggle against the illness for two years. Until now, when I get a cold, I cannot think of any exercise at all as pus forms again. I cannot sit up for very long because my left chest collapsed and ribs were removed. In addition, I do not meet my friends, drinking and hanging around with them, because of my situation like that. When I get home after work, all I can do is just lay myself down for a couple of days. I often wake up at night because I have a sore side. Sometimes, when my body severely ached, I wept and fell asleep.

Attempting Suicide

I thought about committing suicide a few times. While getting the dextrose solution, at the moment my parents went outside, I took out the needle to kill myself. I did so because I heard that blood would drain out when taking out the needle. But I failed as I was discovered doing that. I attempted suicide with electric outlets and tried to throw myself out the window. I could barely manage to walk out of the room on the tenth floor, but I could not kill myself because my parents appeared in my mind's eye. At some point, I gave up on killing myself. I began to believe that a brave man was the one who lived and died with a sound mind. I also thought that a fool was the one who sat idle and died. As Spinoza says, I am living as if I knew that tomorrow the world would go to pieces, I would still plant my apple tree. I don't know when I will die, but I will live to the fullest.

Reading the Bible, I believe I am greatly loved by God although I am sick. I did not complain to God even when the food decayed inside my body and leaked out in indescribable pain. Others complained to God about less serious wounds than mine. But I read the Bible next to them and listened to the preaching of pastors. I didn't know about God's word before, but His word came to me differently when I was lying in bed. I thought God let me get hurt because He loved me so much that He wanted me to overcome the suffering that produced perseverance. Thinking like that, I was glad that my suffering was interpreted as a course that led me to perseverance. I had a strong belief that I would never die. If I would not die despite a great deal of suffering, I should consider overcoming suffering a training course, a test. Thinking like that, every day was not that painful.

I am living with that belief. I have thanked God since I considered my suffering a test. In this belief, I have overcome suffering while reading the Bible. My struggle in the hospital impressed a newly appointed nurse, who had just graduated from college. She said that she had wondered how I could endure such suffering. In May, 1985, I got married to the nurse who had cared for me. My wife, born in Jeonju, quit her job and has dedicated herself to family life. I always thank her because she married me to sacrifice herself for me. After I decided to thank God as I overcame the suffering in the agonizing hospital bed, I thought I have to work for God. However, social life made me gradually keep away from God's work. So, my wife and I promised that if we had a son, we would give our son to God. I feel sorry for him, thinking that he would have to do a lot of work in the countryside and suffer hardships to become a pastor working for God. Sometimes, my eyes are full of tears when I see my three-year-old boy sleeping, feeling sorry for him.

As I got injured, all my family was disturbed. My family was not rich but gentle and warm-hearted. I always feel bad that my younger siblings could not attend school properly because of me. My younger siblings seem to be under the influence of my circumstances. My parents have suffered a lot. They have passionately cared for me, enduring both mental and physical sufferings. When I was in the hospital, my mother suffered beyond description as she came to me after work and cared for me overnight and went to work as a school teacher the next morning. My father suffered from stomach diseases. As he stayed alert because of me, his stomach got better instead.

When I separated from my family after marriage, I was able to ease my parents' worries a little. As I got married, they could live themselves, forgetting about me even for a while! I always tried my best and thought I would do something. However, my life now seems to be just lived rather than to live by myself. I think this situation is my destiny. I would like to kill CHUN Doo-Hwan, thinking him wicked, but there is nothing I can do. I just have that thought because my parents are still alive and now I must make a living as the head of a family with a child. As I try to make a living, I cannot care for other things. I just think I hurt myself, comforting myself.

However, if someone wants to take revenge, I would like to help him.

My strenuous and traumatic life for seven or eight years is beyond description. In 1985, the Regional Development Committee gave me compensation of seven million won. I also received compensation of three million won.

People around me ask how much compensation I received, assuming that it amounts to more than ten million won. That is ridiculous. All my sufferings I have experienced would not be adequately compensated even if someone gave me more than a hundred million won.

I believe that May 18 was self-defense against forced violence. I can say that the students were moderate at first but severely harmed by the soldiers later. I believe that we should consider the students innocent, as they suffered, inhaling tear gas in those hot days. May 18 was meaningful and a great event. Still, when I see students protesting, I stop walking, watch them, and leave when they are done. I am so touched by and grateful to the students when I see them. My doctor tells me that tear gas is like poison to me, dissuading me from joining a protest. Although I am too old to join them, I watch them and stand by them, hoping my standing beside them can support them. I always feel bad for them and grateful to them. I just feel bad because all I can do is just watch them when they are struggling to restore my rights.

V FIERCE BATTLES

2. Gwangju Park

2025. Firearm Training and Command of Local Defense at Gwangju Park

Witness: MOON Jang-Woo (male)
Date of Birth: May 28, 1953 (aged 26)
Occupation: Owner of Sangbo Moonwhasa
(currently in Korea Lifesaving Volunteers)
Date of Record: May 1989

Research & Arrangement by SHIN Bong-Hwa

Overview

MOON Jang-Woo was a platoon leader of the Hakun-dong Reserve Army in 1980. He set fire to the Tax Office on May 20th and then gathered young people and sent them to Naju, Hwasun, Jeonnam Textile, and Ilshin Textile to capture weapons. In addition, after training citizens to use firearms at Gwangju Park, he divided the area into local defense zones and led about 100 citizen militia members to take charge of local defense at the Hungry Bridge in Hakun-dong. However, they surrendered all their weapons at the request of the downtown patrol team of the Province Hall on May 23rd. After that, he fled to his friend's house and surrendered himself on June 26th, suffered severe torture, and was released in April 1981.

Applied to be a Staff Sergeant but Soon Deserted

I was born in Hakun-dong, Gwangju, in 1953 as the third of

four sons and two daughters. Because my father was a doctor of Oriental Medicine, I had a good life. Known as a leader among the kids in the neighborhood, I used to skip school while hanging out with my friends from the sixth grade of elementary school. I thought I could live well enough without going to school, so I quit school in the sixth grade. At first, it was good to just play without going to school. However, when I saw my friends going to school in school uniforms, I envied them and thought I wanted to study. Eventually, I studied on my own and completed my middle school courses with the qualification exam.

After that, I helped with my father's work, and I applied to be a staff sergeant and received education at the Sangmudae Artillery School in 1972. There, math was the most necessary to measure distance when shooting, but I, who did not receive a regular education, had a lot of difficulties in shooting. I managed to pass the artillery sergeant qualification test, but it was still difficult. However, I worked harder than anyone else and received the highest score on the graduation test for the artillery sergeants. I desperately felt that I had to learn during the course of training. In particular, I felt the need to study more because I had to write a diary record in English and Chinese letters when acting on behalf of my superior. I couldn't overcome my regret about learning, so I transferred to Soongmoon High School in my military uniform.

When the 51st Division in Jochiwon was renamed the 32nd Division in the early fall of 1973, one artillery unit was established, and 200 soldiers, including officers and sergeants, applied to transfer to Sangmudae in Gwangju. At that time, I, who had not applied and did not want to go, was transferred.

From the first day on my way to the Jochiwon unit, I had a quarrel with a soldier and beat him, which became known to my superior, so I was beaten. Dissatisfied with the military, and even beaten by my superior, I took out my resentment by beating up the Artillery Lieutenant Colonel. I was afraid that I would immediately be sent to the stockade for assaulting my superior, so I deserted the military. After the desertion, I surrendered to the 5th Division of Yangpyeong, Gyeonggi-do, and spent five months in the stockade. And I was expelled from the military in December 1973. Because I couldn't fulfill the twenty-four months of my military service as a staff sergeant, I was expelled rather than discharged from the military.

Immediately after coming down to Gwangju, I had a physical examination and was transferred to the army reserves. At that time, I met the woman who would become the mother of my children and lived with her, and went to work. After job-hopping, I began working as a sales manager for an advertising agency in 1980. As the branch manager started another business, I took over the company. I was excited about preparing a business plan when May 18 came.

How Could I Endure Injustice?

I met a friend named PARK Kwan-Soo at Samyang Coffee Shop behind the Chungjang-ro Police Box on the afternoon of May 18th. While I was discussing my business plans with him, customers in the coffee shop approached the window and looked outside. We also looked outside, wondering what was going on. Seven or eight students were fleeing with all their might past the Chungjang-ro Police Box, followed by forty to fifty paratroopers chasing the students like hunting dogs. The paratroopers, who couldn't catch the students, caught the passers-by instead and hit them with clubs. They caught even a female student and threw her down mercilessly on the street. They dragged the girl to the underground passage, her clothes peeled off and her bosom exposed. People were watching the scene from all over the surrounding buildings, but no one could protest. I could not say anything either.

However, the paratroopers even caught a man in his forties

or fifties who was riding a bicycle, broke his bicycle, and beat his back mercilessly with clubs. I couldn't stand the boiling anger anymore and shouted at those who were committing atrocities.

"Hey, you sons of bitches. Are you soldiers of the Republic of Korea? Why are you beating innocent people?"

Then even the people from the surrounding buildings shared my anger and cursed the soldiers. At that time, when one of the soldiers looked at me, I flinched. I thought, "Everything will be fine," but, on the other hand, I sat down, smoking and ready to fight.

Immediately, paratroopers armed with bayonets fixed on M16s entered the coffee shop. Seven or eight soldiers, not two or three, flocked in groups. There were ten customers in the coffee shop; most of whom were old, and my friend and I were the only young people. The soldiers approached us and swung their clubs indiscriminately. We had no choice but to get struck. They hit us five or six times with clubs and ordered us to present our ID cards. When we presented our ID cards, a military officer said, "Guys! Let's go." And they left us alone. We were able to avoid a dangerous moment because of him. After that, we returned home late after walking here and there around the protests.

My friend and I decided to meet again at the Samyang Coffee Shop on May 19th, and I went out in a suit. After meeting that friend and discussing some business ideas, I went to the Catholic Center. There were few students there, only paratroopers and the police. As the citizens in the vicinity pointed at the paratroopers and criticized them for the violence so far, the soldiers fired tear gas. When the tear gas detonated, the citizens would flee and then gather again.

Until then, I had been hesitating over whether I should proceed with my business or fight against injustice, while not being able to actively join the protest. However, since I had watched the protests that day and the day before, I couldn't stand still any longer. As a citizen of Gwangju, I felt that the students should be protected and more young people should participate. At last, I concluded that I would fight for my country and people.

Once I had made the decision, I was lighthearted and protested passionately with the demonstrators. When the paratroopers fired tear gas, I threw stones eagerly with other protesters. One time, during a protest, I was chased by paratroopers and was confronted by them in a dead end near the Red Cross Hospital. Two paratroopers rushed at me with their bayonets fixed. Trained in judo and boxing, I felt like I would be beaten to death if I kept still, so I moved quickly and kicked the paratroopers' guns and ran away. I was able to dodge that life-or-death crisis.

That evening, I was trying to get home but was afraid that other protesters might have followed my example and abandoned the protest, so I couldn't go home. Even if I had gone home, I felt that my resolve to fight would have been weakened in the presence of my wife and children. I couldn't find a place to sleep, so I went to sleep in a drain pipe –a large concrete sewer pipe – that was lying at a sewer construction site near Jeonnam Technical High School. I was wearing a suit, so I took off my jacket and slept, careful about getting my clothes dirty. But it was cold, so I went to one of my seniors' houses near Chonnam National University Hospital. On the morning of May 20th, I went back to the downtown from the senior's house.

Arson at the Tax Office

The night of the 20th was the day I was most active. Around 10:30 to 11:00 p.m., I tried to go to Chungjang-ro from the College of Medicine at CNU but went to the front of the Tax Office. Many citizens of all ages had gathered in front of the Tax Office. While walking through the crowd and going to the front of the Tax Office, I suddenly heard gunshots. The paratroopers on both sides of the Tax Office fired. Three young men from the direction of the Labor Office were shot and fell down. The protesters who heard the gunshots did not scatter, but instead screamed and rushed toward the Tax Office. Then the paratroopers who were standing guard outside the Tax Office fled into the Tax Office.

Upset by the sudden gunshots, several young men gathered the people. They cried out to the citizens, "The military must strengthen the national defense with the taxes we paid, but instead, they aim their guns at the hearts of their own people. So, we don't even need the Tax Office. Let's get rid of the Tax Office." A few young men brought a military truck. I sat in the driver's seat and a young man sat next to me. Citizens poured gasoline onto the car and set it on fire.

I was afraid I would get shot if I rushed forward, so I put the car in reverse and sped toward the Tax Office. Then many Molotov cocktails and briquettes were thrown at the Tax Office building. I slammed the car into the entrance of the Tax Office and jumped out of the driver's seat. I got out of the car quickly, but I had a strange feeling, so I jumped over the wall next to the Tax Office. In an instant, bullets fell toward me like rain. They were the bullets the paratroopers who had entered the Tax Office fired. If I had been only one second slower, I would have been torn with bullets. I had crossed the threshold of death once again. But the young man sitting next to me was nowhere to be seen. The Tax Office was on fire, and the surrounding citizens were clapping and cheering.

I went straight to the Labor Office and protested. I heard from the protesters that there were gunshots in front of the Labor Office and also at the New Gwangju Station.

I was exhausted after protesting for so long. I suddenly remembered my family members. In particular, I thought of my older brother, who was physically disabled and lived in Junam village, Jiwon-dong. I went straight to my brother's house, and he and my sister-in-law welcomed me warmly. I was very tired and slept, but I couldn't get a deep sleep.

On the early morning of the 21st, I left for the downtown. I didn't have a car, so I walked toward the downtown for a while. When I arrived at the bus terminal in Hak-dong, I saw protesters riding on a bus with broken windows. Slogans were written on the side of the bus, such as "Let's Kill CHUN Doo-Hwan," "Resign, SHIN Hyeon-Hwak," and "Free KIM Dae-Jung." And some cars had placards on them. Seeing the demonstrators using sticks and boards to beat vehicles in protest, I was filled with joy and pride. I walked up to Seokcheon Bridge in Hak-dong with a proud smile.

After getting a cigarette from a passerby at Seokcheon Bridge, I got in a protest bus. We drove around the city of Gwangju and got off in front of Chonnam National University Hospital. Instead of driving around aimlessly, I felt that I had to move around systematically. I tried to get a car, but there was no car, so I got on a protest bus passing by the Gwangju Stream. In the bus, someone called me and held my hand.

"Bro!"

It was KIM Chun-Guk, a younger friend from my neighborhood. Seeing him, I was very glad and worried at the same time.

"Chun-Guk, you go back home."

"I am all right. Don't you have a family where your children are waiting? So, please, you go back home."

"What are you talking about? I'm fine. What do you know about things like this?"

"What do you think you know?"

Hearing that, I became speechless. He continued to surprise me.

"If you fight for our country and nation, so do I."

I couldn't say anything more when I heard those words full of certainty from him, who I thought was only a youngster.

"O.K. Then you won't regret it, will you?"

"I'll be fine."

"Then, let's die together."

In this way, I joined with him in one heart.

We took the protest car and went to the front of the Province Hall. I saw that the citizens in front of the Tourist Hotel carried bodies of those who had been shot in a wagon as I was standing on the stairs in front of the National Federation of Fisheries Cooperatives.

Around 12:30 p.m., the paratroopers who were guarding the front of the Province Hall suddenly started firing warning shots down toward the floor of the Plaza in front of the Province Hall. There were also quite a few people who were shot down by stray bullets. As the citizens fled to the alleys from the sudden gunshots, now the paratroopers were aiming and shooting at the people. I quickly dodged toward Jin Internal Clinic. I couldn't see Chun-Guk.

There was also an elementary school student at that time, and he dodged bullets so well that there was no need for him to learn individual combat skills. On his way to the National Federation of Fisheries Cooperatives from Jeonnam Ilbo, he crawled on his stomach whenever bullets violently flew toward him, looking out left and right. And he ran toward Jin Internal Clinic. All the citizens applauded and cheered for him.

Leading the Capture of Weapons

I thought that the fight between the paratroopers, who were committing mass shootings with firearms, and us, who were bare-handed, would be like throwing eggs on rocks. In front of Jin Internal Clinic, I delivered a fervent speech to the citizens.

"Everyone, let's talk. I am MOON Jang-Woo, the company commander of the Hakun-dong Army Reserves. Right now, the paratroopers are firing indiscriminately, but we can't just fight with stones or wooden sticks, can we? So, let's all take up arms."

When I shouted out loud, twenty or thirty young people gathered.

"In each police box, police station, and Bangrim-dong in Gwangju, there are arsenal warehouses that can supply companies with weapons. There are also weapons in Ilshin Textile, Jeonnam Textile, Hwasun, and Naju. But the Gwangju police station must have already hid the weapons. There will be a lot of weapons in Hwasun Coal Mine, Naju, and other places, so let's go get them."

The young people also felt the need to seize weapons.

"Whoever is going to Naju, raise your hand."

Then some people raised their hands. They seemed to be the ones who had acquaintances there or who knew the geography of that region well. In this way, they were sent in groups to Naju, Hwasun, Jeonnam Textile, and Ilshin Textile for weapons. And when I asked to meet at Gwangju Park right after bringing weapons, it was around 1:30 p.m., I guess.

After I gathered the young men and sent them to each area, I expected that it would take two to three hours to capture the weapons. After wandering around the downtown by myself, I waited for them at Seokcheon Bridge of Hak-dong, an access to the road from Gwangju to Hwasun, around 3:00 p.m.

As expected, the protesters who went to Hwasun came back armed around 3:20 p.m., with two trucks loaded with firearms, dynamite, and live ammunition, and an LMG[39] in one truck. It looked like the weapons were taken from the Hwasun Coal Mine. I stopped the trucks and unloaded the weapons.

We got several thousand rounds of live ammunition for the LMG that could fire about 480 rounds per minute, and there were several boxes of dynamite. There were 400 to 500 firearms, but there were few M2s or M16s with repeating fire. Most of them

[39] Light machine gun.

were M1s that fired single shots. And as for the live ammunition, there were about twenty to thirty boxes of banana clips with thirty rounds and square clips with twenty rounds. The box was about thirty-five centimeters wide and thirty to forty centimeters high. I was very happy to see the live ammunition and to think that we could fight now. In an instant, many people gathered. I shouted at the citizens.

"Everyone who thinks himself as a citizen of Gwangju, pick up a gun."

Guns and live ammunition were distributed to 50 to 100 citizens there. At that time, KIM Bok-Soo, a junior acquaintance from my neighborhood, appeared in a reserve military uniform. KIM Bok-Soo also picked up a gun. Finally, we were fully armed.

After distributing guns, I gave the citizens some training to prevent gunfire accidents. I taught them when the safety device is locked on an M1, it will not unlock even if the butt plate is impacted. I also taught them that in the case of a carbine, live bullets can fire even when the safety device is locked. So, I told them to avoid any impact to the butt plate of a carbine. In addition, I taught them that even if the clip is removed, one bullet remains in the chamber of the carbine. So, I told them to make sure to remove it after removing the clip. After a rough education like this, I said, "Now that you have received your primary firearms training, let's gather at Gwangju Park, the final gathering place." From there, I loaded the leftover guns with the armed men into two cars and went to Gwangju Park.

Firearm Training and Command of Local Defense at Gwangju Park

When I went to Gwangju Park, the evening sunset shone on the ground of the park. It must have been around 5:00 or 6:00 p.m. In front of the park, an LMG was installed on piled-up flat benches, and 1,500 guns from Ilshin Textile, Jeonnam Textile, and

Naju were piled up to a height of fifty centimeters in front of the stairs of the park.

In addition, eleven Mercedes-Benz express buses were parked toward the downtown. A large number of people of all ages had gathered around them. Including some middle and high school students, about 400 to 500 people were handling rifles in unsafe ways. If anyone looked a little strange, they said, "Who are you?" and aimed the guns. Even more dangerous, many people wore fragmentation grenades on their chests, as seen in movies. If the safety pin had come off while a grenade was attached to the pocket, as if the pin were a ring for carrying the grenade, the entire park would have been in chaos. It was dangerous.

In the meantime, a forty-year-old man was holding a megaphone and teaching the citizens how to operate an LMG. But no one seemed to be paying attention. I, who led the capture of the weapons, took his megaphone and went out in front of the citizens. I intended to establish order and work systematically.

My voice was naturally loud, and I shouted even louder.

"I am MOON Jang-Woo, a citizen of Gwangju who lives in Hakun-dong. I was discharged as a staff sergeant a few years ago, and I am currently serving as a platoon commander in the Army Reserves in Hakun-dong."

When I identified myself like this, all the citizens looked at me.

"The reason I'm standing in front of you with a megaphone is that you're a rabble without a commander. If we act without order now, we will definitely hurt ourselves. The problem is the grenades you have on your chest. If you love and care for Gwangju citizens, the ones who are with the grenades should board the express buses in front of you, please. I beg you earnestly."

It was so chaotic that I had them get in the buses first. I asked them to do it several times in this way, and everyone got in the buses. Except for the citizens on the eleven Benz express buses, those left were asked to stand in a row and then sit down. And I continued,

"Excuse me, but, if you've served in the army, please raise your hand."

Several people raised their hands. When I asked them about their ranks, they were men who were discharged at the ranks of sergeant or staff sergeant.

"If the grenade on your chest explodes, not only you but also innocent citizens will be sacrificed. You don't need grenades now. Let's keep the grenades away from us for each other's safety. These people will retrieve the grenades, so please do not touch them and follow their instructions."

After asking the citizens to excuse me, I had those who had served in the army retrieve the grenades. About 200 recovered grenades were put into boxes and then were managed by one person. The reason that people followed my instructions well, I believe, must have been the invisible power of the person who planned the seizure of the weapons in front of Jin Internal Clinic.

Then, I went into each bus and did firearms training. First, I explained the same contents of training I did in Hak-dong to make the citizens aware of safety accidents. I told them, in case that we would confront martial law forces, to move to another place after shooting because our position would be exposed by the flashes from the muzzles of the rifles when we fired. In addition, we had attached the inner silver foil from packs of cigarettes to the front sight of our guns so we could identify our comrades and not shoot at each other. I also trained them in grenade throwing techniques just in case. The grenade would explode in a few seconds if it was thrown with its safety pin pulled out.

After finishing firearms training, I began to take action to besiege the mountain behind Chosun University, where the martial law forces who withdrew from the Province Hall were stationed.

"Come on! Let's all prepare for what's coming. The martial law forces retreated to the mountains behind Chosun University, but we don't know when they will return. Everyone here, please guard the downtown area, and those on the buses, please follow the lead car."

I divided the citizens into groups of ten and appointed those who had served in the army as group leaders. Then, I led the eleven Benz express buses along the side of the Gwangju Stream, passed the Hakgang Bridge, and stopped them near Chonnam National University Hospital on the road next to South Gwangju Joint Market. When the two buses in front stopped, the buses following them also stopped.

After dropping off eighty citizen militia members from the two buses, I gave simple firearms training and had them guard the local areas around Chonnam National University Hospital. As the buses departed, I deployed two buses each to the South Gwangju railroad station and the patient waiting room at Chosun University Hospital near Hak-dong Jeil Market. Then I went to Hak-dong with five buses. Two were placed on the Seokcheon Bridge in Hak-dong and one by the Soongeui Vocational High School building. After asking the militia members at Soongeui Vocational High School, "Please, don't play any pranks by shooting blank bullets because it would intimidate citizens," I finally led two buses to the Hungry Bridge in Hakun-dong, my stronghold. In this way, we besieged the mountain behind Chosun University, where the martial law forces were stationed.

Regional Defense of Hakun-dong

I went to Hungry Bridge with the citizen militia members on the Benz express buses. I knew the geography well and thought that was a very important point because the martial law forces would pass through that place if they didn't take the most direct route into the downtown. By the time we reached Hungry Bridge, darkness was slowly falling. It was hard to recognize people from a long distance.

As more than eighty militia members got off the bus, local residents welcomed them with applause. We decided to set up a barricade in the middle of the bridge to serve as cover. A white jeep with a Red Cross painted on it was abandoned at the senior citizen center next to the bridge, and there was as much as two dump-truck loads of timber. We brought them to the bridge, put the car in the middle of the bridge, and stacked the timber around it. There was a narrow space for just for one person to pass on either side of the barricade. And there was another abandoned car under Hungry Bridge, so I decided to use it as a command headquarters.

We reorganized the groups again. At first, six groups of twelve people were formed. Then, reserve forces in Hakun-dong and Sotae-dong, and young people in the neighborhood volunteered to form nine groups. But as young people continued to gather, the organization was expanded to eleven groups. There was a total of twelve groups including headquarters. I was the captain of the regional defense of the Hakun-dong Hungry Bridge, and I had YU Hong-Ryeol as my assistant. The reserve forces called me "platoon leader," or others called me "team leader."

After organizing the groups, group leaders were selected, and three live ammunition clips were distributed to each person. Since there were twenty to thirty rounds of live ammunition per clip, about seventy rounds were distributed to each. I entrusted YU Hong-Ryeol with the remaining ten guns and live ammunition, saying, "Don't distribute them to anyone without my permission." After distributing the live ammunition, everyone was told to work for two hours in three shifts, instead of everyone standing guard together.

Finally, I set the password and deployed the militia members to each region: Group 1 was placed at Hungry Bridge, Group 2 at the Hongrim Barbershop under Hungry Bridge in the rear, Group 3 under the bridge at the entrance to Sujeong Mansion, Group 4 at the stone wall of Sujeong Mansion, and Group 5 between Hungry Bridge and Hosanna Kindergarten in preparation for an attack from the direction of Jeungsim Temple. Group 6 was placed at Hosanna Kindergarten, which is closest to the mountain behind Chosun University, Group 7 under the juniper tree next to Hosanna Kindergarten, and Group 8 behind Mudeung Nursery. Also, Group 9 was placed at the main gate of Mudeung Nursery, Group 10 at the Mudeung Church and Taebong Village, and Group 11 at the open space next to the command headquarters. I deployed them strategically around Hungry Bridge in this way.

The residents brought us *gimbap*. It was enough for us to eat for two days. In addition, they brought a few boxes of energy drinks, cigarettes, and even money. We smiled at them and said, "Thank you for your sincerity, but we don't need money. Instead, help the elderly in the senior citizen center." As we had too many cigarettes, we also gave some to the senior citizen center. After filling their stomachs with the rice that residents cooked, the members went to the places where they were assigned in each group to guard each area.

I patrolled every two hours. And every hour I signaled that the area was safe. After one hour, the leader of Group 1 shot a blank, and the leader of Group 2 who heard it shot another blank, and in this way, up to the group leader 11, they also shot a blank. And if there was no problem, I shot two blanks from the headquarters. During the patrol, I went to the Seokcheon Bridge once, but there was nothing wrong. So that evening, the local defense was carried out without any major incidents.

A Fierce Battle with the Martial Law Forces

On the morning of May 22nd, the residents made *gimbap* again. We ate the leftover that we saved from the night before and brought the new *gimbap* to the senior citizen center. Some citizens brought us binoculars from their homes, and some said they would bring shotguns in their homes, but we didn't need shotguns. In these ways, the residents of Hakun-dong responded to us.

After breakfast, we thought the martial law forces would not be able to come down during the day, so we took a nap under the trees near the senior citizen center to be ready for the night guard. The team leaders stood guard duty together at Hungry Bridge.

I was curious about other areas, so I drove to Chonnam National University Hospital. Citizens were still conducting local defense in front of Chonnam National University Hospital. They recognized me and greeted me. When I saw them, I was gratified and returned to my post.

When night came, the crews again guarded the local areas without any change in position. However, on the morning of May 23rd, around 1:30 to 2:00, the sound of military boots of the martial law forces was heard in the village of Suksil on the mountain behind Chosun University. As they crossed the stream, they flashed their lanterns intermittently. It was about 200 meters away from the headquarters, and about 150 meters away from Groups 6 and 7 at Hosanna Kindergarten.

As Groups 6 and 7 discovered the martial law forces, they fired at them first. As the other groups started firing, the martial law forces also fired. There was a fierce battle on both sides. It was a dark night, but the surroundings were lit up by the muzzle flashes from both sides, as if a lot of fireflies flew around on a summer night. There was a fierce battle about half an hour. After a long time, I don't know which side stopped first, but the shooting stopped.

I couldn't move at night, but I thought there might have been casualties. So, I brought two assistants and patrolled the region beginning with Group 1. While on the patrol, I handed out a glass of *Soju*[40] to the crew members, supposing that they were cold. There was nothing wrong as a whole, except that a crew member of Group 4 deployed to Sujeong Mansion was missing. After I looked for him for a while, he came back from checking on the situations of the other groups. Once again relieved, I encouraged them and returned to the headquarters.

That morning, all the crews gathered to make a roll call, and no one was injured, and only the railing of Hungry Bridge had bullet holes. We were in high spirits with a sense of triumph. The residents who couldn't sleep due to the fierce battle in the middle of the night came out with their meals early in the morning with worried expressions.

After breakfast, I looked at the battlefield with the binoculars brought by the residents. I couldn't see any single human shadow, so I went to the battlefield to check the damage to the soldiers. There were only fallen pine trees shot by the bullets, and no traces of the soldiers were found.

I was at the headquarters in despair because I couldn't find any traces of the martial law forces. But a report from a resident of the Taebong Village in Sotae-dong came in. Two soldiers had taken some cooked rice. On hearing this, I organized a special commando force of six with audacity and courage and went to Taebong Village. Near Taebong Village, there were two caves that could accommodate more than 200 people, and we search the caves one by one. When I got to the front of the caves, I was very nervous because I didn't know where the attack would come from. We searched everywhere for thirty to forty minutes, but the soldiers were nowhere to be seen.

---

40) Korean vodka.

Paratroopers Who Came to Spy on Us Were Captured and Handed Over to the Province Hall

On Buddha's Birthday (the 21st), the people who went to Jeungsim Temple to worship Buddha were stranded and were coming down on the morning of the 23rd. However, at around 11:00 a.m., there was a young man in plain clothes among a group of citizens about twenty meters in front of us. One of my crew came up to me and said,

"Sir, there is a suspicious man over there."

"I saw him, too. Pretend you don't know."

We talked casually while smoking. Then he calmly tried to pass in front of us. As he was about to pass us, I snatched him up and knocked him over with my foot. Underneath his plain clothes, his military insignia was exposed. He was a staff sergeant. Meanwhile, another soldier in plain clothes who was following him, ran away in a hurry. Since he was seventy to eighty meters away from us, he couldn't be chased and caught. I fired my M2 automatic rifle in the air. Then the soldier stopped running away and stood still. Several crew members captured him. The soldier trembled with fear. His plain clothes also were taken off to reveal his military insignia, and his underwear was military boxer shorts. They were undoubtedly paratroopers who came to spy in the guise of civilians.

"Where is your hideout?"

"Everyone went over to Jiwon-dong, and only the two of us were left."

"Then where is your equipment?"

"It's under the steel tower of Taebong Village."

Some of the crew went there and brought back all their equipment. There were backpacks, shoes, submachine guns that paratroopers fire as their parachutes fall, and hardtack.

We tied them up with their own ropes. Around eighty to ninety percent of the citizens and other crew members gathered around and said the paratroopers should be killed. Some people were pointing guns at them.

"These men are the same soldiers, but let's not kill them because they are our compatriots," I persuaded them. At that time, two patrol members from the Province Hall came in a jeep. I handed them over along with their equipment to the patrol.

Returning the Weapons after Controversy

At about 1:30 p.m. that day, a patrol vehicle came and said they would retrieve the weapons. Even though we had no intention of returning the weapons, they begged for them, saying, "The weapons are too dispersed, so we will retrieve and redistribute them in order to establish a system." It made sense when I listened to them. The weapons were piled up next to the guard post. About half of the crew members said that they would never accept it. In particular, KIM Chun-Guk and others strongly opposed the idea: "if we return the guns, which are our second life, all that is left to us is death." There was no consensus, so I told the patrol team to come back after a while. In the meantime, I persuaded the crew to "get together with the citizens of Gwangju," and when they arrived two hours later, I returned all the guns between 3:00 and 4:00 p.m. on the 23rd. In this way, the Hakun-dong regional defense force was disbanded.

I loaded about 100 guns and live ammunition in the vehicle and went to the Province Hall with the patrol. Even when returning the weapons, I was very reluctant. When I went to the Province Hall, as I was told, weapons were being returned. Some people came out of the Province Hall.

"You have worked hard all this time."

"What are you going to do with the weapons?"

"We will retrieve the weapons and distribute them again once the situation changes."

"I don't know your age or occupation, but it seems that your idea is different from ours. It's good to maintain order in the Province Hall, the center of Gwangju, but it's a mess here."

"In what sense do you mean a mess?"

"If you have to stay at the Province Hall, the center of the city, if the martial law forces re-emerge, you will have no choice but to be treated like a frog in a well. Trained self-defense forces must stand vigilant at the martial law force's destination. Moreover, it is very problematic even to retrieve weapons from places where they are defending themselves."

"I understand that. It is none of your concern."

Even after hearing that, I felt bad at the thought that something was going wrong.

After I got out of the Province Hall and walked around the downtown, I became curious about the situation in the outskirts of the city. I couldn't go by motorcycle or car, so I rode a bicycle I found in downtown and went to Naju. Instead of going on a main road, I passed through Geumcheon along the local route to Naju and Wangok. I found that protest vehicles in Naju were unable to enter Gwangju. I stayed overnight in Naju.

The people of Naju were also aware of the situation in Gwangju, and everyone was very angry at the martial law forces.

On the night of the 25th, I came back to Gwangju and went to my friend's house in the downtown. I couldn't keep in touch with my home. I thought I would feel weakened if I contacted my family or went home.

On the 26th, I entered the Province Hall and stayed there for about two hours. I just felt like it was in chaos.

A Thoroughly Cautious Fugitive Life

The evening of May 26th was the anniversary of my friend's father's passing, so I went to my friend's place in Jiwon-dong. On the morning of the 27th, I heard that the martial law forces took control of the Province Hall. I could not express my feeling. The feeling of complete defeat in the fight was beyond description. Feeling completely defeated, I wailed. When I went outside, martial law forces on a truck were conducting a search operation.

After drinking with the reserve company commander and local seniors at the reserve company headquarters, I said, "See you later," and left there because I thought it was dangerous to stay. I heard later that the martial law forces attacked the reserve company headquarters thirty minutes after I left. I went to my friend's house. Fortunately, he said his house was safe and told me to stay. In this way, I took refuge in a friend's house who was living as a newlywed in Nongseong-dong.

I contacted my wife who was staying at her mother's and met her. I told my wife about my friend's house and had her memorize the route.

When she came to see me, I told her not to come straight from home but to stop by downtown and then go to Nongseong-dong, then go into someone else's house and check if there was anyone following her. I met my wife a few times like this.

Sometimes I went downtown with my friend. I was very careful because I was on the wanted list, with its bounties on posters in public. I always carried an imported hiking knife with me, thinking that if I had got caught in a check and it became dangerous, I would have killed police officers unconditionally. I thought I had to attack first instead of being attacked by a police officer with a pistol. Although nervous, I carried on with confidence.

However, I heard that, because of me, the reserve company commander was taken away and beaten, and the detectives went to visit my older brother living in Jiwon-dong and treated him harshly. I deeply agonized that I got many people around me in trouble.

In the meantime, broadcasts recommended that people related to 5.18 be turned in, saying they would be generously treated. My wife and my friends, who were tempted by this, recommended that I turn myself in. In my opinion, turning myself in would be like half-death instead of a lenient punishment. I told my wife not to come to me if she wanted me to turn myself in. However, two days later, my wife came back again and suggested that I turn myself in. She looked different than usual in saying that in a situation where I could die if I turned myself in.

Meanwhile, the executives of the YWCA Mountain Club tried to help me escape to Sangtae Village in Mokpo, with which they had a sisterhood relationship. They were going to deliver bags to the students in the Sangtae Village and let me stay there as they left. But I thought I was definitely going to be caught on the way. Knowing that there was no more space for me to stand on, I decided to turn myself in.

Turning Myself in to the Defense Security Command

I was afraid that I would be arrested if I went alone and turned myself in. So, I went to the Intelligence Department of Gwangju Police Station along with the chief of the local district office and the head of the Hakun-dong reserve force on June 26 and turned myself in. After a month as a fugitive, I turned myself in. While I was writing my affidavit in the Intelligence Department, two detectives came in. They even searched my cousin's house in Mukho, Gangwon-do. They suddenly shouted at me, "You bastard, why did you turn yourself in? You should have been caught by us!"

I was immediately handcuffed and taken to the Defense Security Command in a black Hyundai Pony. From that day on, I was tortured worse than death. I was taken to the basement of the Defense Security. A detective had me take off my hiking belt, buckle, and all of my clothes except my underwear. He whipped me with my belt mercilessly on my back. I was whipped hard more than 100 times, and my back was drenched with my blood. After asking me why I turned myself in, he asked me the place where I had been hiding.

"Where have you been for a month?"

"I was in Mudeung Mountain."

"Bullshit. The soldiers searched for you many times, but they couldn't find you."

"No, I like mountains, so I stayed out in nature."

I endured all the tortures with the belief that even if I gave up my life, I would never disclose the names of my friends who hid me.

"Well, how did you get your meals?"

"Of course, I skipped meals or dug kudzu roots to eat many times, and sometimes when I was really hungry, I went out to the city to ask for money from passersby to get ramen, bread, and some side dishes."

"Then, where in Mudeung Mountain have you been?"

"There are six caves between the middle mountaintop and the second reservoir area. I was in the third of the four caves on the right."

I answered plausibly because I was confident about the mountains. In fact, I wanted them to examine the scene. If two or three soldiers had taken me there, I was thinking to escape on the mountain. However, they did not inspect the refuge site.

They beat me without confirming where I had hidden. Not only that, they even subjected me to ant torture. They tied me up, covered my mouth, nose and ears, and placed me on a stretcher and put me on a lawn under a tree full of ants. The red ants clung to me all over my body. I trembled with fear.

Murderous Torture

I was left at Sangmudae with the Joint Investigation Head Quarters on June 28th. As soon as I got there, I began to be tortured. They put handcuffs on me behind my back, laid me upside down on a table, and struck the soles of my feet with a wet pickax handle seventy times. My legs were so swollen that I couldn't stand up, and I lost my sense of feeling. They kept having me stand up and torturing me. Then, they got me down on my knees, and they struck me forty times on each side of my shoulder with the handle of the pickax. Every time they hit me, I fell down and had to stand up again like a roly-poly toy. It was extremely hard to stand up in handcuffs. It took me more than two hours to get up and be knocked down eighty times.

I almost passed out, then they had me sit down in a chair and began to interrogate me. It was a bonus to be beaten if I lied while being questioned. I didn't say I captured the soldiers of the martial law forces, but only said that I had guarded the local area. After the first round of interrogation, I was sent to the guardhouse.

The next day, I was called back to the torture chamber. There were three investigators from the Seoul Joint Investigation Headquarters who seemed to weigh more than eighty kilograms. They questioned my alibi in the same way as in the Defense Security. I just told them that I was in the mountains. They did not listen to me but beat me up. While tying me up, they bent my knees and beat me with a pickaxe handle. Every time I was beaten, it felt as if electricity passed all over my body.

I was called out every two days. When I was called, I went as if a cow being taken to a slaughterhouse. They continued digging into the alibi, but I persisted to the end. They handcuffed me around my bent knees, put square bars between my knees, and began water torture. My head was so heavy that when it went down, they put a towel on my face and started pouring water over it. At first, I held my breath to avoid drinking water but could only do that for a while. My stomach swelled up with how much water I drank. They didn't just pour water. They made me drink water mixed with pepper and red pepper powder and tried to make me confess in every way. However, I could not betray my friends even if I had died. I fainted in a swoon.

I endured until the end of the torture. "Okay, if you say so, I will admit that you stayed in Mt. Mudeung." I won after the severe torture. I was carried into the guardhouse by the military police.

But I was called back again. It was already the fourth time after I had entered the guardhouse. They looked at me and asked me suddenly.

"You know KIM Bok-Soo, right?"

My heart fluttered for a moment because I did not know what KIM Bok-Soo, who served with the self-defense force in Hakun-dong, had said. I couldn't say I didn't know him at all.

"Yes, I know him."

"KIM Bok-Soo has already told us everything, so confess everything truthfully."

"What should I confess?"

"KIM Bok-Soo told me that you were the main culprit in the capture of the weapons."

"There is no such fact."

"Then, you didn't distribute weapons in Hak-dong?"

"There were some weapons there. And I took one and gave others to the people around me. How could I be the main culprit in the capture of the weapons?"

"We won't just sit back. You are telling us some clever lies." They tortured me with so-called chicken roasting. After lightly tying my neck with a rope, they bent my back, tied my hands and feet into an S shape, and hung me from the ceiling. And they turned me relentlessly about 100 or 200 turns. At first, I felt as dizzy as when I was on a swing. However, after turning around for a while, the rope that held me began to unwind and turned faster and faster. I felt as if sky and earth were spinning and driving my head into the ground. I vomited until I was empty.

Torture during Cross-examination

The interrogation continued.

"How many soldiers of the martial law forces did you kill?"

"I didn't kill any of them."

"Didn't you catch them alive and hand them over?"

"I didn't do it."

They brought KIM Bok-Soo to face me, perhaps because the torture did not work. KIM Bok-Soo told them all about the fact that I was the leader of the regional defense of Hakun-dong and caught two soldiers of the martial law forces and handed them over to the Province Hall. The investigators even patted Kim's head and commended him.

"KIM Bok-Soo, you are steady and honest. Want to smoke?"

KIM Bok-Soo told all about the incident while smoking and drinking a beverage. All my lies so far had been revealed, including the fact that I led the capture of the weapons and the firearms training as well as the grenade throwing drills.

When all the facts were revealed, they began to torture me like crazy hunting dogs. They handcuffed me, drew the soles of my feet close together, and placed a square timber ten centimeters in diameter and two meters in length between my legs. One of the investigators bent my head back, and the two over eighty kilograms stood on my legs and rubbed them with the timber. My legs were about to fall apart as they trampled on them. I cried out for the extreme pain, "Hey! You, sons of bitches, kill me with a gun instead. Why are you causing me so much pain?" While I couldn't move, I spat in their faces. Then they kicked my face. They knocked some of my teeth loose.

Even in such a situation, I found superhuman power within me. I stood up under the heavy weight. In doing so, I hurt my back. Because I gritted my teeth and endured the severe pain at that time, I found my back teeth on both sides had broken after I was released.

I was carried into the guardhouse by the military police many times. People in the guardhouse said they would get rice and cigarettes if they went to the Integrated Hospital, so they tried to get themselves taken to the hospital even if they were injured only a little. If they were not in a position to go to the hospital, they would take too much antidiarrheal or headache medicine at one time and were then sent to the hospital. In my case, I was identified as a priority for being sent to the hospital, but I didn't go because I didn't want to be cured by the medicine they gave me. I couldn't eat normally with my hands for a month, so I ate by snapping my hand. And when that was inconvenient, I crouched down like a dog and ate with the one and only thought that I had to survive.

Sentenced to Fifteen Years in Prison for Masterminding a Rebellion

I was interrogated whenever someone who knew me was brought in. I was investigated fourteen times in total, and they conducted on-site inspections in the Hakun-dong area. Prisoners are supposed to receive the prosecutor's record of the investigation for the last time before they are sentenced. Anyone interrogated by prosecutor LEE Cha-Ryang was severely beaten. I was also interrogated by him. As soon as the prosecutor took off my handcuffs, he beat me on the shoulder with a club, saying, "Now,

I see you're MOON Jang-Woo." When he tried to beat me a second time, I grabbed the club.

"Prosecutor, Ive been expecting the investigation report from you. If I had been afraid of your rod, I wouldn't have asked for your record. Ive had countless beatings like this. If you want me to reveal what I haven't revealed yet by using this kind of rod, beat me to the end."

He didn't beat me anymore, perhaps because he was shamed by my words. He offered me a Kent cigarette. When he tried to light the cigarette, I automatically took the lighter, lit his cigarette first, lit mine, turning my head a little to be polite and saying, "Thank you." And I showed him my composure in returning the lighter.

"I wanted to accuse you of smoking imported cigarettes, but I'm an accomplice, so Ill give up that idea."

"Look at this bastard."

"Prosecutor, I am a prisoner, but let me have the report as a respectable human."

"What? Respect! Do prisoners have respect?"

"Before we are prisoners, aren't we humans? Shouldn't our country, becoming a developed country, treat prisoners respectfully?"

"Look at this bastard. Well, let's cut it short, then."

"Ill suggest two conditions to you after I get the record, so please listen. If you don't keep that promise, Ill exercise my right of silence."

"If I break the promise, you'll be the only one who'll suffer."

"I want to believe in your character, prosecutor."

According to the report, which I examined for about an hour and a half, it was written that I dropped out of Hanyang University during my sophomore year. That's how they manipulated me on paper, who had never even been to the main gate of a university.

When the investigation was completed, I proposed the conditions before I signed with my thumb print.

"Let me propose the conditions. Please, delete the two claims that I trained people how to shoot and how to throw grenades."

"Are you kidding? These are the essential points!"

"Didn't you make a promise?"

Then, the prosecutor drew two lines through those sections with a red ballpoint pen and pressed the seal. After that, I was tried in military court. I expected that I would be sentenced to death but was sentenced to fifteen years in prison, which was the lowest sentence for a major figure in a rebellion.

In addition, KIM Chun-Guk, who defended the Hakun-dong area, was sentenced to five years in prison for responding to and following the lead of a rebellion. And KIM Bok-Soo was sentenced to two years.

The Duty of a Prison Guard

After the trial, I was transferred to prison, but I was treated inhumanely in the prison. The problem was the toilet, where everyone could see a person, and the food was worse than a dog's meal. It was so crowded that everyone had to sleep on their sides. Prison guards also treated us like dogs and pigs. One day, while I was reading the Bible because I couldn't sleep, a night-shift prison guard suddenly cursed me.

"You, son of bitch, what are you staying up for?"

I felt sick at the sound and stared at him.

"You, bastard. How dare you stare at me. Stand up."

I was not wearing my jacket, so I stood up awkwardly in my underwear.

"What's your number?"

"2118. What's the matter with you, sir?"

"Cocky bastard. Why the hell are you staring at me like that, you son of bitch?"

"Officer, do you have to curse me like that? You can correct me without cursing like that."

"Look at this bastard."

He brought a club from the ward office where prison officers worked, and told me to put my hand out of the bars. He tried to hit me outside the bars because he was not supposed to open the door at night.

"Do you really have to hit me?"

"Yes, indeed."

I put my hand out through the bars of the cell. When the prison guard lifted the club high and tried to strike it down, I pulled my hand back again to make fun of him. Then the club broke against the iron bars. The prison guard was even more furious and abused me more. I yelled at him.

"Can you write the word 'a prison officer' in Chinese characters?"

"You bastard, are you making fun of me?"

"The Republic of Korea is absurd enough to appoint a prison officer just like you, asshole. Do you even know what the duty of a prison officer is? The Chinese character for the first syllable in a prison officer is 'to teach.' You don't have the ability to teach, so go home and read more!"

While arguing like this, the inmates woke up and said, "You know the bastard's stone stupid," pointing at and teasing him. The prison officer, with a grim face, brought chalk from the ward office and wrote on the bars.

I woke up the next morning and found that our room was marked with "No Drinking Water" and "No Washing." We had breakfast, but they didn't give us a bucket of water, which we usually got every day. We couldn't accept that treatment.

Hunger Strike

I discussed it with the inmates in our room and we decided to fast for five meals. We began what we called a hunger strike. The officials might have been surprised at this because it was the first time anyone had done that in the prison. The prison officials blamed the night-shift prison guard. The reprimanded prison guard summoned me to the counseling room to take it out on me. He ordered me to lie down. As I said I wouldn't, he hit me on my cheek mercilessly. He kept hitting me even though my lips were bleeding. I couldn't stand it and beat him, too. Even the regular prisoners, serving as internal discipline members, joined him and beat me. The inmates in my room kicked the door and protested, perhaps because they heard a three-on-one confrontation. Frightened by the group protests of the inmates, the prison guard stopped beating me and sent me back into the cell. We continued our hunger strike.

It was around the end of October when several people in the room were released. When the number of prisoners in our cell decreased, fifteen prison guards came in with ropes and clubs, trampled on us with their boots, and took us to the security department where they tied all of us up and beat us.

When the incident occurred, about 200 prisoners of conscience went on a hunger strike, demanding better treatment. We demanded correspondence and allowance for visitors, purchase permission, and the right to receive items from the outside. After the whole group fasted for five meals, all the prisoners met with the warden. In accepting all the conditions, the warden demanded we take purification training. We strongly objected to the purification training that treated inmates like animals for eight hours a day. Eventually, we agreed to take a one-hour training course.

After that, visitors were allowed, and we were allowed to write letters once a week with a pencil. The prison guards were also replaced by people with slightly more conscience, but the attitudes of the prison authorities remained the same. Kimchi was made of rotten salted fish and mixed with sand, so we couldn't eat it like that. Only after washing it with water and seasoning it with red pepper paste, could we eat it. The prison gave us such kimchi and sold us good kimchi privately.

There was some conflict between inmates regarding 5.18 inside the prison. Student-inmates such as HEO Kyu-Jung and JEONG Sang-Young spent most of their time reading books. However, prisoners with low educational backgrounds were unable to read books because they could not understand Chinese characters, so they played Go and Chinese chess every day. Sometimes when we played Chinese chess and shouted out, "Checkmate," the student-inmates all looked at us with their eyes wide in disdain. Then we were discouraged by our sins of ignorance and could not say anything.

When I was in prison, prosecutor LEE Cha-Ryang called me out many times. I thought he called me out because there was something missing in the report, but I was told to relax for a while. As he handed over cigarettes, drinks and bread, he said, "Everyone begged for help when I interrogated them, but you were the only one who didn't. This is just a ploy for show, so everyone will be released in one or two and a half years." And he added that I should take care of myself and stay healthy.

Life after Release

I was imprisoned for about ten months but was released on April 3, 1981. When I was released, I found out my wife had cheated on me while delivering yogurt to earn a living. I had no choice but to divorce her and live with my children and my mother. All the lives I had had so far were broken up and scattered, and I had only an empty body, so I did manual labor. After more than four years of manual labor, I met a woman who was working at the City Hall, and got married in February 1986.

I have not recovered from the murderous torture at Sangmudae. When it is cloudy, I feel like something is crawling on my feet and I have no energy. Both my knees and knuckles are swollen. Because I had done yoga to relieve the effects of torture during my imprisonment, I still maintain my health otherwise.

I am working at the Jeonnam branch of Korea Lifesaving Volunteers and serving as the Vice President of the May Gwangju Uprising Comrade Association. Too many organizations regarding May are running, and they have separated into two camps. I hope all related organizations unite in one voice. Also, I believe I have nothing to boast about as one who was involved in 5.18. Compared to the Gwangju citizens, we were just beaten more and imprisoned. All those who were involved in 5.18 should unite with honor and honesty.

V FIERCE BATTLES

3. The Province Hall

3107. Both Legs Cut Off
Witness: PARK Byeong-Jun (male)
Date of Birth: December 13, 1963 (aged 17)
Occupation: Tailor (now a street vendor)
Date of Record: July 1988

Research & Arrangement by YANG Hong-Jin

Overview

At the young age of seventeen, he was shot in the Province Hall at dawn on May 27th.

My Boss's Injury

On May 18, 1980, I was sewing at a *machikova*[41] where people made suits. After graduating from middle school, I got a job at this factory to learn sewing skills and contribute to the household.

My father didn't have a job due to knee arthritis, so my family had financial difficulties. We were a family of four brothers, similar in age, so it was overwhelming for my father and mother to teach all of us.

Daeheung Tailor Shop was in the Goryeo arcade building in

[41] *Machikova* is a Japanese word referring to a small factory. Many employees of Gwangju in the 1970s-80s worked in the small manufacturing industry like a *machikova*.

Chungjang-ro, and the factory was in Bangrim-dong. Id been working here for three years. There were only a few people working in the factory, so we were always busy with a lot of work. And because the factory owner's residence was in the factory, we stayed with the boss's family as if we had been one family together. It had been three years since I began sewing. I got a pretty decent salary, then. I did not necessarily want to spend money, so I gave almost all of it to my mother. Also, I had nothing to do except to go back and forth between my house and the factory.

It was probably around noon, my boss came in panting while I was busy with a lot of work to do. Red blood flowed from his forehead. He put his arms around the wound and leaned against the front door helplessly. He was about to collapse. Seeing this, I stopped sewing, rushed to him, and asked what was going on. I was too shocked to treat his wounds. I was surprised and did not know what to do. I wiped out the bloodstains from his forehead with a piece of cloth.

"There were a lot of demonstrators on Chungjang-ro and Geumnam-ro, so I joined the demonstrators toward Geumnam-ro to hang around with them. Then the martial law forces fired tear gas, beating citizens with clubs without mercy. I could not escape and was hit by a tear gas canister. While the citizens and soldiers were pushing back and forth, I escaped from the martial law force's violence. Chased by the paratroopers, I ran over through buildings or fences at random. I couldn't go into the downtown and came to Bangrim-dong."

After listening to the story, I wondered why the martial law forces beat the citizens with clubs and why the citizens were demonstrating. But I couldn't ask my boss about those things.

As if possessed by a goblin during the day, I felt both bewildered and surprised at the same time.

His wife and I cleaned his wounds and stopped the bleeding

first with bandages and adhesive tapes. My colleagues who worked together at the factory also swore at them, "What bastards they are!" I didn't understand why the soldiers were beating citizens. I couldn't figure out why demonstrators were treated like this.

The boss worriedly told us not to come to the factory the next day. I was usually so busy that I didn't have time to rest. So it was hard to believe that I should rest for a few days until I heard it from him.

After that, I left the factory and walked along the stream of Bangrim-dong. On the way I wondered why the citizens were demonstrating, so I decided to go to the downtown that day instead of going straight home.

When I went to the intersection by the former City Hall from the Bullo-dong Bridge, the protestors were fighting against the police, throwing stones, shouting "CHUN Doo-Hwan, step down" and "Lift the martial law." I wandered around the alley and watched them fighting. I just wondered who CHUN Doo-Hwan was and why they were asking him to step down. Also, I wondered what the martial law forces were and why they should raise their voice in unison against them? Although I was young, I could guess that the protestors were violently demanding something.

After looking around for a long time, I saw protesters scattering from tear gas. And I walked home via Seongha Mansion in Sa-dong.

The Factory Closed

On the morning of May 19th, I went to the factory, wondering if it was true that the boss had told me not to come the previous day. To get to the factory in Bangrim-dong, I had to pass through the bridges of Bulo-dong, Yangrim-dong, Hak-dong, and Bangrim-dong, so I walked along the river, and the martial law forces were encamped on both sides of each bridge. Seeing them, I was filled with the hostility that I couldn't define. I still wondered what kind of people these soldiers were and why they hit the citizens recklessly. As a bus passed through the Hakgang Bridge, the martial law forces stopped the bus, got on the bus, and checked the passengers' IDs. They caught three young men and took them off the bus. I didn't know what happened to those people because I only saw them and went to Bangrim-dong. When I entered the factory, the boss got angry because I had come even though he had told me not to come to work. He said if people wandered around the city, young and old, they would be arrested, beaten, and dragged away. So, he told me to go home quickly.

I went home on foot, thinking that there was no reason for the martial law forces to drag and beat a guy like me. I felt weird not working. For a person who worked every day, it was rather strange not to work.

At around 7:00 p.m., my friend YU Byeong-Seop and I went to the Catholic Center in downtown. He ran a shop that repaired refrigerators, TVs, electrics, and electronics in the neighborhood we lived in. He was my age, and he worked with his older brother.

I heard that the city was agitated, but it was difficult to figure out what was going on from what I had seen that day and the previous days. So I waited for Byeong-Seop until he finished his work and suggested that we go out together to downtown. I also thought of going out to Geumnam-ro and looking around the downtown. Between the Tourist Hotel and the Korea Bank, citizens, riot police, and martial law forces were confronting each other. The riot police and soldiers surrounded the citizens as if besieging them. The soldiers were at the underground shopping center and near the Gwangju Bank while citizens gathered at the Geumnam-ro 1st Street and Geumnam-ro 2nd Street, throwing stones. The martial law forces and the riot police did not care about the strong waves of citizens, throwing tear gas grenades, beating the citizens, and mercilessly stomping them with their military boots.

How ruthlessly they threw apple grenades[42] as they approached the citizens! Stuck in the crowd, I could not escape that scene. I was hit by an apple grenade, fell down, and lost consciousness. It was at a Chinese restaurant that I regained consciousness. I remember the restaurant was behind the Catholic Center, and Byeong-Seop was next to me. If it had not been for Byeong-Seop, I would have been dragged away by the paratroopers on the spot. Thinking of that, I felt dizzy. Even after regaining consciousness, I vomited, gasped, and had difficulty breathing for a long time.

After a while, I came to my senses, left the restaurant, and went back home with Byeong-Seop's support along the dark streets.

With the Protesters

I lay in bed until noon the next day and relaxed myself a bit. Unlike usual days, it was difficult to enjoy the leisurely rest. Being at home was rather frustrating. I did not mention anything to my family about being hit by the tear gas grenade the previous day. It was obvious that I would not be able to go outside if I had told them that story.

The cries of the citizens were vivid in my ears, and the ferocious images of those harsh martial law forces filled my head. I wondered whether the citizens continued to fight like they had done the previous day, and whether there had been any change that day. And it seemed that my curiosity would be satisfied only by going outside. Even at home, my father and mother were listening to the news outside. They told me not to go outside.

It was past 7:00 p.m. in the evening and I went out to the Province Hall with Chun-Sam. Heavily armed martial law forces were viciously guarding the Province Hall. However, the movement of citizens had already been intensified like roaring waves. They

---

[42] Spherical tear gas grenades (literally "apple bomb" in the Korean idiom) with the pin on top; thus, they look like an apple.

continued to throw stones toward the plaza in front of the Province Hall and the fountain, mobilized vehicles to set fire to them, and drove them toward the military cordon.

The vehicles on fire sometimes smashed into trees, not reaching the fountain, and exploded with flames and roaring sounds. Then the martial law forces threw out a huge amount of pepper fog from armored vehicles and fired tear gas canisters while the citizens threw stones in response. After watching the protesters for a while, Chun-Sam asked me to go home. I suggested waiting a little longer, saying that if we got out of a fire pit like this in the wrong direction, it would be worse than not going, but Chun-Sam opposed me implacably. Reluctantly, I escaped to the back alley of the Catholic Center and parted with Chun-Sam at the Gwangju Tax Office. Chun-Sam later told me that he had escaped into the back alley of the Province Hall at that time.

Citizens in front of the Gwangju Tax Office also set fire to oil barrels and pushed them toward the Province Hall. They also set fire to jeeps and trucks and started them toward the Province Hall. From there, I actively shouted slogans and joined the protesters, too. It had been a long time since MBC had already been engulfed in flames, but I followed the protesters past MBC to Mudeung Stadium. I had no intention of going home. We passed by Mudeung Stadium and kept going around shouting slogans. From the moment I joined the protesters, I could vaguely see the reason why the martial law forces were sent to Gwangju to commit all kinds of atrocities. I also learned that this was a tactic of CHUN Doo-Hwan to make an example by punishing the Gwangju citizens. I also understood why citizens later set fires and pushed the vehicles toward the Province Hall. They couldn't stand such things anymore after witnessing the martial law force beating pedestrians with clubs and even beating them while naked except for their underwear, as if the protesters were subhuman.

I went to the intersection at the entrance of CNU to protest, and then to Gwangju Station. The KBS building was on fire. The citizens said that broadcasting companies that engaged in distorting information should be burned. They set fire to branches covered with cotton and threw them at the building. They also threw Molotov cocktails and stones, but I did not throw anything and just watched. At dawn, I thought I had to go home.

I walked from Gwangju Station to my house. When my father saw me, he severely scolded me, "Do you have a death wish?" I had breakfast without saying anything and went out again.

Stealing Weapons from the Monopoly Office

It was May 21st. We went to the park around 10:00 a.m. People riding in the protest vehicles pounded wooden sticks and shouted slogans, such as "Get Out, Martial Law Forces," "Resign, CHUN Doo-Hwan," and "Guarantee the Three Labor Rights."

I thought I should get into a vehicle, too. Just then, an intercity bus with about fifteen people on board passed by. I waved my hand and they let me into the bus. A young man said that we needed weapons in Gwangju now and needed to go to the Monopoly Bureau to get weapons. Three people, including me, agreed to the young man's words. Only three people got off at the Monopoly Bureau and broke the large glass in the main building and went inside. No one was there. Not knowing where the arsenal was, I just followed the two of them. The three of us went down to the basement of the Monopoly Bureau, broke the lock to the warehouse, stole two M1s and around fourteen carbines, and headed to the industrial complex intersection. At that time, I had no fear. When Gwangju citizens were shot to death by the martial law forces, I thought stealing weapons was not a crime. I remember being surprised to see a student in a high school uniform was taken to the Red Cross Hospital the previous day, shot in the head, only showing the white of his eyes. I was burning with resentment, thinking that we could not be defeated.

When I heard that the student who was brought to the Red

Cross Hospital was shot by the martial law forces at the Province Hall, a thought came across my mind since I was a young man with blood boiling just like the student: "What would have happened if I had fought like that student?"

I thought that no one should die in disgrace. After receiving a gun at the industrial complex intersection, they told me to go to the park and get live ammunition, so I got in a van. I parted with the people I was riding with at first. And since I heard that the van was going to the park, I got in the van and got one clip of live ammunition at the park. There were many people in the park, and weapons that seemed to have been stolen were piled up here and there. A young man who said he had been discharged from the military handed out guns. He didn't teach us how to operate a gun but seemed to hand out bullets only to those who could hold a gun. And he didn't even tell us where to go to fight. I was given a gun and bullets, but I was at a loss as to how to fight. The three men who stole the weapons from the Monopoly Bureau were all scattered and I knew nobody. After hesitating for a while, I handed the gun and bullets to someone else. Even though he didn't ask for them, I did so because the gun became a heavy burden to me since I neither knew how to handle a gun nor could find anyone who could give me instructions.

I left the park and went alone to the Red Cross Hospital and the previous City Hall Intersection. People were being taken to the hospital, bleeding from gunshot wounds and at the brink of death. I felt so nauseous that I could not look at the horrible scene. How could Gwangju become like that!

From May 22nd to the 25th, I roamed the streets from home to downtown. I had everything in my eyes as I saw it, but I still didn't know what to do. I thought about what I could do at such a time, but I was not qualified to appear in front of the already armed citizens. A person who could not use a gun on the battlefield was as good as dead!

At around 6:00 p.m. on May 26th, I went to the house of my friend JIN Kyeong-Mo who lived in Dolgogae. He was a friend of mine who sewed suits like me. I stayed at his house talking about what I had seen and heard, and then came out after a while. Protesters were going around broadcasting to ask people to gather at the Province Hall. My friend said he would give me a ride home and put me on the back seat. However, the bike chain broke in front of the Wolsan-dong Police Box, and I parted with him and walked home from there.

Let's Defend Gwangju to the Death

When I got home, my father saw me and scolded me.

"How many times have I told you to stay home but you went out! You are coming this late. Don't you know what's happening these days!"

Then I just bowed my head and ran out of the house. I was thinking of taking a breath for a minute before going inside. As soon as I got down from the house, I took Jungang-ro and went down toward the Korea Bank.

There, I met the protesters I saw while leaving Kyeong-Mo's house earlier. There were about 400 to 500 people, and they were easily recognizable because some people among them seemed to be carrying banners and broadcasting to the crowd. I also joined the protesters and walked to the Province Hall. It was probably around 7:30 p.m. I sat at the fountain and listened intently to Mr. PARK Nam-Sun, who was speaking while holding a 37-caliber pistol. PARK Nam-Sun exclaimed:

"Anyone who is afraid, or who has children or wives, please go home."

I didn't even need time to think about this. I had no fear or desire to go back home. It was my desire to defend Gwangju City from death and save the lives of citizens. Although I had not been active after May 21st, I came to believe it was my own job while seeing the wounds and dead bodies of the citizens. Therefore, I was not scared to gather strength to defend the Province Hall and Gwangju together with the citizens gathered there. We thought that it was our duty to fight to the best of our ability even if the martial law forces came back. However, I momentarily thought, "I am going to die here."

I found that about 100 people remained at the fountain after Mr. PARK Nam-Sun's speech. The 100 people remaining at the fountain entered the YMCA building, which is a gym now. A former officer who had just been discharged from the military taught us how to shoot. It was not an actual training with guns, so I had to understand it just by guessing. I thought I would have been able to handle a gun if I had been to the military. But because anyone who could fire even a single bullet was needed at the moment, I paid attention to him. When I thought about the whole situation later, I couldn't help but feel regretful about how clumsy the armed forces of the citizens were. Our gun control techniques were so lax that only a few people could fire even one shot properly.

After the gun shooting training was over, we ate ramen and received seven Eunhasu cigarettes. As far as I know, at around midnight about fifty people got some sleep, and the other fifty went into the Province Hall. I also lay down in the gym to get some sleep. How long did I sleep? Someone came and shouted, "The martial law forces have come!" So I picked myself up. People who woke up hearing this sound rushed into the Province Hall at once. We received a carbine and bullets at the guard post in front of the main gate of the Province Hall. At that time, we didn't care who gave us the guns because if the martial law forces came, they would shoot us, and we would shoot them all together. We got the guns with a sense of tension to use them to defend ourselves and the Province Hall.

The Martial Law Forces with Armored Vehicles and Tanks

There were flower beds placed about twenty meters apart from each other in front of the Province Hall. I hid behind a flower bed and aimed my gun. Shortly thereafter, armored vehicles, tanks, and trucks of the martial law forces came into the downtown with a roaring sound. They approached the Province Hall, shooting at it. As their bullets flew toward us, someone inside the Province Hall shouted at us to come inside. I lowered my head and entered the Province Hall. In the order we entered, we were organized in groups of twelve people.

After receiving orders to guard the police station in the back alley of the Province Hall, twelve people went there. The police station in the back alley of the Province Hall was under construction, and there was no one there when we went in. There was a post, so some people, including myself, went in there, and the others went into the police station building. The martial law forces approached about three meters away from us but couldn't find us. They wore white bands around their helmets and magazines crisscrossed on their chests. At that time, none of us at the post could handle a gun. First of all, they were people who had never fired a gun before, and actually it was also difficult to shoot at people. As we were all the same human beings, I really felt the difference between the trained and untrained. As the martial law forces passed by the post, we crawled silently from the post back to the basement of the police station. From that moment on, I was gripped by fear. Without even realizing where I was going, I escaped to the basement. Since I was wearing white pants, an off-white T-shirt, and slippers, I was nervous that I could easily be seen in the dark.

We gathered our strength and opened the door and entered. The uniforms of the riot police were piled up like a mountain. I went up there and fell asleep. I couldn't figure out why I fell asleep, but I think I did so because I was very nervous and thought that it would be safe to hide in the basement. I woke up at the sound of the martial law forces coming and firing at random. It was not that the martial law forces came directly to me and fired their guns. Then I looked around. There was no one next to me. My heart plummeted. I was overwhelmed by a sense of fear. There was a door next to where I was sleeping, so I opened the door. People belonging to my group gathered in that place decorated like an office. They also didn't say a word but only exchanged tense eyes with each other. Some were hiding under desks and in cabinets, and one was lying on the bed on the left. They seemed to have given up on getting out altogether. I was just thinking that too. We might think that the outcome of the battle was too obvious in a situation where so many troops invaded and took over the city.

I went beside the person lying on the bed and crouched with my hands clasped. It was probably when I laid down my gun and lay flat on my back. At this time, along with the sound of kicking on the door, a blaring sound expanded and echoed loudly in my ears. A soldier came into our place. He fired his gun at my legs without hesitation. Even now, I sometimes wonder whether the martial law soldier fired the gun like that on purpose or did it out of a sense of duty, but I'm still unsure. The moment I was shot in the legs, I thought of my home and my mother. Two soldiers came in and dragged away me and the person next to me just as we had been shot. I don't know what happened to the others. After being shot, there was no time to think of anyone else.

Injury

When I regained consciousness and woke up after three days at the Integrated Military Hospital, I found myself lying in the intensive care unit. A defense soldier was by my side taking care of me. I asked him when I came here. He said that it was May

27th, which was three days before, and he said he always goes to work at 7:00 a.m., and I had come in when the helicopter landed at the drill ground of the Integrated Military Hospital around the time he came to work that day. As I recall, the time when I was shot was around 3:00 a.m., so I wondered where I had been for four hours. A strange ominous feeling crossed my head. I wondered if they had been trying to do something to me.

My legs hurt so much that I lost consciousness. All I knew was that I had been shot, but I had no idea that something would go wrong with my legs. My parents came to visit me, maybe because the hospital contacted them. The Integrated Hospital did not allow a visit at the time. It seems that the hospital officials tried to prevent even a single bit of confidential information from leaking under close supervision.

When my parents looked at me, they were astonished. Other patients were not allowed visitors, but I could meet my family since I had to have my legs operated on with the permission of my guardians.

Amputation of Both Legs

Since the nerves in my two legs that had been penetrated by the bullets did not work well, I could not even stand properly. The hospital director, a colonel, looked at me and told me that I had to go through skin graft surgery as I seemed quite young. When I looked at the legs, bullet fragments were stuck all over the place. So they could not be removed. And there were several cuts. I thought to myself, "That can't be true that I can't use my legs at all." But for some reason, MOON Byeong-Guk, an orthopedic surgeon, came and said that he had to amputate my legs when only a few days had passed after I regained consciousness.

Later, I heard that Major MOON Byeong-Guk has been running a private hospital in Hwasun. My father and mother wept and begged the doctor to preserve my legs as much as possible. Even after the first operation, the legs were rotted down to the ankles. The arterial nerves were cut, and there was nothing to be done. Therefore, during the second operation, the ankles were amputated. But a few days later, the doctor said that my legs would be amputated. Hearing this, I thought that I would rather die on the operating table. I had no desire to live. The right leg was amputated at the ankle and the left leg at the knee. I had to spend six months of painful days in the Integrated Hospital.

In the early days of investigation at the hospital, I was mainly asked about the details of the time when I was caught at the Province Hall. The investigators didn't bother me much or treat me badly. Since I was young and my legs were amputated, it seems that they treated me better than others. But it was a few days later. Two investigators slammed the door into the room where I was lying and shouted, "Who is PARK Byeong-Jun?" Then two of them grabbed me, pushed the bed, and took me to the corner. I couldn't even sit down at the time, so I laid down with my legs outstretched. The two investigators slapped me in the face without mercy.

"Why didn't you tell us you stole the guns from the Monopoly Bureau? A man who came with you to take the guns told us everything about it. So tell us!"

Then again, they hit my upper body repeatedly without mercy. I intentionally didn't tell them what had happened at the Monopoly Bureau to avoid any bad consequences, but the man I went with just told them my name and what had happened at the Monopoly Bureau.

I lied that Ive never done that. Later, being handcuffed and tied with a rope, the man was brought to where I was, and the investigators made a cross-examination. Reluctantly, I told them that I had gone to the Monopoly Bureau and taken guns. Then the investigators had me sit on the bed, gave me a criminal identification number, and took pictures. After that, they never came to me, and I stayed relatively comfortable compared to others.

When I think about what happened at the hospital, there were a lot of bitter and awkward moments, but I have a couple of anecdotes I remember the most.

While an escort soldier taking care of me pushed the wheelchair and went out to get air for me, another patient the escort soldier was in charge of escaped the hospital. I remember the escort soldier hated me thereafter because his senior official severely berated him. The person who escaped was captured again, but the person shook the hospital upside down.

Some professors shared meals that they had been provided from outside, but only what they couldn't eat, and only when it was a few days old. So we all had diarrhea. Nothing would have happened if they had shared the meals on time. I had never felt resentful like that to professors. Not all professors were like that, but the attitudes of the learned people living in a group disappointed me a lot. The actual reality of the people who boasted of their intelligence fell far short of expectations.

While taking a taxi after leaving the Integrated Hospital, it was difficult to recognize Yang-dong Market in downtown Gwangju. I don't know for sure if it had been a while since I was hospitalized or if I were out of my mind, but the city looked very unfamiliar.

I was taken to the Red Cross Hospital and had surgery to remove my knee joint. After that, I had to undergo dozens of surgeries to fix my right ankle. Because of the side effects of the surgeries, the pain was indescribable when I inadvertently touched the surgical site. At some point, I had surgery to remove flesh from my back and attach it to my leg, which was called microsurgery. Moreover, in January and July, during the change of seasons, the pain was so severe that I could not move easily. After a couple of months in the hospital, I was transferred again to Christian Hospital.

No one told me that I could be cured. I underwent four or five more surgeries under the diagnosis that the name of the disease was unknown. Later, because there was no nerve in my legs, tubes were placed in my legs, and my legs lay flat. And a follow-up operation was performed when something like a stone grew on the heel of my foot. Now, with prosthetic legs, I am able to move a little bit. Since I don't know when I will have to take medicine and have surgery again, I haven't done anything for over eight years. It is regrettable that I trained myself to make a living with my body....

I'm making a living selling hot dogs now, but I can never bring my legs back.

Working as a Founding Member of the Injured Association

I am one of the fourteen members of the May 18 Gwangju Uprising Injured Association since its inception. When it was founded at Mujin Church in 1982, we all put in the first priority to be revealing the truth of the Gwangju People's Uprising by exposing that the CHUN Doo-Hwan administration was the cause of the Gwangju Incident,[43] instead of compensation for damages. And we found the significance of the Injured Association in encouraging the members' passionate struggle. For now, we believe the significance of the Injured Association is to find traces of how the citizens of Gwangju have been sacrificed rather than to receive compensation. The current administration should reveal CHUN Doo-Hwan's crimes in detail. I think that would be possible only when people have a strong desire for democracy. No one starves these days. I believe that if we blindly seek something to eat, history will not develop but stagnate.

---

43) "Gwangju Incident" (*Satae* in Korean) is a derogatory term used by those who intend to show disapproval of the people's democratic uprising. This interview was conducted when the term's disparaging intention was not widely known even to those who willingly participated in the uprising.

For this purpose, the May 18 Gwangju Uprising Injured Association and the May Youth Comrade Association are constantly shouting the slogan, "Arrest CHUN Doo-Hwan and LEE Soon-Ja" in front of the National Assembly building, and struggling through hunger strikes demanding democratization. Since an injured person knows the feelings of other injured ones, only those who have fought with their bodies will know the meaning of our struggle. Our struggle will continue until the day comes when people can live with freedom, and I will continue to fight with limping legs.

3. The Province Hall

2014. An Attack on the Province Hall by a Middle School Commando

Witness: CHOI Dong-Buk (male)
Year of Birth: 1965 (aged 15)
Occupation: Middle school student (currently college student)
Date of Record: October 1988

Research & Arrangement by YANG Hong-Jin

Overview

CHOI Dong-Buk, a third-year student at Mujin Middle School, was selected at a young age as a commando to attack the Province Hall. He was caught by the paratroopers and stabbed with a bayonet and beaten all over his body.

Martial Law Forces, Disband

I was in my third year at Mujin Middle School in 1980. When I went to school on May 19th, I was told to go home after class in the morning for some reason. Without offering an explanation, the school told us to go home and not to come to school for a few days and study by ourselves.

My home was in Juwol-dong. I dropped my backpack at home and went back out to the street. It was cloudy. I recalled the day before when I had gone to Geumnam-ro and seen college students battle paratroopers by throwing stones, and I suspected that it was not irrelevant to school being cancelled earlier that day.

I went to the Daechang Gas Station near Daeseong Elementary School. There citizens and paratroopers confronted each other, and I saw stones and tear gas flying around. I watched citizens and paratroopers pushing and shoving each other for about twenty minutes. The citizens were pushed toward Gwangju Park. As this was happening, I kept following the protest procession from a little distance. In front of the park, there the battle between the paratroopers and citizens continued. About 200 students and citizens would not leave the place as they shouted slogans such as, "Violent Police, Disband," and "Martial Law Forces, Disband."

After a while, the paratroopers were attacked by the citizens and began to retreat. One paratrooper, lagging behind his group, was driven to the side of the stream. There he fell into the stream. The citizens cheered for the victory and booed the soldiers. Soon after, dozens of paratroopers charged in anger toward the citizens. The citizens who saw this scattered.

Even an Old Man Abused Brutally Like a Dog

In the square in front of a gymnasium in a park, a young man was caught by a paratrooper, kicked by military boots and beaten with a club. The paratrooper shouted at him that he would not let him live, and beat him uncontrollably with his club. An old man who saw this stepped forward, begging the soldier to stop beating the young man, saying he was his grandson. Then the soldier began beating the helpless old man with his club.

"Is this old man sick enough to die? Bastard! Dare to say that he is your grandson?"

Some of the paratrooper's fellow soldiers joined in, and they stomped on the old man's back with their military boots and kicked him mercilessly. The old man screamed and fell down. I witnessed the scene while amidst the citizens on the way to the hilltop of the park. The citizens who saw this sight became angry and threw stones at the paratroopers. Everyone cried out, "Do not kill the citizens," and "Disband." Then, the paratroopers rushed toward the citizens with raised clubs. I quickly ran to the Daechang Gas Station next to the Daeseong Elementary School. As I ran around seeing what was happening here and there, it had started raining softly before I was aware. It was around 9:00 p.m. Citizens came out with lumber, glass bottles, kitchen knives, clubs, and pickaxes, and prevented vehicles from moving at the Daechang Gas Station in order to make it easier to confront the paratroopers when they came.

I went back to Yang-dong Market from there. The stalls in Yang-dong Market were almost all closed, and people were in a commotion in the streets. When I was among the people, a jeep with ten or more paratroopers suddenly came, beating them with clubs and taking them randomly. I was caught with other people because I couldn't escape in that mess. About ten people were caught, of which I was the youngest. One citizen looked at me and said to the paratroopers.

"Let the kid go. He has nothing to do with this."

"Why are you here?"

"I was on my way from school."

I answered, but I was very scared as I had seen a few times people severely abused and beaten by the paratroopers. I thought I was near to dying, but they didn't beat me.

One paratrooper told me to go back home.

"Why are you walking around late in the evening? Everyone who wanders around at this hour must die! Go back home!"

I ran without looking back. As I walked home, I thought about various things. Why are those paratroopers stomping on the citizens so cruelly? For what are they doing that? The image of the old man collapsed on the ground was still vivid.

Paratroopers Harassing Girls in the Street

On the 20th, I was taking my bag and about to leave home. Then my mother said,

"Study at home. It is dangerous to go outside. You'd better not go out today."

I replied that I would be back soon and went out. The image of the old man whom I had seen in the park the day before, beaten and dragged by the paratroopers, was haunting me. I had learned that the soldiers were supposed to defend the country and protect the citizens, but these soldiers were harming the citizens. I saw the brutality of the paratroopers and thought that I would also join the citizens and fight against the paratroopers. I passed the park and went toward the Taepyeong Theater.

Paratroopers were stationed in front of the Taepyeong Theater. At that time, two girls were passing by on the sidewalk. A member of the paratroopers accosted the girls.

"You look so pretty. Where are you going?"

The girls walked faster as if to run away without answering him, bending their heads to look down defensively. Then the paratrooper approached the girls and shouted at them,

"Hey! Bitches, you aren't answering me!"

He was chasing after the girls who were already startled and running, shouting, "Catch them!" When the citizens saw this and shouted to save the girls, the paratroopers disappeared. Meanwhile, about fifteen to sixteen people were captured by the paratroopers, beaten with clubs so badly, with all their clothes but underwear stripped off, with their hands up. I thought that it was dangerous for me to go around watching such scenes. But my anger gradually grew when I saw the brutality of the paratroopers. I returned home at 8:00 p.m. that evening.

I, a Third-year Middle School Student, Participated in the Militia

Around 6:00 a.m., the 21st of May, I heard a siren resounding loudly from the side of the Baekun-dong roundabout near my home. Hearing the sound, I got out and went into the street, and

I saw the Baekun Police Box on fire. People were watching it in a commotion. On one side, a truck that came in from the outskirts was set on fire because the people said the car was from Gyeongsang-do. The sound of the explosion of a gas container roared, and the flames soared. Even though it was early in the morning, the citizens were full of anger. I went back home, had my breakfast, and went out again despite my mother's objections.

Since I had first gone out in the morning, the citizens who had gathered at the Baekun-dong roundabout were angry with the soldiers, holding pickaxes, clubs, and knives, the tops of their heads wrapped in cloth. They were ready to attack any paratroopers at any time if they showed up. At the bus terminal across from Daedong High school, I saw citizens in black masks arguing with the bus company to get buses. After seeing this, I went to the Kkachi Pass.

Soldiers were stationed at Saenam Church. Citizens wielded various tools like wooden sticks, and battled with stones against the paratroopers. The citizens were filled with anger and fought fiercely, as if they would not back down. The paratroopers were pushed back and retreated toward Naju. I felt that was odd.

At that time, a military ambulance was passing like a bullet from the downtown to Naju. Citizens stopped the car. Then they told the soldier in the car to get out. The soldier had been injured on his head and was bleeding profusely. When a citizen tried to beat the soldier, the driver stepped forward.

"I am a soldier at Sangmudae. I didn't want to be a soldier. I just did what I was told. Now, a person is hurt, so please just let us go."

"Present your military doctor's ID! And your pistol!"

"I have no pistol."

At this time, the citizens agreed to send the wounded soldier on his way. The citizens who had shaken with indignation at the soldiers let the injured soldier pass at once.

I began to clearly understand why the citizens were angry, and I stayed with them in the procession. While walking to the Shinwoo Apartments, I saw citizens pounding their various vehicles with their improvised wooden clubs. People in the cars appealed for participation.

"Let's go to the Province Hall. Citizens, please get on these vehicles." They were screaming out and raising their voices.

"Let's tear CHUN Doo-Hwan to death."

Seeing a few vehicles passing by, I wanted to go to the Province Hall. I took an express bus. In the bus, I met five friends from my neighborhood and school. The bus I was riding in went in front of the Catholic Center. There were no paratroopers in front of the Catholic Center. However, there was still a fight going on in some places in front of the Province Hall and Jeonil Building.

We moved from the Catholic Center via Gwangnam-ro and turned toward Daein Market. Citizens gave boxes filled with drinks and rice balls to the people in the vehicles. After sharing the food, we were even more full of spirit. After eating, we got back on the bus and moved to the main gate of Chonnam National University. They told me that the soldiers would shoot us if we went inside the campus, so we went only to the entrance of it. I thought I should not enjoy roaming around the downtown in a vehicle. I felt that I had to do something. I wanted to help defeat the paratroopers who killed Gwangju citizens. But I still didn't know what to do.

I Received a Gun and Went to Firearms Training

It was 2:00 p.m. when we went to the Province Hall after moving around from CNU to Baekun-dong. At Gwangnam-ro, I got out of the car and walked to the main branch of Hanil Bank. Citizens continued to be pushed back in the ongoing battle. Here,

I saw the corpse of a man spread out. A paratrooper dragged the corpse and loaded it onto a truck. Red blood clots were tangled all over his body, reflecting a strange glow in the sunlight. I couldn't even open my eyes and look. It was the first time I had seen a dead body, so I felt nauseous. The military truck went toward the Province Hall. The citizens who everywhere found bodies with gunshots were outraged and said they should no longer stand by.

Vehicles that citizens were riding also came out from various parts of the city like triumphant generals. A truck loaded with citizen militia arrived at Hanil Bank. They brought carbines, TNT, grenades, and pistols. A twenty-seven-year-old young man in a reserve army uniform handed out guns to the people gathered in front of the Hanil Bank.

"The citizens of Gwangju can no longer be shot and killed. Only those who can protect the citizens of Gwangju and those who can risk their lives should receive guns."

Young men reached out their hands and rushed to the man in the reserve army uniform. I also asked for one. Then the man in a reserve army uniform said,

"You're still young. Can you fight and put your life on the line?" He looked down at me reluctantly. Then he gave others carbines and live ammunition.

I kept standing there. I asked for a gun with a nervous look, assuring him that I could fight. Later he gave me a carbine and thirty rounds of live ammunition. Those who received guns rode jeeps and went to the Gwangju Park to receive training on how to shoot. In the square in front of the Gwangju Park, about 300 to 400 people were waiting to receive firearms training. I was trained in how to operate a gun and how to use a grenade. After about thirty minutes, I also practiced with live bullets. For the practice, we were given five shots to try to hit a target on the wall. I got it right with no misses.

Proudly Chosen as One of the Thirty-Two Commandos at the Age of Fifteen

It was said that the citizen commandos were selected according to how well they shot. The shooting practice lasted about an hour. Then I participated in the test for selection. There were spaces for men with excellent marksmanship, except for those who had a wife and children or were the oldest sons in a family. I was a fifteen-year-old middle school student and the only child in my family, but I hid the fact that I was the only child. I also passed the commando squad test in which thirty-two people were selected. I had no fear. In just a few days, I was no longer a young middle-schooler, but a militia member filled with justice and wrath. The commander, who appeared to be a former military officer, gave strict instructions to the selected commandos not to return alive. He distributed to us a *Taegeukgi*, a carbine, and two grenades. And he gave a radio to a jeep and taught the driver how to operate a signal to contact the headquarters. In addition, he taught him how to operate a radio to report the situation of the paratroopers to the headquarters at any time.

The selected commandos went to Geumnam-ro. Citizens hid in the alleys of Geumnam-ro and watched the confrontation between the paratroopers and the militia. The commandos decided to break through the military demarcation line of the paratroopers around the Province Hall, the Jeonil Building, and the Tourist Hotel. A jeep with seventeen people did not go straight to the Province Hall, but passed through Dongmyeong Girls' Middle School and went to Seoseok Elementary School first. In front of our jeep, a truck carrying thirty unarmed citizens was going somewhere. In the jeep, we honked at the vehicle in front and asked where it was going.

"We have to go to Hwasun and take the weapons from the Hwasun Mining Plant."

They went waving their hands to encourage us to fight well.

We couldn't come up with a clear plan on how to fight, but we all agreed to break through the military demarcation line somehow.

Our vehicle came out of Seoseok Elementary School and went to Jang-dong. Then, another group of our commandos suddenly charged in their vehicle toward the Province Hall. The truck I was riding in sent a pre-determined signal shot to stop them from going there. We told them it was not the right time. However, they ignored this and went on toward the Province Hall. Then, the paratroopers shot and killed the driver. Two students ran out and threw canisters of tear gas at the Province Hall. But they were also shot as they tried to escape to the Jang-dong Gas Station. I was in the jeep and tried to fire at the paratroopers to save them, but I couldn't because I was out of live ammunition. I contacted the headquarters by radio. I asked them to send me grenades. We tried to send an injured person to the hospital, but we had no vehicle available to go to the hospital. After a while, a bus with citizen militia came and took him to the hospital.

Commandos Attack the Province Hall

Then, I was given live ammunition. A helicopter roared in the sky.

"Citizens, please restrain yourself. Because of a few hooligans, the country is in crisis. Everyone, please go back home."

Enraged, we started shooting at the helicopter. From this time on, I became confident and started shooting without hesitation. When I went from the Nongjang Bridge to the underground shopping center, I saw a fire engine burning. Perhaps someone had set it on fire by making a hole in the fuel tank.

At that time, I heard a radio from the headquarters that a commando on vehicle number 1 had been shot. He said he had been attacked while charging toward the Province Hall. Upon hearing this news, we resolutely said, "We will go to the Province

Hall." Then the headquarters said, "Don't come. There should be no more sacrifices." After a moment's hesitation, a gunshot was heard. When I turned around, I saw that the person riding with me was dead. We were outraged. After moving the corpse to the Christian Hospital, we opened fire at the Jeonil Building and proceeded forward. However, the only result was that three more commandos were killed. For a moment, I thought, "I'm going to die too."

Geumnam-ro was sometimes as quiet as the dead after the cries of the people who had been shot down, and other times gunshots continued like the popping of roasting beans. However, thousands and tens of thousands of eyes were hiding and watching the Province Hall. I requested support from the headquarters, but I didn't get any reply. A convoy of citizens came wearing the armbands of the Red Cross Hospital to treat the fallen citizens. Dozens of people were carried away by car.

A young man from the third block of Geumnam-ro said that only twenty-one people could get on the truck and go to the Province Hall. He said that only those willing to risk their lives to fight should come forward. About fifty people ran out and shouted to get in the car. The young man fired a gun and said there was only space for twenty people. Shortly thereafter, a truck with the twenty people drove toward the Province Hall. Again, I heard gunshots vibrating through the air. The people in the truck were shot and killed. We couldn't accept defeat.

The five of us in the jeep headed toward the fountain to break through the military demarcation line. While we were rushing to the fountain, the engine of the vehicle suddenly stopped. While stalled there, I tried to contact the headquarters. There was no response.

When we started driving again, the driver was shot dead by the paratroopers. Then the person next to him took the steering wheel instead, and we ended up being thrown into the fountain.

The jeep overturned and tipped into the fountain. Three people died while trying to get out of the vehicle. I was stuck in the fountain, struggling to get out of the car. I had a hard time getting out, and I crawled down to the fountain. Guns from the Province Hall fired one after another. I couldn't even raise my head for fear of being shot, so I crawled toward the Suhyup Bank. Dodging bullets, I crawled madly. When I came to the front of the Suhyup Bank, three paratroopers stomped on my hand with their boots. They stabbed my arms with bayonets and kicked me with their boots. They took off my jacket and dragged me to the YMCA. I couldn't even raise my head as they struck me on the head with the butts of their rifles. They were mercilessly beating me all over my body.

When I arrived at the YMCA, they put me at the entrance. They made me stop moving and fired at my feet. At that time, I was so agitated that I didn't even realize I was being shot. Other shots were fired into my leg and knee. The two men next to me were shot dead on the spot. At that time, I was almost unconscious. The paratroopers used the Jeolla dialect.

"Don't pretend you're dead, you bastard!"

I faintly heard their voices. I was so barely conscious that my body was limp. I could barely feel my body. After a while, the paratroopers took me to the YMCA and pushed my head into the toilet bowl in the bathroom. They seemed to think I was dead.

At that time, they seemed to retreat in a hurry, shouting, "Load the bodies quickly!" They left me behind. After a while, citizens came into the bathroom, seeing me where I had been pushed into the toilet, and murmuring among themselves. They struggled to get my head out of the toilet. My head wouldn't come out easily. At that moment, I only thought, "I'm dead now." When my head did come out, I said, "Help me." Then, the people were very surprised. They took me to a hospital on Geumnam-ro.

I received emergency treatment at the hospital and slept for one night. When I woke up, a doctor was there.

"Who are you?"

"I am a member of the 1st platoon of the commandos."

"You must live and be an eye-witness," the doctor told me.

The next morning, I told the doctor that I'd like to be discharged from the hospital. Then, a jeep came to the hospital and drove me to my home in Baekun-dong. As we approached the entrance of the village, my mother ran from the railroad tracks. As she ran over to the side of the jeep and saw me, she wailed.

When I got home, I was very hungry. I asked for water. She said I shouldn't drink water. Nevertheless, I implored her and ended up drinking two bowls of water. Then I ate a lot. My uncle came home, saw me, and took me to the Christian Hospital. Because there was no room, I was treated on the floor. My full consciousness returned, and my body gradually improved.

More than the Injury, the Cold Eyes around Me Hurt My Heart

After the Gwangju Uprising was suppressed and the paratroopers took over the city of Gwangju, the security forces came to the hospital in early June of 1980. The doctor told me ahead of time that if anyone asked where I had been shot. I was told to say that I had been shot at home, and he told me that only lying would save me. I was with my parents at the time, so I wasn't worried about anything dangerous. I just did what the doctor told me to do. But the security officer didn't believe me. The security officer came for several days and tried to take me away. My father firmly stopped him, insisting that the boy knows nothing. Knowing this situation, the doctor forced me to leave the hospital and stay home.

After returning home, I couldn't attend school because I was recovering for about six months. Although I was in my third year of middle school, I barely studied for the entrance exam for high school. However, I applied to an academic high school. The Provincial Education Committee found out that I had participated in May 18 and informed the school that I could not be admitted. I had no choice but to submit an application to the vocational school of Jeonnam Engineering High School, but the application was not accepted there, either. My test scores weren't bad enough for me to fail to be admitted to high school. In fact, my grades were much better than when I had been in my third year of middle school when I couldn't study.

Feeling miserable, I entered Soongeui Vocational High School. I began to realize what the essence of education policy was and started to become cynical. I began to become increasingly critical of what hindered the growth of a human being with such inhumane treatment. Maybe that's why I began to become disillusioned with the educational system while in high school, even though the subjects there didn't fit my aptitude to some degree. I began to become a problematic student who challenged the teachers' words. I think maybe the teachers' views of me were stranger than my view toward them was.

The school told me that I could study at home and that they would have me graduate from school anyhow. In other words, they advised me to take a voluntary leave and study at home while they kept my academic register as it was. I didn't want to continue to go to school, either. This did not mean that I was not interested in studying at all. I liked to read books, and I could understand well if I studied a little more.

After finishing the first semester of my sophomore year in high school, I went to Seoul. A friend of mine who was in a higher grade than me was a laborer at Daewoo Heavy Industries, so we lived together in Seoul. I decided to prepare for the entrance exam for Daewoo Industries, thinking that I might get a job, too. The following year, I passed the exam and got a job at Daewoo Industries. Manual labor did not fit my aptitude, so it was difficult to find the sense of reward than I had expected.

After three months, I came down to Gwangju. I prepared for the university entrance exam at home. I didn't go to school, but I got a high school diploma. Such treatment by the school was strange even when I think about it now. Because my actions as a student were not bad enough to be expelled from school, it seemed to me that they kept my academic registration in good standing.

The following year, I was admitted to the College of Engineering at Chonnam National University. But my mother never allowed me to go to CNU, saying the university is known as a school where students hold demonstrations. She felt so much sorrow for the wounds that I received on May 18, and she suffered seeing the process of my growth thereafter, saying I shouldn't be hurt anymore. Reluctantly, I entered the Department of Nuclear Medicine at Mokpo University, and now I am immersed in my studies and working part-time at the Radiology Department at Korean Hospital. I take pride in being on the path of medicine and will make sure that I shall become a medical practitioner who can take care of the wounds of the weak and poor. Whatever the path I take, wherever I see someone sacrifice and plunder the people, I will always take up arms. For now, I do my best to focus on my studies, but my earnest wish is to become a true medical practitioner who heals the suffering of the people struggling in society. As anyone who has suffered can know pain, I will never spare myself to take care of the wounds of the powerless because I have suffered from the difficulty of not being able to walk right.

V CRITICAL CONSCIOUSNESS

4. Gwangju Young Women's Christian Association (YWCA)

3109. To Take Up Arms for Democratization

Name: CHEON Young-Jin (male)
Date of birth: November 23, 1960 (aged 19)
Occupation: College student (currently working at Korea Credit Guarantee Fund)
Date of Record: August 1988

Research & Arrangement by SHIM In-Taek

Overview

He participated in the student demonstration as a CNU student and took part in demonstrations at the main gate of CNU and the downtown area on May 18th. Later, when Gwangju became liberated temporarily, he joined a downtown rally and entered the Province Hall on May 26th. After that, he was given a gun and engaged in a gunfight with the martial law forces at the YWCA. After the gunfight, he was arrested and imprisoned in the Sangmudae guardhouse.

From Chonnam National University to Downtown

On the morning of May 18th, 1980, I was sleeping because I was exhausted from a series of demonstrations. PARK Kwan-Hyeon, who was the president of the student council of CNU, which I attended, showed his excellent ability to bring students together while gathering their demands for democratization. Therefore, not only conscious and activist students but also ordinary students followed him well. I followed him in the ongoing demonstration. The issue of our protests could, in a word, be brought down to a desire for democratization, and the opaque democratic process of the government authorities only accelerated our enthusiasm for demonstrations. Throughout this process, I became more and more fatigued, and I felt extremely tired due to the torchlight protest in which I participated on May 16th. In addition, I was sleeping until late on the morning of May 18th, so I didn't know that martial law had been expanded nationwide.

At that time, my family was running a salt shop in front of Seogang Health Community College, and my father, opening the store, said, "Oh, why are there soldiers in front of the college?" When I heard the sound in my sleep, I thought, "The martial law has been extended across the country." When I woke up and got out of my room, I saw soldiers wearing paratroopers' military boots and M16 rifles in front of the main gate of Seogang Health Community College.

I finished breakfast and headed to CNU because the student council's announcement, "Let's gather in front of CNU at 10:00 a.m. on the day when martial law is extended," was already delivered through various leaflets and word of mouth.

As a CNU student, I left for school with some sense of responsibility and curiosity. But when I got on the bus, I had mixed feelings. It seemed that the dream of democratization, which was about to be realized, and the path to a just world seemed far away.

I arrived at school around 10:00 a.m. The students' demonstration had not yet begun. Tents of the soldiers had been set up next to the university stadium, and about ten soldiers in combat uniforms and helmets stood in front of the university, probably carrying bayonets or clubs. The students were hanging around for some time, and a while later, when someone shouted a slogan, the students who had been in a commotion began to demonstrate.

We first sang, "Let's Get Together and Become One," which we used to sing at every protest at the time and sat on the bridge in front of the school's main gate and began a sit-in protest, following someone's lead. We sat on the bridge singing a lot of songs. A little later, a man from the soldiers, who appeared to be a commander, ordered us to disband. As we sat still, he told us, it being unclear whether he used a microphone or not, that they'd do something to us if we didn't disband in a few minutes. There was not a large number of us. We were about 100 to 200. But we kept sitting-in, as was our usual means of demonstrating. Then suddenly the soldiers (we didn't know at the time they were paratroopers) started to chase us with clubs, shouting "Charge!" The sound of their military boots was completely different from that of the riot police, who protected us for safety and order during the torchlight demonstration.

Seeing that sight, we ran away in chaos. In the middle of running frantically, I looked back and found an old man stopping a soldier from taking a student in front of the bridge. And the soldier pushed him away with his shoulder.

The scattered students gathered and began the protest again. There was neither a leader nor any command, but we protesters gathered again. When the soldiers chased us, we scattered and ran away again. By doing this, we realized how different they were from the riot police. They were really quick when they ran to us; and when someone was caught, they beat them with clubs.

Around that time, someone suggested we should go downtown. We judged that it would be better to go downtown than to fight with soldiers at school. And we hurried to the downtown area.

Around that time, more students and some citizens joined us, and the number of protesters reached 300 to 400.

It was about noon when we changed our course toward Salesio

High School to go into downtown. The soldiers at CNU seemed to have got the information about our course. The riot police blocked us and fired tear gas at us indiscriminately, as we were heading toward Gwangju Station via Salesio High School. So we dispersed.

I went downtown through a maze-like alley.

Sporadic protests were already underway downtown. There were about ten groups of small demonstrators, each group of which was about 100 to 200. The protesters were pushed back and forth, and when we met each other, we joined together with a shout of joy. In this way, the size reached 1,000, but when soldiers chased us, we were pushed back.

Being pushed back, the protesting group to which I belonged threw stones and broke down Gyerim-dong Police Box and another police box, and attacked a police motorcycle.

We were pushed to Sansu-dong, where we found a bus crowded with the riot police. We protesters surrounded the riot police's bus because we were not afraid of the riot police at all as we protested against soldiers who were throwing themselves at us. The protesters were pushed to Sansu-dong and scattered. Only about 200 people were left. The riot police were sitting motionless in the parked bus. They were sitting there even though the demonstrators told them to come out. Only then did the riot police come out as the protesters mercilessly knocked on the bus doors and rapped on the wire mesh of the bus.

I supposed there was a commander, but we couldn't see such a person. The protesters disarmed all of the riot police and had them sit down on the street.

The demonstrators were divided in opinion on how to deal with the riot police. The opinions were evenly divided into two. One side suggested exchanging the captured riot police for citizens or students who had been captured; and the other side suggested just releasing the riot police because they were innocent.

In the end, it was agreed that the riot police and the citizens or students should be exchanged. The riot police sat helplessly on the street during the discussion, saying "Oh my goodness, oh my goodness."

Ten minutes after we detained the riot police, a truck came and released soldiers. The protesters asked the soldiers to exchange the citizen captives for the riot police. But the soldiers walked slowly toward the protesters and told them to release the riot police unconditionally. The protesters continued to shout and sang, chanting "Exchange the Captives" because they would not comply with the demand of the soldiers. Then suddenly the soldiers shouted, "Charge!" and pulled out their clubs and ran toward us.

The protesters threw stones at the soldiers, but they ran toward us while being hit by the stones. When the protesters saw the sight, they forgot the riot police and began to run away in chaos again. I ran away through the alley like everyone else, and the sound of soldiers' military boots followed along with the sound, "ouch, ouch!" from behind. I couldn't afford to look back because I was so busy running, but the person who was running behind me must have been caught. And the soldiers, as they did in the downtown, targeted only one person at a time here as well, chased him to the end and mercilessly beat the person with clubs.

I went back to downtown, mixed with other protesters and was pushed around by the soldiers. Because there were protesters and soldiers everywhere, I was afraid of being pushed toward the soldiers if I was unlucky. So, I escaped to the basement of the Catholic Center. There was nowhere else to escape.

There was a restaurant in the basement of the Catholic Center, and when I entered the restaurant, the female owner of the restaurant told me not to leave and sit down. The woman brought me a bowl of *Seolleongtang* and I ate it. Maybe everyone who came in there got a free meal.

After leaving the restaurant, I called home not only because I was curious about the family situation but also because my parents might worry about me. Fortunately, nothing had happened at home. I told my parents that I was going to Songjeong-ri because my friend was there. And I went to Songjeong-ri by bus No. 5.

My friend's house was in a village called Usan-dong in Songjeong-ri. Usan-dong was completely a remote area at that time. It had a good environment, so I often visited there with my friends.

Three or four friends including me gathered at my friend's house in Usan-dong on that day. We used to argue with each other when we had a few drinks to claim whose idea was right. So on that day we talked about this and that as we usually had done. We mainly talked about the protest and the violent and inhuman deeds of the soldiers that took place that day. In fact, till that day we all had not known much about CHUN Doo-Hwan. However, we began to think that he might be an authoritarian figure while we took part in the protest, hearing of and shouting the slogans of "CHUN Doo-Hwan, Resign!" and "Release KIM Dae-Jung!" However, we shouted the slogans without a sense of desperation. In fact, the reason why my friends and I joined the demonstration stemmed from a sense of responsibility and aspiration for democratization of this land.

The next morning (May 19th), I called home because I stayed at my friend's house at that time and was very curious about the situation of the downtown as well. My father told me to just stay in Songjeong-ri. I stayed in Usan-dong, Songjeong-ri because I was so tired from running around, being chased, and following the protesters all day long the day before without having proper meals, and my father also advised me to stay there. While I remained in Usan-dong, I heard that city buses in Gwangju were not running and that the citizens protested in the downtown area every day. Hearing the news, I thought that I shouldn't just sit back there, so I walked from Songjeong-ri to Gwangju on May

20th. Many people came out on foot or by bicycle.

There were no city buses running when I arrived in Gwangju, as I had heard. After parting with my friends, I walked straight home to Yangrim-dong. I stayed at home that day even though the citizens gathered and protested every day in the downtown.

Gwangju Liberated

The next day (May 21st), around 10:00 a.m. (?), I went outside and saw that the situation had turned around. The cruel soldiers were only around the Province Hall. The citizens were beating vehicles, of which the windows were all broken, and running around to gather more citizens. In my neighborhood, middle-aged women made *gimbap* for the protesters who rode in the vehicles. The deaconess of a local church, which was located next to my house, also made *gimbap*. And the neighbors provided food to the protesters who drove in my neighborhood. I continued to participate in protests in front of the Province Hall. Sometime in the afternoon, I heard the announcement, "Machine guns were installed on the roof of the CNU Hospital to take over the Province Hall this evening. So citizens should not come out." And countless gunshots rang out that night.

When I came out the next morning, the citizens had taken over the Province Hall. I want to clarify that my memory is not clear enough to describe the situation from then until the afternoon of May 26th in detail and chronologically, even though I went downtown almost as if I went to work while having meals at home and attended citizens' rallies in downtown and happened to witness corpses. On the very first day of the liberation after the Province Hall was taken over, I came out of my house and went around. The place that I visited that day was CNU Hospital.

When I went to the hospital, the morgue was already full of bodies of the people who died during the uprising, and the bodies that could not be moved to the morgue were scattered in the front yard of the morgue. Some of the bodies had died from gunshots. The bodies were all bluish with ice placed in their necks and armpits, probably to prevent the bodies from decomposing due to the weather.

I remember that rallies were held in front of the Province Hall every day, and citizens gathered immediately when they were informed of the time of the rallies. I didn't know other details because I always was alone but remembered that someone came out to host the events. Many people came out and gave some speeches. One came out and said, "Everyone, we should have done this when PARK Chung-Hee was alive, but we did nothing at that time. Then why are we doing this now?" And when the citizens booed, the person got down. The square in front of the Province Hall was filled with citizens, and students lined up and shouted, "Order."

A mobile strike unit (or the citizen militia), which seemed to be newly organized after the takeover of the Province Hall, went around wearing clothes, military helmets, and riot helmets that the riot police had left. The mobile strike unit initially drove around, beating the vehicles with bats instead of guns, but as the mobile strike unit was officially organized, they carried guns in jeeps or trucks. When they rode in a jeep, they maintained the positions such that one person stood guard with a gun and the other members sat in a row behind him. I remember that ordinary citizens did not ride in vehicles around this time.

The Last Battle

Many posters were put up in front of Namdo Arts Center. The contents of the posters included that the U.S. sent a warship to Busan to help Gwangju. I think I saw the *Fighters' Newsletter*, but I don't remember the details.

While I was wandering around without a destination, I saw a hand-written leaflet posted in front of Namdo Arts Center at around 4:00 or 5:00 p.m. on May 26th, saying, "College Students, Gather at the YWCA." So I went to the YWCA, thinking about doing something.

When I arrived at the YWCA, some students were sitting and talking about the Gwangju Uprising. I naturally joined their conversation. And when there were about twenty people gathered, I entered the Province Hall led by KIM Yoon-Ki, who was in the mask dance club at CNU (I got to know his name at the military guardhouse in Sangmudae), and someone called Mr. YANG, without any procedure for investigation or identification check. I think people could go into the Province Hall when a certain number of people gathered regardless of time. I spoke with KIM Yoon-Ki and other leaders naturally and headed to the Province Hall, but until that time I didn't even think that the two were leaders.

Since the citizen militia was already organized, the area around the Province Hall was orderly, and the mobile strike unit wearing riot helmets were driving around. There were quite a lot of people inside the Province Hall, most of whom were young people, and I was told that there were women too, but I didn't see many of them.

In the middle of the Province Hall, PARK Nam-Sun, the head of the situation center, was conducting affairs in his military uniform, pointing in the direction with a pistol in his hand, saying, "Hey, come here. Do it this way." But it was at the military guardhouse in Sangmudae that I found out he was PARK Nam-Sun, the head of the situation center. It was because every time he was called out alone, he came back beaten up, so I asked others, "What's wrong with him?" and they said he was PARK Nam-Sun, the head of the situation center. As we gathered in the Province Hall, the late spokesman YOON Sang-Won came and explained the situation to us. And he made it clear once again by saying, "Without firm determination, it is difficult for us to get through the current situation. Those of you who have no firm determination can leave now." Spokesman YOON Sang-Won was dressed casually and had no gun, but when he said he wouldn't hold anyone who wanted to leave, the atmosphere suddenly seemed to become chilly.

I had entered the Province Hall in anticipation of being assigned a mission. However, I was not assigned any mission, but only ordered to wait after YOON Sang-Won's briefing. I met KIM In-Soon there and talked about this and that. And then we had dinner somewhere on the second floor of the Province Hall.

KIM In-Soon and I kept talking after dinner. I learned that he had graduated from Seoseok High School in the same year as me. He was very knowledgeable, and he said he attended church. We talked and slept on the floor of the Province Hall. He covered himself with his brown jacket, and I just slept in a t-shirt.

While I was sleeping, I heard that the martial law forces had come. After receiving an M1 rifle and ten rounds of live ammunition each, we organized groups of ten to twenty people and followed the leaders to the YWCA. The sound of gunfire was already coming from the outskirts.

In our group, there were LEE Yeon, whom I had met in the Province Hall, and HAN Jeong-Man, whom I had met when we ate. And there was also a reserve, who was the platoon leader of our group. There was also a student in work clothes who attended CNU. I didn't know how he got out of the Province Hall, but he ran away without being caught, and I have seen him several times since then.

Having been assigned to a room, I put my gun on the wall and was leaning against the wall. Until then, I didn't have a thought at all that I would shoot or I would die even though I had seen so many dead people. However, I was just very scared. I heard gunshots in the middle of the night, and a female voice from a speaker, "Citizens, the martial law forces are coming in," drove me to extreme fear. All sorts of thoughts came to my mind. Instead of any logic or systematic thoughts, the faces of my family and my home, one by one, came to my mind, and the past I had lived passed like a panorama.

The distant sound of gunfire began to come closer. It was the beginning of the battle in the Province Hall. I heard the sound of gunfire like the popping of roasting beans. After a long time, I was thinking, "Why are martial law forces not coming here?" and then soldiers appeared in front of the YWCA. It was already getting brighter. The soldiers shouted out loud as soon as they appeared in front of the YWCA. "You guys in the YWCA, come on out!" "Get your hands up and come out!" "Everyone inside, surrender," they shouted. I peeked out through the window and saw the soldiers standing in a line under the wall of the alley across the street, pointing guns at the YWCA and staring at it. But no one surrendered.

The battle had finally begun. I didn't know which side fired the first shot. The room was hit by bullets and filled with gunpowder. I came to my senses when I smelled the gunpowder. I thought it was a battle of life or death. But the battle with the martial law forces was not even a contest. I couldn't even dare to shoot and tucked my head on to the wall because of the bullets flying into the room. Then, I heard someone saying in the next room, "Platoon commander! Platoon commander! The platoon commander is dead!" The platoon commander was a reserve and old enough to know how to use a gun. That's why he was selected as the platoon command. However, I only touched a gun when I was a freshman during military training. So, when I heard that the platoon commander was dead, I just thought that we were all dead now. At that time, the martial law forces had already entered the first floor of the YWCA.

The soldiers kept shouting, "Come out with your hands up! Surrender!" But even in that short moment I thought with pride, "If I come out with my hands up here, it's to surrender."

By that time, I was in a daze, so I didn't know which room

I heard it from, but someone said, "Here we go! Here we go! We are coming out with our hands up! Don't shoot!" Then in our room as well, someone said "Let's get out, let's get out!" We couldn't hesitate any longer with pride or something. We didn't have a choice at the very crossroads of life and death. LEE Yeon, who attended the Department of History at CNU, and everyone in our room went out with our hands up.

When we were taken downstairs, there were people who had been caught earlier than us. There, we were forced to kneel down, lower our heads, with our hands being tightly pinioned behind our backs, and we were beaten and dragged out. I was in a state of confusion so that I could not feel the pain when I was beaten. The day was already completely bright. As I was being taken away, I had a glimpse that many citizens were caught and knelt down like strings of fish in front of the Province Hall. I did not see that many soldiers, and there were tanks on one side of the square and buses in the back. As we were tied up and dragged like strings of fish, we could fall because our feet and bodies got tangled. A student from Daedong High School, named Hyang-Hyeon or something, who was tied behind me, fell down. Then, a soldier kicked the student in the face with his military boots without mercy, completely distorting one side of the student's face. Later, when we were in the guardhouse, a scab was formed on his face and it was removed. We kept looking at the ground and being dragged away, and we heard someone from the alley across the street saying, "Hey, Staff Sergeant KIM, come here and have a drink." I turned my eyes in that direction and saw that a box of beer was placed next to the soldier who was talking, and the soldier was drinking beer while holding it in one hand and shooting with the other, like a scene in a movie. It was ridiculous. We were trembling with our heads down.

The soldier who was dragging me replied.

"I drank a lot, too."

"Where?"

"When I went down to the basement of the Tourist Hotel, there was a pile of beer. I drank a lot there."

The basement of the Tourist Hotel seemed to have been a nightclub back then.

Listening to the conversation of the two soldiers, we were dragged to the front of other soldiers in the alley across from the YWCA. We knelt down and lowered our heads in front of them for a few minutes before being brought back to the front of the Province Hall. It seemed that the situation of the Province Hall building had already ended. With my head lowered, I was loaded like a dog on the bus heading to the guardhouse. Even though I couldn't see the situation ahead because my head was lowered, it seemed that soldiers pushed away a foreign reporter who was trying to get on the bus to take pictures, and I heard him say "No."

When I got to Sangmudae by bus, I knelt down and got my head down on the yard for a brief questioning. Five or six men in plain clothes were sitting at the desks on the yard. They called us forward one by one and asked about personal information such as name and age. And then they asked us if we had carried a gun, shot it at the moment we were captured, what kind of activity we did, and where we did it. After that, they wrote the word, "extremist" in red on the back of those who were screened already. As soon as the investigation was over, we were sent to the guardhouse. The person who questioned me was wearing a reddish shirt, and I went through the same process and was sent to the guardhouse.

The Life in Sangmudae Guardhouse

The guardhouse in Sangmudae had six cells that were organized in a fan shape. A structure made of cement was installed at the center that corresponded to the handle of the fan shape, so that the military police could go up there and do guard duty. More than 100 people were imprisoned in the guardhouse, and we had a hard time on the first day because of the guardhouse chief who was short and looked just like the Grim Reaper from Hell. The guardhouse chief made us kneel down in the cell and went around screaming "Don't move!" and took anybody who moved, beating him almost to death. And when the guardhouse chief called anybody's name and he didn't get an answer at once, he beat the person in the same way. As a result, the guardhouse was, in a word, a crucible of madness worse than Hell, and this condition continued until the next morning. By the morning of the 28th, the fatigue of the citizen militia reached its peak. Actually, the citizen militia, who had the last decisive battle at the Province Hall, YWCA, and other places, had not been able to get enough rest or even sleep well before that. In addition, considering we not only underwent a battle at the crossroads of life and death at the dawn of the 27th, but also we were detained in the guardhouse and tormented by the guardhouse chief for a whole day, how could we endure any longer? When the morning of the 28th came, we fell asleep while kneeling, leaning on the people in front of us or losing our balance and falling aside, despite the shouting or beating of the guardhouse chief. Everyone fell asleep like that.

I heard a "thump, thump" sound from somewhere when I fell asleep like that. I woke up, wondering what the sound was. A man stood up and banged his forehead against the wall. That man was KIM Young-Cheol, who worked at the Good Books Cooperatives or somewhere. I was told that he belonged to the uprising leadership and was arrested at the YMCA. When the man banged his forehead against the wall, blood gushed out of his forehead. The guardhouse chief and the military police came in to twist his hands behind his back and take him out. But I didn't know if he was dead or alive. A few months later, a man with a long vertical scar on his forehead was put in our guardhouse. He was the guy,

KIM Young-Cheol.

That was how my guardhouse life began. We lived on, sitting up straight in five rows in the guardhouse. Having to sit like that all day was pretty hard work. I had to suffer from hunger because the amount of food was very small. The food we had was exactly what soldiers ate in the military. However, the amount of food was significantly less than that of soldiers, and we also used military food trays. But instead of serving soup and rice separately, guards put rice in a soup bowl or a rice bowl, and poured the soup on top of it. And two people ate by sitting face to face. So, when it was mealtime, the middle of the five rows was divided to join both sides of the two rows. This way, the original five rows became four rows. After that, we sat facing each other in two rows and were delivered the food trays that came in from the door of the cell. When the military police said, "Start the meal," we said "Thank you for the meal" and then ate. Because of the small amount of food, I spent the whole day thinking about eating. And when adult citizens and students stayed together, we argued a lot over food.

The adult citizens had various occupations, and although students could not be special beings, they had many trivial quarrels because they had differences in basic perceptions when sharing limited meals.

We went on a hunger strike in the guardhouse because of the small amount of food. During the strike, we refused to eat one meal and expressed our demands specifically, such as "Disclose the normal amount of meals and give us the normal amount," "Don't serve meals in bowls that can be used for dogs or pigs. Don't pour soup over rice. Serve soup and rice separately." Then the chief of the guardhouse said, "Come out here those of you who continue to refuse to eat!" It was obvious that we would have been beaten to death if we had come out. But about half of us came out, got beaten up, came back, and ate again. After the strike, the situation improved. The amount of our meals became similar to those of active-duty soldier prisoners (in the guardhouse, there was a cell where only soldiers who committed crimes while serving in the military were imprisoned), and we received our meals on an individual tray. However, no matter how much improvement was made, hell could not turn into heaven. In the meantime, the students and adults were separated. The students were placed in the third room from the one I was in, to the right of the military police on duty.

Shortly after we started living in the guardhouse, a new system was implemented to have a platoon commander in each room. Platoon commanders were needed when serving meals, but they were needed fundamentally for effective control. The number of military police on duty gradually decreased from five or six just after we went in to the guardhouse, to three or four after two or three days, and to one or two after a while. So it was necessary to have a person in charge of each room for more effective control. In fact, the military police would designate one person as a platoon commander of each room, and harassed and changed the commander if there was trouble in the room due to poor control. The platoon commanders were selected by taking turns, but those who were good at controlling played the role longer than others.

In our room, GU Seong-Ju, who was the head of the supply team in the Province Hall during the uprising, served as a platoon commander because of his excellent leadership. New recruits were in charge of the meal. When more rice was served, they used to collect the leftover rice and soup, and distributed them. And if there were leftovers again, they would serve several more trays of meals. And as time went by, the platoon commanders became friends with the military police, and, accordingly, they got an extra bowl of rice – the commanders handed out a few spoons of rice to the obedient or shared them with their acquaintances.

In addition, if someone wanted to be a platoon commander, he would behave badly and cause troubles to oust the current platoon command. Later, when a man of high-rank came and told the military police, "Hey, give them more food," they gave us some more food, and we devoured it and sighed. And after a long time, bread came in because there was too little rice to serve. This time, I felt like I was getting used to the life in the guardhouse with the joy of eating bread.

Not long after we entered the guardhouse, there was a military policeman who was about to be discharged from the military service. When he was alone on duty at dawn, he came to us and said, "Hey guys, you'd better behave yourselves. If you act like a rabble in the cell, what you did outside will be meaningless. Act with fortitude and dignity. I'm from the Jeolla Province, too." In fact, we had just gotten over the fear of death then. In addition, the hunger and the atmosphere of fear continued, and fatigue reached its peak, so we became irrational and just acted disorderly and did not cope with the situation with fortitude and dignity. The admonition of the military policeman, who said that he came from the same province as us, made me reflect a lot on myself. However, acting with fortitude even after being imprisoned was just a thought. In reality, it was difficult to put that thought into action until my life in the guardhouse ended because there were many people imprisoned together in the guardhouse and because we quarreled over trivial things as captives there unlike when we fought outside. But it was also true that things had gotten a lot better over time.

In the guardhouse, we had our own liberal arts classes. The classes were held in the latter part of our prison life, months after our prison life began. Anyone freely talked about what they felt and thought, and HAN Sang-Seok, who moved from another room, talked very well. One of the Chosun University students was not just good at speaking but also singing. KIM In-Soon, whom I mentioned earlier, had a clear political consciousness and was a devout Christian, so he preached a lot about the Bible. HAN Sang-Seok was a Won-Buddhism believer, so he talked a lot about Won-Buddhism.

There were other minor issues as well. We chatted a lot about the uprising, and especially the American issue was newly raised. On the matter of connection between the Gwangju Uprising and the United States, there were criticisms about the attitude of the U.S. as a simple bystander or its support for the brutality of the martial law forces. Anti-Americanism in the student movement was also discussed.

One day, as opinions were divided among the cells, one of the military police officers said, "Professors are good at speaking, so I'd like to suggest that one of the professors here come forward and speak." Then, LEE Sang-Sik, who was arrested as a professor in the Department of History at CNU, went out into the aisle in front of the cells and gave a speech. I can't remember what he said at the time, but he spoke very well anyhow. The professor concluded his speech by saying, "I haven't been able to say what I wanted to say for a long time, but I talked satisfactorily today." This kind of liberal arts classes continued, and our life in the guardhouse was revitalized as we were exposed to the Bible and Buddhist scriptures. At that time, I was able to read the Bible as a whole and was deeply moved by the Heart Sutra, spending much time reading. Various types of books other than religious scriptures were given to us. The Bible was later handed out to us by the Gideons International, so everyone had their own copies of the Bible. I'm sorry to say this, but nothing beat the Bible to be used as a pillow when sleeping.

Once a week, military chaplains came to have a worship service, and they were very good and comforting. One of them, in particular, preached with great enthusiasm. Someone in the guardhouse, who was from a university of education, was released from the guardhouse ahead of us. I was told that whenever people were released, he came to cheer them up and treated them to a glass of *makgeolli*.

Sometimes I spent time meditating. Mediation brought me a small but valuable enlightenment. Through this experience, I could understand the story that the old monks gained enlightenment during meditation while facing the wall. And one day, the military police handed out to us a piece of paper and a ballpoint pen and told us to write a letter home. I wrote down the letter as they told me, "This is.... I am now under protection in Sangmudae." Later I learned that the letter caused a controversy among my older brothers at home because of the handwriting. This situation was understandable considering that my family heard a flurry of shots at dawn and they had not heard from me, their beloved son and brother, for months. For these reasons, they argued over whether it was my handwriting or not. In fact, I had been in prison for a long time, so my handwriting couldn't be the same as before.

Later, visitors were allowed into the guardhouse. When my father came to see me, I cried a lot. While in the guardhouse, I cried one more time later, during LEE Yeon's testimony. However, when my mother visited me later, I rather comforted her and laughed.

However, in the beginning of my life in the guardhouse, it was quite different from this (there was this kind of atmosphere later on, too). But I wanted to leave the jail as soon as possible. I couldn't even talk to the person sitting next to me, and I stayed seated all day long, except for eating. We were not allowed to move freely. There was a locker in the back of the cell. We took off all the clothes we wore and put them in the locker and wore military uniforms. Later, when we were given toiletries such as toothbrushes and soap, we also put them in the locker.

We washed our face in the bathroom inside the cell. If we wanted to go to the toilet, we were allowed to go there in pairs only after reporting, "We want to use the toilet," and being ordered "Go" even though the toilet was inside the cell. Because the seating arrangement was not decided by anyone, we sat down from the front by our own choice. But it was incredibly hot in the summer because there were about 100 people in the cell, so we tried to sit in front of each other, and when the autumn came and the cold wind blew, we tried not to sit in the front seats.[44)]

There were two things I couldn't forget while being imprisoned in the guardhouse. While the life in the guardhouse continued, the movement of inmates continued, too. Some of them were released by suspension of prosecution without being put on trial; and others who had a sudden fever were taken to and returned from the Integrated Hospital, because the contagious disease of typhoid was rampant that summer. As a result, once the number of inmates was reduced to about fifty. Among the inmates who were transferred in those ways, there was Professor LEE Hong-Gil (?), a white-haired man who was transferred to our room. It seemed that he had been badly beaten up before he was transferred because there were black and blue bruises from his calves to the thighs. At that time, someone applied ointment called Antipramine on him. At that time, in fact, a professor was like a god to us.

Even though I can't remember his name, there was a poor boy who was short, as young as about fifteen years old. He tottered and just stared vacantly without answering and stooped his shoulders even when his name was called. The boy was beaten up by the guardhouse chief. I don't know why the boy was singled out by the guardhouse chief, but he told the boy to come out and handcuffed his wrists to the front iron bars so that he couldn't escape (?). And then he said to us "Hey, you guys. I, the guardhouse chief in my thirties at Sangmudae, will imprint you the memory that will be stuck in your head for the rest of your lives." And he started to beat the boy like a dog. At first, the chief hit him randomly with a cudgel, and then he threw it away and hit him with both hands and feet from head to toe indiscriminately. I had never seen anything like that in my life. The boy was totally the punching bag of the guardhouse chief. Although his head wasn't

---

44) The front wall of each cell was only a set of bars, so there was greater air circulation near the front, which made life more comfortable in the summer but more uncomfortable in the winter.

broken, he couldn't even scream and was just beaten, and then fainted. It was really absurd. What was even more absurd was that he had beaten the little boy almost to death and then instructed his subordinate military police to leave his handcuffs locked. So he stayed up all night, handcuffed to the bars, until dawn. He was probably the one who was beaten most severely in the guardhouse. I still remember the guardhouse chief's face clearly.

Among the military police, ordinary workers were just ordinary people before they became the military police, but among them, the wicked had always been evil.

The Process of a Trial

The investigation for my trial began when I was taken to the guardhouse of Sangmudae. The military police in charge came and called us one by one to be interrogated that day, and we were led by the military police into a room next to the yard outside the guardhouse. There was a desk in the room, and the interrogation was usually divided into two or three parts, and investigators in their 30s or 40s in casual clothes asked questions. When we answered, they wrote down our answers with a ballpoint pen. They asked, "You tried to make KIM Dae-Jung the president!" and if I said I didn't, then they said "Hey, son of bitch, I know you did," and then he wrote "Yes." And then he asked, "Did you shout slogans?" and as we answered that we had shouted slogans such as "Lift Martial Law," "CHUN Doo-Hwan, Resign," and "Release Arrested Students," he wrote them down.

About fifteen days after being put in the guardhouse, there was a first release, and I was questioned three or four times in total. I was questioned for the first time between the fifteenth day and a month after being arrested. And I was summoned as a witness during investigations of others. At first, I was summoned as a witness to LEE Yeon, and the summons was about whether LEE

Yeon did or did not fire at the troops in the battle just before being caught at the YMCA. After inquiring into LEE Yeon's family, they found out that LEE Yeon's brother had been involved in something, so they tried to devise a scheme that LEE Yeon fired a gun. In fact, however, LEE Yeon and I were in the same room during the YMCA battle, and as mentioned above, we could not even aim a gun, let alone shoot one. Nevertheless, they called me out, threatened me with various words, and told me to place my thumbprint in the witness column for him shooting. One night, a Staff Sergeant under the prosecutor called me out and punched me to make me place my thumbprint. But I didn't do it to the last. LEE Yeon asked me a favor by saying, "No matter how many times I get beaten, I will say I didn't shoot to the last, so please testify with the truth." At the time, there were rumors that shooting or not shooting was the standard for release and imprisonment. Ultimately, I endured their threats and beatings to the last because my testimony could affect LEE Yeon's fate. Of course, I would have preferred to testify that he fired a gun because I had suffered a lot. That night when I returned from being beaten by the Staff Sergeant for not signing with my thumbprint, tears came out themselves, and I cried.

Nevertheless, LEE Yeon and I were on the same trial together because we were classified as the YMCA group. The judge said to LEE Yeon, "You shot a gun." And when LEE Yeon said, "I didn't shoot. I said so when I was being investigated, and CHUN Young-Jin, who was a witness, testified to that fact." Then the judge said, "Okay," and moved on.

Next was YOO Jae-Won, my high school friend, who had a radio set in the situation room. According to him, he overheard a radio communication of the martial law forces through the radio set, and if the soldiers made a radio call between themselves about where they were going, he misled them by telegraphing again that the citizen militia was going there. But he said he selected me as a witness and asked me to testify that he had never used a radio set. Because I thought testifying like that would be advantageous to him, I denied firmly that he had ever used a radio set. When writing a report, they ordered us to write where we were caught and what activities we did. But later, in writing about "what was your purpose in doing such a thing?" they wrote their pre-planned scheme: "We attempted to do something with KIM Dae-Jung in some way" or "We planned to do something by taking advantage of the confusion." As far as I know, dissidents, university professors, and executives of the Settlement Committee were investigated somewhere else.

When we were escorted to court, as when we had been sent to be questioned, they called those of us who had a trial on a particular day one by one and then tied us up with a rope. And about seven to ten military police escorted us both front and rear. The trial was done by dividing us into several groups. I was tried in the so-called YWCA Group, which consisted of those caught at the YWCA; JEON Yong-Ho, NA Myeong-Kwan, KIM Seong-Seop, and others who were involved with the *Fighters' Newsletter*, Deulbul Night School, and the College of Commerce at CNU; HAN Jeong-Man who attended the College of Commerce at CNU, LEE Yeon, and so on, who had nothing to do with either the *Fighters' Newsletter* or Deulbul Night School.

I'm not sure whether there was a lawyer for me at the time of the trial, but the judge was in a military uniform with a colonel's rank, and the prosecutor was also in a military uniform. In my case, I didn't have much to say, so it took about thirty minutes to finish. Later, I heard that my father had been in the audience. But I couldn't see him.

As for the case of KIM Yoon-Ki, those who were brought to trial together with him told me that he had said, "It's ridiculous," to the presiding judge in his final statement. I don't remember what I said in my final statement, but I just remember it was simple. My father said that I put my hands behind my back.

The prosecutor asked that I be sentenced to five years at the maximum and three years at the minimum in prison, and I was sentenced to two years at the maximum and a year at the minimum in prison. But I was released after receiving a remittal of punishment at the final trial (at that time I was nineteen years old because my birthday had not passed, and this fact seemed to have played a decisive role in my release). Just before I was released, I was transferred to a prison that I once dreamed of and imprisoned there for seven to ten days. After that, as I was ordered to take a leave of absence by the university president's authority, I was not able to attend university and spent time reading some books that I borrowed from acquaintances. However, I returned to university in 1982, and now, having graduated, I am working for a company.

VI. WITH THE DEAD

1. Sangmugwan (the Province Hall)

1029. Guarding Corpses ___ **JEONG Tae-Ho**

2. The Red Cross Hospital

1030. I Managed Corpses at the Red Cross Hospital ___ **JEONG Jun**

VI WITH THE DEAD

1. Sangmugwan (the Province Hall)

1029. Guarding Corpses
Witness: JEONG Tae-Ho (male)
Year of Birth: 1961 (aged 19)
Occupation: College student (a worker in a secondhand store)
Date of Record: April 1989

Research & Arrangement by SHIN Bong-Wha

Overview

From May 21st, he boarded a pepper-fog vehicle and took pictures of the situation in Gwangju, and from May 23rd, he guarded corpses at the Province Hall as a member of the Corpse Team. He also participated in rallies, night patrols, security guarding, procuring medicine, and broadcasting on the streets. He was captured by the martial law forces on May 27th and released on July 3rd, 1980.

Abandoned as if Orphans

My father, a trainee reporter for the newspaper *Dong-A Ilbo*, and my mother, a teacher, lived together without getting married and gave birth to my sister and me. In 1961, the year I was born, my mother was married to another man because my father was dispatched to Vietnam as a war correspondent. After my mother got remarried to another man, my sister and I had no choice but to grow up with my mother's parents, abandoned as if orphans.

Whenever my sister and I sometimes saw my mother, we had to call her auntie. So we did not have much affection for our parents. My father returned after ten long years but soon married another woman.

I graduated from elementary and middle schools in Hongseong, Chungcheongnam-do, near my mother's family. Strongly independent, I thought I could continue to attend school only if I had a specialty, and I was able to enter Daejeon Physical Education High School without difficulty since I had trained in gymnastics since childhood. In addition to gymnastics, I was healthy and well-built because I exercised a lot, playing tennis and swimming. After graduating from high school, I could no longer stay with my mother's family, so I lived alone and got admitted to the Department of Physical Education at Chosun University.

In 1980, I was a sophomore at Chosun University and lived in Chunghyo-dong, a neighborhood village under Mudeung Mountain Villa. Chunghyo-dong was far from the downtown, so I didn't know what was going on there. But sometimes, I could see students protesting on campus or in downtown. Until then, I just looked on at the students' protest, thinking that it was banging one's head against a wall.

May 20th was the day when I promised to meet a girl attending Ewha Women's University in Seoul, with whom I only had exchanged letters without knowing her face. Around 9:00 a.m., I passed through the back alley behind the Dong-gu District Office. Tear gas powder spread on the street as if telling of a fierce battle the previous day. After passing by that site, I went to Chungjang-ro to get to the Goryeo Coffee Shop across from the Gwangju Post Office, where I was supposed to meet the girl. I hardly saw any paratroopers or citizens in Chungjang-ro. The girl I had promised to meet did not show up, and I went out from the coffee shop with disappointment.

In front of the Gwangju Post Office, about 100 paratroopers, who had not been there earlier, were stationed. The paratroopers saw me and suddenly chased me. Panicked for a moment, I ran into a beauty salon on the second floor of the building across the street. Fortunately, the owner of the beauty salon told the paratroopers, "This is my son." So I was able to dodge that crisis. The old woman walked me to the front of the National Federation of Fisheries Cooperatives building.

I took a bus in front of the National Federation of Fisheries Cooperatives to go to my father's house in Gyerim-dong and saw paratroopers guarding every street. Out of curiosity, I got off in front of Jungang Elementary School. I avoided the places where the paratroopers were stationed and went to the crossroad in front of the Korea Bank. There, the paratroopers beat up citizens, loaded them into trucks, and dragged them somewhere. After they were dragged away, enough shoes to fill a wagon were scattered all over the place.

I was terrified, but I went to Gwangju Park to grasp the situations of other places. I found armed paratroopers were all over the place. At around noon, a military truck carrying paratroopers was standing in the middle of the road, and a taxi following behind honked its horn. Immediately after that, seven or eight martial law soldiers got off the truck and started smashing the taxi windows. When the angry driver protested, the paratroopers brutally beat the driver.

When I saw the violence of the paratroopers, I was upset with anger, thinking "No way! They should not have done that." Knowing how cruel the suppression of the Bu-Ma Democratic Uprising was, as I had heard from my friend, I felt something ominous.

Getting on a Pepper-Fog Truck

Witnessing the brutality of the paratroopers, I left my house on May 21st to go to the downtown. I went to Gwangju Park on a protest vehicle passing by at Sansu-dong Five-way Intersection. There were many protest vehicles in Gwangju Park, including pepper-fog trucks. I thought that it would be safe to ride a pepper-fog truck, so I got on the truck right away. There were seven protesters in the truck, including SONG Il-Kwon, a bus driver working for the Gwangju Express Bus. The rest seemed to be students of CNU and Chosun University.

We got on the pepper-fog truck and pulled it over in the alley of the Im-dong Administrative Office. One of the passengers asked us to take pictures of the current situation and keep them as evidence, so we gladly agreed. I also felt the need to maintain photographs for documentation. The bus driver brought a camera from somewhere. Immediately, our group went out into the downtown as a group. The paratroopers were stationed at the Province Hall, and there were a lot of citizens on the street.

At around 1:00 p.m., citizens pushed away the paratroopers and tried to burn the Jeonnam Ilbo building, but someone said, "This building is property of Jeonnam, so let's leave it as it is." And the citizens agreed and broke only the shutters of the Korea Exchange Bank.

After that, we saw a high school student in an armored vehicle brought from Asia Motors, moving toward the paratroopers, waving a *Taegeukgi*. Soon after, his head was cut off by a gunshot from a paratrooper. At that time, I couldn't see the gun being fired, and I was too stunned to take a picture.

After we saw the scene, we thought we should let citizens know about it. I paid money to borrow a microphone from Gyerim Radio. While going around residential areas of Sansu-dong and Gyerim-dong, we cried, "A high school student was shot dead by a paratrooper."

I took pictures in every critical situation.

It seemed that our group in the pepper-fog truck was the first to enter the Province Hall. It was around 6:00 a.m. on May 22nd.

Believing that our truck was bulletproof, we drove around the Fountain Plaza before entering the building as the leading group. The Province Hall was as quiet as death. We were followed by several other vehicles.

Procuring Medicines

There were many injuries and deaths on May 22nd, perhaps because of the previous day's battle. So there was a shortage of medicines. Just in time, Gwangju Pharmacy in Chungjang-ro contacted us to come and get medicines. My team pull over the pepper-fog truck next to the Province Hall and took a truck to Gwangju Pharmacy. We entered the warehouse of Gwangju Pharmacy and brought a lot of IV kits, gauze, and bandages. We distributed IV kits to the CNU Hospital and the Christian Hospital, and gauze and bandages to private hospitals.

Returning to the Province Hall, we were told that Gwangju would run out of gas. Hearing that martial law troops were lurking in Chosun University in which there was a gas tank, we took a Fiat to find out the movements of the martial law forces. Entering the Chosun University stadium, we drove around very quickly. The stadium was scattered with cooking utensils and leftover chicken scraps left by the paratroopers. We couldn't get to the main building and arrived in front of the Reserve Officers Training Corps (now the university gymnasium) where the gas tank was. There were piles of clothes worn by the paratroopers. We judged that there were no soldiers and went to the Province Hall to inform others of this.

We also heard that the situation on the outskirts of Jiwon-dong had gotten worse. It was around 8:00 or 9:00 p.m. when we took the pepper-fog truck and passed the last bus stop in Jiwon-dong. Two martial law soldiers suddenly appeared and put their guns on us. The martial law forces also held guns in the back of the truck, and we were completely surrounded. They fired all at once.

We believed the truck was bulletproof, so we weren't holding guns. The Gwangju Express bus driver said, "This is our fate. Everyone, hold tight," and then he turned the truck around and began to drive frenetically toward the downtown. Numerous bullets flew but only pierced the ceiling of the truck, not hitting us directly. One of the members was hit by debris and bleeding. As we drove like a bullet, the martial law forces no longer chased us. The pepper-fog truck was shot and destroyed by the gunshots of the martial law forces.

Returning to the Province Hall, we thought we had to arm ourselves to defend against the armed martial law forces. We loaded K303s and LMGs into a military jeep and conducted night patrols. One of the members involved in the Situation Room at the Province Hall carried a pistol. Receiving information that jewelry shops were being robbed, we patrolled the downtown and banks. Also, when we had any notice that there was a suspicious person, we immediately went out, but most of them were drunkards.

Guarding Corpses

Our party, which had been active together, was assigned to other teams and all scattered. I worked with a few girls on the corpse team to guard the corpses. I was scared at first, but later I thought of the girls as my comrades. The bodies were often taken over from the CNU Hospital and the Red Cross Hospital. When a body came in, the investigation team examined it and moved it to the alley between the main building of the Province Hall and the civil service office. We stuffed its eyes, nose, and mouth with cotton to prevent secretions from flowing out of the body. We placed vinyl under the bodies. We also covered with vinyl decomposed and smelly bodies. Many were shot, their limbs cut off. There was also a body stoned to death. When families of the corpses appeared, we washed and clothed them, made coffins for them, covered the coffins with white cloth, put on the *Taegeukgi*, and handed them over to the Sangmugwan. Until May 26th, 147 bodies were handed over to the Sangmugwan, and families of eleven bodies did not appear. Among them, there were two female bodies, and no family members appeared to the end. Since the bodies could not be identified by the faces, we identified them with their belongings, clothes, and shoes. With funds that had been raised, we bought coffins and *Taegeukgis* at a funeral home near the Red Cross Hospital or Yang-dong Market. We ran short of coffins, so we brought coffins made of veneer plates from the Chosun University Hospital.

At that time, we were told that there was a body in the field near Daedong High School in Baekun-dong (currently near the Veterans Hospital). I went out on a search with a few crew members. It was a body of a man who was quite old, and it could not be recognized as it was temporarily buried in soil between the hills. The family of the body did not appear until the evening of May 26th.

In addition, when injured people were brought to the Province Hall, emergency treatment was performed first, and the seriously injured people were taken to hospitals. Since there were already many patients at the Red Cross Hospital, many patients were mainly sent to the CNU Hospital.

Not only was I in charge of the corpses, but I also prepared broadcasting facilities for a rally and put posters in the downtown. In addition, I took a CNU bus with a female student of Songwon College and broadcasted on the street. The contents of the broadcast were to ask families to come and identify the bodies and to inform people of the situation as it had occurred that day.

The Poison Needle Incident

On May 24th, a Colonel and the Director of the Integrated Military Hospital asked for oxygen support, as there were many injuries and deaths due to a friendly fire incident among soldiers. The director said that he would guarantee our identities. So we took the oxygen that we obtained from hospitals and went in with armed mobile patrol unit members. At the entrance of the Hwajeong-dong Industrial Complex, there were tanks and armored vehicles, and wooden barricades had been erected. We handed oxygen tanks over to the military at the entrance of the Integrated Hospital.

I heard a rumor that a person had collapsed from a poison needle in the Province Hall around 4:00 p.m. on May 25th (editor's note: the witness is confused about the incident, which happened in the morning). When I went there, he was already being sent in a car to the CNU Hospital. I got in a car with a few people and followed him to the emergency room of the CNU Hospital. After seeing the person who had been poisoned, I got treatment for my swollen feet. My feet were so swollen that my shoes couldn't come off, so I had to tear them with a knife to heal my feet. When I returned to the Province Hall, I heard that the person poisoned by a needle had disappeared.

It was probably that night. We got the information that the situation in Yu-dong had gotten worse. Two members of the citizen militia went out to guard the outskirts, and we received a radio that two civil militia members had been shot at the Yu-dong Three-way Intersection. I went to the Yu-dong Three-way Intersection, armed with a few crew members, around 11:00 p.m. Behind the trees at the Yu-dong Three-way Intersection, we heard only the sound of gunfire. There was only a military jeep the two militia members had ridden, but no one was seen. We judged them dead as we could not find them. We returned to the Province Hall.

On the Early Morning of May 27th

On the early morning of May 27th, I was so tired from the

street broadcasting the previous day that I was sleeping with seven or eight people in the press conference room on the second floor of the civil service room at the Province Hall. Suddenly, I heard a noisy clang from the piano in the auditorium. When I hurried to the auditorium, one person was shot in the back and collapsed, and it seemed like a bullet penetrated his abdomen. On my way to the Situation Room, thinking that I had to carry him to hospital, I found two martial law soldiers, with bands around their helmets, standing on the stairs in the passage. The martial law soldiers found me and tried to shoot. I said to them, "Don't shoot. There is a patient here." But they pointed their guns at us. The sound of bullets was loud, flying by and bouncing off the railing. Sensing that the situation was serious, I crouched down and went to the press conference room. I went into the bathroom next to the press conference room. The bathroom was already full of people.

For a moment, I thought I could escape. People I was with suggested going into the sewer toward the Boy Scouts League building next to the Province Hall. When I quickly opened the window, I found that the martial law forces were in front of the Sangmugwan, and there was a transformer on the wall. We sensed that it was dangerous to go through the sewer. We decided to come back to take the food we had there and go to the roof of the auditorium to hide.

But it was already too late. Two martial law forces came to the front door and fired. Bullet shards bounced.

"Raise your hands and come out!"

We all raised our hands at this without even attempting to use a gun. I was third in the line. Then a lieutenant in front of us began to shoot. The person right in front of me fell down. They pulled us out and ordered us to sit on the second-floor railing and climb down the railing. I did so with people from other places. They fired at us and beat us countless times. At first, they shot with M16s, but after entering the Province Hall, they took away the carbines we had and fired at us. It seemed that they changed their guns to say that many people died from a friendly fire incident among the citizen militia members.

The martial law forces dragged us to the side of the main building of the Province Hall. There were already about 150 of the citizen militia captured there. The martial law forces wrote something on our backs. And they checked our belongings and took watches or money if we had it, and they took my watch.

From then on, they started beating us murderously. As I was kneeling, the martial law force stabbed me with a bayonet in my left arm. Rather than feeling the pain, I desperately hoped to be killed quickly. We got on a military bus around 5:00 or 6:00 a.m. There were three people on one seat and two in the aisle, a total of eight or nine people were seated in a row, and in the middle, soldiers kept an eye on us and fired blanks.

Murderous Torture at Sangmudae

We were dragged to Sangmudae. Soldiers first interrogated us and took our photos. We were immediately sent to the military police brigade. There were about eighty people in the guardhouse. They were students, shoeshine boys, and restaurant workers. JEONG Dong-Nyeon was one of them.

The suffering began in the brigade. We had to sit straight, and they beat our hands brutally even when our eyes moved slightly. It was common to be stomped by military boots or beaten by clubs. We were sometimes hung upside down from iron bars.

We were interrogated every day, and they forced us to admit to fabricated information.

"You killed two martial law forces and took away weapons and medicines, so put a thump print here."

I said I didn't participate in the demonstration at all and I was in the Province Hall because I had nowhere to sleep. At that time, they beat me with desks and stools, and they even threw a cup in my face while I was drinking water. The hardest thing to bear was being poked with a needle around my fingernails and the torture of hanging from the ceiling by the handcuffs on my wrists.

I still have the scars on my wrists. Also, as I was beaten more than eighty times with a pickaxe handle, my buttocks were so severely bruised that my underwear and flesh stuck tight to each other. Because of such tremendous pain, I only thought, "I wish I could be killed quickly." They said, "We can endure our labor because we take turns. No matter what happens to your body, don't feel sorry about it," and they perpetrated tremendous violence toward me.

When I went for the interrogations, I memorized the statements I made the previous day and thought about how much less I would be beaten that day. Beaten by the military police and the investigators, I got injured every day.

I was so hungry there. There was only about a spoonful of rice served with a slice of kimchi occasionally. From some point on, they rationed out bread, and I endured the pain in waiting for the bread. Perhaps those who were there at that time will never forget the bread.

Once a week, military doctors came to see the health conditions of the inmates. When a military doctor came, I lied, "I am in stage three of pulmonary tuberculosis." The military doctor nodded his head as if he felt bad for the bruises all over my body.

Transferred to the Integrated Military Hospital

With the help of the military doctor, I was transferred to the Integrated Military Hospital. Five people were transferred from Sangmudae, and all the way down to the hospital, it was nice to see people out there living freely. But when I thought about my situation, I felt like I was going crazy. X-rays were taken at the Integrated Hospital and the results were not abnormal, but the head of the surgical department hospitalized me, and I was transferred to a ward. The patients in the ward mainly had gunshot wounds. There was also a woman named KIM Yoon-Hee, who said she was attending the Department of Psychology at CNU.

White rice was served for dinner that day. Lying on the bed and looking at the white rice was like a dream. I asked other patients repeatedly, "Are they giving us this rice?" I couldn't eat well thinking about the people suffering at Sangmudae.

One day, a man named SHIN Myo-Seop, who was beaten so many times by soldiers that he went out of his mind, shouted a slogan, "Guarantee Freedom of the Press. Step Down, SHIN Hyeon-Hwak." And soldiers ran straight to him, beat his head with the butt plates of their rifles, and beat him with clubs. After that incident, the atmosphere in the hospital room, which had been depressed, gradually improved.

I was still interrogated at the Integrated Hospital, but I insisted that I didn't participate in the demonstration to the end. On July 1st, I was moved to Sangmudae again. I was sent to the infantry school auditorium instead of the military police brigade. There I attended lectures along with others. A general came to give us a lecture himself. The next day, I was forced to write a memorandum stating that "I was never beaten at Sangmudae" and was released on July 3rd.

Life after Release

I immediately went to the Red Cross Hospital for treatment. There was no specific physical trauma, but there was no place on my whole body that was fine. One day, I was lamenting my situation, so I drank alcohol and shouted slogans in the downtown, "Step Down, CHUN Doo-Hwan." Passing through Chungjang-ro to the Red Cross Hospital, I mistakenly went to a maternity clinic.

As I entered, the director came out and slapped me on the cheek and reported me to the police box. After a while, a police squad car came. I was taken to the Gwangju Police Station. Detectives did background checks.

"Isn't this the bastard who suffered and was released?"

Then he handed me over to the Daeeui-dong Police Box. I was interrogated while drunk.

"You crazy bastard, why are you wandering around like this at a time like this!"

The head of the police box cursed and slapped me on the cheek. I couldn't just be beaten silently.

"Hey, I was hurt by CHUN Doo-Hwan, then should I be beaten by you again?"

I also slapped his cheek as hard as I could. His glasses fell down to the floor and broke. He got mad and told his crew to complete a police report and send it to the prosecutor, but the police officer who investigated me told me to be cautious, and I was released from the police box two days later.

After that, I drank alcohol if I had only one hundred won in my pocket. Feeling tired of the repetitious life, I entered Baekyang Temple on the condition that I would help to get firewood. Even when I was in Baekyang Temple, I shuddered to see the detectives coming to catch me and to torture me in my dreams whenever I was asleep.

Even if I tried to stay still, I felt like I was going crazy because I remembered what had happened back then. I sought liquor again. I drank alcohol to suppress my suffering and so I could fall asleep when I became unconscious.

My body was still in pain and not getting better. With no one to take care of me and no money, my condition deteriorated. Whenever exposed to the wind, I have wondered if something went wrong with my stomach since I was stomped on the belly by the soldiers' military boots. As a result, I cannot sit for a long time, and it is so difficult to empty my bowels.

On January 14th, 1982, I received a conscription notice for training in the 31st Division for six weeks. During the training period, I was beaten especially much, as I was on the list of those who needed special attention. I went out of my mind, as I was sick and tired of being beaten up. After that, there was no hard training or beatings.

After six weeks of training, I received further training at the Cheongsong Detention Center. At that time, 150 of the 174 trainees were dispatched to the Ministry of Justice, and I was assigned to Uijeongbu Prison. From the third month of living in Uijeongbu Prison, I began to feel mentally disturbed. The prison officials sent me to the National Medical Center, first to the surgical department and then to the psychiatric department. While I was in the ward, I kept running away. In order to discharge me from the unit, the army admitted me to the Capital Integrated Hospital. Even from there, I kept running away, so they handcuffed me. Even after receiving treatment and recovering my health, when I saw the guards beating inmates, I remembered being tortured in Sangmudae in 1980. So I would beat the guards and run away. Because I ran away so many times and was locked up in a military prison, my discharge was delayed by six months, to February 1985.

For the Alienated People

After being discharged, I spent time at Daeseongam[45] in Seoul. Even then, I often went to a police box, broke windows, and beat police officers when I was drunk.

Even now, I can't work because my health does not allow it, so I have to take ten days off a month. If I overwork even a little, my whole-body aches and I can't control my body. My left arm,

45) A small Buddhist temple.

which was stabbed with a bayonet, sometimes feels inflamed and becomes numb.

I came to Gwangju last fall and am living here. I tried to commit suicide several times because I don't know what I'm going to do to support myself, but even that didn't go as planned. My life motto is to live an upright and simple life. Therefore, I refuse to become a clever intellectual who uses flattery to gain money and power. I want to help the underprivileged in this land, by doing whatever I can do. In particular, I want to go to Flower Village (Kkottongnae) in Chungcheong-do and volunteer with lepers.

I think that May 18 was a case where numerous people were sacrificed by just a few blinded by power. They still don't realize their faults. Although the government is asking us to report the casualties of May 18, the government should first identify and compensate the injured and arrested people like me who are clearly identifiable.

The saddest thing, considering what happened in 1980, is that we cannot see historical evidence in the photos taken by our party in the pepper-fog truck. If the photos had been kept well, they would have been released by now, but I suspect that they were lost. I wish I had known the name of the Gwangju Express Bus driver who kept the camera.

VI WITH THE DEAD

2. The Red Cross Hospital

1030. I Managed Corpses at the Red Cross Hospital

Witness: JEONG Jun (male)
Year of Birth: 1955 (aged 25)
Occupation: Unemployed
Date of Record: January 1989

Research & Arrangement by LEE Jong-In

Overview

He was caught in front of the Catholic Center by paratroopers and dragged to Sangmudae. After being released on the 21st, he managed and regulated the treatment of corpses with his friends at the Red Cross Hospital.

Gwangju Citizens Subject to Tyranny and Violence

It was about 2:00 p.m., Monday, May 19th. I was walking with my friend toward Geumnam-ro, speaking with him, after stopping by somewhere near Mido Motel and getting my work done. As we got to Geumnam-ro, the martial law forces standing in military uniforms came into sight.

About a regiment of the martial law forces were standing in arms in two rows all over Geumnam-ro. At that moment we were about to pass by the Dong-gu District Office. The martial law forces who were standing guard in front of the office blocked the street to Geumnam-ro.

With a puzzled look, my friend and I were standing in the middle of the people flooding in when the street was blocked.

The growing number of the citizens began to buzz. They were just concerned about the situation with fear and anxiety.

I muttered to myself, "If the situation continues like this, something will probably happen." I kept looking around.

After a while, a captain told his soldiers something, and the martial law forces opened the street toward the Catholic Center. They urged us to pass quickly.

The citizens rushed out to go faster, buzzing to each other. I got out of there safely, but I could not see my friend. I looked back and tried to find him, but he was out of sight.

Suddenly, the martial law forces blocked the street again and threatened the citizens who were trying to go out. My friend was stuck there.

I tried to go to Mido Motel behind Geumnam Mansion, but I glanced around Geumnam Mansion where three or four young men, who looked like employees of Mido Motel, were beaten and stomped by the soldiers' military boots. At that moment, my legs shook and my heart pounded. I entered the entrance of Geumnam Mansion quickly. Just then, paratroopers chased me into there. A first lieutenant and a staff sergeant of the paratroopers caught another citizen and me and asked, "What is your occupation?"

I answered them immediately in fear, thinking that I would be beaten if I had hesitated.

"I am a businessman. I have a business," I answered. Then, they demanded that I present my ID. I quickly pulled my ID out of my pocket and showed it to them. With their eyes wide open, they urged me to tell the truth.

"Aren't you a student?"

"Why are you saying that? We are not students."

As I answered him bluntly, the First Lieutenant shouted at us, saying, "They always say they are not students. But right after being released, they throw stones and protest!"

"We are so busy that you have to go now. We are not students at all." We appealed to them, and they let us go more easily than we expected.

Breathing a sigh of relief, I entered the management office of Geumnam Mansion. My senior colleague KIM Chang-Soo was there.

When KIM Chang-Soo and I came out of the office, the paratroopers chased us again. One of them grabbed KIM Chang-Soo by the collar and spat out words irritatingly, "You must be a student. Certainly."

I was so upset that I protested against him,

"He is my senior colleague. How can you treat a person of his age like that?"

Then, the paratrooper struck me with his club mercilessly, blaming me for having too many excuses.

We Will Kill All the Gwangju Bastards

While being beaten up like that, I saw a female college student came down from the upper floor of Geumnam Mansion, carrying a book, which looked like a piano lesson book, stuck on her waist. But the paratroopers acted violently even to her with no reason.

As citizens were beaten and pushed away for a while, the citizens who came out in the street protested and threw stones at the paratroopers. They picked up bottles scattered around and threw them, shouting out. Nevertheless, the paratroopers did not like to stay back. Instead, about six of the paratroopers screamed like hell.

"We will kill you all."

Then they chased the citizens who were throwing stones and bottles. The female college student, my senior colleague, and me were held by the paratroopers. They ordered my senior colleague and me, shouting, "Unbuckle your belt."

As we unbuckled our belts, they snatched them away.

They ordered us to raise our hands above our heads. We were dragged without reason to the front of the Tourist Hotel in Geumnam-ro, with our hands up above our heads and our heads down.

On the way to the Tourist Hotel in Geumnam-ro, the paratroopers deployed near the hotel struck us randomly with their buttstocks. They kicked us all over our bodies with their military boots.

"We should kill all these bastards," they said and cursed us.

Around twenty young men and citizens who had already been dragged there by the paratroopers were sitting with their heads down on the ground.

The female college student, my senior colleague, and I also stayed still with our heads down on the ground and our hands on our backs, in the same position as the others. I didn't think anything but just did what they told me to do out of fear.

How long had it been? The van of a police task force squad stopped before us. The twenty young men and citizens, the college student, my senior colleague, and I were forced to get into the van.

"Where are we going?" I thought and sat blankly.

The van headed to the Gwangju Police Station. All we who were captured could do was stay helplessly in the detention room of the Gwangju Police Station. With my head up, I silently looked around. Not only the detention rooms, but also every space was full of captives, regardless of gender. We could not breathe properly, just stay silent and dispirited.

It seemed that curfew had been moved up to 9:00 p.m. And

when it was past 9:00 p.m., ten riot police buses got ready in front of the Gwangju Police Station.

A great number of citizens and students kept in the detention rooms were forced to get on the ten buses. We had to put our head on the back of the person ahead of us, holding their back pockets. We did so because they did not want us to see anything. Anyone who raised their heads or removed their hands from the pockets was beaten by clubs without fail.

The ten riot police buses were instantly filled with the people and quickly transferred to a military base. At first, I didn't know we were headed toward a military base. We were transferred with our hands bound, three or four of us sitting on top of one another on each seat.

While being transferred, the buses stopped suddenly. At the moment, I quickly looked out the window. It was at the roundabout in front of the Gyerim Police Box.

Four or five paratroopers got on the bus we were on. As if we had complained to the paratroopers, they screamed at us, "You think we, the 3rd Airborne Troop, are pushovers? We should kill all you bastards."

The paratroopers' tyranny and violence did not stop there. They began to beat the people, beginning from the first row. More than two-third of the citizens and students in the bus were struck in the back and shoulders.

After beating us with clubs for a while, they threatened us, saying with a weary and tired look, "We will kill all the Gwangju bastards." They repeated the word "kill" in every sentence.

Seeing that, the officer in charge of the transfer, who was from the Province Police Department, said, "How can you beat the captives again? Don't beat them anymore." Then the paratroopers hurled vulgar abuse at him.

My Life at Sangmudae

After that, the four or five paratroopers got off, and I sensed that the bus continued to run for a while. At that moment, I looked out the window. The bus was heading toward the main gate of the 31st Division.

As the bus stopped, a military policeman came up to the bus and asked, "How many buses came?" One of the officers in charge of the transfer answered, "Ten."

Confirming that, the military policeman told him to go to Sangmudae because the 31st Division was already full of captives, so they could not accept any more.

Because I sat in the second seat, I could see and hear about the situation in detail.

Turning back from the 31st Division, the buses left for Sangmudae. After a long time, we arrived in front of the Joint Investigation HQ in Sangmudae. Then, all the captives looked up and out the windows. I also looked out. The military police forces in raincoats, holding pickaxe handles in their hands, were standing in two rows at the doors of the buses.

I didn't know when it started, but it was drizzling outside the window. The military police forces were just waiting for us to get off and come to them quickly. And they urged all the people to get off quickly. In addition, they ordered us to get off with our heads on the hips of the person in front of us.

Except the first person who led the way, all the other people took the same stance, got off, and were gathered in a dark auditorium-like place.

In that place, we were ordered by corporals and privates second class. The soldiers made us stand in one row for each group. Then, they told us to get all our belongings out from our pockets and to hold them in both hands. We did what they told us to do. Then, the soldiers who were waiting began to search us. Looking at the belongings in our hands, they suddenly struck the hands that held our belongings, saying "OK. OK." All the belongings fell down on the floor.

Some people stooped for the fallen belongings. Then, the soldiers together beat up the ones who stooped as if they had been waiting for it.

In the end, the soldiers cowardly and shamelessly committed violence toward the people on the pretext of their stooping.

Seeing that, the people stood still so they would not get beaten. Then, the soldiers pocketed the money and valuables fallen on the floor.

I murmured to myself.

"Surely, they are doing that and won't give our things back."

Feeling injustice and resentment and even thinking how ridiculous it was to take our belongings, all of us felt almost hopeless.

I did what they told me to do and never resisted them so as to be beaten less. The auditorium was packed with about a thousand people. Most of the people were injured. The injured were easily found: some were bleeding from bayonets wounds, some limping in pain, some with distorted faces, and some with internal harm and invisible pain.

While I looked around and saw the injured, a soldier came in.

"Anyone injured, raise up your hand."

So, the injured were transferred somewhere else. The other people remained in the auditorium-like place. After the injured went out, the soldiers inflicted more suffering on us. We had to remain still, crouching until our heads could reach the hips of the people in front of us. We had to do whatever the soldiers told us to do for two days.

That was a horrible place where neither resistance, excuses, nor reasons were allowed.

The next day, people came with rice, introducing themselves as from the "Korea Women's Association." They provided us with pickled radishes for a side dish.

That was the only time we had rice. Except for that time, we had to have hardtack as an emergency ration instead of rice. When we went to the toilet, they made us move in a group of twenty, blindfolded, holding the people in front of us. No individual movement was allowed at all.

Around 2:00 p.m. on the 21st, we were suddenly called out to the drill ground. We went out to the drill ground in a rush all together.

At the podium, there stood a brigadier general and a major general from Korea Army HQ, and each of them said a few words.

"Both the previous situation before you were carried to this place and the present situation are very turbulent. The Gwangju citizens have occupied all the public buildings, so the current situation is very dangerous. However, we've made a negotiation to set you free under the condition that you will promise never to join the protest by signing with your thumbprint. Your families are waiting at the main gate. Once you are released, I ask you to stay calm," they said.

But, in fact, I was released at the rear gate instead of the main gate. I walked toward Yudeok-dong. Citizens took vans, wearing bands around their heads, at the Yudeok-dong Intersection.

Seeing them, I finally realized that the situation had changed. The citizens shared rice balls with us. I did not like to eat them, so I didn't take one and walked straight to the Hwajeong-dong National Housing Corporation Apartment where my senior colleague lived. I took a shower, got a meal from him, and slept.

A Corpse with No Head, Only Two Teeth

The next day, on the afternoon of the 22nd, I went out from Hwajeong-dong. While I was hanging about to go downtown, I saw a truck with citizens coming. I quickly raised my hand and stopped the truck.

"I was released yesterday," I said. Then, they told me to get on. I found that there were lots of beverages and bread on one side of the truck. The truck entered downtown. On the way to the downtown area, I saw people I knew in the intersection of Geumnam-ro. They were going somewhere in a Red Cross Hospital ambulance.

I quickly got off and stopped the Red Cross Hospital ambulance. In the ambulance were my junior colleagues JEONG Chan-Ho, KIM Young-Ho, OH Jong-Ho (the driver). I quickly got on the Red Cross Hospital ambulance and heard in detail from them about the situation so far. I saw citizens roaming in vehicles all over downtown Gwangju.

In the meantime, my junior colleagues had guarded the dead, transferred the wounded to hospitals safely, and helped them get treatment.

I went to the Red Cross Hospital with them in the ambulance. Entering the hospital, I saw Mr. PARK Nam-Sun carrying corpses to the morgue with young people and guiding the wounded to the hospital. He was doing a lot of work.

I had known Mr. PARK Nam-Sun, so I approached him and said hello.

"I will work hard in charge of the Red Cross Hospital with my junior colleagues. So, sir, you don't need to worry about things here. Hand your duty over to me. I will do my best," I said. Then, Mr. PARK Nam-Sun agreed, handed his task over to me, and left the hospital. Since then, serving as a commander-in-chief at the Red Cross Hospital, I managed the situation. The dead were carried to the Red Cross Hospital morgue.

I was in charge of the whole downtown area, in particular, the outskirts of the areas of Seobang and Hwajeong-dong. We put a red cross mark on each ambulance and jeep and wore white coats. We also wore armbands with a cross mark on our right arms.

The Red Cross Hospital was crowded with the wounded and the dead. Not only that, other hospitals were full of the wounded and were short of rooms, so many patients were laid on newspaper or clothes spread on the floor. The hospital capacity was limited, but the wounded flooded in to the hospitals.

In addition, although there were many nurses, the hospitals were short of workers, with a lot of work delayed because of a great number of patients. Whenever needed, we were immediately sent to help the nurses. I ordered a man to guard the entrance of the morgue to control access and guard the corpses. First of all, when a dead person was carried in, we identified the body. When the deceased had an ID, we wrote down the name, address, and age. If not, we wrote down individual particularities or the color of their clothes.

For example, we wrote down the brand of the shoes, the color and type of the pants, estimated the age of the deceased, and described the shape of the faces with a marker on large white paper. And we put the papers on the wall of the construction site next to the Red Cross Hospital. The morgue was filled with the smell of rotting corpses. Ladies in the neighborhood near the Red Cross Hospital made ice packs and brought them to the hospital, so the ice packs were piled up in the morgue. But the stink and rotting smell never disappeared.

The hospital was always in confusion. That day, I was busy with miscellaneous affairs, moving here and there. Two foreigners came into the Red Cross Hospital, with cameras hanging around their necks, and carrying big bags. They came to me and asked, "We'd like to take pictures of the morgue. Please, help us." I asked them for their IDs. They reassured me that they were journalists, showing their IDs, proving that one was a journalist from the United Press International (UPI) and the other from the *Ashahi Shimbun* in Japan.

"It is not difficult for us to help you. But we will be perplexed if you just take pictures ostensibly and do not publish them. Also, we don't know how accurately you will present the photos. Are you sure you are reporting the situation accurately?"

"Don't worry. We are examining the current situation very accurately and sending our reports to our countries."

They answered my questions clearly. The two were war correspondents, so we had no difficulty understanding each other. They spoke Korean well. I brought them into the morgue.

There were two morgue rooms with over twenty corpses in each room, each the size of about seven *pyeong*.

All the corpses were of 5.18, each covered with plastic. The rooms looked misty with fog caused by the water vapor from the ice packs piled up in each room.

The two journalists began to take pictures with their camera lights on. I helped them and uncovered the plastic on the corpses. While uncovering the plastic one by one and taking pictures, we found a corpse with no head. There were just two teeth, and the whole body was covered with marks of violence. I could not keep looking at it and ran out of the morgue. The journalist from the *Ashahi Shimbun* also followed me.

But the UPI correspondent kept taking pictures. When I was smoking, sitting under the tree in the hospital courtyard, the journalist from the *Ashahi Shimbun* came and sat beside me. He was shedding tears.

"They [the soldiers] have gone too far," he said, continuing to cry. I lent him my handkerchief to wipe his tears. He sat with a worried look, got up, and asked me for help.

The UPI correspondent came out of the morgue after taking pictures. The *Ashahi* journalist and I went back to the morgue again. After taking all the photos they wanted, they and I thanked each other politely. They promised to publish the pictures without fail and they left.

A Baby with a Twinkle in His Eyes

It was probably on May 23rd.

Two women I might have seen somewhere came to the Red Cross Hospital. They said they were not hurt.

They were young ladies around the age of twenty-one or two. They told me that they came to help the wounded in the hospital. They were kind and admirable, so I welcomed them and guided them to help the nurses and the wounded. The two ladies took care of the wounded and worked hard. They didn't say a word of complaint.

At around 2:00 or 3:00 p.m. that day, we got a call from Seobang. It was said that a lady carrying her baby on her back was shot by the paratroopers on her way toward the prison.

Upon receiving that message, four of us, including JEONG Chan-Ho, took a jeep with stretchers and dashed off. I could see citizens holding guns all over the downtown. Armed citizens were standing near the Province Hall. I could also see the citizen militia pacing up and down anxiously as they looked at the jeep driving fast.

When we arrive at Seobang, the neighbors were carrying on their backs the lady who had been shot. The lady seemed to be shot in the back of her head. She was bleeding a lot.

The people around said that she was in danger because she had bled too much. I quickly checked her pulse. Her heart seemed to have stopped already. I thought to myself that she was gone.

The eyes of the baby, who seemed to be her son, twinkled at

us. He just looked at his mom, knowing nothing. First, we carried the lady and baby into the jeep and headed to CNU Hospital. After we handed her to the hospital staff, the baby rolled his eyes here and there and began to cry, "Mom, mom," as if he were distressed by the hospital atmosphere.

The baby was whining and crying plaintively. The lady's face was covered with blood, so she could not be identified. It was even difficult to estimate her age.

I handed the baby over to a doctor and told him that the baby is the son of the lady. And I returned to the Red Cross Hospital.

That day, I also cared for the wounded. My senior colleague JEONG Cheol-Nam, who lived across the Bullo-dong Bridge, appeared, almost dead. He was beaten with clubs by the paratroopers when they entered Gwangju. His whole body turned black with bruises. He said that he had heard that I was taking care of the wounded at the Red Cross Hospital, so he had come to the hospital for treatment. I asked a doctor to take good care of him.

The doctor gave him moderate treatment, saying plainly, "This man just has bruises. There are too many patients here. But he is not that serious."

JEONG Cheol-Nam was not even considered a patient. After simple treatment, he went back home.

Receiving Warm Applause from the Gwangju Citizens

It was probably the afternoon of the day after the journalists visited (the researcher's note: It was on May 23rd).

We got a message from the situation room in the Province Hall. They commanded us to carry all the identified corpses placed in coffins from each hospital to the fountain in front of the Province Hall. Upon receiving the message, I immediately went to a funeral home in Yang-dong to buy coffins. Many people had already bought coffins, and just a couple of coffins were left. The owner told me to take them for free.

I instructed my junior colleagues to mobilize trucks or any other vehicles to get coffins. When we gathered some coffins, we began to lay the corpses in the coffins. We placed forty to fifty corpses in coffins.

Most of the corpses had become so bloated that they did not fit the coffins. A corpse that looked like a middle school student was shot in the shoulder. It was said that he had been shot while looking on at a protest. A tall corpse did not fit the coffin, so the coffin lid did not close. Neighbors watched us laying the corpses in the coffins, and some brought us *Taegeukgis* they kept in their houses. We put some *Taegeukgis* over the coffins. We also entirely covered the corpses with *Taegeukgis*.

Most of the corpses were young, and occasionally there were some old people. And we also found some children's corpses. We managed to lay them in the coffins and began to loaded the coffins into the vehicles. There were five vehicles loaded with the coffins. So, we brought two family members for each of the dead and left the Red Cross Hospital with the headlights of the vehicles on.

We passed by Taepyeong Theater, Chungjang-ro Police Box, and Hanil Bank, and proceed to the fountain of the Province Hall. Then, I held a megaphone and shouted to the citizens gathering along Geumnam-ro and near the Province Hall, "Here the patriotic Gwangju citizens are passing now. They were shot dead and mistreated by the paratroopers. My dear fellow patriotic Gwangju citizens! Please, express your condolences to the deceased."

A great number of the Gwangju citizens gathered around the fountain of the Province Hall, and they seemed to be having a rally.

Someone who looked like a college student was giving a speech on the podium. When the people shouted that the funeral vehicles were passing, the citizens cleared the way to let the vehicles to pass by. All the citizens stood up and sang the national anthem, and the surrounding area of the Province Hall became solemn all at once. The buses drove around the fountain once and unloaded the coffins. Coffins with corpses and corpses without coffins were placed in a row in front of the Province Hall and Sangmugwan. Getting off the vehicles, we had a funeral rite by burning incense and paying a silent tribute to express our condolences. After the rite was over, I stood looking around the Province Hall. A student came to me and began to shout aloud to the citizens, "Let us applaud these gentlemen for doing the hard work at the Red Cross Hospital."

Unexpectedly, we received a round of applause. The student suddenly walked around with a donation box, asking the citizens for donations. The citizens actively responded to him.

The student brought the donation box and suddenly held out the box to me. I quickly refused it.

"How could I receive this! I will never take it."

But the student stubbornly insisted. I hesitated for a moment and said to him, "Then, let me go to the hospital and ask the doctor what to do. I will be back. Wait for me." I went to the Red Cross Hospital by car. I asked about it to the director of the hospital.

"The citizens have given us a donation. Should we accept that?"

"Both you and we are volunteering. You should never accept that."

The doctor answered me selflessly. Listening to him, I immediately went back to the Province Hall and explained the situation to the student. Nevertheless, the student continued to insist that I accept the donation. I went to the Red Cross Hospital again and explained the story in detail to the director, and he said to me reluctantly, "Then, you can accept it but use it to buy fruit and give them to the wounded."

I came back to the fountain of the Province Hall. I accepted the donation and thanked the citizens so much. The chair of the funeral preparation committee, Mr. CHOI Kyu-Han (the funeral bus driver), and I entered the Province Hall with the donation box and took it to the office identified as the "accounting office."

Seeing me entering the office, Mr. CHA Seong-Won followed me.

We counted the money from the donation box in the office. All counted, it amounted to about a million won, including all the coins. We decided that I should receive four hundred won to buy fruit for the wounded, and the chair of the funeral preparation committee took the rest for the funeral. We exchanged the receipts with each other and left the accounting office of the Province Hall.

Upon coming out of the Province Hall, I took an ambulance and went to the fruit and vegetable market on the other side of the Intercity Public Bus Terminal. We fully loaded the ambulance with fruits like Korean melons and tomatoes and went to the CNU Hospital, the Chosun University Hospital, and the Christian Hospital to distribute the fruit. We brought the leftovers back to the Red Cross Hospital.

Two ladies working in the kitchen squashed the fruits into juice and shared it with each hospitalized patient and all the wounded. We all felt proud.

INDEX

R

S

T

Y

PARTICIPANTS

CO-EDITORS

KIM Yeon-Min
Robert Grotjohn

ADVISORY COMMITTEE

CHOI Jeong-Gi
KIM Hyeong-Joo
HAN Seung-Hee

TRANSLATORS

AHN A-Ram
BAEK Seung-Hyun
CHU Yeon-Ji
HAN Min-Jeong
JO Ye-Rok
KANG Eui-Huack
KANG Yoon-Suk
KIM Baeg-Seung
KIM Eun-Hey
KIM Eun-Young
KIM Han-Byeol
KIM He-Ra
KIM Ja-Young
KIM Myeong-Seo
KIM Seong-Hoon
KIM Yeon-Min
KWAK Ku
LEE Hyun-kyung
LEE Joo-Ri
LEE Ju-Eun
LEE Myeong-Ha
LEE Seon-Yeong
LEE Seong-Hyeon
LEE Sook-In
LEEM Eun-Ha
LIM Jin-Ah
MIN Tae-Un
MUN Young-Hee
NA Yoon-Hee
NAH Hee-kyung
OH Mi-Ra
OH Se-Rin
PARK Jin-Suk
PARK Mi-Kyung
ROH Seung-Hee
SHIN Keun-Young